Lecture Notes in Artificial Intelligence   10643

Subseries of Lecture Notes in Computer Science

More information about this series at http://www.springer.com/series/1244

Gita Sukthankar · Juan A. Rodriguez-Aguilar (Eds.)

Autonomous Agents and Multiagent Systems

AAMAS 2017 Workshops, Visionary Papers
São Paulo, Brazil, May 8–12, 2017
Revised Selected Papers

 Springer

Editors
Gita Sukthankar ⓘ
University of Central Florida
Orlando, FL
USA

Juan A. Rodriguez-Aguilar ⓘ
IIIA-CSIC
Bellaterra
Spain

ISSN 0302-9743   ISSN 1611-3349   (electronic)
Lecture Notes in Artificial Intelligence
ISBN 978-3-319-71678-7   ISBN 978-3-319-71679-4   (eBook)
https://doi.org/10.1007/978-3-319-71679-4

Library of Congress Control Number: 2017960858

LNCS Sublibrary: SL7 – Artificial Intelligence

Printed on acid-free paper

This Springer imprint is published by Springer Nature
The registered company is Springer International Publishing AG
The registered company address is: Gewerbestrasse 11, 6330 Cham, Switzerland

Preface

AAMAS is the leading scientific conference for research in autonomous agents and multiagent systems, which is annually organized by the non-profit organization, the International Foundation for Autonomous Agents and Multiagent Systems (IFAA-MAS). The AAMAS conference series was initiated in 2002 by merging three highly respected meetings: the International Conference on Multi-Agent Systems (ICMAS); the International Workshop on Agent Theories, Architectures, and Languages (ATAL); and the International Conference on Autonomous Agents (AA).

Besides the main program, AAMAS hosts a number of workshops, which aim at stimulating and facilitating discussion, interaction, and comparison of approaches, methods, and ideas related to specific topics, both theoretical and applied, in the general area of Autonomous Agents and Multiagent Systems. The AAMAS workshops provide an informal setting where participants have the opportunity to discuss specific technical topics in an atmosphere that fosters the active exchange of ideas.

This book compiles the most visionary papers of the AAMAS 2017 workshops. In total, AAMAS 2017 ran 18 workshops. To select the most visionary papers, the organizers of each workshop were asked to nominate up to two papers from their workshop and send those papers, along with the reviews they received during their workshop's review process, to the AAMAS 2017 workshop co-chairs. The AAMAS 2017 workshop co-chairs then studied each paper carefully, in order to assess its quality and whether it was suitable to be selected for this book. Notice that not all workshops were able to contribute to this volume. The result is a compilation of 15 papers selected from 10 workshops, which we list below.

- The 22nd International Workshop on Coordination, Organization, Institutions, and Norms in Agent Systems (COIN 2017)
- The 4th International Workshop on Agent-Mediated Electronic Commerce and Trading Agents Design and Analysis (AMEC/TADA 2017)
- The 18th International Workshop on Multi-Agent-Based Simulation (MABS 2017)
- The 8th International Workshop on Optimisation in Multiagent Systems (OptMAS 2017)
- The 10th International Workshop on Agents Applied in Health Care (A2HC 2017)
- The 19th International Workshop on Trust in Agent Societies (Trust 2017)
- The 17th International Workshop on Adaptive Learning Agents (ALA 2017)
- The 1st International Workshop on Teams in Multi-Agent Systems (TEAMAS 2017)
- The 10th International Workshop on Agent-Based Complex Automated Negotiations (ACAN 2017)
- The 4th International Workshop on Exploring Beyond the Worst Case in Computational Social Choice (EXPLORE 2017)

We note that a similar process was carried out to select the best papers of the AAMAS 2017 workshops. While visionary papers are papers with novel ideas that propose a change in the way research is currently carried out, best papers follow the style of more traditional papers. The selected best papers may be found in the Springer book LNCS 10642.

The AAMAS 2017 workshops are the second AAMAS workshop series to publish their (selected) papers in the form of a collective book. We hope that this book can better disseminate the most notable results of these workshops and encourage authors to submit top-quality research work to the AAMAS workshops.

August 2017   Gita Sukthankar
                                                    Juan A. Rodriguez-Aguilar

Organization

AAMAS 2017 Workshop Co-chairs

Gita Sukthankar   University of Central Florida, USA
Juan A. Rodriguez-Aguilar   Artificial Intelligence Research Institute, Spain

AAMAS 2017 Workshop Organizers

COIN 2017

Felipe Meneguzzi   Pontifical Catholic University of Rio Grande do Sul,
                               Brazil
Wamberto Vasconcelos   University of Aberdeen, UK

AMEC/TADA 2017

Sofia Ceppi   The University of Edinburgh, UK
Chen Hajaj   Vanderbilt University, USA
Ioannis A. Vetsikas   National Center for Scientific Research (NCSR)
                               "Demokritos", Greece
Esther David   Ashkelon Academic College, Israel
Valentin Robu   Heriot-Watt University, UK

MABS 2017

Graçaliz Pereira Dimuro   Universidade Federal do Rio Grande - FURG, Brazil
Luis Antunes   University of Lisbon, Portugal

OptMAS 2017

Archie Chapman   University of Sydney, Australia
Sebastian Stein   University of Southampton, UK
Long Tran-Thanh   University of Southampton, UK
William Yeoh   New Mexico State University, USA
Roie Zivan   Ben-Gurion University of the Negev, Israel

A2HC 2017

Sara Montagna   University of Bologna, Italy
Eloisa Vargiu   Fundació Eurecat - eHealth Unit, Spain
Marcia Ito   BM Brazil/Faculty of Technology of São Paulo, Brazil
Daniel Castro Silva   University of Porto, Portugal
Pedro Henriques Abreu   University of Coimbra, Portugal
Michael Ignaz Schumacher   University of Applied Sciences Western Switzerland,
                               Switzerland

Trust 2017

Jie Zhang	Nanyang Technological University, Singapore
Murat Sensoy	Ozyegin University, Turkey
Rino Falcone	ISTC-CNR, Rome, Italy

ALA 2017

Tim Brys	Vrije Universiteit Brussels, Belgium
Anna Harutyunyan	Vrije Universiteit Brussels, Belgium
Patrick Mannion	Galway-Mayo Institute of Technology, Ireland
Kaushik Subramanian	Georgia Institute of Technology, USA

TEAMAS 2017

Ewa Andrejczuk	IIIA-CSIC, Spain
Juan M. Alberola	Universitat Politecnica de Valencia, Spain
Leandro Soriano Marcolino	Lancaster University, UK
Mehdi Farhangian	University of Otago, New Zealand

ACAN 2017

Susel Fernandez Melian	Nagoya Institute of Technology, Japan
Katsuhide Fujita	Tokyo University of Agriculture & Technology, Japan
Naoki Fukuta	Shizuoka University, Japan
Takayuki Ito	Nagoya Institute of Technology, Japan
Minjie Zhang	University of Wollongong, Australia
Quan Bai	Auckland University of Technology, New Zealand
Fenghui Ren	University of Wollongong, Australia
Miguel Angel Lopez Carmona	University of Alcala, Spain
Ivan Marsa Maestre	University of Alcala, Spain
Tim Baarslag	Centrum Wiskunde & Informatica, The Netherlands
Reyhan Aydogan	Ozyegin University, Turkey

EXPLORE 2017

Haris Aziz	University of New South Wales, Australia
John P. Dickerson	University of Maryland, USA
Omer Lev	University of Toronto, Canada
Nicholas Mattei	IBM Research, USA

Contents

Competitive Belief Propagation to Efficiently Solve Complex Multi-agent Negotiations with Network Structure

Ivan Marsa-Maestre[1(✉)], Jose Manuel Gimenez-Guzman[1], Enrique de la Hoz[1], and David Orden[2]

[1] Computer Engineering Department, University of Alcala, Alcalá de Henares, Spain
{ivan.marsa,josem.gimenez,enrique.delahoz}@uah.es
[2] Department of Physics and Mathematics, University of Alcala, Alcalá de Henares, Spain
david.orden@uah.es

Abstract. This paper focuses on enabling the use of negotiation for complex system optimisation, whose main challenge nowadays is scalability. Although multi-agent automated negotiation has been studied for decades, it is still a challenge to handle in a scalable and efficient manner negotiation problems involving many issues with complex interdependencies. This is a clear obstacle for the use of automated negotiation in complex networks. This paper proposes a novel perspective on the negotiation process as a *competitive belief propagation* process, where the whole negotiation is modelled as a factor graph and distributed belief propagation techniques (BP) are used to yield a solution. We show that the model adequately suits both simple and complex negotiation settings in the literature, and we validate its efficiency and scalability in a challenging, network structured, channel negotiation setting.

Keywords: Belief propagation · Network-structured negotiations
Wi-Fi channel negotiation

1 Introduction

A wide range of real-world systems can be modelled as dynamic sets of interconnected nodes [14,20]. The adequate management of complex networked systems is becoming critical for industrialized countries, since they keep growing in size and complexity. An important sub-class involves autonomous, self-interested entities (e.g. drivers in a transportation network). The self-interested nature of the entities in the network causes the network to deviate from socially-optimal behaviour. This leads to problems related to unavailability and inefficient use of resources.

Different fields of research are working on these challenges, but, so far, with only mixed success. Optimization techniques are especially suited to

© Springer International Publishing AG 2017
G. Sukthankar and J. A. Rodriguez-Aguilar (Eds.): AAMAS 2017 Visionary Papers,
LNAI 10643, pp. 1–16, 2017.
https://doi.org/10.1007/978-3-319-71679-4_1

address large-scale systems with an underlying network structure, usually with a "divide and conquer" approach [22,24]. However, their performance severely decreases as the complexity of the system increases [21], and with the presence of autonomous entities which deviate from the globally optimal solution, thus harming the social goal. Negotiation techniques are known to be useful to handle self-interested behaviour [1], but scale poorly with problem size and the intricacies of interdependencies [15].

Belief propagation (BP) is a message-passing technique which has been successfully used to solve optimization problems by modelling problem constraints using a graph structure [9]. In our previous work, we used it to improve the scalability of an agent self-preference exploration during an auction-based negotiation process over preference spaces built of hypercube-shaped constraints [18]. In a more recent work [11], the concept was extended to utility hypergraphs, enabling negotiations with more complex shaped constraints. These works contributed to greatly enhance scalability in complex negotiations by modelling utilities as graphs, but did not explore problems which were graph-structured by themselves. In addition, these works used belief propagation to explore the preferences of each agent separately, thus keeping the BP process as a local optimization process, using it to assist in the local search for solutions during the negotiation process. This is coherent with the usual use of BP in cooperative optimization settings.

Our goal is to provide a novel perspective of the multi-agent negotiation process as a *competitive belief propagation*, which can help to efficiently handle conflicts in network-structured settings. In this paper, we contribute to this goal in the following way:

- We define the negotiation problem as a *factor graph F_P* and the negotiation process as a *competitive belief propagation* over the factor graph, and we show how the model suits well-known negotiation settings in the literature (Sect. 2).
- We apply this model to a challenging, network structured complex negotiation setting: Wi-Fi channel negotiation (Sects. 3.1 and 3.2).
- We propose a distributed, scalable approach to use competitive belief propagation to solve the problem (Sect. 3.3).

To test our hypothesis and evaluate the validity of our contribution, we have conducted a set of experiments in a realistic scenario setting (Sect. 4). Our experiments show that the belief propagation approach outperforms a classical nonlinear negotiation approach in terms of solution efficiency and performance. The last section summarizes our contributions and sheds light on future challenges and lines of research.

2 Negotiation as Competitive Belief Propagation

As we said above, our goal is to provide an alternative perspective on automated negotiation as a competitive belief propagation process, so that this process can be mapped naturally to network structured problems. To understand the rationale of this novel perspective, let's see a simple example of the correspondence between the two problems. Consider the classic negotiation game between a buyer agent B and a seller agent S over the price p of an item, and let us assume that they are going to use an alternating offer protocol for the negotiation [7]. Let b_B^0 and b_S^0 the initial agent offers (or *bids*). For a typical bargaining scenario, we will have $b_B^0 < b_S^0$, that is, the buyer wants to pay less than the seller wants to get. During the negotiation, we will expect to see a progressive relaxation of the agents' initial positions (i.e. $b_B^t \geq b_B^{t-1}$ and $b_S^t \leq b_S^{t-1}$) until we reach the point of agreement (i.e. $b_B^t = b_S^t$) or the deadline expires. The relaxation speed of the agents' positions will depend on the different agent bidding strategies (e.g. boulware, conceder, tit-for-tat [2]). This process can easily be seen as a *belief competition*. Both agents start out with different beliefs about how much they want to give or receive for the item (b_B^0 and b_S^0, respectively), and these beliefs get updated through the subsequents iterations of the protocol until an agreement is reached (i.e. the beliefs of both agents match) or the deadline expires. This belief competition perspective can be formalized into a factor graph and a belief propagation process [9], as we will see in the following subsection.

2.1   Negotiation as a Factorized Optimization Problem

Belief propagation (BP) techniques have been shown as successful heuristics for solving *factorized optimization problems*, that is, problems P of the form

$$minimize \sum_{i \in V} \Phi_i(x_i) + \sum_{c \in C} \Psi_c(x_c) \tag{1}$$

where V is a finite set of *variables* and C is a finite collection of subsets of V representing constraints. Φ_i and Ψ_i are real-valued functions called, respectively, *variable functions* and *factor functions*, representing the impact on the objective function of the value of each independent variable, and of combinations of variable values (i.e. interdependencies between variables).

We can easily map to this kind of problem most of the utility or social welfare functions used in automated negotiation, by choosing adequate expressions for the Φ_i and Ψ_i functions. For instance, in the trivial buyer-seller negotiation example above we could choose

$$\Phi_B = \begin{cases} x - R_B & \text{if } x \leq R_B \\ \infty & \text{otherwise} \end{cases} \qquad \Phi_S = \begin{cases} R_S - x & \text{if } x \geq R_S \\ \infty & \text{otherwise} \end{cases}$$

$$\Psi(x_B, x_S) = \begin{cases} 0 & \text{if } x_B = x_S \\ \infty & \text{otherwise} \end{cases}$$

where R_B and R_S are the reservation values of buyer and seller, respectively. In this trivial case, each Φ_i functions account for the preferences of agent i, and the Ψ function represents that a disagreement is the worst possible outcome. Other Ψ functions could be chosen depending on the desired outcome of the negotiation. For instance, we could choose a Ψ function representing a Clarke tax $(\Psi(x_B, x_S) = \frac{x_S - x_B}{2})$, or a fairness metric such as the one defined in [8].

A similar translation can be done in a linear-additive multi-issue negotiation setting, such as the one described in [6,17]. Here there would be a $\Phi_{a,i}(x_{a,i})$ function for each agent a and issue i, corresponding to the valuation function of each agent for each issue. Ψ_i functions would be defined for each issue depending on the desired outcome of the negotiation. For instance, to introduce the aforementioned fairness measure we could define:

$$\Psi(x_B, i, x_S, i) = \begin{cases} \frac{(\Phi_B(x_B) + \Phi_S(x_S))^2 + (\Phi_B(x_B) - \Phi_S(x_S))^2}{2} & \text{if } x_B = x_S \\ \infty & \text{otherwise} \end{cases}$$

Apart from the Φ and Ψ functions, we can also derive the corresponding factor graph F_P of the factorized optimization problem P. This is a bipartite graph with a node per Φ and Ψ function, and links between nodes which share *variables*.

2.2   The Negotiation Process as Belief Propagation

Once the negotiation problem has been expressed as a factorized optimization problem F_P, we can solve it using belief propagation techniques. In particular, we use the min-sum version of BP described in [9], which we reproduce in Algorithm 1 for convenience.

Algorithm 1. min-sum BP

Input : F: bipartite factor graph with edges (i, f) between variable nodes and factor nodes representing constraints N: number of iterations
C: $\{c_i\}$: available color set
Output: S: estimated optimal assignment
Initialize $t = 0$
foreach *edge (i, f) in F* **do**
 | initialize $m_{f \to i}^0(z) \forall z \in C$
end
for $t = 1, 2, \ldots, N$ **do**
 | **foreach** *edge (i, f) in F* **do**
 | | update $m_{i \to f}^t(z) = \Phi_i(z) + \sum_{k \in f_i \backslash f} m_{k \to i}^{t-1}(z)$
 | | update $m_{f \to i}^t(z) = \min_{y \in C^{|f|}, y_i = z} \Psi_f(y) + \sum_{j \in f \backslash i} m_{j \to f}^{t-1}(y_j)$
 | **end**
 | $t = t + 1$
end
Set the belief function as
$b_i^N = \Phi_i(z) + \sum_{k \in f_i} m_{k \to i}^N(z)$ for each variable node i
Estimate the optimal assignment S as
$\hat{s}_i^{N(z)}$ for each variable node i

The min-sum algorithm is a message-passing algorithm which defines a number of messages $m^t_{X \to Y}$ to be passed among nodes of the factor graph F_P throughout the different iterations of the algorithm. We turn the algorithm into a multi-agent negotiation protocol by mapping the graph nodes to agents. In our example, we would map to each negotiating agent A and B the nodes corresponding to its own beliefs/preferences about the issue values, and the nodes corresponding to the Ψ functions (in this case, incentivizing fairness) would be mapped to a mediator agent M. The negotiation would progress via message passing between factor and variable nodes assigned to different agents at each iteration.

3   Scaling Up: BP in the Wi-Fi Negotiation Problem

In our previous work, we proposed Wi-Fi channel assignment as a realistic and challenging benchmark for complex automated negotiations [3,4]. In this setting, different Wi-Fi providers, acting as agents, have to collectively decide how to distribute the channels used by their access points (APs) in order to minimize interference between nodes and thus maximize the utility (i.e., network throughput) for their clients, which will be different kinds of wireless devices (WDs). A Wi-Fi negotiation scenario will be characterized by:

- A Wi-Fi association graph G, which is a geometric graph (i.e., nodes have specific positions in space) with two kinds of vertices, representing APs and WDs. Edges in the graph represent the association of a particular WD to an AP. In Fig. 1 we show a graphical representation of a scenario with 26 APs and 400 WDs.
- An interference graph I, which includes the same vertices as G in the same positions in space, but in this case edges represent potential interferences between devices, and edge weights account for the intensity of these interferences. For detailed description of the Wi-Fi interference model in this setting, the reader is advised to check [13]. The corresponding graph for the aforementioned scenario can be seen in Fig. 2.
- A mapping of access points to different providers, which will be the negotiating agents. The goal of each agent will be to minimize the interference suffered by its APs and their associated WDs. In this paper, we will assume there are two providers.

This is a particularly interesting problem, since it belongs to the family of Frequency Assignment Problems (which has been extensively studied from the perspective of discrete optimization) and it is strongly related to the prominent mathematical graph coloring problem [23] and to distributed constraint optimization models [10]. In the following, we will formally describe the negotiation problem, and the translation of the problem to the belief propagation model.

3.1   Negotiation Domain

For the scope of this work, we assume a multiattribute negotiation domain, where a deal or solution to the problem is defined as the set of attributes (*issues*),

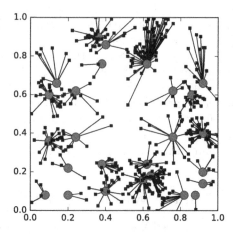

Fig. 1. Wi-Fi association graph G for an scenario with 26 APs and 400 wireless devices.

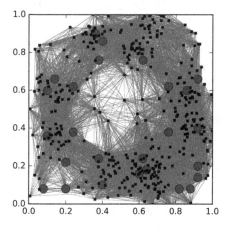

Fig. 2. Wi-Fi interference graph I for an scenario with 26 APs and 400 wireless devices.

and each one of them can be in a certain range. In our case, for a channel assignment problem with n_{AP} access points, a solution or deal S can be expressed as $S = \{s_i | i \in 1, ..., n_{AP}\}$, where $s_i \in \{1, \ldots, 11\}$ represents the assignation of a Wi-Fi channel to the i-th access point.

As stated above, we assume that there are two network providers or agents (commonly Internet Service Providers, ISPs), thus APs belong to one of the agents. Each provider only has control over the channel assignment for its own access points. According to this situation, $P = \{p_1, p_2\}$ will be the set of agents that will negotiate the channel assignment. We find adequate to focus in the two-provider case because there are more works in complex bilateral negotiations than for the multilateral case (three or more agents).

Finally, each one of these agents p_i will compute its utility U_{p_i} for a certain solution according to the model described in [4,13]. As we showed in our previous works, the problem settings (high cardinality of the solution space and attribute interdependence) will make the utility functions highly complex, with multiple local optima.

3.2 Channel Negotiation as a Factorized Optimization Problem

Given that U_{p_i} depends on the sum of the interferences suffered by their APs and their associated WDs, and that those interferences are caused by nearby APs and WDs using the same channel to transmit, intuitively we need to avoid using the same (or similar) channels in nearby devices. More specifically, we have to avoid using "close" channels in devices whose associated vertices in the interference graph I are connected, specially if the weight of the connecting edge is high.

This is quite similar to the *Threshold Coloring Problem* (TSC) [19], which is depicted in Fig. 3. In this problem, we have an undirected graph and a set of available colors (in the example, red, green and blue), with an associated interference matrix, which assigns an interference value for the occurrence of any pair of colors in any edge of the graph. The goal of the TSC problem is to find a coloring which minimizes the maximum interference per node (the optimal solutions for the example problem can be seen shadowed in the figure). Our hypothesis is that, by translating the problem of channel assignment to this problem, we will find suitable solutions in a reasonable time. We will have as the available color set the different Wi-Fi channels, and as the color interference matrix the co-channel interference index [13].

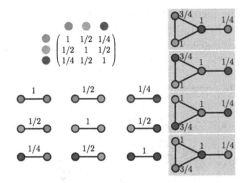

Fig. 3. Example of the Threshold Spectrum Coloring problem (TSC). (Color figure online)

The translation from the Wi-Fi channel negotiation problem to the TSC problem is not straightforward. First of all, the variable/issue sets for both problems are different. TSC assumes all colorings are possible, while in Wi-Fi channel negotiation only channels chosen by the APs are negotiated, since all WDs associated to a given AP will use the same channel to communicate. To account for this, we propose to do a *compactation* of the interference graph I. That is, we will derive a *compact graph* C from the graph I as follows:

- We will have a vertex in the graph C for every AP vertex in the graph I.
- Two vertices in C will be connected if and only if there was an edge in I; (a) between them, (b) between one of the APs and one of the WDs associated to the other AP, or (c) between WDs of the two APs.

Such a compact graph for the example given in Figs. 1 and 2 is shown in Fig. 4. In addition, we will introduce edge weights in graph C according to two different strategies:

- *Uniform BP translation (BPu):* we will assume that each existing edge between vertices i and j in the compact graph C has an associated weight $w_{ij} = 1$. This is the simplest possible translation (all edges equal), which loses most information from the interference graph I, so we expect it to give the less optimal results, but also to be the most efficient in terms of computation time.
- *Weighted BP translation (BPw):* in this case, we will assign to each edge between vertices i and j in the compact graph C a weight w_{ij} equal to the number of edges in graph I between them, between one of the APs and one of the clients associated to the other AP, and between WDs of the two APs. This is a reasonable choice, since it will prioritize the edges between APs which have more potential interferences, but it is still a much more efficient choice computationally than evaluating the real interference between APs and their WDs.

The last step for the formalization is to translate the coloring of the compact graph C to a factorized optimization problem. To do this, we use our vertices representing APs as variables (which can take different values depending on

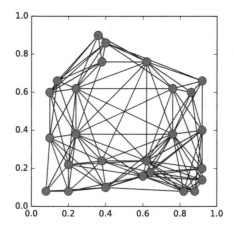

Fig. 4. Compact graph C for an scenario with 26 APs and 400 wireless devices.

which channel the AP uses to transmit) and the edges between pairs of vertices (which represent interferences between APs) as constraints. According to this, we define the corresponding functions as follows:

$$\Phi_i(s_i) = 0$$

$$\Psi_C(s_i, s_j) = w_{ij}c(s_i, s_j), \forall C \equiv (i, j)$$

That is, we use a constant zero value for each variable function, and we use the product of the weight of the corresponding edge in the compact graph and the co-channel interference between the chosen channels (see [13] for details) for each factor function. With this formulation, we try to mitigate the impact of using "close" channels in close APs, which is coherent with the Wi-Fi interference model. It is worth noting that this formulation differs from the TSC problem, given that here we try to minimize the sum of the contributions for all nodes in the graph, while pure TSC aims to minimize the maximum contribution for any single node in the graph. However, as shown in [19], sum minimization is a good heuristic to minimize the maximum in this context, and therefore successful techniques proposed for TSC can be used here as benchmarks.

Finally, we need to build the factor graph F_P of our problem, which is a bipartite graph with *variable nodes* in one side of the partition and *factor nodes* corresponding to the constraints in the other side of the partition. Links between both partitions occur between a constraint and the variable nodes it refers to. For instance, in the graph example given in Fig. 3, the resulting factor graph F_P would be as shown in Fig. 5.

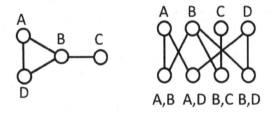

Fig. 5. Factor graph F_P (right) for our example TSC problem.

3.3   A Scalable Negotiation Using Belief Propagation

To solve the factorized optimization problem we have proposed for our Wi-Fi negotiation scenario, we would have to apply the min-sum algorithm for BP [9]. The problem with applying directly the min-sum BP algorithm to our problem is that the algorithm only has correctness and convergence guarantees when the solution is unique and the factor graph is a tree. Although solution uniqueness can be achieved with randomized weights as suggested in [9], most of our scenarios do not create tree factor graphs. The usual junction tree technique used in machine learning to address this problem [25] is not applicable here, because it is centralized, which is not scalable (neither desirable) for competitive negotiation scenarios where sharing of private information should be minimized.

Taking this into account, to ensure convergence and correctness of the algorithm, we propose to divide the factor graph into trees using a distributed, gossip-inspired technique [5]. The technique we propose works as follows:

- All AP nodes in the compact graph C are initialized to the *unassigned* state, which means they do not belong to any tree.
- Nodes in *unassigned* state respond to the behaviour:

• Decide with probability p whether to start a new tree (therefore changing their status to assigned) or to wait a random time.
• Upon receiving a message from an *assigned* neighbour (that is, a neighbour already belonging to a tree), switch to assigned status and acknowledge the membership to the tree.

- Nodes in *assigned* state respond to the behaviour:

• Decide with probability p whether to invite a random subset of its (not already-invited) neighbors to its tree or to wait a random time.

This technique asynchronously divides the compact graph C into a set of disjoint trees, from which tree factor graphs can be derived so that BP converges. Of course, when we work with the resulting set of trees, we lose the information about the influencing factors Ψ_{ij} corresponding to components c_i and c_j which are neighbors in the compact graph but have ended up in different trees. To minimize the impact of this simplification, we iteratively introduce this effect in the functions Φ_i of the frontier nodes (that is, the nodes in a tree which are neighbors of nodes in other trees). That is, the belief propagation process is repeated several times in an iterative manner, and at each iteration K the frontier nodes are assigned a variable function $\Phi_i^K(s_i)$ which is computed as follows:

$$\Phi_i^K(s_i) = \sum_{j \in \aleph(i)} \Psi_{ij}(s_i, \hat{s}_j^{K-1})$$

Where $\aleph(i)$ is the set of neighbors of component c_i in the compact graph and $\hat{s}_j^{K-1}$ is the optimal assignment for neighbor c_j for the previous execution of the BP algorithm.

Computation of the Φ_i^K functions is performed at each corresponding provider agent for the AP i. Computation of the $\Psi_{C_{ij}}^K$ functions when APs i and j belong to different providers is randomly assigned to one of the provider agents to avoid agent manipulation of the belief propagation process.

Fig. 6. Polytechnic school building plan. (Color figure online)

4   Experimental Evaluation

To validate our approach and assess the contribution of our mechanisms, we have conducted a set of experiments of the Wi-Fi real-world setting we used in [3], which uses the real layout of the first floor plant of our University (Fig. 6). The real positions of deployed APs are displayed with green dots, ranging their signal coverage from red (high coverage) to light blue (very low coverage). Note that the center of the plan represents a central courtyard, so it has low signal coverage. For the position of WDs we have considered that we have users attending classes in classrooms and also some students are located randomly in the building (resting, in the cafeteria, studying...). For this last group of students, we have considered that there are 100 students randomly located in the building following a uniform distribution. For the students in classrooms, we have tested several scenarios varying randomly the ratio of classrooms being used (ρ, with $\rho \in [0.25, 0.5, 0.75, 1.0]$). As there are 48 classrooms in the building, we have considered scenarios with 12, 24, 36 and 48 classrooms. For each classroom, we have deployed 25 students in each one randomly using a normal distribution around the center of each classroom and a standard deviation normalized to the size of the scenario of 0.05. In Table 1 we show a summary of the real-world scenarios under study. Finally, as the specific random classrooms under use could affect the results, we have tested three experiments for each value of ρ, so the total number of deployments studied has been 12. In each setting, APs have been randomly assigned to the two providers.

We are interested in evaluating the performance of BPu and BPw in comparison with the well-known technique called *Simulated Annealing* (SA) [12,16]. For a further description of how this technique has been deployed, see [4]. More specifically, we are interested in evaluating the performance of these techniques in terms of the normalized utility (U_n) that they can achieve in a certain

Table 1. Summary of scenarios of the real-world setting.

Scenario	ρ	# Classrooms	# WD
1, 2, 3	0.25	12	400
4, 5, 6	0.5	12	700
7, 8, 9	0.75	12	1000
10, 11, 12	1.0	48	1300

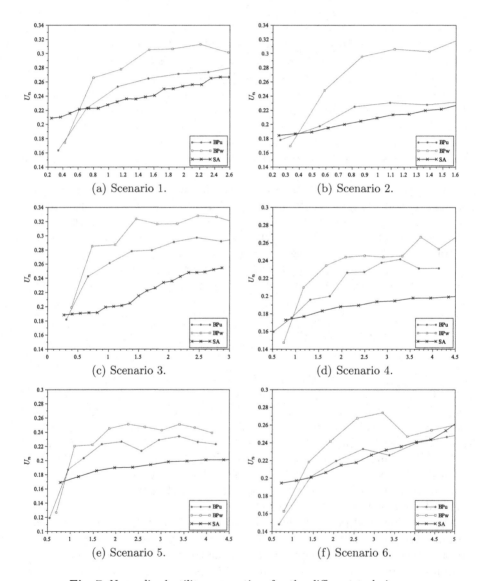

Fig. 7. Normalized utility versus time for the different techniques.

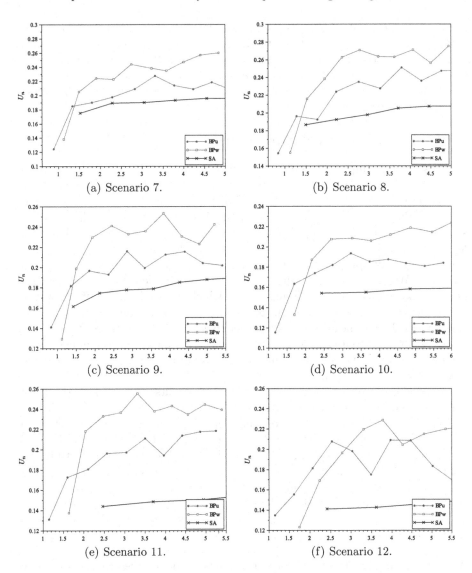

Fig. 8. Normalized utility versus time for the different techniques.

computation time. The different values for the computation time have been obtained running the techniques with a different number of iterations.

Note that the normalized utility is defined as the sum of utilities for all nodes in the network (APs and WDs) divided by the graph order, i.e. divided by the number of nodes in the graph. Figures 7 and 8 show this comparison for the 12 scenarios under study. Results show that, except for the shortest runs where BP obtains worse results than SA, in almost all cases, BP is able to obtain a better performance (higher U_n) than SA for the same computation time.

Comparing BPu with BPw we can conclude that BPw always outperforms BPu. This expected result is due to the fact that the compact graph of BPw includes more information than its counterpart of BPu. As a consequence of these results, we consider that the use of Belief Propagation, specially in its BPw setting, is very useful, as its efficiency is higher than the well-known, successful approach SA.

5   Conclusions and Future Work

Our research attempts to enable the use of complex automated negotiations in the management of complex systems with network structure, which are of increasing interest in many disciplines. One of the biggest challenges for this is the scalability of complex negotiation mechanisms when facing the large utility spaces and complex interdependencies of such systems. To address this challenge, in this paper we propose a novel perspective for the negotiation process as competitive belief propagation, which maps naturally to settings with a graph structure. We also propose an efficient mechanism to implement this competitive belief propagation process in large settings, which takes advantage of gossip-like techniques. Finally, we validate our approach on a realistic and challenging setting: Wi-Fi channel negotiation. Experiments show that our approach achieves better results that well-known successful nonlinear negotiation techniques in less computation time, which is a significant advance for the success of negotiation mechanisms in these settings.

Although our experiments yield satisfactory results, there is still plenty of work to be done in this area. We are interested in evaluating more sophisticated strategies than BPu and BPw for weighting the compact graph, in order to get as close as possible to the real interference model without imposing too much computational complexity in the mechanism. We want also to study the influence of different graph properties (e.g. diameter) in the performance of the BP techniques. Finally, we are interested in evaluating the strategic properties of the mechanisms, to see how the belief propagation process performs when agents are allowed to "lie" in their messages in order to try to influence the outcome of the mechanism to their advantage.

Acknowledgments. This work has been supported by the Spanish Ministry of Economy and Competitiveness grants TIN2016-80622-P, TIN2014-61627-EXP, MTM2014-54207 and TEC2013-45183-R, and by the University of Alcala through CCG2016/EXP-048.

References

1. An, B., Lesser, V., Sim, K.M.: Strategic agents for multi-resource negotiation. Auton. Agent. Multi-Agent Syst. **23**(1), 114–153 (2011)
2. Baarslag, T., Dirkzwager, A., Hindriks, K.V., Jonker, C.M.: The significance of bidding, accepting and opponent modeling in automated negotiation. In: Proceedings of the Twenty-First European Conference on Artificial Intelligence, pp. 27–32. IOS Press (2014)

3. De La Hoz, E., Gimenez-Guzman, J.M., Marsa-Maestre, I., Orden, D.: A realistic scenario for complex automated nonlinear negotiation: Wi-Fi channel assignment. In: Proceedings of the the Ninth International Workshop on Agent-based Complex Automated Negotiations (ACAN2016), Singapore (2016)
4. De La Hoz, E., Marsa-Maestre, I., Gimenez-Guzman, J.M., Orden, D., Klein, M.: Multi-agent nonlinear negotiation for Wi-Fi channel assignment. In: Proceedings of the 16th International Conference on Autonomous Agents and Multiagent Systems, AAMAS 2017, International Foundation for Autonomous Agents and Multiagent Systems, Sao Paulo, Brazil (2017)
5. Demers, A., Greene, D., Hauser, C., Irish, W., Larson, J., Shenker, S., Sturgis, H., Swinehart, D., Terry, D.: Epidemic algorithms for replicated database maintenance. In: Proceedings of the Sixth Annual ACM Symposium on Principles of Distributed Computing, PODC 1987, New York, NY, USA, pp. 1–12 (1987)
6. Faratin, P., Sierra, C., Jennings, N.R.: Using similarity criteria to make issue trade-offs in automated negotiations. Artif. Intell. **142**(2), 205–237 (2002)
7. Fatima, S., Kraus, S., Wooldridge, M.: Principles of Automated Negotiation. Cambridge University Press, Cambridge (2014)
8. Fujita, K., Ito, T., Klein, M.: A secure and fair protocol that addresses weaknesses of the nash bargaining solution in nonlinear negotiation. Group Decis. Negot. **21**(1), 29–47 (2012)
9. Gamarnik, D., Shah, D., Wei, Y.: Belief propagation for min-cost network flow: convergence and correctness. Oper. Res. **60**(2), 410–428 (2012)
10. Grubshtein, A., Meisels, A.: A distributed cooperative approach for optimizing a family of network games. In: Brazier, F.M.T., Nieuwenhuis, K., Pavlin, G., Warnier, M., Badica, C. (eds.) Intelligent Distributed Computing V: Proceedings of the 5th International Symposium on Intelligent Distributed Computing - IDC 2011, pp. 49–62. Springer, Heidelberg (2012). https://doi.org/10.1007/978-3-642-24013-3_6
11. Hadfi, R., Ito, T.: Complex multi-issue negotiation using utility hyper-graphs. JACIII **19**(4), 514–522 (2015)
12. Hattori, H., Klein, M., Ito, T.: Using iterative narrowing to enable multi-party negotiations with multiple interdependent issues. In: Proceedings of the 6th International Joint Conference on Autonomous Agents and Multiagent Systems, AAMAS 2007, pp. 247:1–247:3. ACM, New York (2007)
13. de la Hoz, E., Gimenez-Guzman, J.M., Marsa-Maestre, I., Orden, D.: Automated negotiation for resource assignment in wireless surveillance sensor networks. Sensors **15**(11), 29547–29568 (2015)
14. Kinney, R., Crucitti, P., Albert, R., Latora, V.: Modeling cascading failures in the North American power grid. Eur. Phys. J. B-Condens. Matter Complex Syst. **46**(1), 101–107 (2005)
15. Klein, M., Faratin, P., Sayama, H., Bar-Yam, Y.: Negotiating complex contracts. Group Decis. Negot. **12**(2), 111–125 (2003)
16. Lang, F., Fink, A.: Learning from the metaheuristics: protocols for automated negotiations. Group Decis. Negot. **24**(2), 299–332 (2015)
17. Lopez-Carmona, M.A., Marsa-Maestre, I., Ibañez, G., Carral, J.A., Velasco, J.R.: Improving trade-offs in automated bilateral negotiations for expressive and inexpressive scenarios. J. Intell. Fuzzy Syst. **21**(3), 165–174 (2010)
18. Marsa-Maestre, I., Lopez-Carmona, M.A., Velasco, J.R., de la Hoz, E.: Effective bidding and deal identification for negotiations in highly nonlinear scenarios. In: Proceedings of the 8th International Conference on Autonomous Agents and Multiagent Systems - Volume 2, AAMAS 2009, International Foundation for Autonomous Agents and Multiagent Systems, Richland, SC, pp. 1057–1064 (2009)

19. Orden, D., Marsá-Maestre, I., Giménez-Guzmán, J.M., de la Hoz, E.: Spectrum graph coloring and applications to WiFi channel assignment. CoRR abs/1602.05038 (2016)
20. Osorio, C., Bierlaire, M.: Mitigating network congestion: analytical models, optimization methods and their applications. In: 90th Annual Meeting, No. EPFL-TALK-196049 (2011)
21. Pelikan, M., Sastry, K., Goldberg, D.E.: Multiobjective estimation of distribution algorithms. In: Pelikan, M., Sastry, K., CantúPaz, E. (eds.) Scalable Optimization via Probabilistic Modeling, pp. 223–248. Springer, Heidelberg (2006). https://doi.org/10.1007/978-3-540-34954-9_10
22. Schaller, B.: New York City's congestion pricing experience and implications for road pricing acceptance in the United States. Transp. Pol. **17**(4), 266–273 (2010)
23. Tuza, Z., Gutin, G., Plurnmer, M., Tucker, A., Burke, E., Werra, D., Kingston, J.: Colorings and related topics. Handbook of Graph Theory. Discrete Mathematics and Its Applications, pp. 340–483. CRC Press, Boca Raton (2003)
24. Vytelingum, P., Ramchurn, S.D., Voice, T.D., Rogers, A., Jennings, N.R.: Trading agents for the smart electricity grid. In: Proceedings of the 9th International Conference on Autonomous Agents and Multiagent Systems: Volume 1, International Foundation for Autonomous Agents and Multiagent Systems, pp. 897–904 (2010)
25. Zheng, L., Mengshoel, O.: Optimizing parallel belief propagation in junction treesusing regression. In: Proceedings of the 19th ACM SIGKDD International Conference on Knowledge Discovery and Data Mining, KDD 2013, ACM, Chicago, Illinois, USA, pp. 757–765 (2013)

Stable Configurations with (Meta)Punishing Agents

Nathaniel Beckemeyer$^{(\boxtimes)}$ (iD), William Macke, and Sandip Sen

The Tandy School of Computer Science, The University of Tulsa, Tulsa, OK, USA
{nate,william-macke,sandip}@utulsa.edu

Abstract. We consider an adaptation of Axelrod's metanorm model, where a population of agents choose between cooperating and defecting in bilateral interactions. Because punishing incurs an enforcement cost, Axelrod proposes using metanorms, to facilitate the stability of a norm of punishing defectors, where those who do not punish defectors can themselves be punished. We present two approaches to study the social effects of such metanorms when agents can choose their interaction partners: (a) a theoretical study, when agent behaviors are static, showing stable social configurations, under all possible relationships between system parameters representing agent payoffs with or without defection, punishment, and meta-punishment, and (b) an experimental evaluation of emergent social configurations when agents choose behaviors to maximize expected utility. We highlight emergent social configurations, including anarchy, a "police" state with cooperating agents who enforce, and a unique "corrupt police" state where one enforcer penalizes all defectors but defects on others!

Keywords: MABS workshop · Multi-agent systems · Cooperation
Norm emergence · Network topologies · Metanorm
Metapunishment · Punishment

1 Introduction

With the burgeoning of participation and activities in online social networks, there is increasing interest in understanding how interactions between individuals can give rise to emergent social structure and phenomena [3,4,10], such as information cascades [7], as well as the influence individuals have on others [9]. Concomitantly, researchers have used agent-based models and simulations to study how behavioral traits and interaction decisions can shape the dynamics of social networks. The goal of these research is to understand the dynamics of network connections and topologies [13,15,18], information flow [5,19], or to characterize the emergence of conventions or norms [1,11,12,17,21] or cooperative behavior [14,16]. While some of these research analytically prove convergence or equilibrium or formally derive rational agent behaviors [8,16,18], others use

© Springer International Publishing AG 2017
G. Sukthankar and J. A. Rodriguez-Aguilar (Eds.): AAMAS 2017 Visionary Papers,
LNAI 10643, pp. 17–30, 2017.
https://doi.org/10.1007/978-3-319-71679-4_2

extensive experimental evaluations to understand the nature of emerging behaviors and topologies in networks of self-interested agents [1,14,15].

A number of these studies investigate scenarios where the network topology changes based on strategic or exploratory rewiring of connections by agents seeking more beneficial partnerships [15,17,18]. Interaction between neighbors on networks are often represented as a stage game [11,12].Some of these studies on norm emergence have also considered agents who use punishments and sanctions to facilitate convergence to social welfare maximizing outcomes for these games [14,20]. The use of punishments to facilitate norm emergence goes back to the work of Axelrod [2] who observes *"A norm exists in a given social setting to the extent that individuals usually act in a certain way and are often punished when seen not to be acting in this way."* Axelrod observes that punishing norm violators can be costly and hence free riders, who do not punish violators but rely on others to do so, may proliferate. He then suggested the use of a *metanorm*, a norm to punish those who do not punish norm violators (we refer to this as *metapunishment*)! Mahmoud et al. [14] have used resource-aware, adaptive use of metanorms to promote cooperation in peer-to-peer resource sharing networks, when individuals may have incentives to defect.

Our goal in this paper is to investigate how the ability to rewire as well as the use of punishment and metapunishment can result in the emergence of different network topologies between different types of agents. We consider the following agent types connected in a network: *cooperators* who always cooperate with their neighbors, *defectors* who defect against all neighbors, *punishers (corrupt)* who are cooperating (defecting) agents that also punish, and metapunish if that option is available. A link is created between two agents if any one of them wants to interact with the other. Each agent interaction is represented as a stage game with a payoff matrix representing a social dilemma: mutual cooperation is preferable to mutual defection but there is incentive to defect against a cooperator. When punishment is allowed, the situation corresponds to an extensive form game, where an agent has the option to punish a defecting neighbor. When metapunishment is allowed, an agent can metapunish a neighbor who do not punish its defecting neighbors. Punishment and metapunishment have costs to the enforcer, which are less than the corresponding costs to the recipient.

In the present study, we make the two following assumptions: Only one agent is necessary to choose another as a neighbor, or, equivalently, both agents must agree to cease interacting; and agents, once having selected a strategy, do not change their behavior. We assume the former following initial work in [6], wherein only one agent must choose to interact in order to connect to the other agents. Additionally, one can imagine a variety of real world scenarios corresponding to bilateral agreement, such as a group in a social network where leaving brings a substantial cost to the user, reputation or otherwise, which forces the user to interact with others he or she may not like. This formulation of the problem also allows for an interesting new aspect of the game: oppression. With mutual consent required to terminate a link, one party can defect and enforce norms upon another without this parties permission. Additionally, we find the choice of static strategies a reasonable formation because people tend to maintain a mostly constant persona when interacting with their neighbors.

Similar work was performed by Galán et al. in [13]. We note, however, that their work focused on stable norms resulting from static topologies; our paper considers the converse question of the stable topologies that result from rewiring connections while agents follow static behaviors. The network characterizations that they present are also unsuitable for our model due to the fact that, in our work, the networks either initialize as fully connected or links can be added as agents deem rational, as opposed to constant topologies. For example, since all agents of a particular type behave in the same manner in our model, they will all make the same decisions as to which other agents to connect to or attempt to disconnect from—contrasting the probabilistic behaviors used in their work. Consequently, analyses of the resultant clustering coefficients, numbers of triples, or other metrics are uninteresting. Another key difference between the two works is that the agents in their work change strategies by the genetic forces of selection and mutation; in our work, however, behaviors only change in the experimental analysis due to rational choice, and are constant in the theoretical analysis.

The paper is organized as follows. In Sect. 2, we present the configurations that will result when agents cannot change their type but can change their connections. These situations are amenable to algebraic solutions and we can precisely derive the network topologies that will arise by the rewiring process. We consider all possible game scenarios conforming with the social dilemma mentioned above and for various cost of making a new connection. We highlight interesting resultant networks for situations where there is (a) no punishment, (b) punishment but not metapunishment, and (c) metapunishment. In Sect. 3, we present experimental results showing converged network topologies where in addition to rewiring their connections, agents can also myopically change their types to maximize the utility they expect to receive given their current neighbors (these scenarios do not lend them to similar algebraic analysis as in the case of fixed agent types). We find interesting converged topologies such as a *police state* where few punishing agents keep other agents from defecting, as well as an oddball *corrupt police state* where a lone (meta)punishing agent prevents others from defecting but itself defects against all others! An associated interesting observation is the relative frequency with which the different converged topologies result when punishment is used with or without metapunishment. We conclude with a brief discussion of future work.

2   Theoretical Analysis

2.1   Specification

Game Mechanics. Starting with an initial network of fully connected agents, the game proceeds in many rounds. In each round, an agent interacts with each of its neighbors. An agent, *Player A*, can either choose to cooperate or defect against its neighbor, *Player B*. Choosing to defect gives *Player A* the temptation reward and *Player B* the hurt value, and choosing to cooperate gives the baseline reward to both players. When the punishment option is present, each interaction has a second stage, wherein, if *Player A* chooses to defect against *Player B*, then *Player B* has the opportunity to punish *Player A*.

Finally, if the metapunishment option is present, each round has a second phase. Each player, *Player A*, observes the interactions of each other agent, *Player B*—specifically, whether *Player B* chose to punish. If *Player B* chose not to punish a defector, then *Player A* has the opportunity to metapunish *Player B*. Metapunishment enables agents to encourage other agents to punish those agents who defect.

An agent has to pay a linking cost r for each of its link to a neighbor. If a link to a neighbor brings negative utility, then an the agent will try to cut that link at the end of a round. If both agents in a linked pair attempt to cut a link, the link will be eliminated. If only one agent, however, attempts to cut that link, then the link will remain.

Agent Strategies. For a description of the payoffs used in this game, see Table 1.

Table 1. Glossary of payoffs. If a payoff contains the letter on the left, then the payoff includes the reward for the interaction on the right (the payoffs are additive). For instance, dh indicates that the agent both defected and was defected against.

b	The baseline—the reward for cooperation on both sides
d	Defecting
h	Being defected against (harmed)
dp	Defecting and being punished
he	Being defected against and enforcing
m	Being metapunished
M	Metaenforcing

Each agent type in the population has a type or strategy which cannot be changed. Without punishment, there are two agent types: *cooperator* types always cooperate and *defector* types always defect.

In the case of basic punishment, the *cooperator* type agents cooperate but do not enforce punishment. The *defector* type agents defect but do not enforce. There are two additional types: The *punisher* and *corrupt*. The *punisher* type agents cooperate and enforce punishment. The *corrupt* type agents defect and enforce punishment.

In the case of metapunishment, the agent types are the same as those in the basic punishment case, but the *punisher* and *corrupt* types both metapunish as well while other agent types do not.

2.2 Payoff Topologies

No punishment. We first examine the case of no punishment. Table 2 represents the payoff matrix for this scenario.

Table 2. Payoffs without punishment

	cooperator	defector
cooperator	(b, b)	(h, d)
defector	(d, h)	(dh, dh)

Because there is no punishment, the only options are passivity and defection. b is simply the baseline. d is the baseline plus the temptation reward, which is included to incentivize agents to defect. h is b plus the hurt value, included to incentivize agents to punish. So, we make the following assumptions:

1. The temptation reward is greater than 0, or equivalently, $d > b$
2. The hurt value is less than 0.

From these assumptions, we can conclude that $d > b > h$ and, furthermore, that $d > dh > h$, since dh is simply $b + hurt\ value + temptation\ reward$

These conditions lead to six meaningful placements of the linking cost, r, and five unique topologies:

1. $r > d$: The network is empty because the linking cost is higher than the maximum possible reward from a link.
2. $d > r \geq dh, b$: The defecting agents form links with the passive agents in order to gain the temptation reward, d
3. $d, dh > r > b$: The defecting agents form links with themselves (for dh) and the passive agents (for d).
4. $b > r \geq dh, h$: The defecting agents connect to the passive agents, and the passive agents connect to themselves.
5. $b, dh > r > h$: A complete network is formed (the defecting agents will forcibly connect to the passive agents).
6. $h > r$: A complete network is formed.

Punishment. In this section, we examine the case of basic punishment. Table 3 represents the payoff matrix for this scenario.

Table 3. Payoffs with basic punishment

	cooperate	punish	defect	corrupt
cooperate	(b, b)	(b, b)	(h, d)	(h, d)
punisher	(b, b)	(b, b)	(he, dp)	(he, dp)
defector	(d, h)	(dp, he)	(dh, dh)	(dhp, dhe)
corrupt	(d, h)	(dp, he)	(dhe, dhp)	$(dhpe, dhpe)$

In addition to the assumptions made in the previous section, we assume that enforcing and being punished cost the agent, and that it is worse for an agent to be punished after defecting than for an agent to enforce after being defected against:

1. The enforcement cost is less than 0.
2. The punishment cost is less than the enforcement cost.
3. $he > dp$: Total payoff for the punisher is greater than that of the punished.

From these assumptions, we can conclude that $d > b > h > he > dp > dhp > dhpe$, that $d > dh > h$, and that $dh > dhe > he$. These orderings suggest 13 possible placements for the linking cost, which lead to 10 different topologies. An interesting few selected results follow.

Agents who punish can, in some configurations, prevent defecting agents from connecting to themselves. Figure 1(a) shows a sample configuration wherein the *punisher* agents are not connected to defecting agents, but the *cooperator* agents are. An interesting note about Fig. 1(a) is its similarity to a hub network, where the *cooperator* agents are the hub, and the other agents do not interact outside of their own groups.

In general, punishment is a highly effective method for agents to defend themselves against defection. Figure 1(b) represents the most connected network wherein agents who defect, *corrupt* and *defector* agents, still connect to the *punisher* agents.

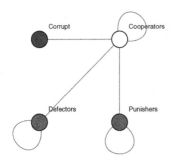

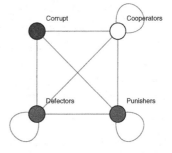

(a) $d, b, dh > r \geq dhe,$ $he, dp, dhp, dhpe$
This is an example of a network where punishers are safe from defection.

(b) $d, b, dh, h, dhe, he > r \geq dp, dhp, dhpe$
This topology is the most connected network wherein agents still defect against punishers.

Fig. 1. Interesting topologies from basic punishment.

Metapunishment. In this section, we examine the case of metapunishment. Table 4 represents the payoff matrix for this scenario.

Table 4. Payoffs with metapunishment

	cooperate	punish	defect	corrupt
cooperate	(b,b)	(m,M)	(h,d)	(hm,dM)
punish	(M,m)	(b,b)	(eM,dpm)	(he,dp)
defect	(d,h)	(dpm,eM)	(dh,dh)	$(dhpm,dheM)$
corrupt	(dM,hm)	(dp,he)	$(dheM,dhpm)$	$(dhpe,dhpe)$

In this section, similarly to the case of basic punishment, we assume additionally that it costs to meta-enforce and to be metapunished, and that being metapunished for neglecting to punish is worse for an agent than for an agent's meta-enforcing. That is,

1. The meta-enforcement cost is less than 0.
2. The metapunishment cost is less than the meta-enforcement cost.
3. $M > m$: Being metapunished is worse than meta-enforcing.

From these assumptions, we can conclude that $d > b > h > he > dp > dhp > dhpe$, that $d > dM > M > m > hm > dpm > dhpm$, that $M > eM > dpm > hm$, that $d > dh > h$, that $dh > dhe > he$, that $dhe > dheM$, and that $dM > dheM > dpm$.

These constraints imply 113 possible placements for the linking cost, which lead to 73 unique topologies. In the following paragraphs, we highlight notable results.

Metapunishment can destabilize previously stable topologies. Figure 2(a) shows one circumstance in which *punisher* agents will not connect to *cooperator* agents in contrast to the case of basic punishment. Specifically, the *cooperator* and *punisher* agents used to receive b when they interacted; however, in this case, metapunishment reduces the payoffs below the linking cost.

Additionally, metapunishment can entirely cease interactions between *punisher* agents and nonpunishing agents. As an example, Fig. 2(b) contains no connections between the *punisher* agents and the *defector* agents nor the *cooperator* agents. This topology is also remarkable because the temptation reward is sufficient to offset the meta-enforcement cost, as evidenced by the connection from the *corrupt* agents to the nonpunishing ones. This phenomena is interesting because the *corrupt* agents are punishing agents for not punishing the *corrupt* agents.

An interesting side effect of metapunishment is that the *defector* strategy may actually present a way for agents to defend themselves. In Fig. 2(c), the *defector* agents are not connected to the *punisher* agents. The *cooperator* agents also are connected to the *punisher* agents. This connections implies that the meta-enforcement cost is, alone, insufficient to prevent *punisher* agents from linking to *cooperator* agents. Additionally, the *corrupt* agents are, connected to the *punisher* agents. This connection implies that the hurt value and enforcement cost are insufficient to prevent a link from forming. Therefore, it is the

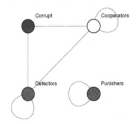 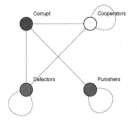 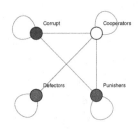

(a) d, b, dh, dhe, dM, $dheM > r > h$, he, dp, dhp, $dhpe$, M, m, hm, eM, dpm, $dhpm$

This topology demonstrates metapunishment can halt agents connected with only basic punishment from connecting now.

(b) d, b, dh, h, dhe, he, dp, dhp, dM, $dheM$, $> r >$ $dhpe$, M, m, hm, eM, dpm, $dhpm$

A topology wherein the meta-enforcement cost prevents *punisher* agents from connecting to nonpunishing agents.

(c) d, b, dh, h, dhe, he, dp, dhp, $dhpe$, dM, $M > r >$ m, hm, eM, $dheM$, dpm, $dhpm$

This topology shows the power of *defector* agents to thwart metapunishment.

Fig. 2. Interesting topologies from including metapunishment

combination of hurt value, enforcement cost, and meta-enforcement cost that does prevent the link from the *punisher* to the *defector* agents from forming—a combination that can only occur with agents using the *defector* strategy.

3   Experimental Analysis

The above analysis assumed agent types were static. To understand the emergent topologies when agents could myopically adapt their types to optimize payoff given their neighbors types, we ran simulations varying various parameters. During rounds, agents would follow this algorithm:

```
procedure AGENT_BEHAVIOR()
maxUtility = Utility(currentStrategy)
maxStrategy = currentStrategy
for strategy in Strategies do
  if Utility(strategy) > maxUtility then
    maxUtility = Utility(strategy)
    maxStrategy = strategy
  end if
end for
if maxStrategy != currentStrategy then
  currentStrategy = maxStrategy
  return
end if
for link in CurrentLinks do
  if Utility(link)<0 then
    removeLink()
    return
  end if
```

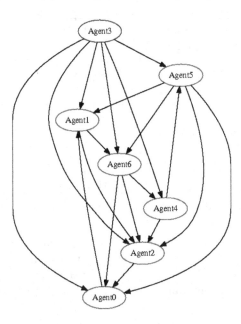

Fig. 3. One Way Corrupt Police (Red-*cooperator*, Violet-*corrupt*). (Color figure online)

end for

LinkToRandomAgent()

Where the utilities of links are defined by the values in the payoff matrices given in Sect. 2, and the utility of a strategy is simply the sum of all of the links of an agent, assuming that the agent adopts that strategy. In a round agents make their decisions sequentially. The order of turns was decided randomly at the beginning of each round. Simulations were run with both simple punishment and meta-punishment and with various numbers of agents. Each simulation ran for 1000 rounds. Only simple graphs were used; i.e., if Agent 1 connected to Agent 2, then Agent 2 could not connect to Agent 1. Each agent was assigned a random strategy at the beginning of the game.

3.1 Observed Stable Configurations

All experiments produced one of three stable configurations: *Anarchy* indicates all agents are defecting, *Police State* refers to a few punishing agents and the rest neutral, and *Corrupt Police State* refers to exactly one agent defecting and punishing while the rest are neutral.

The three stable configurations mentioned above could form different topologies: *Complete Network, Empty Anarchy, One way corrupt police*. In the complete network, all agents linked with all other agents. Any of the three configurations could form with this topology. Empty anarchy was an anarchy network without any agent linking to any other agent. The one way Corrupt Police was the most

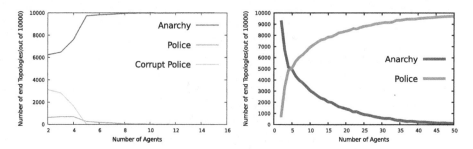

Fig. 4. End Topologies with different # of agents: Punishment only (Left), Metapunishment included (Right). Parameters: Base 0, Defection Reward 3, Defection Hurt 1, Punishment Cost 2, Punishment Hurt 9, Linking Cost 0.

interesting of the three topologies. It was a corrupt police state, but none of the cooperators were willingly linked to the corrupt police officer. Thus we had one group of agents that would link to only agents of their own type, but were being stabilized and exploited simultaneously by an outside agent. See Fig. 3.

3.2   Conditions for Network Development

An important goal of the experimental analysis was to observe what conditions were required for each of the three stable configurations to emerge.

Figure 4 shows the relative frequency of emergence of different stable configurations as we vary the number of agents in the network. Without metapunishment, as the number of agents increases, the number of configurations that result in anarchy also increases. We will discuss this phenomena in detail below. With metapunishment, increasing the number of agents increases the likelihood of a police state emerging. Presence of more metapunishers force non-punishers to start punishing; thus with more agents present there is an increase in frequency of the emergence of police states.

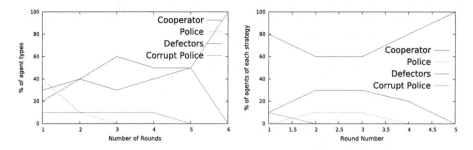

Fig. 5. % of agent types as Anarchy develops, 10 agents: punishment only (Left), with Metapunishment (Right). Parameters: Base 10, Defection Reward 1, Defection Hurt 3, Punishment Cost 3, Punishment Hurt 12, Linking Cost 0.

Anarchy. Due to the randomness of allocation of initial agent types, the initial number of agent types may not be equal. The initial agent type distribution is likely to be more skewed particularly for small agent populations. If there were too many defectors at the beginning, anarchy developed from large numbers of agents defecting. When a punisher links with a defector, one of two things happen: the defector stops defecting or the punisher stops punishing. When there are far more defectors than there are punishers, it becomes much more likely that the punisher will have to back down and stop punishing at some point. For small populations there are more chances of very few defectors in the initial population, whence the network may evolve to a state different from anarchy. With larger populations, there are more agents that can defect in the early rounds of the game and it becomes harder for the punishing agents to maintain order. With large enough numbers of agents, the end topology is almost always anarchy. Hence, all figures of networks developing are shown with 10 agents. Anarchy was by far the most common of the three stable configurations that formed without metapunishment. When metapunishment was included, the frequency of anarchy networks drastically decreased because of reasons listed below. The percentage of different agent types in sample runs that evolved Anarchy networks, with or without metapunishment, are shown in Fig. 5. Modified parameters are used when observing network developments to reduce the anarchy development rate.

Police. The convergence to a police state was facilitated by an initial state of a large number of punishers. These punishers would have to immediately link with each other in order for the police state to form, because otherwise the punishers would want to become defectors. If two punishers link with each other, neither will defect to avoid being punished by the other. However if a punisher is linked only with non-punishing agents, then it will become a defector for the Utility boost. From there they would force all defecting agents to become neutral as they connected to them. When metapunishment is included, punishers gain the ability to force other agents to become punishers. This aides the development of police networks and increases their relative frequency. Sample runs that evolved the Police state are presented in Fig. 6.

Corrupt Police. The corrupt police state developed from an initial state of a large number of agents who were defecting and punishing. As these agents linked with others, they forced those agents to become neutral to avoid punishment. When two of these agents connect, one will back down and become neutral while the other will remain a defector and punisher. A sample run that evolved a Corrupt Police network is shown in Fig. 7.

This demonstrates one of the more interesting outcomes of the game: Corruption will not tolerate company while non-corruption requires it. In the corrupt police network, all "corrupt police officers" will eliminate each other until only one remains, while the police network requires multiple interacting "officers". The corrupt police network was only stable without metapunishment. If metapunishment exists, then the corrupt police officer will have to punish neutral

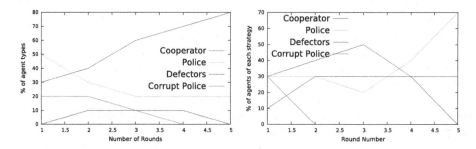

Fig. 6. % of agent types as Police state evolves, 10 agents: punishment only (Left); with Metapunishment (Right). Parameters: Base 10, Defection Reward 1, Defection Hurt 3, Punishment Cost 3, Punishment Hurt 12, Linking Cost 0.

agents for not punishing it. This in turn forces the neutral agents to become punishers, and hence the corrupt police network does not emerge with metapunishment.

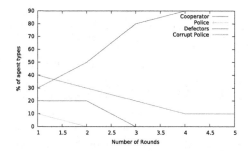

Fig. 7. % of agent types as corrupt police configuration develops (simple punishment); 10 agents. Parameters: Base 10, Defection Reward 1, Defection Hurt 3, Punishment Cost 3, Punishment Hurt 12, Linking Cost 0.

4   Conclusions

We investigated the effect of rewiring and behavior adoptions on the emergent topology of networked self-interested agents interacting in a social dilemma scenario with and without punishment and metapunishment options. When agent types were fixed, we identify, using algebraic calculations, interesting topologies that result under various relationships between agent interaction payoffs and rewiring costs. Such derivations are not forthcoming when agents can change their types myopically to maximize payoffs given their neighborhood. We run a suit of experiments and observe the emergence of different classes of network topologies. Particularly interesting are the police and corrupt police states and their relative abundance with and without the option of metapunishment.

We plan to investigate unilateral elimination of links which should allow for cooperators to thrive more frequently. We will analyze mixed, rather than pure strategy types, where agents defect with some probability $0 < p < 1$. We will also study a broader class of social dilemmas, including the prisoner's dilemma and the Hawk-Dove game. In Sect. 2, we assumed all types are present in equal numbers; we will analyze non-uniform distribution of agent types. Finally, we intend to perform analyses similar to those done by Galán et al. in [13]: Allowing for nondeterministic behavior could lead to some highly intriguing resultant social networks and network properties. Combining all of these future directions, characterizing networks with unilateral links could additionally prove fascinating.

Acknowledgments. We would like to thank the University of Tulsa and in particular the Tulsa Undergraduate Research Challenge (TURC) for financial support of this project.

References

1. Airiau, S., Sen, S., Villatoro, D.: Emergence of conventions through social learning - heterogeneous learners in complex networks. Auton. Agent. Multi-Agent Syst. **28**, 779–804 (2014). https://doi.org/10.1007/s10458-013-9237-x
2. Axelrod, R.: An evolutionary approach to norms. Am. Polit. Sci. Rev. **80**, 1095–1111 (1986)
3. Baetz, O.: Social activity and network formation. Theor. Econ. **10**(2), 315–340 (2015)
4. Barabasi, A.: Network Science. Cambridge university press (2016)
5. Belardinelli, F., Grossi, D.: On the formal verification of diffusion phenomena in open dynamic agent networks. In: Proceedings of the 2015 International Conference on Autonomous Agents and Multiagent Systems, AAMAS 2015, Richland, SC, International Foundation for Autonomous Agents and Multiagent Systems, pp. 237–245 (2015)
6. Berninghaus, S., Vogt, B.: Network formation and coordination games, March 2003
7. Borge-Holthoefer, J., Baos, R.A., Gonzlez-Bailn, S., Moreno, Y.: Cascading behaviour in complex socio-technical networks. J. Complex Netw. **1**(1), 3–24 (2013)
8. Brooks, L., Iba, W., Sen, S.: Modeling the emergence and convergence of norms. In: IJCAI, pp. 97–102 (2011)
9. Cha, M., Haddadi, H., Benevenuto, F., Gummadi, K.P.: Measuring user influence in Twitter: the million follower fallacy. In: ICWSM 2010: Proceedings of international AAAI Conference on Weblogs and Social (2010)
10. David, E., Jon, K.: Networks, Crowds, and Markets: Reasoning About a Highly Connected World. Cambridge University Press, New York (2010)
11. Delgado, J.: Emergence of social conventions in complex networks. Artif. Intell. **141**(1–2), 171–185 (2002)
12. Epstein, J.M.: Learning to be thoughtless: social norms and individual computation. Comput. Econ. **18**(1), 9–24 (2001)
13. Galán, J.M., Łatek, M.M., Rizi, S.M.M.: Axelrod's metanorm games on networks. PLoS ONE **6**(5), 1–11 (2011)

14. Mahmoud, S., Miles, S., Luck, M.: Cooperation emergence under resource-constrained peer punishment. In: Proceedings of the 2016 International Conference on Autonomous Agents & Multiagent Systems, AAMAS 2016, Richland, SC, International Foundation for Autonomous Agents and Multiagent Systems, pp. 900–908 (2016)

15. Peleteiro, A., Burguillo, J.C., Chong, S.Y.: Exploring indirect reciprocity in complex networks using coalitions and rewiring. In: Proceedings of the 2014 International Conference on Autonomous Agents and Multi-Agent Systems, AAMAS 2014, Richland, SC, International Foundation for Autonomous Agents and Multiagent Systems, pp. 669–676 (2014)

16. Ranjbar-Sahraei, B., Bou Ammar, H., Bloembergen, D., Tuyls, K., Weiss, G.: Evolution of cooperation in arbitrary complex networks. In: Proceedings of the 2014 International Conference on Autonomous Agents and Multi-Agent Systems, AAMAS 2014, Richland, SC, International Foundation for Autonomous Agents and Multiagent Systems, pp. 677–684 (2014)

17. Savarimuthu, B.T.R., Cranefield, S., Purvis, M., Purvis, M.: Norm emergence in agent societies formed by dynamically changing networks. In: Proceedings of the 2007 IEEE/WIC/ACM International Conference on Intelligent Agent Technology, IAT 2007, Washington, DC, USA, IEEE Computer Society, pp. 464–470 (2007)

18. Sina, S., Hazon, N., Hassidim, A., Kraus, S.: Adapting the social network to affect elections. In: Proceedings of the 2015 International Conference on Autonomous Agents and Multiagent Systems, AAMAS 2015, Richland, SC, International Foundation for Autonomous Agents and Multiagent Systems, pp. 705–713 (2015)

19. Tsang, A., Larson, K.: Opinion dynamics of skeptical agents. In: Proceedings of the 2014 International Conference on Autonomous Agents and Multi-Agent Systems, AAMAS 2014, Richland, SC, International Foundation for Autonomous Agents and Multiagent Systems, pp. 277–284 (2014)

20. Villatoro, D., Andrighetto, G., Sabater-Mir, J., Conte, R.: Dynamic sanctioning for robust and cost-efficient norm compliance. In: Proceedings of the Twenty-Second International Joint Conference on Artificial Intelligence - Volume One, IJCAI 2011, pp. 414–419. AAAI Press (2011)

21. Villatoro, D., Sen, S., Sabater-Mir, J.: Topology and memory effect on convention emergence. In: IAT (2009)

KILT: A Modelling Approach Based on Participatory Agent-Based Simulation of Stylized Socio-Ecosystems to Stimulate Social Learning with Local Stakeholders

Christophe Le Page[1,2](✉) and Arthur Perrotton[3,4](✉)

[1] CIRAD, UPR Green, 34398 Montpellier, France
christophe.le_page@cirad.fr
[2] CIRAD, UPR Green, University of Brasilia, Brasilia, Brazil
[3] CIRAD, UMR Astre, 34398 Montpellier, France
arthur.perrotton@cirad.fr
[4] Center for Applied Social Sciences,
University of Zimbabwe, Harare, Zimbabwe

Abstract. A new approach is introduced under the slogan «Keep It a Learning Tool» (KILT) to emphasize the crucial need to make the purpose of the modelling process explicit when choosing the degree of complicatedness of an agent-based simulation model. We suggest that a co-design approach driven by early-stage and interactive simulation of empirical agent-based models representing stylized socio-ecosystems stimulates collective learning and, as a result, may promote the emergence of cooperative interactions among local stakeholders.

Keywords: Participatory agent-based simulation · Social learning
Stylized landscape · Role-playing game · Companion modelling

1 Introduction

An agent-based simulation is said to be "participatory" as soon as some decisions of the agents are entrusted to the participants. A typology of simulations has been proposed by Crookall and his colleagues [1]. They distinguished two types of simulations depending on who controls it, and where the focus is. When the simulation is mainly controlled by the computer, the focus of interaction can be set on computer-participant interactions (participants observe the simulation run in the manner of a cinema audience), or on participant-participant interactions (participants can intervene while the simulation runs or at intervals provided during the run). In any of these cases, the flexibility of the simulation remains limited. A second type is when the simulation is mainly controlled by the participants. The focus of interaction can then be set on computer-participant ("flight simulator" for which generally only one user interacts continuously with the simulation), or on participant-participant. In that last case, participants will be confronted with concrete situations, acted out by the organizers of the participatory simulation workshops, which they must react to.

© Springer International Publishing AG 2017
G. Sukthankar and J. A. Rodriguez-Aguilar (Eds.): AAMAS 2017 Visionary Papers,
LNAI 10643, pp. 31–44, 2017.
https://doi.org/10.1007/978-3-319-71679-4_3

This type of interactive participatory agent-based simulation is very similar to what is called a computer-assisted role-playing game in the framework of the companion modeling approach [2–4]. As pointed out by Barreteau [5], there is a striking correspondence between the features of an agent-based simulation and a role-playing game session: agent/player, role/rule, game-turn/time-step, game board/interface. This similarity is due to the fact that, from a formal point of view, a role-playing game is a kind of multi-agent system: it is composed of interacting entities, evolving in a shared environment, each one seeking to achieve a specific goal. Apart from the simulation of agents' decisions, the computerization may also support the following features: (i) recording the decisions of human agents, which enables computing performance indicators (results of their actions) and "replaying" the session during the debriefing; (ii) simulating the dynamics of the resources; (iii) visualizing the updated state of the resources and the positioning of the agents, possibly according to points of view specific to each type of players [6].

In computer science, participatory agent-based simulation represents a fertile ground for improving the techniques of Artificial Intelligence related to supervised learning such as inverse reinforcement learning or support vector machines [7]. Introducing assistant agents with learning abilities can help eliciting the behavior of human participants and also supporting them to make decisions during the course of the simulation [8]. Participatory agent-based simulation sessions have been successfully used as an experimental framework to extract interaction patterns in negotiated (written) elements between participants [9].

By integrating the HubNet module into the NetLogo platform, which allows interconnecting several identical user interfaces to the same simulation, Wilensky and Stroup [10] paved the way for using participatory simulation to facilitate the learning of complex systems to students. One of the first applications of HubNet is called Gridlock[1]. It is a simulation of car traffic in real time where each student controls a traffic light while the teacher controls the global variables, such as speed limit and number of cars. The group is challenged to develop strategies to improve traffic and discuss the different ways of measuring the traffic quality [11]. Another example of the educational potential of interactive multi-agent simulations is given by the experiment on the spread of a contagious disease conducted with US high school students [12]. A network of miniature communicating computers (tags) allows simulating the spreading of a virus among the participants, each of them wearing a tag as a bracelet, only one being initially infected. Participants are challenged to meet as many people as possible without getting sick. To stimulate experiential learning, students were told nothing about how the virus moved from one tag to another, the degree of contagiousness, the possibility for latency.

In such an immersive configuration, the space of interactions does not have to be "re-presented" to the participants. In most of the applications of participatory agent-based simulation anyway, space has to be explicitly represented into the model. This is of particular importance when the target system is a socio-ecosystem. The distribution of a participative multi-agent simulation on several computers is an

---

[1] http://ccl.northwestern.edu/netlogo/models/HubNetGridlockHubNet.

efficient way of staging information asymmetry between participants. It is then interesting to observe if participants take the initiative to share certain information - initially private - with others. When the objective is to improve the mutual understanding between the participants, it becomes critical to encourage direct interaction between them and to stimulate exchanges. Representing a common visualization space and a support to materialize the decisions of the players with pawns and tokens, a large game board (so that everyone can sit around) is a configuration that answers perfectly to this need. For instance, the environment of the *SAMBA* model, developed in Vietnam [13, 14], consists of a rectangular support filled with cubes, each of the six faces representing a land cover. Players then manipulate the cubes directly to signify the changes in land use corresponding to their actions. But when the simulation includes ecological and/or hydro-physical processes not directly under the control of the players, manually updating the environment by an operator is a tedious operation that causes dead times for the participants.

Using a digital game board provided by the projection on a horizontal flat surface of the computerized representation of the environment was recently tested in rural Zimbabwe. Before presenting the participatory agent-based simulation approach that was conducted with local actors to foster social learning, we propose a review of the applications of participatory agent-based simulation in the field of socio-ecological science, distinguishing its uses with scholars and with stakeholders. We stress the importance to clarify two fundamental features that are interconnected: the degree of realism of the model and the purpose of the modelling process.

2 Abstract, Stylized and Realistic Representations of Space in Agent-Based Models of Socio-Ecosystems

The representation of the environment can range from purely abstract landscapes to realistic ones integrating spatial data from geographical information systems. In the case of an abstract world, the environment of the model does not refer to any particular landscape, like in the *ReHab* participatory simulation tool [15], where harvesters have to collect a resource in an imaginary landscape that is also a nesting and breeding ground for a migratory bird under the protection of rangers (see Fig. 1a).

In an intermediate case, the implicit reference to a given socio-ecological system results in equivalent proportions in the distribution of the modalities of each landscape characteristics (primarily the land use) and possibly also in the similarity of the space configuration, with the integration of typical spatial patterns. For instance, in the *BUTORSTAR* model, the impacts on avifauna of the management of reed beds resulting from decisions made by farmers, reed collectors, hunters and naturalists are simulated in a stylized representation of the Camargue wetland [16]. Similarly, in the *SylvoPast* gaming tool [17] featuring conflicts of interest between a forester and a shepherd in the context of fires' prevention in the Mediterranean region, the proportions of the different types of vegetation cover (see Fig. 2b) are based on empirical data, so that the stylized environment of the model represents an archetypical grazed Mediterranean forest.

It is also the case of the *NewDistrict* interactive and asymmetric agent-based simulation [19] where the impacts of peri-urban development on biodiversity are

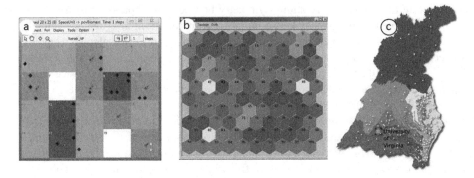

Fig. 1. The three types of environment in participatory agent-based simulation: (a) abstract, like in the *ReHab* game [15]; (b) stylized, like in the *SylvoPast* game [17]; (c) realistic, like in the uva bay game [18].

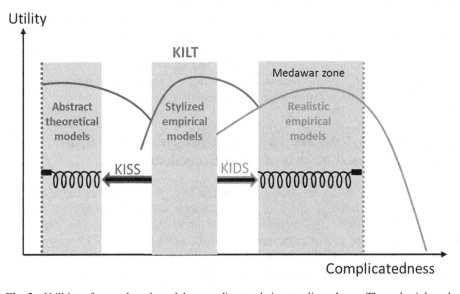

Fig. 2. Utilities of agent-based models according to their complicatedness. The red, pink and blue lines represent the utility functions of the abstract theoretical models, the stylized empirical models and the realistic empirical models. The black springs within the areas of effective use of abstract theoretical models and realistic empirical models symbolize the retraction force exerted by the *KISS* and *KIDS* principles [adapted from 32]

investigated in a stylized landscape. Three ecological processes are simulated (bee colonization, bird migration and water quality), with participants playing the roles of mayor, building contractor, farmer, forester and ecologist, each one equipped with a specific computer interface representing the landscape according to a point of view specific to its activity.

Recent technological advances [20, 21] have reinforced a trend that emerged some fifteen years ago [22–24] to move towards spatially-explicit agent-based models representing realistic landscapes by associating them with GIS. Extensions to integrate spatial data from GIS have been added to the main existing platforms (NetLogo, Mason, RePast). New platforms have been developed focusing mainly on these aspects: GAMA [25] and MAGéo [26]. This type of data-intensive models are becoming more and more popular, due to the increased availability of data, the computing power of computers and the increasing demand from policy-makers and managers for policy and scenario analysis [27]. A recent and emblematic example is the *uva bay game*, a large-scale agent-based participatory simulation of the Chesapeake Bay socio-ecosystem [18]. The game allows players to take the roles of stakeholders, such as farmers, developer, watermen, and local policy-makers, make decisions about their livelihoods or regulatory authority and see the impacts of their decisions on their own personal finances, the regional economy, fish and crab populations and overall bay health. Figure 1c shows the locations of the players (white dots) in one of the 8 watersheds represented in the model.

3   Involvement of Local Stakeholders: Adjusting the Degree of Complicatedness of the Model to Its Purpose

All the examples presented in the previous section were firstly developed to be used with students, for educational purpose. It is quite common to note a dual use of participatory agent-based simulation in the field of socio-ecological science: either support to the implementation of experiential learning in classrooms to teach students who are unfamiliar with the interdependencies of ecological and social dynamics, or a direct use with the actors of the socio-ecosystems. For instance, two gaming sessions of *BUTORSTAR* involving stakeholders of Étang de Vendres were organized, with the aim of increasing their capacity to adopt modes of interactions favoring adaptive management of the environment [28]. This duplication of the target audience (students and local actors) was also performed with *SylvoPast*, *NewDistrict* and *uva bay game*. In these three cases, the tool used with students and local stakeholders was strictly the same. In other cases, the tool initially designed to be used with stakeholders has to be adapted to meet the educational needs of both schoolchildren and the general public. This was for instance the case for the computer-assisted role-playing game designed by a group of researchers and biosphere reserve managers in Ushant Island (Brittany, France) to investigate consequences of land-use changes and fallow land encroachment on landscape, traditional activities and biodiversity [29, 30].

Even when the tools are similar, there is a shift in the purpose of conducting participatory simulation with stakeholders, who are definitively knowledgeable, rather than students. Generally, simulation is viewed as a mean to support experimentation by conducting *what-if* analysis that are not pre-determined, and not anymore as a mean to gain experience [31]. It does not make much sense to discuss the appropriate degree of complicatedness of a model supporting participatory agent-based simulation with stakeholders without specifying the type of stakeholders to be involved and without clarifying the purpose of their involvement [32]. Most commonly, the stakeholders involved are policy-makers and/or managers and the purpose is to gain insight about the functioning of the target socio-ecosystem as a basis for policy and scenario analysis related to agriculture and natural resource management [33].

In such a context of use, the *KIDS* ("Keep it Descriptive Stupid") approach [34] is undoubtedly relevant: models should be as complicated as necessary to answer the specific research question, with mid-levels of complicatedness providing the highest benefit per unit of modeling effort, which is reflected by the existence of what was called the "Medawar zone" [35]. On the other hand, the popular admonition *KISS* ("Keep It Simple, Stupid") that enjoins modelers to fight against their propensity to endlessly refine their model [36] is especially valid for theory-building and education purposes. A common idea is that choosing an intermediate posture in between these two zones of efficiency (see Fig. 2) may jeopardize the achievement of one purpose or the other. The empirical details in such models may hinder the theory building purpose and the stylized components may limit their applications in policy support [32].

Yet we believe there is a *raison d'être* for this type of intermediate stylized empirical agent-based models, which is to stimulate social learning through their co-design with local actors. Social learning has become a central concept in discourse on management issues related to the complexity of socio-ecosystems. Yet the theoretical and practical development of the concept is problematic [37, 38]. Most publications attempt to define its meaning, or to account for its realization in a given situation. Referring to the theory of communicative action [39], the different definitions of social learning emphasize the role of dialogue and intercommunication between group members in facilitating the perception of different representations and the development of collective problem-solving skills [40]. In this perspective, the relational dimension of learning is essential [41].

We advocate that, to fulfill its role of intermediate object allowing exchanges of viewpoints among participants, the model must be connected to reality in a stylized form so that each user can find ways to project features of the socio-ecosystem that make sense for him. To mark the specificity of this approach, we introduce the acronym *KILT* for Keep It a Learning Tool!

The *KILT* approach consists in initiating the process with an over-simplified stylized yet empirically grounded model that enables tackling the complexity of the target socio-ecosystem with a tool that has the status of a sketch. It provides the main features of the final version; however, it is clearly unfinished: there remains an important work of progressive shaping and improvement so that it acquires its final form and becomes usable with people who were not involved in its design.

In this approach, participatory simulation is used from an early stage of the process, as a strategic method to facilitate the co-design. A first version of a stylized agent-based model, deliberately simplistic, is designed by a group of 2–3 researchers. Handled as a participatory simulation tool (the actions of the agents are decided by the participants), it is introduced to a group of local actors to gather their suggestions to adjust it so that it enables discussing an issue related to the target system that was collectively formulated. A group of co-designers is then set up and the model is fine-tuned through a series of successive workshops. Once the design of an operational version is achieved, the tool is introduced to the other kinds of local actors as a support for communication.

To illustrate such a process, we will now present a recent implementation that took place in Zimbabwe.

4 Kulayijana: "Teaching Each Other"

A companion modelling process has been thought to create a fair and balanced communication arena in which local communities and protected area managers would exchange constructively on issues related to the coexistence between human populations and wildlife in the periphery of Hwange National Park, Zimbabwe.

Co-designed with a group of 11 villagers, the agent-based model represents the interactions between agricultural activities, livestock practices and wildlife. The model runs in an abstract virtual landscape that does not integrate specific details of the area, but shares fundamental features with two adjacent areas: a communal area and a forest. To motivate the participation of local actors involved in the co-design of the simulation tool, we chose to initiate the process by crash-testing with them a voluntarily simplistic version, not including some factors that clearly impact the result of their activities, especially crop losses due to extreme climatic events or crop raiding by elephants. During the first test of the game, these on-purpose omissions led to overly positive results of the players, who had all "enriched" dramatically. Although this was very pleasing to everyone, all participants acknowledged it was clearly unrealistic. Drawing on this, the participants engaged in a process of refining the game to make it more realistic while remaining "playable". This process lasted more than a year, with a set of iterative co-design workshops to test and improve the successive versions.

In the context of workshops organized in rural areas in countries such as Zimbabwe, the use of a computer is not always simple. In terms of ease of use, a non-computerized game is much more interesting, and as mentioned above, the use of a physical game board usually improves the direct interaction among the participants. During the co-design process, we therefore introduced a computer-free version with a game board. In this configuration, it was necessary to manually carry out the updates related to crops and fodder growth processes, losses of crop production due to climatic hazards and raiding by elephants, cattle predation by lions, water levels in ponds according to the input of rainfall data, which considerably slowed down the game and made its use very tedious. The local actors themselves felt that this mode of operation was not suitable and requested the return of the computer support. This challenging request was addressed by the use of a short focal projector allowing the horizontal projection of the computerized environment. With the stylized environment projected on a horizontal support, the players were able to position the artefacts making it possible to materialize their actions: the positioning and guarding of their cattle, the sowing and harvesting on their five plots, and the collective guarding of their communal paddock at night to prevent crop raiding by elephants (cf. Fig. 3).

The final version of the role-playing game was tested and validated with other villagers who were not involved in its co-design. In February 2016, a game session involving protected area managers from the study area was co-facilitated by 3 local members of the co-design team. One of them expressed his feelings before this event: *"It's our game, we are proud of what we have done. It shows our life, what we need*

Fig. 3. The virtual game board of the *Kulayinjana* agent-based model [42]

and what we have to live with [wildlife]. I hope they will like the game and see ways we can play together". At the end of the session, one of the managers said: "*This game is great, it could be useful for me to understand better the way they [the villagers] use my forest, and if we could play together and discuss, we could produce good management plans*" [42].

5   Discussion

The case study in Zimbabwe suggests that the horizontal projection of the environment on a physical support serving as a digital game board is an innovation that greatly benefits the implementation of participatory agent-based simulation in stimulating interactions. Other applications are currently underway. In the Poitevin marsh, such type of interactive multi-agent simulation is used to discuss with local stakeholders the relevance of agri-environmental public policies as incentives for farmers to adopt practices favoring the conservation of biodiversity [43]. In the flood plains of the Brazilian Amazon, it is used to better understand how populations adapt their practices to the drastic changes in the hydrographic regime currently observed [44].

In contexts where power asymmetries are strong, strengthening the capacities of the least favored actors constitutes a prerequisite to enable their fair inclusion in concertation processes [45]. Involving them in the co-design of a simplified but still meaningful representation of the socio-ecosystem taking the form of a computer-simulation tool requires some specific attention. Involving heterogeneous participants (here researchers and local actors) in a balanced co-design process is challenging. The rewards, in terms of learning, make the effort worthwhile [46]. Such a process exhibits features that may foster social learning: small group work, multiple sources of knowledge, egalitarian atmosphere, repeated meetings, open communication, unrestrained thinking [47]. The interviews conducted with the 22 local farmers who participated to the three workshops organized to test the "*Kulayijana*" tool indicated that it was found useful (75%) or very useful (25%), that it served as an opportunity to think (40%), learn (28%) and open new perspectives (12%). The self-learning dimension, which was also highlighted by the members of the co-design team, was therefore confirmed by the players [42].

Because social learning entails individual learning, measuring it is very challenging [47]. Scholz [48] recently proposed an analytical framework to monitor and compare the results of participatory approaches with respect to social learning, adding to the definition proposed by Reed [38] in looking for a convergence in the direction of individual learning. Most of the existing work aiming at assessing to what extent participatory modeling can support social learning is based on the use of conceptual diagrams (causal loop diagrams; stock/flow diagrams, cognitive maps), through a statistical analysis of the distributions of concepts' categories in the individual diagrams and in a diagram collectively built [49–51]. Involving local actors in activities like drawing relationships among conceptual entities can be abstruse, especially for those who only had access to rudimentary education. In such a context, we believe it is more suitable to use a concrete playable model.

Visual representations easily grasped by the participants can facilitate socially constructing shared meaning [52, 53]. The constructionist philosophy of learning advocates for mixing media in the model construction: translating one media into another can illuminate one media model formulation by seeing it in terms of another way of formulating it [54]. In the Zimbabwean case presented above, the introduction of a non-computerized version of the model at some stage of the co-design process (see Fig. 4) contributed to reinforce the sense of ownership of the computerized version by mitigating the black-box effect inherent to the use of such high-tech tool.

Fig. 4. Non-computerized (left) and computerized (right) versions of the Kulayinjana model

Providing detailed realistic representations may tend to keep the local actors focusing on some particular features that could distract them from taking a critical distance needed to debate issues in depth and not just superficially. Moreover, tackling conflict situations requires stepping back from the peculiarities on which the existing tensions could easily crystalize. On the contrary, purely abstract representations are likely to appear completely unrelated to the practical difficulties faced by the local actors. A stylized representation constitutes an interesting compromise between these two extremes.

The *KILT* approach does not fall within the scope of the two classical orientations of science, namely theory-oriented science and policy-oriented science (see Fig. 5).

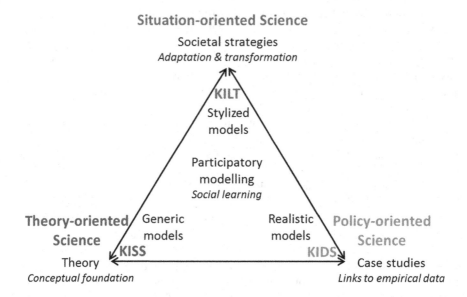

Fig. 5. The scientific orientation inherent to the KILT approach (adapted from [55])

Theory-oriented science -for which the KISS approach is well suited- is intended to consolidate generic knowledge. Policy-oriented socio-ecological science, which aims at supporting policy-makers by assessing the effects of various management rules, will mainly gain from modeling processes implemented according to KIDS principles. Issues arising from local stakeholders could be more properly dealt with by the KILT approach, where the social learning could foster mutual understanding and common agreement leading to collective action.

6   Conclusion

Deeper work is needed to investigate if and why the co-design with local actors of stylized models through the early use of participatory agent-based simulation triggers more effectively social learning. Difficulties arise from the complexity and context-dependence of processes influencing social learning. Moreover, the existing approaches to measuring social learning focus on cognitive learning while neglecting the social-relational dimensions of learning. With the *KILT* approach, the focus is specifically set on how interactive settings of participatory agent-based simulation processes could facilitate social learning. Among the features that account for fostering social learning in collaborative natural resource management, small group work, repeated opportunities to interact, open communication and unrestrained thinking are highlighted [56].

When a small group of researchers from different disciplines engage with local actors in the co-design of stylized models, it has to be very clearly stated that the main purpose is to foster communication through social learning. If any participatory modelling process can potentially lead to such an effect, it is still not so common to set it as the core goal [57]. This situation-oriented science hinges on a transdisciplinary practice in the sense that societies do not know the boundaries that science imposes on them [58].

References

1. Crookall, D., Martin, A., Saunders, D., Coote, A.: Human and computer involvement in simulation. Simul. Gaming **17**, 345–375 (1986)
2. Bousquet, F., Barreteau, O., D'Aquino, P., Etienne, M., Boissau, S., Aubert, S., Le Page, C., Babin, D., Castella, J.-C.: Multi-agent systems and role games: collective learning processes for ecosystem management. In: Janssen, M.A. (ed.) Complexity and Ecosystem Management. The Theory and Practice of Multi-Agent Systems, pp. 248–285. Edward Elgar Publishing, Cheltenham (2002)
3. Barreteau, O., Le Page, C., Perez, P.: Contribution of simulation and gaming to natural resource management issues: an introduction. Simul. Gaming **38**, 185–194 (2007)
4. Barreteau, O., Le Page, C., D'Aquino, P.: Role-playing games, models and negotiation processes. J. Artif. Soc. Soc. Simul. **6**(2), 10 (2003)
5. Barreteau, O.: The joint use of role-playing games and models regarding negotiation processes: characterization of associations. J. Artif. Soc. Soc. Simul. **6**(2), 3 (2003)
6. Le Page, C., Abrami, G., Barreteau, O., Becu, N., Bommel, P., Botta, A., Dray, A., Monteil, C., Souchère, V.: Models for sharing representations. In: Etienne, M. (ed.) Companion Modelling. A Participatory Approach to Support Sustainable Development, pp. 69–96. Quæ, Versailles (2011)
7. Berland, M., Rand, W.: Participatory simulation as a tool for agent-based simulation. In: ICAART 2009: Proceedings of the International Conference on Agents and Artificial Intelligence, pp. 553–557 (2009)
8. Guyot, P., Honiden, S.: Agent-based participatory simulations: merging multi-agent systems and role-playing games. J. Artif. Soc. Soc. Simul. **9**(4), 8 (2006)
9. Guyot, P., Drogoul, A., Honiden, S.: Power and negotiation: lessons from agent-based participatory simulations. In: Fifth International Joint Conference on Autonomous Agents and Multiagent Systems (AAMAS 2006), pp. 27–33 (2006)
10. Wilensky, U., Stroup, W.: Learning through participatory simulations: network-based design for systems learning in classrooms. In: Proceedings of the Computer Supported Collaborative Learning Conference (CSCL 1999), pp. 667–676. Lawrence Erlbaum Associates, Mahwah (1999)

11. Wilensky, U., Stroup, W.: NetLogo HubNet Gridlock HubNet model. Center for Connected Learning and Computer-Based Modeling, Northwestern University, Evanston, IL (1999)
12. Colella, V.: Participatory simulations: building collaborative understanding through immersive dynamic modeling. J. Learn. Sci. **9**, 471–500 (2000)
13. Boissau, S., Lan Anh, H., Castella, J.C.: The SAMBA role play game in Northern Vietnam. Mt. Res. Dev. **24**, 101–105 (2004)
14. Castella, J.C., Trung, T.N., Boissau, S.: Participatory simulation of land-use changes in the Northern Mountains of Vietnam: the combined use of an agent-based model, a role-playing game, and a geographic information system. Ecol. Soc. **10**(1), 27 (2005)
15. Le Page, C., Dray, A., Perez, P., Garcia, C.: Exploring how knowledge and communication influence natural resources management with REHAB. Simul. Gaming **47**, 257–284 (2016)
16. Mathevet, R., Le Page, C., Etienne, M., Lefebvre, G., Poulin, B., Gigot, G., Proréol, S., Mauchamp, A.: ButorStar: a role-playing game for collective awareness of reedbed wise use. Simul. Gaming **38**, 233–262 (2007)
17. Etienne, M.: SYLVOPAST a multiple target role-playing game to assess negotiation processes in silvopastoral management planning. J. Artif. Soc. Soc. Simul. **6**(2), 5 (2003)
18. Rates, C.A., Mulvey, B.K., Feldon, D.F.: Promoting conceptual change for complex systems understanding: outcomes of an agent-based participatory simulation. J. Sci. Educ. Technol. **25**(4), 610–627 (2016)
19. Becu, N., Frascaria-Lacoste, N., Latune, J.: Distributed asymmetric simulation—enhancing participatory simulation using the concept of habitus. In: The Shift from Teaching to Learning: Individual, Collective and Organizational Learning Through Gaming Simulation, pp. 75–85 (2014)
20. Heppenstall, A., Crooks, A., See, L.M., Batty, M. (eds.): Agent-Based Models of Geographical Systems. Springer, Dordrecht (2012)
21. Crooks, A.: Agent-based models and geographical information systems. In: Brunsdon, C., Singleton, A. (eds.) Geocomputation: A Practical Primer, pp. 63–77. SAGE, London (2015)
22. Ligtenberg, A., Bregt, A.K., Van Lammeren, R.: Multi-actor-based land use modelling: spatial planning using agents. Landscape Urban Plann. **56**, 21–33 (2001)
23. Gimblett, H.R.: Integrating Geographic Information Systems and Agent-Based Modeling Techniques for Simulating Social and Ecological Processes. Oxford University Press, New York (2002)
24. Brown, D.G., Riolo, R., Robinson, D.T., North, M., Rand, W.: Spatial process and data models: toward integration of agent-based models and GIS. J. Geogr. Syst. **7**, 25–47 (2005)
25. Taillandier, P., Vo, D.-A., Amouroux, E., Drogoul, A.: GAMA: a simulation platform that integrates geographical information data, agent-based modeling and multi-scale control. In: Desai, N., Liu, A., Winikoff, M. (eds.) PRIMA 2010. LNCS, vol. 7057, pp. 242–258. Springer, Heidelberg (2012). https://doi.org/10.1007/978-3-642-25920-3_17
26. Langlois, P., Blanpain, B., Daudé, E.: MAGéo, une plateforme de modélisation et de simulation multi-agent pour les sciences humaines. Cybergeo Eur. J. Geogr. (2015). http://cybergeo.revues.org/27236
27. Schlüter, M., McAllister, R.R.J., Arlinghaus, R., Bunnefeld, N., Eisenack, K., Hölker, F., Milner-Gulland, E.J., Müller, B., Nicholson, E., Quaas, M., Stöven, M.: New horizons for managing the environment: a review of coupled social-ecological systems modeling. Nat. Resour. Model. **25**, 219–272 (2012)
28. Mathevet, R., Le Page, C., Etienne, M., Poulin, B., Lefebvre, G., Cazin, F., Ruffray, X.: Des roselières et des hommes. ButorStar: un jeu de rôles pour l'aide à la gestion collective. Rev. Int. Géomatique **18**, 375–395 (2008)

29. Gourmelon, F., Chlous-Ducharme, F., Kerbiriou, C., Rouan, M., Bioret, F.: Role-playing game developed from a modelling process: a relevant participatory tool for sustainable development? A co-construction experiment in an insular biosphere reserve. Land Use Policy **32**, 96–107 (2013)

30. Gourmelon, F., Rouan, M., Lefevre, J.-F., Rognant, A.: Role-playing game and learning for young people about sustainable development stakes: an experiment in transferring and adapting interdisciplinary scientific knowledge. J. Artif. Soc. Soc. Simul. **14**(4), 21 (2011)

31. Ören, T.I.: Uses of simulation. In: Sokolowski, J.A., Banks, C.M. (eds.) Principles of Modeling and Simulation, pp. 153–179. John Wiley & Sons (2008)

32. Sun, Z., Lorscheid, I., Millington, J.D., Lauf, S., Magliocca, N.R., Groeneveld, J., Balbi, S., Nolzen, H., Müller, B., Schulze, J., Buchmann, C.M.: Simple or complicated agent-based models? A complicated issue. Environ. Model Softw. **86**, 56–67 (2016)

33. Lusiana, B., van Noordwijk, M., Suyamto, D., Mulia, R., Joshi, L., Cadisch, G.: Users' perspectives on validity of a simulation model for natural resource management. Int. J. Agric. Sustain. **9**, 364–378 (2011)

34. Edmonds, B., Moss, S.: From KISS to KIDS – an 'Anti-simplistic' modelling approach. In: Davidsson, P., Logan, B., Takadama, K. (eds.) MABS 2004. LNCS, vol. 3415, pp. 130–144. Springer, Heidelberg (2005). https://doi.org/10.1007/978-3-540-32243-6_11

35. Grimm, V., Revilla, E., Berger, U., Jeltsch, F., Mooij, W.M., Railsback, S.F., Thulke, H.-H., Weiner, J., Wiegand, T., DeAngelis, D.L.: Pattern-oriented modeling of agent-based complex systems: lessons from ecology. Science **310**, 987–991 (2005)

36. Axelrod, R.: Advancing the art of simulation in the social sciences. In: Conte, R., Hegselmann, R., Terna, P. (eds.) Simulating Social Phenomena. Lecture Notes in Economics and Mathematical Systems, vol. 456, pp. 21–40. Springer, Heidelberg (1997). https://doi.org/10.1007/978-3-662-03366-1_2

37. Kilvington, M.J.: Building capacity for social learning in environmental management. Ph.D. Lincoln University, Canterbury, New Zealand (2010)

38. Reed, M., Evely, A., Cundill, G., Fazey, I., Glass, J., Laing, A., Newig, J., Parrish, B., Prell, C., Raymond, C., Stringer, L.: What is social learning? Ecol. Soc. **15**(4), r1 (2010)

39. Habermas, J.: The Theory of Communicative Action, vol. I. Beacon, Boston (1984)

40. Daré, W.S., Van Paassen, A., Ducrot, R., Mathevet, R., Queste, J., Trébuil, G., Barnaud, C., Lagabrielle, E.: Learning about interdependencies and dynamics. In: Etienne, M. (ed.) Companion Modelling. A Participatory Approach to Support Sustainable Development, pp. 205–229. Quæ, Versailles (2011)

41. Bouwen, R., Taillieu, T.: Multi-party collaboration as social learning for interdependence: developing relational knowing for sustainable natural resource management. J. Commun. Appl. Soc. Psychol. **14**, 137–153 (2004)

42. Perrotton, A., de Garine Wichatitsky, M., Valls-Fox, H., Le Page, C.: My cattle and your park: co-designing a role-playing game with rural communities to promote multi-stakeholder dialogue at the edge of protected areas. Ecol. Soc. **22**(1), 35 (2017)

43. Hardy, P.-Y., Souchère, V., Dray, A., David, M., Sabatier, R., Kernéis, E.: Individual vs collective in public policy design, a cooperation example in the Marais Poitevin region. In: Sauvage, S., Sánchez-Pérez, J.M., Rizzoli, A.E. (eds.) 8th International Congress on Environmental Modelling and Software, Toulouse, France (2016)

44. Bommel, P., Bonnet, M.-P., Coudel, E., Haentjens, E., Kraus, C.N., Melo, G., Nasuti, S., Le Page, C.: Livelihoods of local communities in an Amazonian floodplain coping with global changes. From role-playing games to hybrid simulations to involve local stakeholders in participatory foresight study at territorial level. In: 8th International Congress on Environmental Modelling and Software, pp. 1140–1147 (2016)

45. Barnaud, C., Van Paassen, A.: Equity, power games, and legitimacy: dilemmas of participatory natural resource management. Ecol. Soc. **18**(2), 21 (2013)
46. Druckman, D., Ebner, N.: Onstage or behind the scenes? Relative learning benefits of simulation role-play and design. Simul. Gaming **39**, 465–497 (2008)
47. Muro, M., Jeffrey, P.: A critical review of the theory and application of social learning in participatory natural resource management processes. J. Environ. Plann. Manag. **51**, 325–344 (2008)
48. Scholz, G.: How participatory methods facilitate social learning in natural resource management. An exploration of group interaction using interdisciplinary syntheses and agent-based modeling, Osnabrück, Germany (2016)
49. Vennix, J.A.M.: Group Model Building: Facilitating Team Learning Using System Dynamics. Jonh Wiley & Sons Ltd., Chichester (1996)
50. Mathevet, R., Etienne, M., Lynam, T., Calvet, C.: Water management in the Camargue Biosphere Reserve: insights from comparative mental models analysis. Ecol. Soc. **16**(1), 43 (2011)
51. Scholz, G., Austermann, M., Kaldrack, K., Pahl-Wostl, C.: Evaluating group model building exercises: a method for comparing externalized mental models and group models. Syst. Dyn. Rev. **31**, 28–45 (2015)
52. Black, L.J.: When visuals are boundary objects in system dynamics work. Syst. Dyn. Rev. **29**, 70–86 (2013)
53. Black, L.J., Andersen, D.F.: Using visual representations as boundary objects to resolve conflict in collaborative model-building approaches. Syst. Res. Behav. Sci. **29**, 194–208 (2012)
54. Wilensky, U., Papert, S.: Restructurations: reformulations of knowledge disciplines through new representational forms. In: Constructionism 2010, Paris (2010)
55. Schlüter, M., Müller, B., Frank, K.: How to use models to improve analysis and governance of social-ecological systems-the reference frame MORE (2013)
56. Schusler, T.M., Decker, D.J., Pfeffer, M.J.: Social learning for collaborative natural resource management. Soc. Nat. Resour. **16**, 309–326 (2003)
57. Brugnach, M.: From prediction to learning: the implications of changing the purpose of the modelling activity. In: Proceedings of the iEMSs Fourth Biennial Meeting: International Congress on Environmental Modelling and Software (iEMSs 2010), pp. 547–553. International Environmental Modelling and Software Society (2010)
58. de Sartre, X.A., Petit, O.: L'interdisciplinarité comme méthode de compréhension des interactions entre natures et sociétés. In: Hubert, B., Mathieu, N. (eds.) Interdisciplinarités entre Natures et Sociétés, pp. 367–386. P.I.E. Peter Lang, Bruxelles (2016)

Thwarting Vote Buying Through Decoy Ballots
Extended Version

David C. Parkes[1], Paul Tylkin[1(✉)], and Lirong Xia[2]

[1] Harvard University, Cambridge, MA, USA
`ptylkin@g.harvard.edu`
[2] Rensselaer Polytechnic Institute, Troy, NY, USA

Abstract. There is increasing interest in promoting participatory democracy, in particular by allowing voting by mail or internet and through random-sample elections. A pernicious concern, though, is that of *vote buying*, which occurs when a bad actor seeks to buy ballots, paying someone to vote against their own intent. This becomes possible whenever a voter is able to sell evidence of which way she voted. We show how to thwart vote buying through *decoy ballots*, which are not counted but are indistinguishable from real ballots to a buyer. We show that an Election Authority can significantly reduce the power of vote buying through a small number of optimally distributed decoys, and model societal processes by which decoys could be distributed. We also introduce a generalization of our model to non-binary election outcomes.

1 Introduction

The goal of participatory democracy [9,11] is to engage citizens more frequently and with more granularity in the decision-making processes of government bodies. Technologies that can help with this transition are those that support voting from the home by mail or over the internet, and that make use of *random sample elections*, in which a representative subsample of the population is tasked with voting on a particular issue, allowing participatory democracy to function without everyone needing to be concerned with every issue.

A pernicious concern, though, is that of *vote buying*, where a bad actor attempts to gain improper influence in an election by purchasing ballots from voters and paying them to vote against their intent. The practical implications of this are manifold, since the social construct of elections relies on the perception of reliability and fairness. Vote buying has been an everlasting threat to democracy; for example, a survey shows that in the 1996 Thai general elections

---

This is an extended version of *Thwarting Vote Buying through Decoy Ballots*, which was presented at the EXPLORE 2017 workshop at the 16th Int. Conf. on Autonomous Agents and Multiagent Systems (AAMAS 2017) and the Proc. 26th Int. Joint Conf. on Artificial Intelligence (IJCAI 2017).

© Springer International Publishing AG 2017
G. Sukthankar and J. A. Rodriguez-Aguilar (Eds.): AAMAS 2017 Visionary Papers,
LNAI 10643, pp. 45–66, 2017.
https://doi.org/10.1007/978-3-319-71679-4_4

"one third of households were offered money to buy votes at the last general election" [13]. Schaffer [14] mentions that *"[Vote buying]... is making an impressive comeback...it seems, a blossoming market for votes has emerged as an epiphenomenon of democratization"*. New technologies can make the situation worse. For example, web platforms can serve as middlemen, digital currency supports anonymous payments, and abundant data coupled with machine learning can help buyers discover entrapment schemes as well as identify voters to target with offers.

In this paper, we show that vote buying can be thwarted by distributing *decoy ballots*, which are not counted, in addition to real ballots. A vote buyer will not know whether a ballot is real or decoy, and thus, decoys (if sold) may deplete a buyer's budget. Voters who know that they have a decoy ballot are motivated to sell their ballots to a buyer, both for reasons of profit and out of civic duty, wanting to maintain the election's integrity. David Chaum earlier introduced the notion of random sample voting, and proposed decoy ballots in order to address the potential problem of vote buying in remote elections generally and for random sample voting in particular [4]. He has also introduced the key notion of *proof of decoy* (see Sect. 2). We study how to distribute decoy ballots, and analyze the power of this approach.

We assume that real ballots impose a high cost on society, for the reason that it takes effort for citizens to become informed about an issue and vote appropriately, thus representing their considered opinion on an issue.[1] Without the willingness to invest this effort, methods of participatory democracy may ultimately fail. For example, a simple calculation for the US shows that if we assume that 200 M people will participate, and there are about 12,000 issues to decide per year,[2] then assuming that voters are willing to engage three times a year, we have a maximum of 50,000 voters per issue. At this scale, vote buying, especially on contentious issues, may pose a severe problem.

Turning to decoy ballots, we model these as costly but not so costly that the number of decoys to distribute cannot be considered as a design decision of the Election Authority. The cost of decoys comes about because, to be effective, voters need to be willing to go to the effort to sell the ballot (and thus, cast the ballot and prove which way it was cast) if approached by a buyer. But because any decoy ballots are not counted, we assume it is less cognitively expensive for a voter to form an opinion.

Although we situate our discussion in a societal context, similar themes can be imagined for economies of AIs [12], where it is desired to elicit and fairly aggregate multiple opinions, but would not be scalable to request input from every agent all the time.

Our Contributions. Focusing mostly on the binary outcome case, we provide a formal model of vote buying, including a characterization of the vote buyer's

---

[1] In some approaches to random-sample voting this cost comes also about as a result of needing to physically mail ballots.

[2] This represents the approximate voter population and the number of issues before Congress per year, assuming 2 issues per bill.

behavior and an optimal policy for distributing decoy ballots by the Election Authority (EA). In addition, we model two societal processes by which decoys could be distributed—these approaches freeing the EA of any concern that it could be seen to be biasing the outcome of an election when distributing decoys in any way other than reflecting a random sample of the population. In simulation, we show that the EA can make effective use of decoy ballots to maintain election integrity (e.g., reducing the probability that the buyer changes the outcome to less than 1%). For the optimal defense, we are able to achieve this by adding a small number of decoys that are proportional in quantity to the number of ballots the buyer can afford to buy. Interestingly, a "civic duty defense" that allocates decoys to a random subset of those who request one is almost as effective as the optimal defense in which the EA optimizes the distribution of voter types that receive decoys. We also provide a generalization of our model to the three-outcome case, prove that a *buy the expected winner* strategy is optimal for elections with simple voter types, and provide numerical results illustrating the strategy of both the buyer and the EA in equilibrium.

Related Work. There are numerous studies on vote buying, for example [8, 15, 16, 19]. These include game-theoretic models of vote buying, but none that consider the role of decoy ballots. In the work by Dekel *et al.* [6], the game is played by the candidates themselves buying votes, Groseclose and Snyder [10] study vote buying in legislative bodies and analyze the optimal coalition size. Vicente [18] studies the incumbency advantage in a vote buying game. Within AI, the problem studied here related to studies of control (manipulation of the election structure, including changing the candidate slate) and bribery (voters are paid by an interested party to vote a certain way) as studied in computational social choice [2, 7]. In particular, the *lobbying* problem considers an election with a binary outcome on a number of issues, and the vote buyer has a total budget that can be expended across all issues [1, 3, 5]. Ours is a special case with a single issue, but whereas previous research has focused on using computational complexity as a barrier against bribery and control, we adopt a game-theoretic model and study the power of decoy ballots. There is also a conceptual connection with work on *security games* [17], where the approach is to use game theory to design optimal strategies to prevent losses from terrorist attacks.

2   The Model

We assume that there is a large population of possible voters, and, for now, assume that this is a binary choice election with possible votes YES and NO. For expositional simplicity, we assume that all voters who receive a real ballot will place a vote. Similarly, we assume that every voter for whom it is profitable to sell a ballot (decoy or otherwise) will try to sell the ballot.[3]

---

[3] It is simple to generalize the model so that the voters who cast ballots are sampled uniformly from those who receive ballots, and similarly for those who try to sell ballots.

The voters. Each voter i has an immutable, publicly-observable *voter type*, θ_i, which indicates the probability that a random voter with this type will vote YES. We can think about θ_i as the prior that a voter will vote YES before she has carefully considered the merits of an issue. Voter types are drawn independently from a *voter type distribution* with probability density f, assumed to have full support on $[0, 1]$. We assume without loss of generality that $E_f[\theta] < 1/2$, i.e., that the outcome of the election without any interference by a buyer and with enough real ballots is NO.

The buyer. We model a single, budget-limited buyer. Given our assumption that $E_f[\theta] < 1/2$, we consider the interesting case of a *YES-buyer*, meaning that the buyer wants the election outcome to be YES. To keep things simple, we assume the buyer can find the voters with ballots, and will offer the same price $p > 0$ to each voter in some subset of these voters. The buyer has a budget B, representing the number of ballots that he can afford to purchase at price p, and has no utility for unspent budget. The buyer selects a random subset of voters if more respond to the offer than he can afford.

Conditioned on whether a voter's intent is to vote NO or YES, and whether they have a real or decoy ballot, all voters have the same utility function in regard to whether or not to sell. In particular, simple analysis yields that this ordering of the minimum price that a voter will require in order to agree to sell a ballot is real-NO > real-YES > decoy-YES > decoy-NO. For example, any price that is acceptable to a "real-YES" voter (real ballot, intent to vote YES) is also acceptable to "decoy-YES" and "decoy-NO" voters. Ballots from decoy-NO voters are the cheapest to buy.[4]

Based on this, the real-NO votes—and the only ones the buyer is interested in—are the most expensive ballots to buy. Because of this, we assume the buyer will set price p high enough for a real-NO voter to agree to sell if approached. This could be set based on market research, for example.

The game form. The voters who receive a real ballot are a random subset of the population, and thus with types that follow f. The choice of how to distribute decoy ballots is, in general, a design decision. Let ψ denote the density function for this decoy ballot distribution. Modeled as a sequential-move game, the election proceeds in three stages:

(1) The EA distributes some number of real and decoy ballots, with the number and type distribution of real ballots assumed fixed, but the number of decoy ballots, and perhaps type distribution ψ a design decision.

---

[4] To understand this ordering, suppose that a voter with a real ballot has a cost for selling, representing the possibility of being caught. In addition, voters that intend to vote NO prefer not to vote YES. Thus, real-NO ballots are the most expensive votes to buy. Amongst decoys, decoy-YES ballots are more expensive to buy than decoy-NO ballots because a voter who would vote NO (if she had a real ballot) has a value for depleting the budget of a YES-buyer. This is not the case for a voter who would vote YES.

(2) The buyer learns who has received a ballot (possibly a decoy) and chooses to offer price p to each voter in some subset of voters who have (real or decoy) ballots. The voters who receive an offer decide whether or not to sell. The buyer breaks ties at random if multiple voters agree to sell.

(3) Both real and decoy ballots are cast, and the real ballots are tallied to determine the outcome. The buyer makes payments to voters who agreed to sell and provide a proof that they vote YES.

Both distribution f and the type of each voter is common knowledge. Our analysis will focus on the subgame perfect equilibrium of this game. Throughout, the voters have a simple equilibrium behavior—agree to sell if offered a price p (which will, in equilibrium, be high enough to be acceptable.)

Proof of decoy. We assume the existence of a *proof-of-decoy*, which lets a voter with a decoy choose to prove that she has a decoy. This is required to mitigate the "fear of being caught selling a ballot"— that way, a voter with a decoy can prove to a vigilante that she is not selling a real ballot. On the other hand, there is no way to prove the authenticity of a real ballot. This property is easy to support through standard cryptographic primitives; see, for example, Chaum [4].[5]

EA and Buyer objectives. We take as the objective of the EA that of maintaining election integrity, and thus *minimizing the probability that the buyer changes the election outcome*. In contrast, the interests of the buyer are diametrically opposed, and he wants to *maximize the probability that the outcome of the election is changed*.

3   Buyer Analysis

Given the buyer's objective, the best response of the buyer to the EA is to maximize the expected number of real-NO ballots that he buys, given his budget B and knowledge about voters' types (probability of voting YES). Let $\mathcal{I} \subseteq [0, 1]$ denote the subset of voter types from which the buyer buys; in particular, the buyer will buy every ballot held (real or decoy) by voters of these types. Let n_r denote the number of real ballots and n_d the number of decoy ballots. The buyer wants to select the subset $\mathcal{I}$ to solve:

$$\max_{\mathcal{I}} \int_{\mathcal{I}} \frac{n_r}{n_r + n_d}(1 - \theta)f(\theta)d\theta \text{ s.t. } \int_{\mathcal{I}} n_r f(\theta) + n_d \psi(\theta)d\theta \leq B. \quad (1)$$

In this way, the buyer maximizes a quantity that is proportional to the expected number of real-NO ballots purchased, subject to the total budget.

---

[5] The asymmetry in having proof-of-decoy without proof-of-authenticity is important to prevent a buyer from using coercion to buy only real ballots, while at the same time allowing a voter with a decoy ballot to sell without fear of being accused of acting against the social good. A voter will never choose to reveal that she holds a decoy to a buyer, since doing so would remove the chance of a sale.

Let $h(\theta)$ denote the *probability that a ballot is real-NO given type θ*. By Bayes' rule, and recalling that the buyer has knowledge of f and ψ, this is

$$h(\theta) \stackrel{\text{def}}{=} P(\text{real} \wedge \text{NO}|\theta) = \frac{n_r(1-\theta)f(\theta)}{n_r f(\theta) + n_d \psi(\theta)}. \tag{2}$$

Given a set $I \subseteq [0,1]$, let $h(I)$ denote the set $\{h(\theta)\}$ for $\theta \in I$. Let $h(I_1) < h(I_2)$ mean that every value in I_1 is strictly less than every value in I_2.

Lemma 1 (Buyer Optimality). *The optimal buyer strategy in the subgame perfect equilibrium is to buy in order of decreasing $h(\theta)$ until the budget is exhausted.*

Proof. Suppose not, i.e., suppose that there is a set $J \subset \mathcal{I}$ and a set $J' \not\subset \mathcal{I}$ such that $h(J') > h(J)$. Then, the buyer could strictly increase his objective by buying J' instead of J.

We assume w.l.o.g. that if a YES-buyer has to choose between buying two subsets of $[0,1]$ for which $h(\theta)$ is equal, he will buy the subset with lower θ. Let $\mathfrak{M} \stackrel{\text{def}}{=} \int_{\mathcal{I}} f(\theta)d\theta$ denote the fraction of real ballots that the buyer buys. By 'election bought', we refer to the event that the buyer buys enough real ballots to change the outcome (with n_r real ballots); by 'correct outcome is NO', we refer to the event that the election outcome is NO (with $n_r + n_d$ real ballots).

Lemma 2. *The probability that the buyer changes the outcome in the subgame perfect equilibrium is given by*

$$P(\textit{buyer changes outcome})$$
$$= P([\textit{election bought}] \wedge [\textit{correct outcome is NO}])$$
$$\approx P\left(\frac{n_r(1 - 2\mathfrak{M}) - 2(1 - \mathfrak{M})\mu_Y)}{2\sqrt{n_r(1-\mathfrak{M})\mu_Y(1-\mu_Y)}} < Z < \frac{(1-2\mu)\sqrt{n_r + n_d}}{2\sqrt{\mu(1-\mu)}}\right), \tag{3}$$

where $Z \sim \mathcal{N}(0,1)$, $\mu \stackrel{\text{def}}{=} E_f[\theta]$, and $\mu_Y \stackrel{\text{def}}{=} \frac{1}{1-\mathfrak{M}} \int_{[0,1]\setminus\mathcal{I}} \theta f(\theta)d\theta$.

Proof. Let the type distribution of the unbought types be given by

$$f_Y(\theta) \stackrel{\text{def}}{=} \begin{cases} \frac{f(\theta)}{1-\mathfrak{M}} & \text{for } \theta \in [0,1] - \mathcal{I} \\ 0 & \text{for } \theta \in \mathcal{I} \end{cases}. \tag{4}$$

To model votes, we introduce the shorthand notation $X_i \multimap f(\theta)$ to denote the hierarchical model $\theta_i \sim f(\theta); X_i \sim \text{Bern}(\theta_i)$. The probability that the buyer changes the outcome is given by

$$P(\textit{buyer changes outcome})$$
$$= P([\textit{election bought}] \wedge [\textit{correct outcome is NO}])$$
$$= P\left(\left[\frac{\sum_{i=1}^{(1-\mathfrak{M})n_r} V_i}{n_r} + \mathfrak{M} > \frac{1}{2}\right] \wedge \left[\frac{\sum_{j=1}^{n_r+n_d} W_j}{n_r + n_d} < \frac{1}{2}\right]\right), \tag{5}$$

where $V_i \multimap f_Y(\theta)$ and $W_j \multimap f(\theta)$. We can use the Normal approximation to the Binomial to obtain

$P(buyer\ changes\ outcome)$

$$\approx P\left(\frac{n_r(1 - 2\mathfrak{M} - 2(1 - \mathfrak{M})\mu_Y)}{2\sqrt{n_r(1 - \mathfrak{M})\mu_Y(1 - \mu_Y)}} < Z < \frac{(1 - 2\mu)\sqrt{n_r + n_d}}{2\sqrt{\mu(1 - \mu)}} \right). \qquad (6)$$

This allows us to compute the probability the buyer changes the election outcome, which is determined by the fraction of real ballots that he is able to buy given a defense.

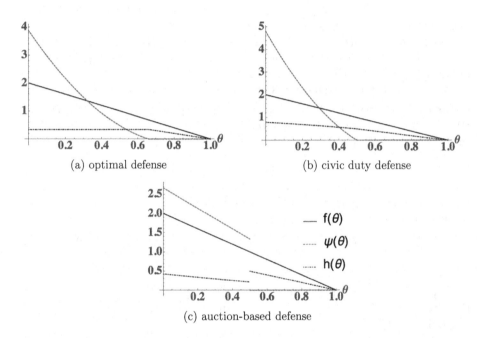

(a) optimal defense

(b) civic duty defense

(c) auction-based defense

Fig. 1. Examples of type distribution $f(\theta)$, decoy distribution $\psi(\theta)$, and desirability to buyer $h(\theta)$ for (a) an optimal defense, (b) a civic duty defense with max type requesting a decoy $x_C = 0.5$ and 10% decoy ballots, (c) an auction-based defense with max type assigned a decoy $x_A = 0.5$ and 50% decoy ballots. Here $f = \text{Beta}(1, 2)$.

4   Optimal Decoy Distribution

In this section, we assume that the EA can design defense distribution ψ, and study the equilibrium of the vote-buying game where the EA chooses an optimal defense given that the buyer will best respond.

Definition 1 (Canonical Defense). *Defense ψ is* canonical *if there is some* x, $0 \leq x \leq 1$, *s.t.* $h(\theta) = \min(1 - x, 1 - \theta)$.

See Fig. 1(a) for an illustration of a canonical defense. Let supp(g) denote the support of distribution g. Define the following two properties for ψ:

(P1) $h(\theta)$ has the same value for all $\theta \in \text{supp}(\psi)$.
(P2) $\min_{\theta \in \text{supp}(\psi)} h(\theta) \geq \max_{\theta \notin \text{supp}(\psi)} h(\theta)$

Lemma 3. *Any defense ψ satisfying both P1 and P2 is canonical.*

Proof. We assume that ψ satisfies P1 and P2, and show that $\text{supp}(\psi) = [0, \text{xx}_0]$ for some $x_0 \in [0, 1]$, i.e., we must have $0 \in \text{supp}(\psi)$, $\text{supp}(\psi)$ must be contiguous, and the left endpoint of $\text{supp}(\psi) \overset{\text{def}}{=} [x_0, x_0]$ is 0 (i.e., x_0 must be 0). Assume that ψ is a defense that satisfies both P1 and P2.

Since $\forall \theta \notin \text{supp}(\psi), h(\theta) = 1 - \theta$ and $\forall \theta \in \text{supp}(\psi), h(\theta) \leq 1 - \theta$, this tells us that P2 requires $0 \in \text{supp}(\psi)$. Otherwise, $h(0) > \max_{\theta \in \text{supp}(\psi)} h(\theta) \geq \min_{\theta \in \text{supp}(\psi)} h(\theta)$, which contradicts P2.

Next, assume for contradiction that $\text{supp}(\psi)$ is not contiguous. Then, consider the first two intervals $J_1 \overset{\text{def}}{=} [x_1, x_2]$ and $J_2 \overset{\text{def}}{=} [x_3, x_4]$, with $J_1, J_2 \subseteq \text{supp}(\psi)$. By P1, $h(\theta)$ has the same value $\forall \theta \in \text{supp}(\psi)$. Call this value y. First, we examine the special case of $x_1 = 0$. Then, we have

$$y \leq (1 - x4) < (1 - x3) \leq \max_{\theta \notin \text{supp}(\psi)} h(\theta), \qquad (7)$$

i.e., $y < \max_{\theta \notin \text{supp}(\psi)} h(\theta)$, but this contradicts P2.
So then, suppose that $x_1 \neq 0$. Then, we have

$$y \leq (1 - x_4) < (1 - x_3) < (1 - x_2) < (1 - x_1) \leq \max_{\theta \notin \text{supp}(\psi)} h(\theta), \qquad (8)$$

i.e., $y < \max_{\theta \notin \text{supp}(\psi)} h(\theta)$, but this contradicts P2.
Finally, assume for contradiction that $\text{supp}(\psi) = [x_1, x_2]$, and consider $x_0 < x_1$ (i.e., $x_1 > 0$). We have $h(x_0) > 1 - x_1$, and then $h(x_0) > \min_{\theta \in \text{supp}(\psi)} h(\theta)$, contradicting P2.

Lemma 4. *If the buyer buys all ballots in* $\text{supp}(\psi)$, *then there is a canonical defense ψ' with the same value.*

Proof. Let ψ be a non-canonical defense. Suppose that $\text{supp}(\psi) \subseteq \mathcal{I}$, and let $d = \min_{\theta \in \text{supp}(\psi)} h(\theta)$. By Lemma 1, the buyer buys all ballots with $\theta \leq 1 - d$. Now let ψ' denote a canonical defense, and let $h'(\theta) = \frac{n_r f(\theta)(1-\theta)}{n_r f(\theta) + n_d \psi'(\theta)}$. Now $\min_{\theta \in \text{supp}(\psi')} h'(\theta) \geq d$ by P1. Thus, the buyer still buys all ballots with $\theta \leq 1 - d$, including all of the decoys distributed according to ψ'.

Lemma 3 characterizes canonical defenses in terms of the properties defined above. Lemma 4 shows that if the buyer can buy up all decoys, then how they are distributed no longer matters.

Fixing the number of real ballots n_r, the EA's remaining choices are about n_d and ψ. We now state our main characterization result.

Theorem 1. *For a given n_r, n_d, and buyer budget B, the optimal strategy of the EA in the subgame perfect equilibrium is canonical.*

Proof. Assume for contradiction, that there is a non-canonical ψ that is better than any canonical defense. Let k be an index, and consider a sequence of defenses $\{\psi_k\} = \{\psi_0, \psi_1, ...\}$, where $\psi \stackrel{\text{def}}{=} \psi_0$. We will show that we can define a finite sequence that obtains a canonical defense at least as good as ψ. Let $h_k(\theta)$ denote the function h that corresponds to ψ_k.

Let $\mathcal{I}_k \subseteq [0, 1]$ denote the set of intervals that are best for the buyer given ψ_k (solving for the buyer's objective subject to his budget). If the buyer buys all ballots in $\text{supp}(\psi_k)$, then by Lemma 4, we can modify ψ_k to form a canonical ψ_{k+1} with the same value, and we are done.

Suppose otherwise, and that in addition ψ_k does not satisfy P1 and P2. That is, we have:

(P0) the buyer does not buy all ballots in $\text{supp}(\psi_k)$, and one or both of
($\neg$ P1) $h_k(\theta)$ takes on multiple values for $\theta \in \text{supp}(\psi_k)$
($\neg$ P2) $\min_{\theta \in \text{supp}(\psi_k)} h_k(\theta) < \max_{\theta \notin \text{supp}(\psi_k)} h_k(\theta)$.

By P0, we can construct some interval $S_k \subseteq \text{supp}(\psi_k)$ (the *source set*), where the buyer is not buying all ballots, and an interval $T_k \subseteq \mathcal{I}_k$ (the *target set*), such that $h_k(S_k) < h_k(T_k)$ (and thus, $S_k \cap T_k = \varnothing$). Let $R_k = \text{supp}\psi \setminus \mathcal{I}_k$ be the remaining subset of $\text{supp}(\psi)$ that the buyer is not buying. We must have $\text{argmin}_{\theta \in \text{supp}(\psi_k)} h_k(\theta) \subseteq R_k$. The existence of T_k follows from $\neg P1$ because $\exists \theta \in \mathcal{I}_k$ for which $h_k(\theta) > \min_{\theta \in \text{supp}(\psi_k)} h_k(\theta)$ (the existence is guaranteed by values of $\theta \in \text{supp}(\psi_k)$ that are greater than the minimum), and thus we have $\max_{\theta \in \mathcal{I}_k} h_k(\theta) > \min_{\theta \in \text{supp}(\psi_k)} h_k(\theta)$. If $\neg P2$, then by buyer optimality (Lemma 1), $\text{argmin}_{\theta \in \text{supp}(\psi_k)} h_k(\theta) \subseteq R_k$. In both cases, $\text{argmin}_{\theta \in \text{supp}(\psi_k)} h_k(\theta) \subseteq S_k$.

We pick $\epsilon_S, \epsilon_T > 0$ to define a move of a uniform slice of ψ density from S_k to T_k such that,

(i) $\int_{\theta \in S_k} \max(0, \psi_k(\theta) - \epsilon_S)\, d\theta = \int_{\theta \in T_k} \epsilon_T\, d\theta$ [mass conservation]
(ii) $h_{k+1}(S_k) < h_{k+1}(T_k)$ [target set still preferred by buyer to source set]

By continuity (except possibly on a set of measure 0) of $h(\theta)$, such an ϵ_S, ϵ_T pair that satisfies (ii) exists. We argue that $S_k \cap \mathcal{I}_{k+1} = \varnothing$. Before the ψ mass is moved, we have $\min h_k(\mathcal{I}_k) \geq h_k(T_k) > h_k(S_k)$. After the move, we have $\min h_{k+1}(\mathcal{I}_{k+1}) \geq h_{k+1}(T_k) > h_{k+1}(S_k)$. The inequality is because the buyer can always exhaust his budget by buying $\mathcal{I}_k$. Thus, we know that the buyer does not buy anything in S_k after the ψ mass has been moved. Let $Q_k \stackrel{\text{def}}{=} \int_{\mathcal{I}_k} (1-\theta) f(\theta) d\theta$. Thus, we have $Q_{k+1} \leq Q_k$ because the only set on which $h_{k+1}(\theta) > h_k(\theta)$ is S_k. In addition, $\min_{\theta \in \text{supp}(\psi_k)} h_k(\theta) < \min_{\theta \in \text{supp}(\psi_{k+1})} h_{k+1}(\theta)$. Because $\forall k \in \mathbb{Z}^+$, $\theta \in [0, 1]$, $h_k(\theta) \geq 0$ the sequence must be finite.

Note that $h_{k+1}(\theta)$ only differs from $h_k(\theta)$ at S_k and T_k, increasing at S_k and decreasing at T_k. We have

$$\min_{\theta \in \mathrm{supp}(\psi_{k+1})} h_{k+1}(\theta)$$

$$= \min \left[\min_{\theta \in S_k} h_{k+1}(\theta), \min_{\theta \in T_k} h_{k+1}(\theta), \min_{\theta \in \mathrm{supp}(\psi_{k+1}) \backslash \{T_k, S_k\}} h_{k+1}(\theta) \right]$$

$$> \min \left[\min_{\theta \in S_k} h_k(\theta), \min_{\theta \in S_k} h_k(\theta), \min_{\theta \in S_k} h_k(\theta) \right] = \min_{\theta \in \mathrm{supp}(\psi_k)} h_k(\theta). \tag{9}$$

Theorem 1 says that for a given n_r and n_d, the optimal design of ψ by the EA is canonical. The next result shows that ψ (and its support, which is $[0, x_o]$, "o" for optimal) can be easily computed given any n_r and n_d.

Theorem 2. *For any given n_r and n_d, the optimal defense of the EA in the subgame perfect equilibrium is given by a decoy ballot distribution with density function*

$$\psi(\theta) = \begin{cases} \frac{n_r}{n_d} \frac{(x_o - \theta) f(\theta)}{1 - x_o} & \text{for } \theta \in [0, x_o] \\ 0 & \text{for } \theta \in (x_o, 1] \end{cases}, \tag{10}$$

where the threshold x_o is determined by the following equation: $\frac{1}{1-x_o} \int_0^{x_o} F(\theta) d\theta = \frac{n_d}{n_r}$ and $F(\theta)$ is the CDF of f.

Proof. We suppose that n_r and n_d are fixed, and solve the expression $h(\theta) = c$ for $\psi(\theta)$, where $\theta \in [0, x_o]$ and $c > 0$, which gives us

$$\psi(\theta) = \frac{n_r}{n_d} \left(\frac{(1 - \theta) f(\theta)}{c} - f(\theta) \right). \tag{11}$$

Now, we need $\psi(\theta)$ to be non-negative on its support, which gives us $c \leq 1 - \theta, \forall \theta \in [0, x_o]$, which implies that $c \leq 1 - x_o$. Further, we need

$$\int_0^{x_o} \frac{n_r}{n_d} \left(\frac{(1 - \theta) f(\theta)}{1 - x_o} - f(\theta) \right) = 1, \tag{12}$$

which implies that $\frac{1}{1-x_o} \left(F(x_o) - \int_0^{x_o} \theta f(\theta) d\theta \right) - F(x_o) = \frac{n_d}{n_r}$, and after integrating by parts and using the fact that $\theta \geq 0$, we obtain $\frac{1}{1-x_o} \int_0^{x_o} F(\theta) d\theta = \frac{n_d}{n_r}$. Also, plugging in $1 - x_o$ for c, we have, $\forall \theta \in [0, x_o]$,

$$\psi(\theta) = \frac{n_r}{n_d} \left(\frac{(1 - \theta) f(\theta)}{1 - x_o} - f(\theta) \right) = \frac{n_r}{n_d} \frac{(x_o - \theta) f(\theta)}{1 - x_o}, \tag{13}$$

as desired.

With this expression, we can determine the power of increasing the number of decoys, n_d, for any voter type distribution f, buyer budget B, and number of real ballots n_r.

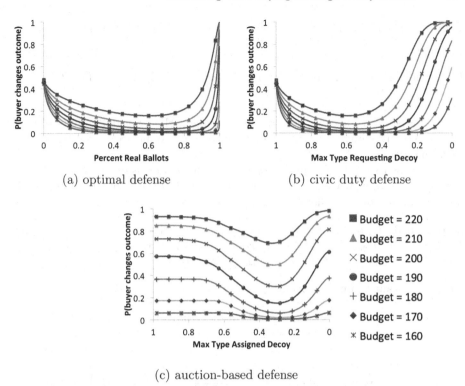

(a) optimal defense   (b) civic duty defense

(c) auction-based defense

Fig. 2. Comparing the power of different defenses, with $f = \text{Beta}(2, 4)$, 1000 ballots in total (some real, some decoy), and different buyer budgets B. (a) Optimal defense, varying the fraction of real ballots. (b) Civic duty defense, with the EA optimizing the number of decoy ballots to use for each value of parameter x_C (the 'max type requesting decoy'). (c) Auction-based defense, with the EA optimizing the number of decoys to use for each value of x_A (the 'max type assigned a decoy').

5   Neutral Approaches

In this section, we consider defenses where the EA does not design ψ, since doing so may be argued as the EA playing too active a role in running the election. Beyond neutrality, these new approaches have the additional advantage of not relying on the EA having knowledge of f.

5.1   A Constrained Defense

We first consider a *constrained defense*:

Definition 2. *Defense ψ is* constrained *if the EA distributes decoy ballots uniformly at random, i.e., $\psi = f$.*

Having a constrained defense implies that $h(\theta) = \frac{n_r}{n_r + n_d}(1 - \theta)$ and $\mathcal{I} = [0, \tau_C]$ for some $\tau_C > 0$, such that the budget is spent, i.e., $F(\tau_C) = B/(n_r + n_d)$.

Definition 3 (Low Budget). *A low budget is a budget where* $\int_{\tau_C}^1 \theta f(\theta) d\theta < \frac{1}{2} - F(\tau_C)$.

Definition 4 (High Budget). *A high budget is a budget where* $\int_{\tau_C}^1 \theta f(\theta) d\theta > \frac{1}{2} - F(\tau_C)$.

In words, for a buyer with a low (high) budget, the expected number of real ballots the buyer buys is lower than (exceeds) the amount needed to change the election outcome.

One way to study the power of a constrained defense is to consider the following question: if the total number of ballots is fixed, what is the optimal mix of real and decoy ballots?

Theorem 3. *Fixing the total number of ballots, the best constrained defense for the EA in the subgame perfect equilibrium is all (one) real ballots for low (high) buyer budget under the Normal approximation (3).*

Proof. We want to find, for fixed $n_r + n_d$,

$$\underset{\{n_r, n_d\}}{\operatorname{argmin}} P(buyer\ changes\ outcome) \tag{14}$$

$$\approx \underset{\{n_r, n_d\}}{\operatorname{argmin}} P\left(\frac{\sqrt{n_r}(1 - 2F(\tau)) - 2(1 - F(\tau))\mu_Y}{2\sqrt{(1 - F(\tau))\mu_Y(1 - \mu_Y)}} < Z\right). \tag{15}$$

If a buyer has low budget, then this means that $\mu_Y(1 - F(\tau)) < \frac{1}{2} - F(\tau)$, which implies that

$$\frac{\sqrt{n_r}(1 - 2F(\tau)) - 2(1 - F(\tau))\mu_Y}{2\sqrt{(1 - F(\tau))\mu_Y(1 - \mu_Y)}} < 0, \tag{16}$$

and $P(buyer\ changes\ outcome)$ is minimized when $n_d = 0$. Similarly, if a buyer has high budget, then this means that $\mu_Y(1 - F(\tau)) > \frac{1}{2} - F(\tau)$, which implies that

$$\frac{\sqrt{n_r}(1 - 2F(\tau)) - 2(1 - F(\tau))\mu_Y}{2\sqrt{(1 - F(\tau))\mu_Y(1 - \mu_Y)}} > 0, \tag{17}$$

and $P(buyer\ changes\ outcome)$ is minimized when $n_r \to 0$.

With a low buyer budget, while a constrained defense makes the buyer buy some decoys, it also leaves unpurchased decoys and reduces the number of unpurchased real ballots, decreasing the accuracy of the result. Thus, decoys are not useful for the EA in this case. On the other hand, the best that the EA can do with a buyer with a high budget is to issue a single real ballot, with the hope that the buyer won't buy it, resulting in a high variance outcome based on the vote of a single voter. Decoys are used, but not to good effect.

5.2   Civic Duty Defense

In this model, the EA makes decoy ballots available to a random subset of those voters who make an explicit request for a decoy.[6] The decision of the EA is thus the number of decoy ballots, but not how to distribute them. Rather, this decision arises through a simple model of a societal process.

In modeling this process, we assume that, for a YES-buyer, there is some distribution of civic-mindedness $\pi(\theta)$, with support on $[0, x_c]$, that determines the probability that a voter will request a decoy, where x_c is a fixed, publicly known quantity ("c" for civic). In particular, we assume for simplicity that $\pi(\theta) \propto x_c - \theta$. This captures the idea that the more extreme an agent's type, the more likely the agent is to request a decoy and thus help preserve the election's integrity.

Via Bayes' rule, the effect on the distribution on types ψ of those who get decoys is $\psi(\theta) = P(\theta|\text{request decoy}) \propto P(\text{request decoy}|\theta)f(\theta) = \pi(\theta) \cdot f(\theta) = (x_c - \theta)f(\theta)$. In fact, there will sometimes be a choice of n_d such that the civic duty defense is optimal. If the EA can choose a number of decoys n_d such that $\frac{n_d(1-x_c)}{n_r} = k$, where k is the normalization constant, then we see the canonical structure, with $h(\theta) = 1 - x_c$, $\forall \theta \in [0, x_c]$. We call the defense obtained via this model a *civic duty defense*. An example of this defense is illustrated in Fig. 1(b).

5.3   Auction-Based Defense

In this variation, the EA makes decoy ballots available to voters via an auction. We assume a simple n_d+1st price auction (when selling n_d decoy ballots), with the EA choosing n_d. The intent is not to model a sophisticated auction, but to adopt a strategyproof mechanism as a model for an idealized market-based approach for distributing decoy ballots to voters. The effect is that decoys go to voters with the highest value for decoys. As with the civic duty defense, the EA who makes use of an auction-based defense chooses the number of decoy ballots but not how to distribute them.

In modeling this societal process, we assume that the value to a voter for a decoy is monotonically increasing as the voter's type θ gets closer to zero.[7] For this reason, we model the effect of the auction as being that there is some threshold $x_A \in (0, 1)$, whereby the decoys are distributed according to voter type distribution f, conditioned on $\theta \le x_A$ ("A" for auction). In particular, for $\theta \in [0, x_A]$, we have $\psi(\theta) \propto f(\theta)$.

---

[6] We leave unmodeled that the buyer could try to interfere with this process. But notice that buying decoys from citizens who participate in this process is not useful because it depletes budget without hope of gaining real ballots. The same argument holds for the auction-based defense.

[7] We continue to assume that a voter's value for using a decoy is less than her value for a real ballot. Because of this, the auction-based process is consistent with our analysis in Sect. 2 in regard to the ordering of minimum acceptable offer price across different kinds of voters.

6   Simulation Results

We describe the results of an extensive simulation study to compare the power of various defenses in preventing a buyer succeeding in changing the outcome of an election. We choose to present results for voter type distribution $f = \text{Beta}(2,4)$, but the analysis is qualitatively unchanged for other distributions, including those with mean voting types in $[0.01, 0.49]$.

Figure 4 fixes the number of real ballots, and shows that vote buying can be successfully thwarted by issuing sufficiently many decoy ballots. The optimal and civic duty defenses are most effective, but even issuing decoys according to the auction-based and constrained defenses substantially reduces the probability of a vote buyer's success. It is interesting that even a small number of decoys, relative to the number of real ballots, can be effective. It also helps with understanding to compare the power of different defenses when fixing the total number of ballots and varying the number of decoy ballots. Figure 2(a) shows the effect of varying the fraction of real ballots when using an optimal defense. Figures 2(b) and (c) show the effect of the civic duty defense and auction-based defence for different values of model parameter x_C (the 'max type requesting a decoy') and x_A (the 'max type winning a decoy'), with the EA optimizing the number of decoys for each value of x_C and x_A, respectively. The auction-based defense is the least effective, but even here there is a range of x_A for which the performance is better than without using any decoys. In Figs. 2(b) and (c), a maximum type of 0 receiving a decoy corresponds to zero decoys.

Fixing the total number of ballots, we can also examine the relative power of the different defenses as a function of the buyer budget. In Fig. 3 (with 1000 total ballots) we see that an optimal defense can use decoys to protect against buyers with around twice the budget of a 'no defense' approach that just uses real ballots. For the civic-duty and auction-based defenses, we fix $x_C = x_A = 0.5$ and pick the best n_d at each point in the graph. The auction-based defense is better than no defense and the constrained defense. The civic-duty defense has good performance, about that of the optimal defense for many buyer budgets.

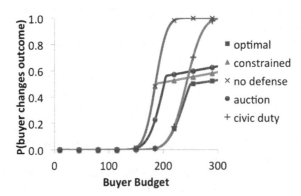

Fig. 3. Comparing the power of various defenses for $f = \text{Beta}(2,4)$, x_C and $x_A = 0.5$, and 1000 total ballots.

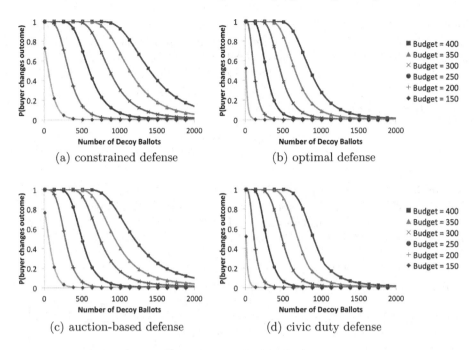

Fig. 4. Using decoys to thwart vote buying, for different buyer budgets (the number of ballots the buyer can buy). The number of real ballots is 750, the voter type distribution is $f = \text{Beta}(2,4)$. (a) Constrained defense, in which decoy ballots are distributed according to $f(\theta)$. (b) Optimal defense. (c) Auction-based defense with $x_{\text{A}} = 0.5$. (d) Civic duty defense with $x_{\text{C}} = 0.5$.

7 Non-binary Election Outcomes

In this section, we consider a generalization of the model presented above to non-binary election outcomes. In particular, suppose that there are three election choices, X, Y, and Z, and assume, without loss of generality, that Z is expected to receive the most votes, followed by Y, followed by X. In this version, we consider the election outcome to be determined by plurality, although an alternative research direction could consider another rule such as single transferable vote.

There are three possible classes of buyers: an X-buyer, who wants the election outcome to be X, a Y-buyer, who wants the election outcome to be Y, and an XY-buyer, who wants the election outcome to be either X or Y. Here, we will discuss only X-buyers, leaving an analysis of the other two classes of buyers to future work.

We model voter types as being a vector of length 3, namely

$$\theta_i \overset{\text{def}}{=} (P(\text{voter } i \text{ votes } X), P(\text{voter } i \text{ votes } Y), P(\text{voter } i \text{ votes } Z)),$$

and use the shorthand $\theta_i[X]$, $\theta_i[Y]$, and $\theta_i[Z]$ to refer to the components of θ_i. Types are drawn from a distribution $g(\theta)$ with full support on a 2-simplex (e.g., a Dirichlet distribution or a discrete distribution with point masses).

Let $\mathcal{J} \subset [0,1] \times [0,1]$ denote the subset of types that the buyer buys. Let $\mathfrak{M} \stackrel{\text{def}}{=} \int_{\mathcal{J}} g(\theta)d\theta$ denote the fraction of real ballots that the buyer buys. Let type distribution of the unbought types be given by

$$
g_\tau(\theta) \stackrel{\text{def}}{=} \begin{cases} \frac{g(\theta)}{1-\mathfrak{M}} & \text{for } \theta \in [0,1] \times [0,1] - \mathcal{J} \\ 0 & \text{for } \theta \in \mathcal{J} \end{cases} . \tag{18}
$$

We use the notation $X_i \multimap f(\theta)$ to denote the hierarchical model $\theta_i \sim g(\theta); X_i \sim$ Categorical(θ_i), and can now specify what it means for the buyer to change the election outcome. As in the proof of Lemma 2, let $V_i \multimap g_\tau(\theta)$ denote the unbought votes, and let $W_j \multimap g(\theta)$ denote all votes. We then have

$P(\text{buyer changes outcome})$
$= P([\text{election bought}] \wedge [\text{correct outcome is } Y \text{ or } Z])$

$$
= P\left(\left[\frac{\sum_{i=1}^{(1-\mathfrak{M})n_r} \mathbb{1}_{V_i=X}}{n_r} + \mathfrak{M} > \max\left(\frac{\sum_{i=1}^{(1-\mathfrak{M})n_r} \mathbb{1}_{V_i=Y}}{n_r}, \frac{\sum_{i=1}^{(1-\mathfrak{M})n_r} \mathbb{1}_{V_i=Z}}{n_r}\right)\right]\right.
$$
$$
\left. \wedge \left[\min\left(\frac{\sum_{j=1}^{n_r+n_d} \mathbb{1}_{W_j=Y}}{n_r+n_d}, \frac{\sum_{j=1}^{n_r+n_d} \mathbb{1}_{W_j=Z}}{n_r+n_d}\right) > \frac{\sum_{j=1}^{n_r+n_d} \mathbb{1}_{W_j=X}}{n_r+n_d}\right]\right), \tag{19}
$$

Recall that in the binary outcome case, we derived a simple characterization for an optimal buyer strategy (Lemma 1). On this basis, we were able to characterize the form of an optimal defense. In the three-outcome case, the strategy space is much richer, so we will discuss a few examples to illustrate some possible buyer strategies.

We first describe a simple vote buying strategy, and then show that it is optimal for simple, *deterministic types* (types where the voters vote for a particular outcome with probability 1).

Definition 5 (Buy the Expected Winner (BEW)). *The* buy the expected winner (BEW) *strategy is to greedily buy the type with the highest probability of voting for the current expected winner of the election, with the current expected winner determined considering the ballots already purchased by the buyer.*

Example 1. Suppose we have two voter types: 1,000 voters of type α: (0.25, 0, 0.75) and 600 voters of type β: (0, 1, 0) and no decoy ballots. Thus, the expected vote count is 250 X votes, 600 Y votes, and 750 Z votes. Table 1 illustrates the expected outcome for different buyer budgets and strategies. The third strategy for each budget above is to buy 200 votes of type α, and then buy four α votes for every three β votes until the budget runs out. This is the BEW strategy, which we can determine is optimal by enumerating all possible buyer strategies.

Example 2: Counterexample to Optimality of BEW. Suppose we have two voter types: 1,000 voters of type α: (0.25, 0, 0.75) and 1,000 voters of type β: (0, 0.26, 0.74) and no decoy ballots. The expected vote count is 250 X votes, 260 Y votes, and 1,490 Z votes. Table 2 illustrates the expected outcome for different buyer budgets and strategies. The buyer is better off buying type β than type α, which shows that the BEW strategy (i.e., buying type α) is not optimal. In fact, buying all type β is optimal, which can be seen by enumerating all possible buyer strategies.We next demonstrate that a refinement of BEW, where the buyer instead buys the type with highest $\max(\theta_i[Y], \theta_i[Z]) - \theta_i[X]$, can also be suboptimal.

Table 1. Illustrative buyer strategies for voter types α: (0.25, 0, 0.75) and β: (0, 1, 0).

Budget	Strategy	$E[\#X]$	$E[\#Y]$	$E[\#Z]$
0	-	250	600	750
400	Buy all α	550	600	450
400	Buy all β	650	200	750
400	Buy 314 α and 86 β	572.25	514	513.75
450	Buy all α	587.5	600	412.5
450	Buy all β	700	150	750
450	Buy 343 α and 107 β	614.25	493	492.75
500	Buy all α	625	600	375
500	Buy all β	750	100	750
500	Buy 371 α and 129 β	657.25	471	471.75

Table 2. Illustrative buyer strategies for voter types α: (0.25, 0, 0.75) and β: (0, 0.26, 0.74).

Budget	Strategy	$E[\#X]$	$E[\#Y]$	$E[\#Z]$
0	-	250	260	1,490
750	Buy all α	812.5	260	927.5
750	Buy all β	1,000	65	935

Example 3: Counterexample to Optimality of Refined BEW. Suppose we have 200 voters of type α: (0.25, 0.75, 0), 100 voters of type β: (0, 0.4, 0.6), and 150 voters of type γ: (0, 0, 1) and no decoy ballots. Then $E(\#X) = 50$, $E(\#Y) = 190$, $E(\#Z) = 210$. Suppose the buyer budget is 111. Table 3 illustrates the expected outcome for different buyer budgets and strategies. The first strategy

is the refined version of BEW. The buyer first buys 20 votes of type γ. Then, we have $E(\#X) = 70$, $E(\#Y) = 190$, $E(\#Z) = 190$. Now, he will buy 39 more ballots of type γ and 52 ballots of type α, resulting in $E(\#X) = 148$, $E(\#Y) = 151$, $E(\#Z) = 151$. So Y and Z are tied, and X has lost. The second strategy is to buy all 100 β votes and then 11 more γ votes. Here, we have $E(\#X) = 161$, $E(\#Y) = 150$, $E(\#Z) = 139$, and X wins. The third strategy, obtained by enumerating all possible strategies, is optimal.

Table 3. Illustrative buyer strategies for voter types α: (0.25, 0.75, 0), β: (0, 0.4, 0.6), and γ: (0, 0, 1).

Budget	Strategy	$E[\#X]$	$E[\#Y]$	$E[\#Z]$
0	-	50	190	210
111	Buy 52 α and 59 γ	148	151	151
111	Buy 100 β and 11 γ	161	150	139
111	Buy 2 α and 109 β	160.5	144.9	144.6

Example 4: Simple (Deterministic) Types. Suppose that we 200 voters of type X: (1, 0, 0), 350 voters of type Y: (0, 1, 0), and 450 voters of type Z: (0, 0, 1), and no decoy ballots. Table 4 illustrates the expected outcome for different buyer budgets and strategies. The third strategy is the BEW strategy, which is optimal here.

Table 4. Illustrative buyer strategies for deterministic voter types, X: (1, 0, 0), Y: (0, 1, 0), and Z: (0, 0, 1).

Budget	Strategy	$E[\#X]$	$E[\#Y]$	$E[\#Z]$
0	-	200	350	450
150	buy all Y	350	200	450
150	buy all Z	350	350	300
150	buy 25 Y and 125 Z	350	325	325

Example 5: Simple (Deterministic) Types with Decoys Suppose that the voter types are the same as in Example 4, but that the EA can issue decoys. We can numerically calculate the optimal EA strategy given the optimal defense. In regard to the optimal defense, this is BEW for some buyer budgets and numbers of decoys, but not always. See Fig. 5 for an illustration of the results. The optimal EA defense is to add the first 450 decoys with only Z type, and

then to begin adding both type Y and type Z decoys. In Fig. 5(a), all decoys
are issued with type Z, and the optimal buyer strategy is to buy more Z ballots
as each of them becomes less valuable— the buyer is playing the BEW strategy,
now incorporating the probability that the ballots are real. In Fig. 5(b), some of
the decoys (for numbers of decoys > 450) are issued with type Y, and the optimal
buyer strategy is sometimes to buy all or nearly all Y ballots instead of Z ballots.
In both cases, we see that the decoy defense is effective in stopping a vote buyer.
The red line corresponds to the threshold where the buyer goes from winning in
expectation to losing in expectation. With no defense, a strategic buyer needs
a budget of 134 ballots to change the outcome of the election (where he would
buy 17 Y ballots and 117 Z ballots). By issuing decoys, the EA can thwart a
vote buyer with budgets including 150 and 300 (with 1,000 total real ballots).

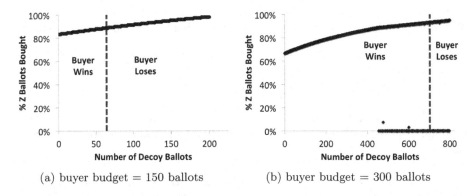

(a) buyer budget = 150 ballots   (b) buyer budget = 300 ballots

Fig. 5. Using optimally-distributed decoys to thwart vote buying in the three-outcome
case. The voter types are from Example 5. In (a), the buyer is playing the BEW
strategy, which is optimal. However, BEW is not optimal for all buyer budgets and
numbers of decoys, as can be seen in (b), where the buyer sometimes buys all or nearly
all Y ballots.

We can prove the optimality of BEW for these simple, deterministic types,
and without decoy ballots. Note that with deterministic types there is no uncertainty about the outcome of the election.

Theorem 4. *For deterministic types and no decoy ballots, the BEW strategy is
optimal for a buyer.*

Proof. We provide a proof for the slightly simpler case of buying fractional ballots (the proof for indivisible ballots follows the same outline). Let X, Y, and
Z refer to the types $(1, 0, 0)$, $(0, 1, 0)$, and $(0, 0, 1)$. Let x, y, and z refer to
the number of ballots cast for each election outcome. We proceed to show that
the BEW strategy minimizes the number of ballots needed for an X-buyer to
change the outcome of the election. Let $\delta_y \geq 0, \delta_z \geq 0$ denote the number of
Y and Z ballots purchased, respectively. The buyer wants to find the minimum
$\delta = \delta_y + \delta_z$ s.t. $x + \delta_y + \delta_z \geq \max(y - \delta_y, z - \delta_z)$.

(Case 1) $x < y = z$. In BEW, the buyer buys Y and Z ballots in equal quantity until winning. In particular, buying $\delta_y^* = \delta_z^* = 1/3(y - x)$ leads to a win for X, since $x + \delta_y^* + \delta_z^* = x/3 + (2/3)y = y - \delta_y^* = z - \delta_z^*$. No strategy using $\delta' < \delta^* = \delta_y^* + \delta_z^* = 2/3(y - x)$ ballots can do better. We have

$$\min_{\delta_y', \delta_z' : \delta_y' + \delta_z' = \delta'} \max(y - \delta_y', z - \delta_z') \geq \min_{\delta_y, \delta_z : \delta_y + \delta_z = \delta^*} \max(y - \delta_y, z - \delta_z)$$
$$= \max(y - \delta_y^*, z - \delta_z^*) = x/3 + (2/3)y > x + \delta',$$

where the first inequality follows because the LHS is more constrained, and the first equality follows because this balances the two components of $\max(\cdot, \cdot)$.

(Case 2) $x < y < z$, and $1/2(x + z) \geq y$. In BEW, the buyer buys $\delta_y^* = 0$ and $\delta_z^* = 1/2(z - x)$ of the Y and Z ballots respectively. This leads to a win for X, with $x + \delta_z^* = z - \delta_z^* = (1/2)(z + x)$ (and $x + \delta_z^* = (1/2)(z + x) \geq y = y - \delta^*$.) No strategy using $\delta' < \delta^* = \delta_y^* + \delta_z^* = 1/2(z - x)$ ballots can do better. We have

$$\min_{\delta_y', \delta_z' : \delta_y' + \delta_z' = \delta'} \max(y - \delta_y', z - \delta_z') \geq \min_{\delta_y, \delta_z : \delta_y + \delta_z = \delta^*} \max(y - \delta_y, z - \delta_z)$$
$$= \max(y - \delta_y^*, z - \delta_z^*) = 1/2(x + z) > x + \delta',$$

where the first inequal. follows because the LHS is more constrained, and the first equality follows because $z - \delta^* \geq y$ and thus it is optimal to only buy Z ballots.

(Case 3) $x < y < z$, and $1/2(x + z) < y$ In BEW, the buyer first buys $z - y$ of the Z ballots, and then splits the remaining purchases equally between Y and Z ballots. In particular, $\delta_y^* = 1/3(y - (x + (z - y))) = 1/3(2y - x - z)$ and $\delta_z^* = (z-y)+1/3(2y-x-z) = z-(y-\delta_y^*)$. Let $\delta^* = \delta_y^* + \delta_z^* = (1/3)y - (2/3)x + (1/3)z$. This leads to a win for X, with $x + \delta^* = (1/3)(x + y + z) = y - \delta_y^* = z - \delta_z^*$. No strategy using $\delta' < \delta^*$ ballots can do better. We have

$$\min_{\delta_y', \delta_z' : \delta_y' + \delta_z' = \delta'} \max(y - \delta_y', z - \delta_z') \geq \min_{\delta_y, \delta_z : \delta_y + \delta_z = \delta^*} \max(y - \delta_y, z - \delta_z)$$
$$= \max(y - \delta_y^*, z - \delta_z^*) = (1/3)(x + y + z) > x + \delta',$$

where the first inequality follows because the LHS is more constrained, and the first equality follows because this balances the two components of $\max(\cdot, \cdot)$.

An immediate corollary (noting that BEW is oblivious to budget) is that BEW also maximizes the advantage for X over the closest other outcome for a buyer with additional budget. We leave to future work to develop a full characterization of the optimal buyer strategy, and, in turn, optimal defense by the EA in the case of three or more outcomes. We do not yet have a characterization of the optimal buyer strategy even for the case of deterministic ballots, once decoys are also introduced.

8 Conclusion

We have presented the first game-theoretic study of the power of decoy ballots in thwarting vote buyers. We have characterized the form of an optimal defense, and compared its power to those of neutral defenses that could be enabled through leveraging simple societal processes to distribute decoy ballots. Our results are positive: decoy ballots are effective in thwarting the power of a vote buyer. Amongst the neutral defenses, the civic duty defense, where decoys are given at random to a subset of those who request such a ballot, seems especially interesting. Topics for future study include understanding defenses under the requirement that they must protect equally against a YES- or NO-buyer, and in settings with multiple buyers, simultaneous polls, and participants with value and cost heterogeneity. For the non-binary outcome case, we have provided some illustrative examples of the new subtleties that arise in modeling the optimal buyer strategy and thus optimal EA defense. There are a number of future directions of interest, including characterizing the optimal buyer and decoy defense strategies for non-binary outcome elections (initially for deterministic types). We expect that the richness of this setting will yield future interesting insights.

Acknowledgments. The Random Sample Voting (RSV) project has done much to encourage and facilitate this work, including convening a number of conference calls and circulating various internal documents. We are grateful to participants at EXPLORE 2017 for helpful discussions, as well as to the reviewers for their suggestions. LX acknowledges the support of the National Science Foundation, under grant IIS-1453542.

References

1. Binkele-Raible, D., Erdélyi, G., Fernau, H., Goldsmith, J., Mattei, N., Rothe, J.: The complexity of probabilistic lobbying. J. Discret. Optim. **11**, 1–21 (2014)
2. Brandt, F., Conitzer, V., Endriss, U., Lang, J., Procaccia, A.D. (eds.): Handbook of Computational Social Choice. Cambridge University Press, Cambridge (2016)
3. Bredereck, R., Chen, J., Hartung, S., Kratsch, S., Niedermeier, R., Suchý, O., Woeginger, G.J.: A multivariate complexity analysis of lobbying in multiple referenda. J. Artif. Intell. Res. **50**, 409–446 (2014)
4. Chaum, D.: Random-sample voting (2016). http://rsvoting.org/whitepaper/white_paper.pdf
5. Christian, R., Fellows, M., Rosamond, F., Slinko, A.: On complexity of lobbying in multiple referenda. Rev. Econ. Des. **11**(3), 217–224 (2007)
6. Dekel, E., Jackson, M.O., Wolinsky, A.: Vote buying: general elections. J. Polit. Econ. **116**(2), 351–381 (2008)
7. Faliszewski, P., Rothe, J.: Control and bribery in voting. In: Brandt, F., Conitzer, V., Endriss, A., Lang, J., Procaccia, A.D. (eds.) Handbook of Computational Social Choice. Cambridge University Press, Cambridge (2016)
8. Finan, F., Schechter, L.: Vote-buying and reciprocity. Econometrica **80**(2), 863–881 (2012)

9. Goel, A., Lee, D.T.: Towards large-scale deliberative decision-making: Small groups and the importance of triads. In: Proceedings of the 2016 ACM Conference on Economics and Computation, EC 2016, Maastricht, The Netherlands, pp. 287–303, 24–28 July 2016

10. Groseclose, T., Snyder, J.M.: Buying supermajorities. Am. Polit. Sci. Rev. **90**(2), 303–315 (1996)

11. Lee, D.T., Goel, A., Aitamurto, T., Landemore, H.: Crowdsourcing for participatory democracies: Efficient elicitation of social choice functions. In: Proceedings of the Second AAAI Conference on Human Computation and Crowdsourcing, HCOMP 2014, 2–4 November 2014

12. Parkes, D.C., Wellman, M.P.: Economic reasoning and artificial intelligence. Science **349**(6245), 267–272 (2015)

13. Phongpaichit, P., Treerat, N., Chaiyapong, Y., Baker, C.: Corruption in the public sector in Thailand perceptions and experience of households. Political Economy Center. Chulalongkorn University, Bangkok (2000)

14. Schaffer, F.C. (ed.): Elections for Sale: The Causes And Consequences of Vote Buying. Lynne Rienner Publishers, London (2007)

15. Schaffer, F.C.: Why study vote buying? In: Schaffer, F.C. (ed.) Elections for Sale: The Causes And Consequences of Vote Buying, pp. 1–16. Lynne Rienner Publishers, London (2007)

16. Stokes, S.C., Dunning, T., Nazareno, M., Brusco, V.: Brokers, Voters, and Clientelism, chap. 8. What killed vote buying in Britain and the United States? Cambridge University Press, New York (2013)

17. Tambe, M.: Security and Game Theory: Algorithms, Deployed Systems, Lessons Learned. Cambridge University Press, Cambridge (2011)

18. Vicente, P.C.: A model of vote-buying with an incumbency advantage (2013). http://www.pedrovicente.org/vb.pdf

19. Vicente, P.C.: Is vote buying effective? evidence from a field experiment in West Africa. Econ. J. **124**(574), F356–F387 (2014)

Efficient Evaluation of Influenza Mitigation Strategies Using Preventive Bandits

Pieter Libin[1,2](✉) [iD], Timothy Verstraeten[1] [iD], Kristof Theys[2] [iD],
Diederik M. Roijers[1] [iD], Peter Vrancx[1] [iD], and Ann Nowé[1] [iD]

[1] Artificial Intelligence lab, Department of Computer Science,
Vrije Universiteit Brussel, Brussels, Belgium
{pieter.libin,tiverstr,diederik.roijers,peter.vrancx,ann.nowe}@vub.ac.be
[2] Department of Microbiology and Immunology, Rega Institute
for Medical Research KU Leuven - University of Leuven, Leuven, Belgium
kristof.theys@kuleuven.be

Abstract. Pandemic influenza has the epidemic potential to kill millions of people. While different preventive measures exist, it remains challenging to implement them in an effective and efficient way. To improve preventive strategies, it is necessary to thoroughly understand their impact on the complex dynamics of influenza epidemics. To this end, epidemiological models provide an essential tool to evaluate such strategies *in silico*. Epidemiological models are frequently used to assist the decision making concerning the mitigation of ongoing epidemics. Therefore, rapidly identifying the most promising preventive strategies is crucial to adequately inform public health officials. To this end, we formulate the evaluation of prevention strategies as a multi-armed bandit problem. Through experiments, we demonstrate that it is possible to identify the optimal strategy using only a limited number of model evaluations, even if there is a large number of preventive strategies to consider.

Keywords: Epidemiological models · Preventive strategies
Pandemic influenza · Multi-armed bandits · Reinforcement learning

1 Introduction

The influenza virus is responsible for the deaths of half of a million people each year [1]. Additionally, seasonal influenza epidemics cause a significant economic burden [2]. While influenza is typically confined to local epidemics, it can cause a pandemic when a novel strain emerges that has the ability to spread rapidly among a susceptible human host population [3]. Pandemic influenza occurs less frequently than seasonal influenza but the outcome with respect to morbidity and mortality can be much more severe, potentially killing millions of people worldwide [4]. Therefore, it is essential to study mitigation policies to control pandemic influenza epidemics.

G. Sukthankar and J. A. Rodriguez-Aguilar (Eds.): AAMAS 2017 Visionary Papers,
LNAI 10643, pp. 67–85, 2017.
https://doi.org/10.1007/978-3-319-71679-4_5

For influenza, different preventive measures exist: i.a., vaccination, social measures (e.g., school closures) and antiviral drugs. However, the efficiency of these measures greatly depends on their availability, as well as on epidemiological characteristics. Furthermore, governments typically have limited resources to implement such measures. Therefore, it remains challenging to formulate prevention strategies that make effective and efficient use of these preventive measures while putting as little strain on the available resources as possible.

To improve the development of preventive strategies, it is necessary to thoroughly understand the complex dynamics of influenza epidemics. To this end, epidemiological models are commonly used. Such models study the effects of preventive measures *in silico* [5,6].

Epidemiological models are frequently used to assist the decision making concerning the mitigation of ongoing epidemics (not only for influenza, e.g., the H1N1/09 influenza pandemic [7], but also the 2014–2016 Ebola epidemic [8], the 2016 yellow fever outbreak [9], etc.). Therefore, rapidly identifying the most promising preventive strategies is crucial. This however, can be at odds with the accuracy of the models.

There are two main types of epidemiological models that are frequently applied: *compartment models*, which divide the population into discrete homogeneous states (i.e., compartments) and describe the transition rates from one state to another, and *individual-based models* that explicitly represent all individuals and their connections, and simulate the spread of a pathogen among these individuals. While individual-based models are usually associated with a greater model complexity and computational cost than compartment models, they allow for a more accurate evaluation of preventive strategies [10–12]. It is therefore highly preferable to use individual-based models whenever computational resource constraints permit. In order to make it feasible to use individual-based models, it is essential to use the available computational resources as efficiently as possible.

The outcome of the simulation of a preventive strategy in a stochastic individual-based model, is a sample of that strategy's *outcome distribution*. In the literature, a set of possible prevention strategies is typically evaluated by simulating each of the strategies a predefined number of times (e.g., [13]). However, this can allocate a large proportion of computational resources to explore the effects of highly sub-optimal strategies.

We therefore propose to apply *reinforcement learning* [14] with *multi-armed bandits* [15]. Reinforcement learning is the study of how to balance exploitation (i.e., further simulating the effects of what we believe to be the best preventive strategy to obtain more accurate results) and exploration (i.e., simulating the effects of other strategies to see whether they might actually be better than our current best). By using this framework, we aim to reduce the number of required model evaluations to determine the most promising preventive strategies. This reduces the total time required to study a given set of prevention strategies, making the use of individual-based models attainable in studies where it would otherwise not be computationally feasible. Additionally, faster evaluation can also free up computational resources in studies that already use individual-based models, capacitating researchers to explore different model scenarios. Considering a wider range of scenarios increases the confidence about the overall utility of prevention strategies.

In this paper, we formulate the evaluation of preventive strategies as a multi-armed bandit learning problem in Sect. 3. The utility of this new method is confirmed through experiments in the context of pandemic influenza in Sect. 4, using the popular FluTE individual-based model [10]. Our results show that we can quickly focus our computational resources on the optimal prevention strategy. We thus conclude that our method has the potential to be used as a decision support tool for mitigating influenza epidemics.

2   Background

This section provides background on the application domain (i.e., finding mitigation strategies for pandemic influenza using epidemiological models) and learning methods (i.e., multi-armed bandits) approached in this study.

2.1   Pandemic Influenza

Influenza is an infectious disease caused by the influenza virus. The primary prevention strategy to mitigate seasonal influenza is to produce vaccine prior to the epidemic, anticipating the virus strains that are expected to circulate. This vaccine pool is used to inoculate the population before the start of the epidemic. As influenza viruses are constantly evolving, the stockpiling of vaccine to prepare for a pandemic is not possible, as the vaccine should be specifically tailored to the virus that is the source of the pandemic [16]. Therefore, before an appropriate vaccine can be developed, the responsible virus needs to be identified [16]. Hence, vaccine will be available only in limited supply at the beginning of the pandemic [16]. Additionally, vaccine shortage can be induced by problems with vaccine production (e.g., the vaccine contamination in the United States in 2004–2005 [17]). While pandemic influenza has been studied and modeled extensively, there are still many aspects with respect to mitigation strategies that remain to be investigated [13,18]. Furthermore, awareness was raised recently about certain parameters and assumptions used in epidemiological models to be too conservative to explore the full epidemic potential of pandemic influenza, and as a result evaluate mitigation strategies overly optimistic [19]. These concerns indicate that the reevaluation of preventive strategies, taking into account more realistic assumptions, is warranted.

The severity of pandemic influenza, the limited availability of vaccine and an extensive set of open research questions render this field a primary target to evaluate preventive strategies more efficiently.

2.2   Epidemiological Models

Epidemiological models are an indispensable tool to investigate how pathogens spread through a population and to evaluate mitigation strategies. Epidemiological models are therefore crucial tools to assist policy makers with their decisions [20,21]. Modeling epidemiological processes can be approached by means of individual-based models or compartment models. Compartment models divide the population into discrete homogeneous states (i.e., compartments) and describe the transition rates from one state to another. Compartment models can be formulated as differential equations and thus form a mathematical framework to model epidemics. Individual-based models, on the other hand, explicitly represent all individuals and their connections and simulate the spread of a pathogen among this network of individuals. Individual attributes influence the way the contact network evolves temporally and spatially. Additionally, the infection progress and the different stages associated with this progress is modeled per individual. Individual-based models allow to evaluate therapeutic and preventive interventions on the level of individuals. Compartment models generalize on population level and represent the expectation of epidemiological outcomes, while individual-based models are able to represent individual heterogeneity. Modeling a greater level of heterogeneity is usually associated with a greater model complexity and computational cost, but allows for a more accurate evaluation of preventive strategies [10–12,22,23]. The result of a model evaluation is referred to as the model outcome. The relevant model outcomes greatly depend on the policy makers' research questions (e.g., prevalence, proportion of symptomatic individuals, morbidity, mortality, cost).

2.3   Modeling Influenza

There is a long tradition to use individual-based models to study influenza epidemics [5,6,13], since it allows for a more accurate evaluation of preventive strategies. A main example is FluTE [10], an influenza individual-based model that has been the driver for many high impact research efforts over the last decade [5,6,24]. FluTE implements a contact model where the population is divided into communities of households [10]. The population is thus organized in a hierarchy of social mixing groups where the contact intensity is inversely proportional with the size of the group (e.g., closer contact between members of a household than between colleagues). FluTE also supports worker's commute and the travel of individuals, both model components that can be parameterized from census data. FluTE's contact network can be informed by population census data, and geographical regions as large as the United States can be modeled [10]. Next to the social mixing model, FluTE implements an individual disease progression model, where different disease stages are associated with different levels of infectiousness. To support the evaluation of prevention strategies, FluTE allows the simulation of both therapeutic interventions (i.e., vaccines, antiviral compounds) and non-therapeutic interventions (i.e., school closure, case isolation, household quarantine). FluTE is a highly customizable simulator in which all model components can be configured in great detail.

2.4 Multi-armed Bandit

The multi-armed bandit problem [25] concerns a k-armed bandit (i.e., a slot machine with k levers) where each arm A_i returns a reward r_i when it is pulled. As each arm returns rewards according to a particular reward distribution, a gambler wants to play a sequence of arms to maximize her/his reward. A strategy to play such a sequence of arms is called a *policy*. Such policies need to carefully balance between exploitation (i.e., choose the arms with the highest expected reward) and exploration (i.e., explore the other arms to potentially identify even more promising arms).

Multi-armed bandits have been proven useful to model many empirical cases: i.a., the organization of clinical trials such that patient mortality is minimized [26], resource allocation among competing stakeholders [27], adaptive routing [28], A/B testing [29] and automated auctioning [30].

One of the simplest bandit learning algorithms is the ε-greedy policy [14], this policy selects the greedy arm (i.e., the arm with the highest expected reward) with probability $1 - \varepsilon$ and explores the non-greedy arms with probability ε. Another popular policy is UCB1 (i.e., Upper Confidence Bound) [15]. UCB1 considers the uncertainty of each arms' value (i.e., the uncertainty of the expected reward) by selecting the arm with the highest upper confidence bound. The upper confidence bound for an arm A_i is computed as $\bar{x}_i + \sqrt{c\frac{ln(n)}{n_i}}$ where $\bar{x}_i$ is the sample average of A_i, n_i is the number of times A_i was played and n is the overall number of plays [15]. The second term is an exploratory term, which decreases when arm A_i is being pulled sufficiently. This promotes the exploration of arms for which the estimated expected reward is uncertain.

3 Methods

To optimize the evaluation of prevention strategies, it is important to identify the best strategy using a minimal amount of model evaluations. Therefore, we propose to formulate the evaluation of prevention strategies as a multi-armed bandit problem. The presented method is generic with respect to the kind of epidemic that is modeled (i.e., pathogen, contact network, preventive strategies). The method is evaluated in the context of pandemic influenza in the next section.

3.1 Preventive Bandits

Definition 1. *A multi-armed bandit problem [15] consists of $n = |\{A_0, ..., A_n\}|$ arms and a (time-independent) reward distribution $P(r|A_i, \theta_i)$ for each arm, where θ_i are the parameters of the distribution. At each time step, t, an agent (i.e., gambler) chooses and plays an arm A_i, and receives a reward, r_t sampled (independently) from $P(r|A_i, \theta_i)$. The reward distributions' parameters are unknown to the agent.*

The goal in a multi-armed bandit is to optimize the cumulative sum of rewards. In order to do so, it must select arms that exploit its current knowledge about θ_i, i.e., by picking the best arm it has seen so far. However, it must also explore, in order to discover arms that are better. Because the rewards are received stochastically, the agent must never exclude the possibility that its current estimates are wrong.

In our setting, we want to find the optimal preventive strategy from a set of strategies by evaluating the strategies in an epidemiological model.

Definition 2. *A stochastic epidemiological model E is a function $\mathcal{C} \times \mathcal{P} \to \mathbb{R}$ where: $c \in \mathcal{C}$ is a configuration, $p \in \mathcal{P}$ is a preventive strategy and the codomain $\mathbb{R}$ represents the model outcome distribution.*

Note that a model configuration $c \in \mathcal{C}$ describes the entire model environment. This means both aspects inherent to the model (e.g., FluTE's mixing model) and options that the modeler can provide (e.g., population statistics, vaccine properties, basic reproduction number).

Our objective is to find the optimal preventive strategy from a set of alternative preventive strategies $\{p_0, ..., p_n\} \subset \mathcal{P}$ for a particular configuration $c_0 \in \mathcal{C}$ (corresponding to the studied epidemic) of a stochastic epidemiological model. To this end, we define a preventive bandit.

Definition 3. *A preventive bandit has $n = |\{p_0, ..., p_n\}|$ arms. Playing arm p_i corresponds to evaluating $E(c_0, p_i)$ by running a simulation of the epidemiological model. Evaluating $E(c_0, p_i)$ results in a sample of the model outcome distribution. The reward of p_i is a mapping of this model outcome (i.e., a sample of the model outcome distribution) using a mapping function $\mathbb{R} \to \mathbb{R}$.[1]*

A preventive bandit is thus a multi-armed bandit, in which the arms are preventive strategies, and the reward distribution is implemented by an instance of a stochastic epidemiological model $E(c_0, p_i)$. We note that while the parameters of the reward distribution are in fact known, it is intractable to determine the optimal reward analytically from the stochastic epidemiological model.

Formulating the evaluation of preventive strategies in terms of a bandit problem provides us with a new framework to reason about this task. The goal is to determine the best preventive strategy (i.e., the prevention strategy that mitigates the pandemic best on average) using as little model evaluations as possible.

3.2 Identifying the Optimal Strategy

Our goal is to identify the optimal strategy for a particular configuration $c_0 \in \mathcal{C}$ while thoroughly exploring all preventive strategies. For this purpose, we explore the use of the popular ε-greedy and UCB1 algorithms.

---

[1] The mapping function allows the model outcome to be represented more conveniently for learning.

4 Experiments

Two experiments were composed and performed in the context of pandemic influenza modeling. More specifically, in these experiments we analyze the mitigation strategy to vaccinate a population when only a limited number of vaccine doses is available (details about this scenario in Sect. 2). The experiments are inspired by the work of Medlock [31].

When the number of vaccine doses is limited, it is imperative to identify an optimal vaccine allocation strategy [31]. In our experiments, we explore the allocation of vaccines over five different age groups: pre-school children, school-age children, young adults, older adults and the elderly.

The experiments share a base model configuration, but differ with respect to a key epidemiological parameter: the basic reproduction number (i.e., R_0). The basic reproduction number represents the number of infections that is, by average, generated by one single infection.

4.1 Influenza Model and Configuration

The epidemiological model used in the experiments is the FluTE stochastic individual-based model (for details please refer to Appendix A). FluTE comes with a set of sample populations, in this experiment we use the sample population that describes a single community consisting of 2000 individuals (for details please refer to Appendix A). At the first day of the simulated epidemic, 10 random individuals are infected (i.e., 10 infections are seeded). The epidemic is simulated for 180 days. During this time no more infections are seeded. Thus, all new infections established during the run time of the simulation, result from the mixing between infectious and susceptible individuals. We assume no pre-existing immunity towards the circulating virus variant. We assume there are 100 vaccine doses to allocate (i.e., vaccine for 5% of the population).

In this experiment, we explore the efficacy of different vaccine allocation strategies. We consider that only one vaccine variant is available in the simulation environment. FluTE allows vaccine efficacy to be configured on 3 levels: efficacy to protect against infection when an individual is susceptible (i.e., VE_{Sus}), efficacy to avoid an infected individual from becoming infectious (i.e., VE_{Inf}) and efficacy to avoid an infected individual from becoming symptomatic (i.e., VE_{Sym}). In our experiment we consider $VE_{Sus} = 0.5$ [32], $VE_{Inf} = 0.5$ [32] and $VE_{Sym} = 0.67$ [7]. The influenza vaccine, as most vaccines, only becomes fully effective after a certain period upon its administration, and the effectiveness increases gradually over this period [33]. In our experiment, we assume the vaccine effectiveness to build up exponentially over a period of 2 weeks [33,34].

We define two experiments: both experiments use the base model configuration as described above. The two experiments differ with respect to their R_0 (i.e., basic reproduction number) parameter. To evaluate our new method, we select 2 values that are used in many studies: $R_0 = \{1.3, 1.4\}$ [5,10,31]. Each experiment thus has its own configuration. With respect to the definition of the epidemiological model (i.e., $E = \mathcal{C} \times \mathcal{P} \rightarrow \mathbb{R}$), we can express these configurations as $c_{R_0=1.3}$ and $c_{R_0=1.4} \in \mathcal{C}$.

4.2 Formulating Vaccine Allocation Strategies

We consider 5 age groups to which vaccine doses can be allocated: pre-school children (i.e., 0–4 years old), school-age children (i.e., 5–18 years old), young adults (i.e., 19–29 years old), older adults (i.e., 30–64 years old) and the elderly (>65 years old). An allocation scheme can be encoded by a Boolean 5-tuple, where each position in the tuple corresponds to the respective age group. When the value is 1 at a position, this denotes that vaccines should be allocated to the respective age group. When the value is 0 at a position, this denotes that vaccines should not be allocated to the respective age group. When vaccine is to be allocated to a particular age group, this is done proportional to the size of the population that is part of this age group.

Some examples: a preventive strategy where no vaccine should be allocated is encoded as $\langle 0, 0, 0, 0, 0 \rangle$, a preventive strategy where vaccine needs to be allocated uniformly across all age groups is encoded as $\langle 1, 1, 1, 1, 1 \rangle$, a preventive strategy where vaccine needs to be allocated exclusively to children is encoded as $\langle 1, 1, 0, 0, 0 \rangle$.

To decide on the best vaccine allocation strategy, we enumerate all possible combinations of this tuple. Since the tuple consists of a sequence of $\{0, 1\}^*$, the tuple can be encoded as a binary number. This enables us to represent the different allocation strategies by integers (i.e., $\{0, 1, ..., 31\}$).

With respect to the definition of the epidemiological model (i.e., $E = \mathcal{C} \times \mathcal{P} \rightarrow \mathbb{R}$), this set of 32 strategies is a subset of $\mathcal{P}$.

4.3 An Influenza Bandit

So far, we defined the model configurations (i.e., $c_{R_0=1.3}$ and $c_{R_0=1.4}$) and the set of preventive strategies (i.e., 32 vaccine allocation strategies) to be evaluated.

Now, let us define the *influenza preventive bandit* B_{Flu}: B_{Flu} has exactly 32 arms (i.e., $\{A_0, ..., A_{31}\}$). Each arm A_i is associated with the allocation strategy for which the integer encoding is equal to i. To conclude the specification of the influenza bandit B_{Flu}, we describe what happens when an arm A_i of B_{Flu} is played:

1. Invoke FluTE with a model configuration $c_0 \in \mathcal{C}$ and the vaccine allocation strategy $p_i \in \mathcal{P}$ associated with the arm A_i (i.e., this is allocation strategy i, using the strategy's integer representation).[2]
2. From FluTE's output, extract the proportion of the population that experienced a symptomatic infection: $\frac{\text{\# symptomatic individuals}}{\text{\# individuals}}$.
3. Return a $reward = 1 - \frac{\text{\# symptomatic individuals}}{\text{\# individuals}}$. Note that the reward denotes the proportion of individuals that did not experience symptomatic infection.

---

[2] Note that the configuration is serialized as a text file, for details on the format of this file, refer to Appendix B.

4.4   Outcome Distributions

To perform an initial analysis concerning the outcome distributions of the 32 prevention strategies, all strategies were evaluated 1000 times for both model configurations (i.e., $c_{R_0=1.3}$ and $c_{R_0=1.4} \in \mathcal{C}$). Note that generating thousands of samples (i.e., 2×32000 in this case) would not be computationally feasible when considering a larger population. This analysis is performed to identify the best strategy, such that we can properly validate the results from our learning experiments.

The outcome distributions are visualized in Figs. 1 and 2 for $c_{R_0=1.3}$ and $c_{R_0=1.4}$ respectively. A violin plot is used to plot the density of the outcome

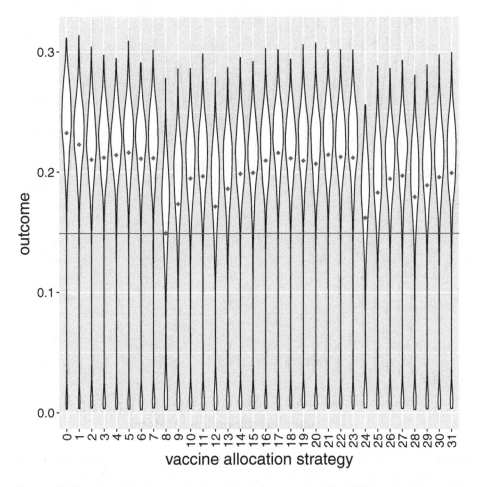

Fig. 1. Violin plot that depicts the density of the outcome distribution for 32 vaccine allocation strategies, considering a model environment with $R_0 = 1.3$. For each density, the sample mean is visualized with a diamond. The sample mean of the optimal strategy is depicted with a horizontal line.

distribution per vaccine allocation strategy. The density for a particular strategy is computed based on 1000 samples of the strategy's outcome distribution. Note that while the distributions have considerable density around the mean of the distribution, there is also quite some density where the outcome is close to 0. This is an artefact of the stochastic simulation: the pathogen is not able to establish an epidemic for certain simulation runs.

Our analysis shows that the best vaccine allocation strategy was identified to be $\langle 0, 1, 0, 0, 0 \rangle$ (i.e., vaccine allocation strategy 8) for both model configurations $c_{R_0=1.3}$ and $c_{R_o=1.4}$.

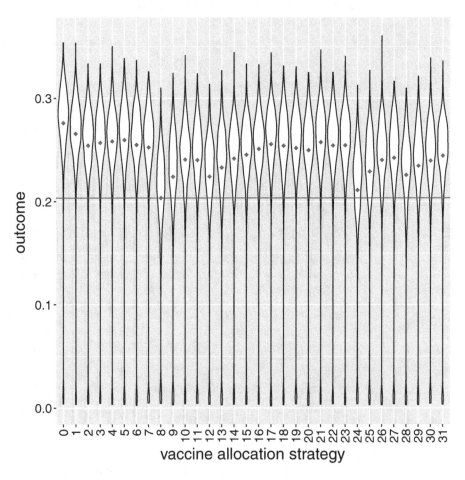

Fig. 2. Violin plot that depicts the density of the outcome distribution for 32 vaccine allocation strategies, considering a model environment with $R_0 = 1.4$. For each density, the sample mean is visualized with a diamond. The sample mean of the optimal strategy is depicted with a horizontal line.

4.5 UCB1 and ε-greedy Experiment

To explore the utility of bandits to evaluate preventive strategies, we average over 500 independent bandit runs for both experiments. For each experiment, we run the ε-greedy ($\varepsilon = 0.1$) and UCB1 algorithm for 1000 iterations.[3]

The average reward reported in the first experiment is visualized in Fig. 3 for both the ε-greedy and UCB1 algorithm. The average reward reported in the second experiment is visualized in Fig. 4 for both the ε-greedy and UCB1 algorithm.

We observe that the average reward starts to increase from iteration 400, for both ε-greedy and UCB1, and continues to increase for the rest of the iterations. However, we also note that the average reward learning curve increases faster for ε-greedy than for UCB1.

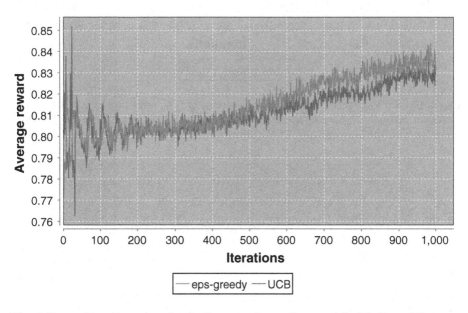

Fig. 3. Reward learning curve for the first experiment (i.e., model with $R_0 = 1.3$), averaged over 500 independent bandits for 1000 iterations. This plot depicts the learning curve for both the ε-greedy and UCB1 algorithms.

In the previous section, the best vaccine allocation strategy was identified to be $\langle 0, 1, 0, 0, 0 \rangle$ (i.e., vaccine allocation strategy 8) for both $c_{R_0=1.3}$ and $c_{R_o=1.4}$. Figure 5 visualizes the percentage of plays of the optimal arm (i.e., vaccine allocation strategy $\langle 0, 1, 0, 0, 0 \rangle$) for the first experiment. Figure 6 visualizes the percentage of plays of the optimal arm (i.e., vaccine allocation strategy $\langle 0, 1, 0, 0, 0 \rangle$) for the second experiment.

---

[3] To remind the reader, each arm involves the invocation of the FluTE simulator, and is therefore associated with a significant computational cost (for details, please see Appendix D).

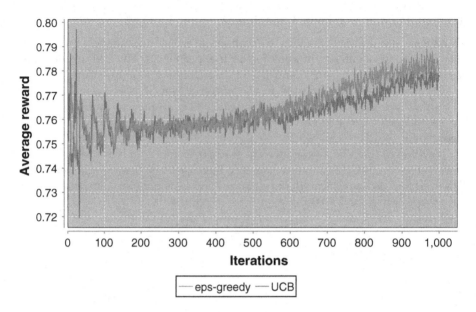

Fig. 4. Reward learning curve for the first experiment (i.e., model with $R_0 = 1.4$), averaged over 500 independent bandits for 1000 iterations. This plot depicts the learning curve for both the ε-greedy and UCB1 algorithms.

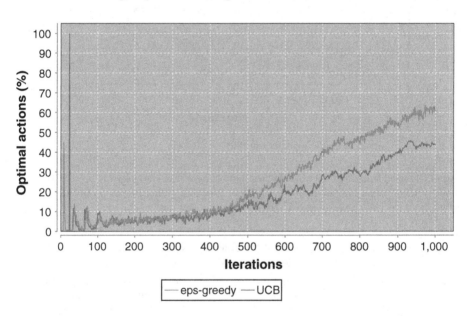

Fig. 5. Optimal action selection learning curve for the first experiment (i.e., model with $R_0 = 1.3$), averaged over 500 independent bandits for 1000 iterations (i.e., the Y-axis depicts the % the optimal action was selected). This plot depicts the learning curve for both the ε-greedy and UCB1 algorithms.

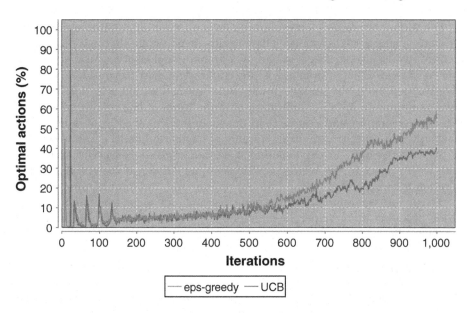

Fig. 6. Optimal action selection learning curve for the first experiment (i.e., model with $R_0 = 1.4$), averaged over 500 independent bandits for 1000 iterations (i.e., the Y-axis depicts the % the optimal action was selected). This plot depicts the learning curve for both the ε-greedy and UCB1 algorithms.

For both of the experiments, ε-greedy ends up selecting optimal actions 60% of the time after 1000 iterations. As we observed for the average reward learning curve, UCB1 also performs worse with respect to the optimal action selection learning curve, reaching only 40–45% optimal action selection.

5   Discussion

Our influenza model, and more specifically the context in which only a limited set of vaccine doses is available, was inspired by the work presented by Medlock and Galvani [31]. However, we consider a much smaller population (i.e., 2000 individuals versus the entire United States), to make it computationally feasible to validate our learning experiments. Furthermore, because of the differences between the model setup presented by Medlock and FluTE, a perfect mapping was not possible. It would therefore not be sound to compare our results directly to the results obtained by Medlock. We were, however, able to reproduce some significant trends. The best strategy identified by our analyses is associated with the allocation of vaccine to children: this is in agreement with Medlock's work.

The analysis of the outcome distributions for the different vaccine allocation strategies shows that there is one optimal strategy $\langle 0, 1, 0, 0, 0 \rangle$. The differences between the means and medians of the different strategies are however not very pronounced. This is related to the limited number of available vaccine doses.

For both of the experiments, ε-greedy ends up selecting optimal actions 60% of the time after 1000 iterations. These results demonstrate that it is possible to identify the optimal strategy using only a limited number of model evaluations, even if there is a large number of preventive strategies to consider. We also observe, that both the average reward and optimal action selection learning curves continue to increase, indicating that the learning has not yet converged. It is however important to stress that, our main interest is not convergence, but to identify the best strategy using a minimal number of model evaluations.

We observe that, in our experiment setting, ε-greedy outperforms UCB1, both with respect to the average reward learning curve and the optimal action selection learning curve.

To support the reproducibility of our research, all source code and configuration files used in our experiments is publicly available (for details, please see the Appendices).

6   Conclusions

We formally defined the evaluation of prevention strategies as a multi-armed bandit problem. We used this formal definition to describe a bandit that can be used to evaluate vaccine allocation strategies with the intention to mitigate pandemic influenza. Two elaborate experiments were set up to evaluate this preventive bandit using the popular FluTE individual-based model. To assess the performance of the preventive bandit, we report an average over 500 independent bandit runs, for the two experiments.

We demonstrate that it is possible to identify the optimal strategy using only a limited number of model evaluations, even if there is a large number of preventive strategies to consider.

We are confident that our method has the potential to be used as a decision support tool for mitigating influenza epidemics. To increase this potential, we aim to significantly extend the features of our tool and framework.

Firstly, while our method is evaluated in the context of pandemic influenza, it is important to stress that both our formalisms and infrastructure can be used to evaluate prevention strategies for other infectious diseases. We expect that epidemics of arboviruses (i.e., viruses that are transmitted by a mosquito vector; e.g., Zika virus, Dengue virus) are a particularly interesting use case for our preventive bandits. Only since recently, Dengue and Zika vaccines are available [35] or in the pipeline [36], and the optimal allocation of these vaccines is an important research topic [37]. Additionally, there exist individual-based arbovirus models [38] that could be readily applied to perform such analyses. We aim to test our approach on these pathogens as well.

Secondly, we aim to make different algorithmic extensions. In this study, we used elemental bandit learning algorithms (i.e., ε-greedy and UCB1). We acknowledge that other algorithms are more suited to identify the optimal action and could potentially learn faster. We created the infrastructure to easily implement and experiment with different algorithms and epidemiological models (details can be found in the Appendices) and we will use this framework to explore the use of other algorithms. Furthermore, the use of stateless reinforcement learning (i.e., bandits) presents us with a stepping stone to consider reinforcement learning where the partial or full state of the epidemiological model (e.g., which people are currently infected, and which measures have already been taken and to what effect) is used to learn preventive strategies that are more reactive towards events that take place in the simulation. We believe that such strategies may prove to be better than the static strategies we used in this study.

Finally, our current preventive bandits only learn with respect to a single model outcome: more specifically, for influenza this is the proportion of symptomatic infections. In the context of influenza, and for many infectious diseases, there is often interest to consider additional model outcomes (e.g., morbidity, mortality, cost). In the future, we aim to use *multi-objective multi-armed bandits* [39] in contrast to the current single-objective preventive bandits. With this approach, we plan to learn a *coverage set* containing an optimal strategy for every possible preference profile the decision makers might have [40]. We aim to design suitable quality metrics [41–43] tailored to the use case of epidemiological preventive strategy learning, to support the entire spectrum of epidemiological models and thus to prevent method over-fitting [43].

Acknowledgments. Pieter Libin was supported by a PhD grant of the FWO (Fonds Wetenschappelijk Onderzoek − Vlaanderen) and the VUB research council (VUB/OZR2714). Timothy Verstraeten was supported by a PhD grant of the FWO (Fonds Wetenschappelijk Onderzoek − Vlaanderen) and the VUB research council (VUB/OZR2884). Kristof Theys was supported by a postdoctoral grant of the FWO (Fonds Wetenschappelijk Onderzoek − Vlaanderen). Diederik Roijers was supported by a postdoctoral grant of the FWO (Fonds Wetenschappelijk Onderzoek − Vlaanderen). Thanks to Roxana Rădulescu, for her careful proofreading and helpful suggestions. Thanks to Karen Goedeweeck, for her careful proofreading. Thanks to all GNU/Python/R/Scala/FluTE hackers for their efforts, useful libraries and excellent tools. The computational resources and services used in this work were provided by the Hercules Foundation and the Flemish Government department EWI-FWO Krediet aan Navorsers (Theys, KAN2012 1.5.249.12.).

Appendix

A FluTE Source

FluTE is a stochastic individual-based model, that is implemented in C++. The original source code, as release by FluTE's author (i.e., D. Chao), is available from https://github.com/dlchao/FluTE. This github repository contains FluTE's C++ source code, GNU/Linux-specific make files and a set of population density descriptions that can be used to simulate particular geographical settings (i.e., 2000-individual population, Seattle, Los Angelos and the entire United States).

Some changes were made to the source code to make our research easier: we organized the source code in a directory structure and added a CMake meta-make file. This CMake build file allows us to build the source code on GNU/Linux and MacOS. These changes are publicly available on the https://github.com/vub-ai-lab/FluTE-bandits github repository.

B FluTE Configurations

To run our experiments, we defined a model environment to evaluate pre-vaccination with little vaccine available, as described in detail in Sect. 4. The pre-vaccination configuration script can be found in the 'configs/bandits' directory of the https://github.com/vub-ai-lab/FluTE-bandits github repository. Note that this configuration script is a python Mako template (http://makotemplates.org/), to enable easy parameterization of the configuration script.

C Bandit Implementation

We implemented a flexible bandit framework in Scala, the code is publicly available on github: https://github.com/vub-ai-lab/scala-bandits. This framework is specifically designed to enable us to easily experiment with new algorithms and environments (i.e., both Scala environments and external environments, such as e.g., the FluTE simulator environment). The repository contains the ε-greedy algorithm, the UCB1 algorithm, the Sutton test environment [14], the FluTE environment and some post processing utilities.

D High Performance Computing

Simulating epidemics using individual-based models is a computationally intensive process. Therefore, our experiments were run on a powerful high performance computing cluster: the Flemish Supercomputer Center. We report that, to make this possible, all software had to be installed (or built) for the high performance computing cluster. We report that our FluTE CMake file allows the generation of efficient code (i.e., using SSE instructions) for all platforms used in our analyses (i.e., MacOS, XUbuntu desktop GNU/Linux and GNU/Linux on the high performance computing cluster).

References

1. Stöhr, K.: Influenza: WHO cares. Lancet Infect. Dis. **2**(9), 517 (2002)
2. Molinari, N.A.M., Ortega-Sanchez, I.R., Messonnier, M.L., Thompson, W.W., Wortley, P.M., Weintraub, E., Bridges, C.B.: The annual impact of seasonal influenza in the US: measuring disease burden and costs. Vaccine **25**(27), 5086–5096 (2007)
3. Nicholls, H.: Pandemic influenza: the inside story. PLoS Biol. **4**(2), e50 (2006)
4. Patterson, K.D., Pyle, G.F.: The geography and mortality of the 1918 influenza pandemic. Bull. Hist. Med. **65**(1), 4 (1991)

5. Basta, N.E., Chao, D.L., Halloran, M.E., Matrajt, L., Longini, I.M.: Strategies for pandemic and seasonal influenza vaccination of schoolchildren in the United States. Am. J. Epidemiol. **170**(6), 679–686 (2009)

6. Germann, T.C., Kadau, K., Longini, I.M., Macken, C.A.: Mitigation strategies for pandemic influenza in the United States. Proc. Nat. Acad. Sci. **103**(15), 5935–5940 (2006)

7. Yang, Y., Sugimoto, J.D., Halloran, M.E., Basta, N.E., Chao, D.L., Matrajt, L., Potter, G., Kenah, E., Longini, I.M.: The transmissibility and control of pandemic influenza A (H1N1) virus. Science **326**(2009), 729–33 (2009). New York

8. Ajelli, M., Merler, S., Fumanelli, L., y Piontti, A.P., E Dean, N., Longini, I.M., Halloran, M.E., Vespignani, A.: Spatiotemporal dynamics of the Ebola epidemic in Guinea and implications for vaccination and disease elimination: a computational modeling analysis. BMC Med. **14**(1), 1–10 (2016)

9. Kraemer, M.U.G., Faria, N.R., Reiner, R.C., Golding, N., Nikolay, B., Stasse, S., Johansson, M.A., Salje, H., Faye, O., William Wint, G.R., et al.: Spread of yellow fever virus outbreak in Angola and the Democratic Republic of the Congo 2015–16: a modelling study. Lancet Infect. Dis. **17**(3), 330–338 (2017)

10. Chao, D.L., Halloran, M.E., Obenchain, V.J., Longini Jr., I.M.: FluTE, a publicly available stochastic influenza epidemic simulation model. PLoS Comput. Biol. **6**(1), e1000656 (2010)

11. Eubank, S.G., Kumar, V.S., Marathe, M.V., Srinivasan, A., Wang, N.: Structure of social contact networks and their impact on epidemics. DIMACS Seri. Discrete Math. Theor. Comput. Sci. **70**(0208005), 181 (2006)

12. Meyers, L.A., Newman, M.E.J., Martin, M., Schrag, S.: Applying network theory to epidemics: control measures for Mycoplasma pneumoniae outbreaks. Emerg. Infect. Dis. **9**(2), 204–210 (2003)

13. Fumanelli, L., Ajelli, M., Merler, S., Ferguson, N.M., Cauchemez, S.: Model-based comprehensive analysis of school closure policies for Mitigating Influenza Epidemics and Pandemics. PLoS Comput. Biol. **12**(1), e1004681 (2016)

14. Sutton, R.S., Barto, A.G.: Reinforcement Learning: An Introduction. MIT Press, Cambridge (1998)

15. Auer, P., Cesa-Bianchi, N., Fischer, P.: Finite-time analysis of the multiarmed bandit problem. Mach. Learn. **47**(2–3), 235–256 (2002)

16. World Health Organization, et al.: WHO guidelines on the use of vaccines and antivirals during influenza pandemics (2004)

17. Enserink, M.: Crisis underscores fragility of vaccine production system. Science **306**(5695), 385 (2004)

18. Biggerstaff, M., Reed, C., Swerdlow, D.L., Gambhir, M., Graitcer, S., Finelli, L., Borse, R.H., Rasmussen, S.A., Meltzer, M.I., Bridges, C.B.: Estimating the potential effects of a vaccine program against an emerging influenza pandemic - United States. Clin. Infect. Dis. **60**, S20–S29 (2015)

19. Miller, M.A., Viboud, C., Balinska, M., Simonsen, L.: The signature features of influenza pandemics: implications for policy. N. Engl. J. Med. **360**(25), 2595–2598 (2009)

20. Garnett, G.P., Cousens, S., Hallett, T.B., Steketee, R., Walker, N.: Mathematical models in the evaluation of health programmes. Lancet **378**(9790), 515–525 (2011)

21. Lessler, J., Edmunds, W.J., Halloran, M.E., Hollingsworth, T.D., Lloyd, A.L.: Seven challenges for model-driven data collection in experimental and observational studies. Epidemics **10**, 78–82 (2014)

22. Rahmandad, H., Sterman, J.: Heterogeneity and network structure in the dynamics of diffusion: comparing agent-based and differential equation models. Manage. Sci. **54**(5), 998–1014 (2008)
23. Willem, L.: Agent-Based Models For Infectious Disease Transmission: Exploration, Estimation & Computational Efficiency. Ph.D. thesis (2015)
24. Halloran, M.E., Longini, I.M., Nizam, A., Yang, Y.: Containing bioterrorist smallpox. Science **298**(5597), 1428–1432 (2002). New York
25. Herbert, R.: Some aspects of the sequential design of experiments. Bull. Am. Math. Soc. **58**(5), 527–535 (1952)
26. Press, W.H.: Bandit solutions provide unified ethical models for randomized clinical trials and comparative effectiveness research. Proc. Nat. Acad. Sci. **106**(52), 22387–22392 (2009)
27. Gittins, J., Glazebrook, K., Weber, R.: Multi-Armed Bandit Allocation Indices, 2nd edn. Wiley, Chichester (2011)
28. Awerbuch, B., Kleinberg, R.: Near-optimal adaptive routing: shortest paths and geometric generalizations. In: Proceeding of the 36th Annual ACM Symposium on Theory of Computing, pp. 45–53 (2004)
29. Kaufmann, E., Cappé, O., Garivier, A.: On the complexity of A/B testing. In: COLT, pp. 461–481 (2014)
30. Blum, A., Kumar, V., Rudra, A., Felix, W.: Online learning in online auctions. Theoret. Comput. Sci. **324**(2–3), 137–146 (2004)
31. Medlock, J., Galvani, A.P.: Optimizing influenza vaccine distribution. Science **325**(5948), 1705–1708 (2009)
32. McLean, H.Q., Thompson, M.G., Sundaram, M.E., Kieke, B.A., Gaglani, M., Murthy, K., Piedra, P.A., Zimmerman, R.K., Nowalk, M.P., Raviotta, J.M., Jackson, M.L., Jackson, L., Ohmit, S.E., Petrie, J.G., Monto, A.S., Meece, J.K., Thaker, S.N., Clippard, J.R., Spencer, S.M., Fry, A.M., Belongia, E.A.: Influenza vaccine effectiveness in the United States during 2012–2013: variable protection by age and virus type. J. Infect. Dis. **211**(10), 1529–1540 (2015)
33. Abbas, A.K., Lichtman, A.H., Pillai, S.: Cellular and Molecular Immunology. Elsevier Health Sciences, Amsterdam (2014)
34. CDC: Key facts about influenza (flu) & flu vaccine. Centers for Disease Control and Prevention, Atlanta (2014)
35. Hadinegoro, S.R., Arredondo-García, J.L., Capeding, M.R., Deseda, C., Chotpitayasunondh, T., Dietze, R., Muhammad Ismail, H.I.H., Reynales, H., Limkittikul, K., Rivera-Medina, D.M., Tran, H.N., Bouckenooghe, A., Chansinghakul, D., Cortés, M., Fanouillere, K., Forrat, R., Frago, C., Gailhardou, S., Jackson, N., Noriega, F., Plennevaux, E., Wartel, T.A., Zambrano, B., Saville, M.: Efficacy and long-term safety of a dengue vaccine in regions of endemic disease. N. Engl. J. Med. **373**(13), 1195–1206 (2015)
36. Cohen, J.: The race for a Zika vaccine is on. Science **351**(6273), 543–544 (2016)
37. Ferguson, N.M., Rodríguez-Barraquer, I., Dorigatti, I., Mier-y Teran-Romero, L., Laydon, D.J., Cummings, D.A.T.: Benefits and risks of the Sanofi-Pasteur dengue vaccine: modeling optimal deployment. Science **353**(6303), 1033–1036 (2016)
38. Chao, D.L., Halstead, S.B., Halloran, M.E., Longini, I.M.: Controlling dengue with vaccines in Thailand. PLoS Neglected Trop. Dis. **6**(10), e1876 (2012)
39. Drugan, M.M., Nowe, A.: Designing multi-objective multi-armed bandits algorithms: a study. In: Proceedings of the International Joint Conference on Neural Networks (2013)
40. Roijers, D.M., Vamplew, P., Whiteson, S., Dazeley, R.: A survey of multi-objective sequential decision-making. J. Artif. Intell. Res. **48**, 67–113 (2013)

41. Roijers, D.M.: Multi-objective decision-theoretic planning. Ph.D. thesis, University of Amsterdam (2016)
42. Vamplew, P., Dazeley, R., Berry, A., Issabekov, R., Dekker, E.: Empirical evaluation methods for multiobjective reinforcement learning algorithms. Mach. Learn. **84**(1–2), 51–80 (2011)
43. Zintgraf, L.M., Kanters, T.V., Roijers, D.M., Oliehoek, F.A., Beau, P.: Quality assessment of MORL algorithms: a utility-based approach. In: Proceedings of the Twenty-Fourth Belgian-Dutch Conference on Machine Learning, Benelearn 2015 (2015)

Adaptive Agents in Minecraft: A Hybrid Paradigm for Combining Domain Knowledge with Reinforcement Learning

Priyam Parashar[1]([✉]), Bradley Sheneman[2], and Ashok K. Goel[3]

[1] Contextual Robotics Institute, University of California, San Diego,
La Jolla, CA 92043, USA
pparashar@ucsd.edu
http://acsweb.ucsd.edu/~pparasha/
[2] American Family Insurance, Chicago, IL, USA
[3] School of Interactive Computing, Georgia Institute of Technology,
Atlanta, GA 30332-0250, USA

Abstract. We present a pilot study focused on creating flexible Hierarchical Task Networks that can leverage Reinforcement Learning to repair and adapt incomplete plans in the simulated rich domain of Minecraft. This paper presents an early evaluation of our algorithm using simulation for adaptive agents planning in a dynamic world. Our algorithm uses an hierarchical planner and can theoretically be used for any type of "bot". The main aim of our study is to create flexible knowledge-based planners for robots, which can leverage exploration and guide learning more efficiently by imparting structure using domain knowledge. Results from simulations indicate that a combined approach using both HTN and RL is more flexible than HTN alone and more efficient than RL alone.

Keywords: Reinforcement learning · Artificial intelligence
Simulation · Adaptive agents

1 Introduction

Hierarchical Task Networks (HTNs) have been used extensively in artificial intelligence applications, specially robotics. They have many advantages which make them a lucrative choice for programming task-level behaviors in structured environments. The biggest one, of course, is that by being hierarchical they are invariant to the low-level agent controllers, which enables re-use of successful plans and simplifies programming. Furthermore, they impose a symbolic and object-oriented structure on world, making higher-level task planning and reasoning easier. Interestingly though this is also one of the major flaws of HTN planner. Classic HTNs follow a strictly structured approach towards task planning, making them incapable of handling dynamic environments. In this paper

© Springer International Publishing AG 2017
G. Sukthankar and J. A. Rodriguez-Aguilar (Eds.): AAMAS 2017 Visionary Papers,
LNAI 10643, pp. 86–100, 2017.
https://doi.org/10.1007/978-3-319-71679-4_6

we experimentally show a way of making HTN plans more flexible by introducing reinforcement learning in the system that can learn new plan segments by exploration. The benefit of such an approach is two-fold, reinforcement learning helps networks learn new plans in dynamic environments and domain knowledge helps guide reinforcement learning towards more fruitful states for faster convergence with fewer data samples.

The obvious question here is why is making HTNs flexible an important endeavour? The short answer is because everyday life is full of chaos and noise. The long answer is that embodied intelligent agents are rapidly moving from industrial sector to personal ones. Robots are being employed in offices, universities, hospitals, etc. to name a few places. These environments are highly dynamic and require agents to be more adaptable and flexible with their assumptions. Agents which can learn, either by demonstrations or exploration, are therefore heavily explored and favored for automating work-flow in named domains [1,5,6,10,19].

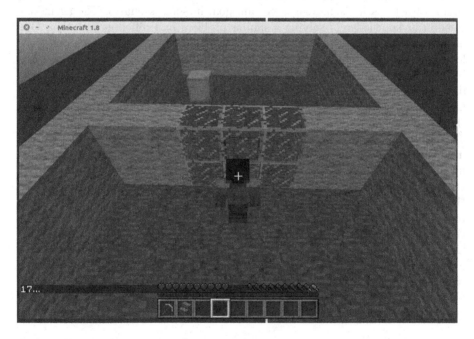

Fig. 1. A view of the Puzzle Room showing the Agent and Gold separated by a Glass Wall

The reason for machine learning gaining ground is the appeal for customization of the robot. Traditionally robots need a very structured environment for reliable accuracy in work which results in substantial setup time, and in some cases a procedure overhaul, before introducing a robot to the work-flow. This process is very different from how human workers are expected to function.

When moving from one to another similar environment, humans tend to explore the surroundings by actions or asking questions until they build a better mental model. Machine learning helps robots by learning from experimentation or demonstrations by non-experts which reduces manual coding effort of experts. Reinforcement learning has been seen as one of the most successful unsupervised methods of learning optimal goal-directed behavior in an unknown environment. The biggest critique of this method has been that reinforcement learners need a substantial amount of domain knowledge, or huge amounts of data, to efficiently understand, manipulate and examine the world and results of actions. This leads to an obvious marriage between the two methods outlined above.

In this paper, we have built an artificially intelligent agent capable of higher-level reasoning and borrowing knowledge from known problems to solve new ones by employing a guided reinforcement learner. We borrow our intuition from the key concept of *scaffolding* in cognitive science. Scaffolding, in its oldest definition [4], means to highlight the actions of master or the learner which contribute more to the success of a task. In our experiments, our agent is asked to plan course of actions for achieving a certain goal in some scenario. The agent has some prior knowledge of solving a similar problem in a different situation. Our algorithm basically compares the new situation to the most similar known problem, and uses the differences along with domain knowledge from its knowledge base to guide exploration of the reinforcement learner by providing rewards or discounts for fruitful actions. As of right now we are providing the most similar known problem manually to the system, leaving the rest of the reasoning up-to the algorithm.

We are exploring two key concepts here. The main hypothesis is that we can use the domain-knowledge stored in HTN to help guide RL better and speed up its learning curve. The other hypothesis concerns focusing of attention at the right level of detail. HTNs by definition are hierarchical and we hypothesize that this information can help in further focusing attention on the right actions to better explore the environment. We elaborate this point in more detail in the Approach section. We would like to point out here that implementing this algorithm on real embodied agents would have required substantial effort in implementing accurate perception, manipulation, etc. While our focus in this paper is to verify our approach and methods first, before adding other unstable components to the pipeline. We have therefore used simulation in this paper for verifying our concept and evaluating the algorithm.

2   Literature Review

Hierarchical Task Networks have been extensively explored in the AI research community in the last few decades, owing to its expressivity [30], speed and efficiency in complex domains, and invariance to lower-level mechanics of execution [9,21,22]. Specifically, HTNs have been popular in robotics due to its ability to re-use plans [31] and accurate task planning in structured domains [16]. Given the complexity of real-world scenarios, the symbolic abstractions used by

HTNs can measurably speed up the planning time [31]. Apart from manipulators, HTNs have been successfully used in improving navigation strategies for mobile robots by reasoning on future actions of the robot [3]. HTNs are also discussed in human-robot interaction community, specially human-guided learning. Humans tend to think of tasks in a naturally hierarchical way, and HTNs have been seen as a fitting format to learn these representations [18].

Reinforcement Learning (RL) [26] is a well known machine learning technique for training appropriate agent behavior using the concept of rewards. The technique is influenced by concepts from psychology where subjects, especially young children, are rewarded for appropriate behavior and penalized for inappropriate actions to help them learn the norms of culture and society [2,24]. In machine learning, this technique is used to provide appropriate reward to the agent depending upon consequences of its actions. This helps the agent learn the correct actions to be taken in different conditions or *states*, as an indirect way of learning the correct cost function associated with the environment and the task. Recently, learning game-playing policies using only visual cues has gained much traction in the community due to its obvious benefits in an unstructured domain [17].

Reinforcement Learning has also seen an increased interest from the robotics community in the last decade. Especially it has been observed that model-based versions of RL seem to do exceptionally well in robotics [14]. Trying to merge together new knowledge with known knowledge-base is not a new endeavour and has been extensively explored in literature. Cognitive scientists recognize that rules coded using higher-level knowledge can help guide lower-level actions for better skill acquisition [25]. In the field of AI, Murdock and Goel [20] used model-based reasoning to localize and guide RL, while Ulam et al. [29] propose fusing RL with domain-knowledge in video games to improve training efficiency. Other authors have modified a flavor of HTN to calculate and update beliefs of success for different methods, and improve re-planning by focusing on the more successful plans [11,15]. Hogg and Nejati propose algorithms to create HTNs in a way such that non-determinism is baked-into the methods by first observing task demonstrations [12,23]. Minecraft platform itself is a very new phenomenon in aiding and exploring different learning methods in the community and [27] is an important recent paper relevant to our mission, highlighting the versatility and ease of use of the platform.

3   Approach

3.1   Hierarchical Task Networks

Hierarchical Task Networks (HTNs) [8,9] are one of the more classic approaches used in the world of planning, especially robotics. HTNs represent the environment in terms of a dictionary of symbolic state variables and plans. This includes a library of *primitive actions* and *methods*. A primitive action is the smallest unit of plan decomposition. A method is a composite action made up of one or more ordered primitive actions or methods. It comprises of two main

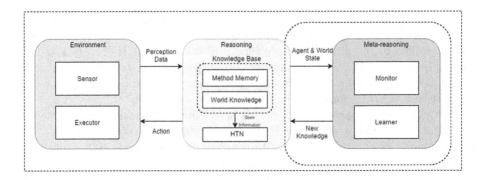

Fig. 2. System architecture

attributes: *pre-conditions* and *effects*. Pre-conditions are a set of environment conditions conditioned on state variables which must be true for a method to be executed. Effects are changes that the method, if executed, would have on the environment variables. Depending upon the goal and the state of the environment HTNs string together these methods to build a complete plan.

In the current context, the HTN uses atomic actions like "move forward", "turn left/right" and "break block in focus". For all experiments in this paper the end-goal of the agent remains same, which is to acquire the gold block.

3.2 Reinforcement Learning: Q-Learning

We have implemented a tabular form of Q-learning for our reinforcement learning purposes in this paper, using the following update formula. s denotes a state from the table, a denotes the action taken in state s, s' symbolizes the next state once action a is executed and $R(s, a)$ is the reward agent received after executing action a while in state s.

$$Q(s,a) = Q(s,a) + \alpha * (R(s,a) + \gamma * \arg\max_{a} Q(s',a') - Q(s,a))$$

The states of the table vary depending upon whether the q-learner is using domain-knowledge or not. World of Minecraft is grid-based and the pure q-learner states consist of the 9 blocks right in front of the agent including the ground blocks, what the agent is staring at, what is the agent holding in its hand and agent's pitch state, i.e. angle at which the agent is staring. For the combination learner, we have also provided states with a count of relevant items within a 5×5 grid around the agent. We have used ϵ-greedy selection strategy, with an exponentially decaying ϵ. After some calibration, our implementation uses a starter ϵ of 0.4 with a decay rate of 0.95 over 1000 iterations, a learning rate, α, of 0.55 and a γ of 0.75. In addition, the Q-values were normalized so as to sum to 50. The ϵ decays as per the following formula, where decay_steps is 100 in our implementation:

$$new_\epsilon = starter_\epsilon * \texttt{decay\_rate}^{\frac{iteration\_step}{decay\_steps}}$$

3.3   Architecture

The architecture, Fig. 2, is divided into three major components: Environment Interface, Reasoning AI and a Meta-Reasoner. This three-layered architecture is similar to traditional AI architectures for metareasoning [7,13]. The environment interface consists of the actual game engine and API, where agent takes actions and uses sensors to perceive surroundings. The simulation is achieved using the rich world of Minecraft with the help of Malmo Platform[1]. The reasoning AI is the actual planner (HTN in our case) that communicates directly with the environment and reasons on environment state and agent-specific variables to build and execute a plan. We have used a stripped down python version of SHOP [22] called PyHop[2] in our implementation. The meta-reasoner is the third hidden component which communicates with the AI and keeps track of internal processes responsible for planning and execution with the help of internal meta-data like error flags and execution trace of planning process. This part emulates the process of debugging run-time error using meta-information as well as deploying a solution just like human developers. The solution, in our implementation, is the Learner module which uses the information provided by meta-reasoner to setup rewards for appropriate states for Q-learning.

3.4   Algorithm

As noted above in Subsect. 3.1, the agent is continually processing current world state with method pre-conditions (within the Reasoning component) before enqueueing any action execution. In a dynamic world, this is where the first break happens. The reality is different from the expected. This raises an error flag followed by compilation of an error message, including level of mismatch, rest of the plan and name of mismatched method. This information is dispatched to the Meta-reasoner, which uses it to grab the pre-conditions of methods queued after the mismatched method in the plan. These states are used as intermediate states or goals for the learner, intuition being that if the learner can find a way to these states the planner can re-use the coded methods to achieve the goal. Moreover, the Meta-reasoner forms a comparison of current scenario to the nearest known scenario encountered in the past which it knows the solution to (Fig. 3).

This comparison helps in creating a secondary level of rewards which is endowed on those actions which make this scenario more like the one already known and solved. A third layer of discounts is formed by looking at or being near *relevant items*. These relevant items are defined by the differences between current and compared scenario and the knowledge base. Any action which leads the agent in direct line of sight of relevant items or brings the agent near relevant items is discounted by some amount. We are discounting the cost, i.e. such a fruitful action costs -0.5 as compared to -1 of normal action, and not rewarding it because we still want the agent to maximize overall reward with minimum

---

[1] https://github.com/Microsoft/malmo.

[2] https://bitbucket.org/dananau/pyhop.

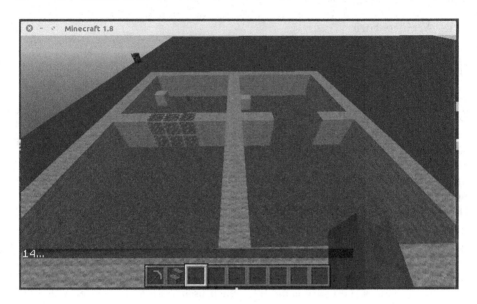

Fig. 3. A view of the compared rooms

Require: s_a: State of the Agent, s_w: State of the World, $method_t$: Current method
to be executed, htn_plan
1: **procedure** PLANNER()
2:     **while** $method_t \neq \varnothing$ **do**
3:         let PC = EXTRACTPRECONDITION($method_t$)
4:         **if** $s_w =$ PC **then**
5:             EXECUTE($method_t$)
6:             UPDATESTATE(s_w)
7:             $method_t \leftarrow$ NEXTMETHOD(HTNPlan, $t + 1$)
8:         **else**
9:             new_method $\leftarrow$ METAAI(s_w, s_a, htn_plan, $method_t$)
10:            ADDNEWMETHOD(htn_plan, new_method)
11:        **end if**
12:    **end while**
13: **end procedure**

Fig. 4. Central planning and execution algorithm

number of actions. An example of fruitful action can be seen in Fig. 6. Once the
q-values are converged above a threshold or once the agent achieves the goal
more than a threshold number of times, this learned policy is then added to the
method library with the mismatched set of state variables as its pre-conditions
(Figs. 4 and 5).

Let us further clarify with the help of an example. Figure 9 is an example
of a plan proposed by the HTN for a scenario where the agent needs to break
the wall before acquiring the gold block. During run-time though, the agent

realizes that the scenario is modified and the plan breaks down while processing `break_the_wall` method. This raises an error flag and a stack-trace is generated describing the breakage point and the reason for breakage. Using these messages, the meta-reasoner deduces that the pre-conditions for `break_the_wall` method were not satisfied. It then looks ahead and grabs the pre-conditions of methods queued after the named method. Meta-reasoner then uses these grabbed pre-conditions to generate reward states for the agent and deploys the RL module which explores the simulated world to learn a new method to bridge the broken plan.

Require: s_a, s_w, htn_plan, $method_t$
1: **procedure** METAAI()
2:     error_level ←
    FINDERRORLEVEL(htn_plan.error_msgs)
3:     **if** error_level = PreconditionMismatch **then**
4:         actions ←
    EXTRACTALLACTIONS(htn_plan.library)
5:         intermediate_states ←
    EXTRACTPRECONDITIONS(All methods in htn_plan queued after $method_t$)
6:         $R(s)$ ← SETUPREWARDS(intermediate_states)
7:         INITIALIZE(QLearner, s_w, $R(s)$, actions)
8:         QLEARNER.ADDSTATEVARIABLE(
    relevant_item_count)
9:         LAUNCH(QLearner)
10:     **else if** error_level = InventoryMismatch **then**
11:         relevant_actions ←
    EXTRACTINVENTORYACTIONS(htn_plan.library)
12:         intermediate_state ←
    EFFECTOFMETHOD($method_t$)
13:         $R(s)$ ← SETUPREWARDS(intermediate_state)
14:         INITIALIZE(QLearner, s_w, $R(s)$, relevant_actions)
15:         LAUNCH(QLearner)
16:     **end if**
17: **end procedure**

Fig. 5. Meta-reasoner algorithm

4   Experimental Setup

Our experimental setup borrows from the classic "room solving" puzzle games which required the player to solve a level by acquiring gold or reaching the exit door by overcoming certain obstacles. For our experiment we created three similar puzzles with varying levels of complexity. We have kept things relatively simple in our puzzle rooms in order to verify our concept rather than robustness of the system. As in the classic puzzles, in this experiment the room is considered solved when the agent successfully acquires the gold block.

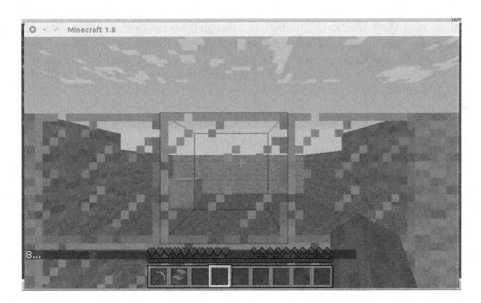

Fig. 6. An example of a fruitful action where the agent is directly staring at the Glass wall

Looking at the decomposition of `break_the_wall` method more carefully in Fig. 9, we can see that not only does this method have pre-conditions specific to execution conditions (for example, do not trigger until agent is right next to the wall) but it also has some *inventory* pre-conditions which require the presence of certain tools for successful action execution. There could be two scenarios here, either that the agent was not able to successfully navigate to the wall, say because of a ditch, or the agent did not have the required tools to successfully execute the method. These two problems require two completely different solutions. While the first scenario might require learning of a whole new method to traverse a ditch, the other only requires playing with different tools to find a valid substitute. This is where the hierarchical nature of HTNs helps guide the learner towards right nature of solution. Depending upon whether the breakage was due to new environmental conditions or agent's limited experience with different artifacts, the Meta-reasoner deploys different kinds of solutions to repair the knowledge-base of the planner.

We thus created two different classes of experimental scenarios to test the hierarchical nature of learning from our system. One class tests the adaptability of methods, by rendering an inventory-listed tool unavailable to the user forcing the agent to improvise by learning a new tool on the fly. The other class operates on problems one level above, changing the world state such that none of the stored methods match the current state, rendering a stored method invalid for our scenario. The agent is then instructed to explore the world and learn an alternate method to achieve its immediate goal.

4.1   Adapting a Known Method

Using our wall-in-the-room setup, we placed the agent and the gold block on opposite sides of this stone wall. We first wrote a plan in which agent uses an "iron axe" tool to first break the wall to access the gold block. To introduce the agent to a new situation, we changed agent's inventory to have a "wood axe" and "steel axe" instead. Thus everything else remains the same except that the agent now has different tools than the one planned for.

4.2   Learning a New Method

We created an environment that was new for the agent but similar to a known scenario stored in HTN memory. We used a simple empty-pair-of-rooms plan to solve a Puzzle Room with a wall in the moddle, as can be seen in Fig. 1. We want to test if the agent can learn the full method from scratch.

4.3   Combination Learner Versus End-to-End Learner

Finally, we want to compare the efficiency of such an architecture versus one which can not reason about the failure of a plan and decides to employ an end-to-end learner which learns a complete plan from breakage point to the final goal. For this we create a new pipeline and run it on the same wall-in-the-room scenario. Instead of reasoning about information gap and learning a bridging method, this pipeline follows a brute learning policy by employing a learner which learns a completely new method from point of failure with its goal as gold block acquisition. We then compare the training time and resultant accuracy between this brute end-to-end learner pipeline with our results from our architecture.

5   Observations, Results and Discussion

Figure 7 shows the comparison between end-to-end learner and our combination learner for the two different method learning scenarios. We would like to point out an interesting observation here, when we compared HTN enriched RL agent with pure RL agent, the pure RL agent resulted in zero percentage of success in completing the mission over 1000 iterations. Our theory is that the proposed scenario was a little too complicated for a simple algorithm like zero-order tabular Q-learning to formulate. The solution required three different actions strung in a row together without missing a beat, which was hard for a no-memory technique to make tractable. Therefore, the results that we show are contrasting between pure RL enriched with room comparison rewards and HTN enriched RL with room comparison as well as fruitful action discounts.

As readers can see in Fig. 7, the Q-values for pure reinforcement learning approach first take a dip before gaining value. This is due to the agent's repeatedly wrong or unfruitful actions which further decrease its confidence in actions.

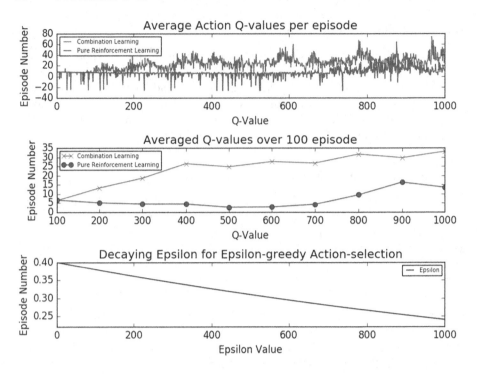

Fig. 7. Comparing action Q-values for different approaches

The topmost plot shows a considerable amount of spikes and jumping around for the Q-values, this is because the ϵ for our action-selection strategy is still pretty high with a lowest value of 0.25. This leads to execution of random actions by the agent, but since our environment's solution relying on a strictly sequential series of actions even one wrong random action can lead the agent down a rabbit-hole with no gains. The most important results can be seen in the second subplot in the figure, where our combination learner performs significantly better than the pure reinforcement learner. We have used an averaged plot of Q-values here to account for randomness introduced by moderately high ϵ value and to display the comparison more clearly.

Our results are very much in line with the findings of Ulam et al. [28,29] where they saw a considerable speed-up of learning process by providing it with internal model and knowledge about the game world. However, our algorithm goes a step beyond the reactive nature of learning described in the paper and outlines an automated way of mining out relevant reward information from successes of the past to promote a deliberative flavor of learning. The proposed approach is also simpler to implement as compared to [12] which requires complete bottom-up construction of new plans. With memory becoming cheap and processing power available in the cloud, our approach holds merit with its quick learning curve. As can be seen in Fig. 8, our agent learns to stay alive for longer quicker, in terms of number of iterations, than pure RL agent. This is important and interesting. Such an observation indicates that even if the agent is not yet proficient in solving the puzzle, it has learnt the boundaries of absolute failure. This is helpful when the sustenance of agent and prolonged exploration is key to learning better solutions.

Moreover, the combination of HTN and RL ends up being more flexible than either HTN or pure RL methods. While classical HTNs are by nature inflexible, and reinforcement learning being very specific to its start and end state, this modular approach lets us re-use the small chunks of methods in any arbitrary sequence to form a plan. The observations of Tessler et al. [27] agree with this claim. The authors have used another hierarchical planner with an advanced flavor of reinforcement learning in their paper which helps support claims about generality of this combination of techniques.

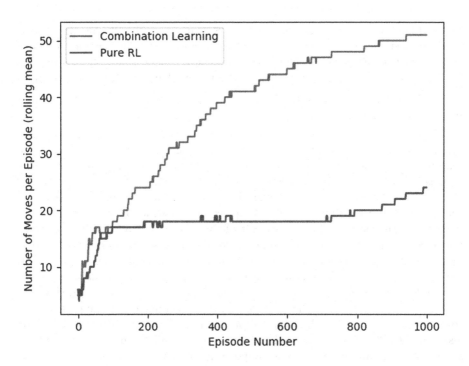

Fig. 8. Number of moves taken by agent per episode

We have not shown the result for first class of experiments since it merely involved simulating same action with different inventory items. Since we were selecting item in a randomised manner, the efficiency, in terms of speed of finding the correct item, was not a measurable evaluation criteria.

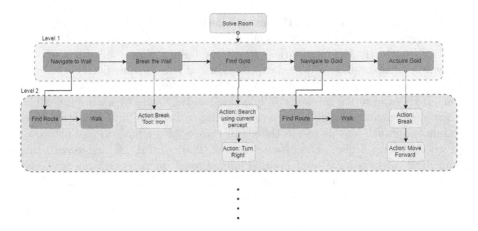

Fig. 9. Plan made for the Wall-in-the-Room Scenario by HTN Planner. Blue boxes symbolize methods and yellow boxes symbolize primitive or atomic actions. This diagram only shows one level of expansion of the plan for explanation purposes, the blue boxes on Level 2 can still be expanded further. (Color figure online)

6   Conclusion

As shown in this paper, using a dedicated diagnostic system and a meta-reasoning component can measurably increase the efficiency of planning systems. This is important because this enables us to have a flexible planner capable of extending and repairing its knowledge base. Such an ability makes it easier for the industry and consumers to use adaptive agents which come with pre-built domain information, ready to work out-of-the-box as well as capable of tweaking that information as per the changes specific to new environment. They can plan well for the situations already seen, and can potentially learn for new situations by exploring. This is a critical missing piece towards enabling agents to handle open-world situations. Additionally, talking from a computation perspective, the guidance that the HTN provides to machine learner helps scope the to-be-explored state-space by a big factor. Such an architecture beats end-to-end learners not only in terms of efficiency but also flexibility, since methods can be strung together in any order to accomplish different tasks.

7   Future Work

Our first item of action is to evaluate this algorithm on an actual embodied agent working in real-world scenarios. We also plan on using richer planning languages with our architecture, which not only are stronger at planning but also provide better diagnostic information of the working of a system. As we said earlier, diagnostics are the backbone of our meta-reasoning component. Rich diagnostic messages, apart from providing internal information, can also be leveraged to create templated explanations to the users to elaborate the purpose of an action.

Machine learning techniques, generally, tend to absorb patterns from data in the form of mathematical policies and functions and usually can not explain the purpose or reason for learnt behavior. By such a hybrid approach, we plan to use the internal diagnostic information along with meta-reasoning layer to be build an interactive learner which can not only exploit exploration but also knowledge from human users to adapt to new situations.

References

1. Argall, B.D., Chernova, S., Veloso, M., Browning, B.: A survey of robot learning from demonstration. Robot. Auton. Syst. **57**(5), 469–483 (2009). https://doi.org/10.1016/j.robot.2008.10.024
2. Becker, W.C.: Parents are Teachers: A Child Management Program (1971)
3. Belker, T., Hammel, M., Hertzberg, J.: Learning to optimize mobile robot navigation based on HTN plans. In: Proceedings of the IEEE International Conference on Robotics and Automation, ICRA 2003, vol. 3, pp. 4136–4141. IEEE (2003)
4. Berk, L.E., Winsler, A.: Scaffolding Children's Learning: Vygotsky and Early Childhood Education. NAEYC Research into Practice Series, vol. 7. ERIC (1995)
5. Breazeal, C., Buchsbaum, D., Gray, J., Gatenby, D., Blumberg, B.: Learning from and about others: towards using imitation to bootstrap the social understanding of others by robots. Learning **11**(1-2) (2006)
6. Breazeal, C., Scassellati, B.: Robots that imitate humans. Trends Cogn. Sci. **6**(11), 481–487 (2002)
7. Cox, M.T., Raja, A.: Metareasoning: Thinking about Thinking. MIT Press, Cambridge (2011)
8. Erol, K., Hendler, J.A., Nau, D.S.: UMCP: a sound and complete procedure for hierarchical task-network planning. In: AIPS, vol. 94, pp. 249–254 (1994)
9. Erol, K., Hendler, J., Nau, D.S.: HTN planning: complexity and expressivity. In: AAAI, vol. 94, pp. 1123–1128 (1994)
10. Fitzgerald, T., Thomaz, A., Goel, A.: Human-Robot Co-Creativity: Task Transfer of a Spectrum of Similarity. In: Proceedings of Seventh International Conference on Computational Creativity, Atlanta, June 2017 (2017)
11. Hayashi, H., Tokura, S., Hasegawa, T., Ozaki, F.: Dynagent: an incremental forward-chaining HTN planning agent in dynamic domains. In: Baldoni, M., Endriss, U., Omicini, A., Torroni, P. (eds.) DALT 2005. LNCS (LNAI), vol. 3904, pp. 171–187. Springer, Heidelberg (2006). https://doi.org/10.1007/11691792_11
12. Hogg, C., Kuter, U., Muñoz-Avila, H.: Learning hierarchical task networks for nondeterministic planning domains. In: IJCAI International Joint Conference on Artificial Intelligence, pp. 1708–1714 (2009)
13. Jones, J.K., Goel, A.K.: Perceptually grounded self-diagnosis and self-repair of domain knowledge. Knowl. Based Syst. **27**, 281–301 (2012)
14. Kober, J., Bagnell, J.A., Peters, J.: Reinforcement learning in robotics: a survey. Int. J. Robot. Res. **32**(11), 1238–1278 (2013). http://repository.cmu.edu/robotics
15. Magnenat, S., Chappelier, J.-C., Mondada, F.: Integration of online learning into htn planning for robotic tasks. In: AAAI Spring Symposium: Designing Intelligent Robots (2012)
16. Magnenat, S., Voelkle, M., Mondada, F.: Planner9, a HTN planner distributed on groups of miniature mobile robots. In: Xie, M., Xiong, Y., Xiong, C., Liu, H., Hu, Z. (eds.) ICIRA 2009. LNCS (LNAI), vol. 5928, pp. 1013–1022. Springer, Heidelberg (2009). https://doi.org/10.1007/978-3-642-10817-4_99

17. Mnih, V., Kavukcuoglu, K., Silver, D., Graves, A., Antonoglou, I., Wierstra, D., Riedmiller, M.: Playing atari with deep reinforcement learning (2013). ArXiv preprint: arXiv:1312.5602

18. Mohseni-Kabir, A., Rich, C., Chernova, S., Sidner, C.L., Miller, D.: Interactive hierarchical task learning from a single demonstration. In: Proceedings of the Tenth Annual ACM/IEEE International Conference on Human-Robot Interaction, pp. 205–212. ACM (2015)

19. Morimoto, J., Doya, K.: Acquisition of stand-up behavior by a real robot using hierarchical reinforcement learning. Robot. Auton. Syst. **36**, 37–51 (2001)

20. Murdock, J.W., Goel, A.K.: Meta-case-based reasoning: self-improvement through self-understanding. J. Exp. Theor. Artif. Intell. **20**(1), 1–36 (2008)

21. Nau, D., Au, T.-C., Ilghami, O., Kuter, U., Murdock, J.W., Wu, D., Yaman, F.: SHOP2: an HTN planning system. J. Artif. Intell. Res. **20**, 379–404 (2003)

22. Nau, D., Cao, Y., Lotem, A., Munoz-Avila, H.: SHOP: simple hierarchical ordered planner (1999)

23. Nejati, N., Langley, P., Konik, T.: Learning hierarchical task networks by observation. In: Proceedings of the 23rd International Conference on Machine Learning, pp. 665–672. ACM (2006)

24. Sidowski, J.B., Wycko, L.B., Tabory, L.: The influence of reinforcement and punishment in a minimal social situation. J. Abnorm. Soc. Psychol. **52**(1), 115 (1956)

25. Sun, R., Zhang, X.: Top-down versus bottom-up learning in cognitive skill acquisition. Cogn. Syst. Res. **5**(1), 63–89 (2004)

26. Sutton, R.S., Barto, A.G.: Reinforcement Learning: An Introduction, vol. 1. MIT Press, Cambridge (1998)

27. Tessler, C., Givony, S., Zahavy, T., Mankowitz, D.J., Mannor, S.: A deep hierarchical approach to lifelong learning in minecraft, CoRR, volume abs/1604.07255 (2016). http://arxiv.org/abs/1604.07255

28. Ulam, P., Goel, A., Jones, J., Murdock, W.: Using model-based reflection to guide reinforcement learning. In: Reasoning, Representation, and Learning in Computer Games, p. 107 (2005)

29. Ulam, P., Jones, J., Goel, A.K.: Combining model-based meta-reasoning and reinforcement learning for adapting game-playing agents. In: Artificial Intelligence and Interactive Digital Entertainment Conference, pp. 132–137 (2008)

30. Williamson, M., Decker, K., Sycara, K.: Unified information and control flow in hierarchical task networks. In: Proceedings of the AAAI 1996 Workshop on Theories of Planning, Action, and Control (1996)

31. Wolfe, J., Marthi, B., Russell, S.: Combined task and motion planning for mobile manipulation. In: International Conference on Automated Planning and Scheduling, pp. 254–257 (2010)

Budget Limited Trust-Aware Decision Making

Taha D. Güneş[ID], Timothy J. Norman[⊠], and Long Tran-Thanh

Agents, Interaction and Complexity Group,
University of Southampton, Southampton, UK
{t.d.gunes,t.j.norman,l.tran-thanh}@soton.ac.uk

Abstract. Utilizing witness information to supplement direct evidence is commonly used to build assessments of the trustworthiness of agents. The process of acquiring this kind of evidence is, however, typically assumed to be cost-free. In practice, agents are budget-limited, and investments in acquiring witness (or reputation) information will affect the budget that can be used for direct interaction. At the same time, acquiring such witness information can help in making better trust decisions. We explore this trade-off, formalising it as a budget-limited multi-armed bandit problem, and evaluate the effectiveness of algorithms to guide this decision process.

1 Introduction

Models of trust in agent societies are designed to support decisions of who to interact with. To better choose interaction partners, historical information about their past performance is necessary for most trust models [1–4]. Accessing interaction histories is not always feasible, however, and may be costly. Agents that query reputation information providers to reduce the uncertainty associated with limited knowledge will incur costs, at least in terms of time to decision: evaluating the trustworthiness of others is resource-dependent [5]. The question then is how to take into account information retrieval costs, resource limits and the properties of an agent society to guide the process of deciding whom to interact with.

Numerous models have been proposed to effectively discover trustworthy partners that do not consider resource constraints. In a recent and insightful review, Yu *et al.* [1] characterise these approaches as *greedy* and *dynamic*. The most common greedy approach is, in general, to progressively pick the best option that the agent has. Agents start by exploring trustees randomly, gradually shifting towards those that have higher reputation. Dynamic approaches tend to divide effort between *exploration* and *exploitation*. According to Yu *et al.*, there are few dynamic approaches except for those that use reinforcement learning. A recent example is the model proposed by Sen *et al.* [6], in which they consider a supply chain and employ a Budget-Limited Multi-Armed Bandit BL-MAB algorithm [7] to manage the explore/exploit trade-off. This is one of the first approaches that considers cost associated with invoking the services of trustees. They do not, however, consider the process of acquiring witness information, or

© Springer International Publishing AG 2017
G. Sukthankar and J. A. Rodriguez-Aguilar (Eds.): AAMAS 2017 Visionary Papers,
LNAI 10643, pp. 101–110, 2017.
https://doi.org/10.1007/978-3-319-71679-4_7

the costs associated with this. In other recent research, strategies for acquiring witness information within cost constraints have been explored that are robust to biases in reports due to effects such as hearsay evidence [8]. This research focusses exclusively on the trust assessment and information fusion problem, however, eschewing the question of deciding who to trust.

There are several different metrics used to judge an agent as trustworthy that have been considered in the literature. In this work, we consider an agent to be *trustworthy* if it acts according to the truster's expectation most of the time; e.g. by consistently providing a satisfactory service. Reputational reports from third parties can aid in the generation of these expectations, but may be misleading for decision makers if, for example, the witness is not reliable [5]. To limit the complexity of the problem we address, however, we assume that witness information is unbiased.

Our starting point in this research is algorithms developed to solve budget-limited multi-armed bandit (BL-MAB) problems. We explore algorithms that combine direct and indirect evidence of agent performance and evaluate trustworthiness on-the-fly within cost and budget constraints; the aim being to maximise the number of successful interactions. Our assumed setting is as follows. The decision maker has an infinite number of tasks that can only be completed through out-sourcing to service providers, but it has a fixed budget for the completion of tasks. Each service provider handles a task with some fixed cost. Ratings of prior performance of these service providers can be purchased from a central authority. Given these constraints, the decision maker's goal is to have as many tasks as possible completed within budget. Therefore, the decision maker must spend its budget strategically to identify and utilise high-performing service providers.

The rest of the paper is organised as: First, we formulate this decision-making problem in Sect. 2. Then the algorithms that we developed are proposed in Sect. 3, later in Sect. 4 we show our findings and in Sect. 5 we discuss them in detail. Lastly, we conclude our investigation in Sect. 6.

2   Budget-Limited Trust Decision Making

Given that our focus is on the problem of selecting good (trustworthy) agents within hard budgetary constraints, we intentionally use a simple model of evidence and trust assessment. We also formalise the model from the perspective of a single agent (the decision maker) making service selection decisions. The environment in which this agent operates consists of a set of agents, $\mathcal{A} = \{1, \ldots, n\}$, that offer functionally equivalent services, but that vary in performance. We assume that the performance of a service provider can be judged as success/failure once invoked by the decision maker. Given binary performance assessments, a common means to build a model to predict future performance (i.e. trustworthiness) is through Subjective Logic (SL) [9]; this is the trust assessment model we adopt.

In SL, an opinion held by some decision maker, i, about an agent, j, regarding some issue is a tuple $\omega_{i:j} = \langle b_{i:j}, d_{i:j}, u_{i:j}, a_{i:j} \rangle$, where $b_{i:j}$ is the belief mass associated with i's view that j will succeed in future, comparable interactions (aka. *belief*), $d_{i:j}$ is that associated with future failure (aka. *disbelief*), $u_{i:j}$ is the belief mass associated with i's *uncertainty* where $u_{i:j} = 1 - (b_{i:j} + d_{i:j})$, and $a_{i:j} \in [0, 1]$ is the prior, or base rate. The evidence used to construct binomial opinions are represented as a pair $\langle r_{i:j}, s_{i:j} \rangle$ where $r_{i:j}$ is the number of *positive* interactions that i experienced with j and $s_{i:j}$ is the number of *negative* interactions. The belief masses, $b_{i:j}$, $d_{i:j}$ and $u_{i:j}$, are computed using the formulae:

$$b_{i:j} = \frac{r_{i:j}}{(r_{i:j} + s_{i:j} + 2)} \tag{1}$$

$$d_{i:j} = \frac{s_{i:j}}{(r_{i:j} + s_{i:j} + 2)} \tag{2}$$

$$u_{i:j} = \frac{2}{(r_{i:j} + s_{i:j} + 2)} \tag{3}$$

We can generate a single-valued, normalised trust assessment that can be used to rank and select from among individuals by distributing the uncertainty between belief and disbelief via our base rate, thus:

$$\tau_{i:j} = b_{i:j} + a_{i:j} \cdot u_{i:j} \tag{4}$$

Given that we consider the trust decision problem from the perspective of a single agent, we typically refer to τ_j as the trust that our decision maker has in agent $j \in \mathcal{A}$, that r_j is the number of positive experiences our decision maker has with j, etc. The exception is when we refer to an agent we call the *oracle*, $\mathcal{O}$.

As a proxy for querying for reputation reports from witnesses to the performance of agents in $\mathcal{A}$, we use a single reputation provider: the oracle. The oracle has some amount of evidence about each agent in the environment $\{\langle r_{\mathcal{O}:1}, s_{\mathcal{O}:1} \rangle, \ldots, \langle r_{\mathcal{O}:n}, s_{\mathcal{O}:n} \rangle\}$. The certainty of the opinions held by $\mathcal{O}$ is parameterized by K; i.e. for each $\langle r_{\mathcal{O}:j}, s_{\mathcal{O}:j} \rangle \in \mathcal{O}$, $r_{\mathcal{O}:j} + s_{\mathcal{O}:j} = K$. This is, of course, a significant simplification of the process of acquiring evidence from witnesses. Normally, it would be necessary for the decision maker to build a model of each other agent *as a witness* (a different issue from that of being a service provider), then use these in order to discount opinions from different sources. This would, however, introduce unnecessary complexity to our model; we argue that this simplification enables us to focus on our central question of budget-limited trust decision making.

We formalize our decision problem as a budget-limited multi-armed bandit [7], which aims to maximize the total amount of reward within a budget by pulling arms of a slot machine. Pulling an arm is a metaphor for interacting with either a reputation provider or invoking the service of some provider (trustee). The objective is to maximize the total number of successful interactions that truster agent makes with trustees given the available budget. The truster can request information about trustees from the *Oracle* or interact with agents directly. Information from *Oracle* supports future decisions only: it provides no reward. The truster, therefore, needs to decide how to invest its budget: querying the *Oracle* or directly interacting with trustees.

Suppose that the cost of querying the *Oracle* is d, the cost of interacting with a trustee directly is c, and the agent has a budget, B. Given some algorithm A, the number of direct interactions N_i^B and witness information retrievals N_O^B are bounded by the budget B; that is:

$$P\left(\sum_i^n N_i^B(A) \cdot c + \sum_i^n N_O^B(A) \cdot d \leq B\right) = 1. \tag{5}$$

The optimal algorithm, A^*, is an algorithm that maximizes total reward (total number of successful interactions), such that:

$$A^* = \arg\max_A \sum_i^n \mathbf{E}[N_i^B(A)] \cdot \mu_i - \sum_i^n \mathbf{E}[N_O^B(A)] \tag{6}$$

3   The Algorithms

In this section, we formalise the algorithms that we investigated for this particular problem: the first (A_{greedy}) randomly picks trustees and tends to stick with honest agents, two other algorithms ($A_{\epsilon_{1,2}}$) are allocating budget for witness information to bootstrap their knowledge about the environment. All of the algorithms that are described below comply the restriction of not overspending the fixed budget (Eq. (5)). The normalised trust assessment calculation shown in Eq. (4) is used in each algorithm to calculate the density of reward.

A_{greedy}: The greedy algorithm is a popular approach for trust-aware decision making [1]. The version that we implemented is an extension of random exploration. Initially, normalised trust assessments of all agents are equal. For this reason, the first interaction that algorithm performs is to randomly pick a trustee agent. Based on the outcome of the first interaction, future iterations of A_{greedy} may be directed to explore other agents or stick with the same one. These selections are determined by picking the most dense arm which is $i = \arg\max_i (\tau_i)$, as in BL-MAB epsilon-first approaches [7]. The Oracle's opinions are not queried in this algorithm. We consider this algorithm as a baseline for other algorithms and formalised in Algorithm 1.

A_{ϵ_1}: The ϵ-first algorithm (shown in Algorithm 2) allocates its budget based on a ratio of exploration/exploitation, ϵ, where the exploration budget is ϵB and the remainder of the budget $B - \epsilon B$ is reserved for exploitation. In exploration as long as exploration budget is not exhausted, an agent is selected randomly and the reputation information about that agent is gathered from the *Oracle*. (The same agent is not queried twice.) The cost of witness information retrievals, d, is deducted from the exploration budget for each transaction. Depending on the exploration budget and the number of agents in the environment, there may be some budget left; if so, this is added to exploitation budget. The exploitation phase is then bounded by the remaining budget, where the cost of each interaction is c. This phase is identical to A_{greedy}, where the most dense arm is pulled and the density of this arm may change as a result.

A_{ϵ_2}: This algorithm (shown in the Algorithm 3) differs from A_{ϵ_1} in the exploitation phase only. Rather than looking for the densest arm, it randomly samples arms according to their density. This may lead to more information about other trustees being acquired, increasing the chance of exploring more of the population.

Algorithm 1. Trust-Aware Budget-Limited Greedy Algorithm - A_{greedy}

1: $t \leftarrow 1$;
2: **Exploration phase:**
3: **Exploitation phase:**
4: **while** $B_t \geq c$ **do**
5:     $i = \arg\max_i(\tau_i)$;
6:     interact with i and update $\langle r_i, s_i \rangle$;
7:     $B_{t+1} \leftarrow B_t - c$;
8:     $t \leftarrow t + 1$;
9: **end while**

Algorithm 2. Deterministic Trust-Aware Budget-Limited ϵ-First Algorithm - A_{ϵ_1}

1: $t \leftarrow 1$;
2: $B^{explore} \leftarrow \epsilon B$;
3: $B^{exploit} \leftarrow B - B^{explore}$
4: **Exploration phase:**
5: $A = \mathcal{A}$
6: **while** $B_t^{explore} \geq d$ **and** $A \neq \{\}$ **do**
7:     randomly select $i \in A$
8:     $\langle r_{\mathcal{O}:j}, s_{\mathcal{O}:j} \rangle \leftarrow$ query $(\mathcal{O}, i)$
9:     $r_i \leftarrow r_i + r_{\mathcal{O}:j} \quad s_i \leftarrow s_i + s_{\mathcal{O}:j}$;
10:     $B_{t+1}^{explore} \leftarrow B_t^{explore} - d$;
11:     $A \leftarrow A \setminus \{i\}$;
12:     $t \leftarrow t + 1$;
13: **end while**
14: $B^{exploit} \leftarrow B^{exploit} + B^{explore}$;
15: **Exploitation phase:**
16: **while** $B_t^{exploit} \geq c$ **do**
17:     $i = \arg\max_i(\tau_i)$;
18:     interact with i and update $\langle r_i, s_i \rangle$;
19:     $B_t^{exploit} = B_t^{exploit} - c$;
20:     $t \leftarrow t + 1$;
21: **end while**

---

4 Simulation Results

To evaluate our algorithms, we conducted experiments to investigate: the advantages and disadvantages of investing budget in acquiring witness information; choosing reputation versus direct experience in varying budget scenarios;

Algorithm 3. Trust-Aware Budget-Limited ϵ-First Algorithm - A_{ϵ_2}

1: **Exploration phase:**
2: Same as A_{ϵ_1}
3: **Exploitation phase:**
4: **while** $B_t^{exploit} \geq c$ **do**
5:     $i \leftarrow$ weighted random sample set $\{\tau_i, ..., \tau_n\}$;
6:     interact with i and update $\langle r_i, s_i \rangle$;
7:     $B_{t+1}^{exploit} \leftarrow B_t^{exploit} - c$;
8:     $t \leftarrow t + 1$;
9: **end while**

Table 1. Simulation environment

Description	Parameter	Value
Budget	B	300
Oracle knowledge	K	100
Direct interaction cost	c	3
Witness information cost	d	1
Total number of trustees	N	160

the knowledge acquired by each algorithm; and the factors that affect an optimal ϵ. Each experiment was repeated 1000 times and the average taken to minimise influence of noise. The parameters in Table 1 are selected for our experiments. We defined the behaviours of the agent as honest, random, malicious with numbers of 10, 50 and 100. Behaviours are distributed normally such that the mean of an honest agent is selected randomly from range $[0.5, 1.0]$ and for dishonest agents $[0, 0.5]$ with standard deviation 0.1. The amount of evidence from the Oracle is distributed normally with a mean 100 and a standard deviation 20.

4.1 Optimal ϵ

Our results indicate that investing some budget in acquiring witness information can yield an increase in reward. In Fig. 1a, the ϵ-first algorithm A_{ϵ_1} performed better than other algorithms for some values of ϵ for a budget of 300; Here A_{ϵ_1} gains the maximum reward with $\epsilon = 0.1$. The total reward is, however, sensitive to the choice of ϵ.

We then investigated whether the choice of a good ϵ, depends on the budget, B. As shown in Fig. 1b, we varied the budget up to 600 to explore how this affects the optimal ϵ. We found no clear dependency between budget and ϵ: a peak reward is obtained near to $\epsilon = 0.1$ in Fig. 1a, regardless of budget. We conclude that ϵ does not depend on available budget.

4.2 Environment Exploration

Exploration of the environment varied significantly in each algorithm. Since the budget is limited, all algorithms had to interact with a certain number of agents.

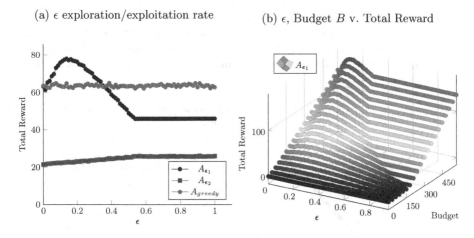

(a) ϵ exploration/exploitation rate   (b) ϵ, Budget B v. Total Reward

Fig. 1. Exploration vs. Exploitation comparison

As shown in Fig. 3[1], A_{ϵ_2} used its budget for more exploration than A_{ϵ_1} which spent more of its budget on exploitation, and hence acquired more evidence about specific service providers. Algorithm A_{greedy} followed a similar pattern as $A_{\epsilon_{1,2}}$ with the exception of the peak around 95. The reason for these peaks in the amount of evidence acquired about individual service providers is that both $A_{\epsilon_{1,2}}$ query the Oracle. The evidence that A_{greedy} acquires varies from 0 to 100 in an decreasing manner.

4.3   Performance over Time

We investigated the probability that an interaction is successful over time. In Fig. 2b, A_{greedy} became more successful over time as it starts to identify better performing service providers from a random initial selection; this drops to zero at the end simply because A_{greedy} has exhausted its budget. The other algorithms, $A_{\epsilon_{1,2}}$, invest budget at the start of the simulation on exploration (querying the Oracle), and hence receive no reward. During the exploitation phase, however, the probability of a successful interaction was relatively static for both ϵ-first algorithms.

The total reward acquired by A_{ϵ_1} was higher than our benchmark reference A_{greedy}, as shown in Fig. 2a, and this was consistently the case regardless of budget. On the other hand, the performance of A_{ϵ_2} was significantly worse than either of the other algorithms.

The formulation of our problem is the reason for the delayed-reward effect: all, zero reward, interactions with the Oracle occur before any exploitation of the knowledge acquired. This provides a reasonable outcome if the environment

---

[1] The maximum frequency in the figure is capped at 5 for clarity of presentation; the number of agents for which the decision maker has no evidence is often significantly higher than 5.

is static throughout; i.e. the availability of service providers does not change, and service providers have infinite capacity to complete tasks. In environments where agents may leave or join, or where their service offerings may change over time, strategic interleaving of exploration and exploitation may be beneficial.

(a) Cumulative Reward v. Time

(b) Probability of having successful interactions v. Time

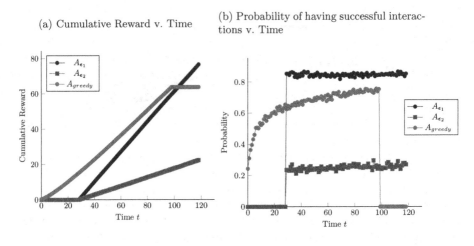

Fig. 2. Performance over time

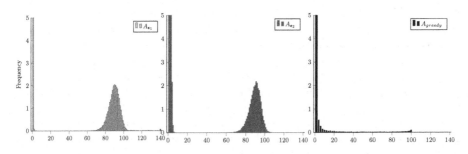

Fig. 3. Histogram of evidence $(r_i + s_i)$ in $[0, 140]$

5   Discussion

Optimal stopping in the class of problems referred to as the "secretary problem" resembles our problem of picking the right ϵ. In secretary problems [10] the applicants are interviewed one by one. The goal of the interviewer is to employ the best candidate. In these problems, however, each applicant is interviewed only once, and a decision to employ can only be made at that time. There are some similarities, however: the employer is not aware of the level of expertise of each applicant. Having agents leaving the environment is a challenging problem.

The environment that is dynamic requires trusters to trade-off continuing to interact with the current, best service provider or trying others.

Our environment is not dynamic, and this is a very strong assumption. In any practical system agents may enter and leave the system. Indeed, malicious agents may exploit this ability: they may create new identities to *whitewash* a poor reputation, or even collude with other agents to increase their perceived standing [11]. An important avenue for future research is to investigate how algorithms are robust to these kinds of attacks.

We adopted Subjective Logic as the basis for our trust model. There are other models, however, that may be employed. Wang and Singh's model [12], for example, takes conflicting evidence into account in computing a trust rating. One area for future research is to explore the interactions between the trust model employed and the algorithm used to spend a limited budget on acquiring direct and indirect evidence.

We plan to try different scenarios of witness information propagation not only environments that have a global reputation provider, but also the environments such that trustees have opinions about each other. The challenge of having opinions of trustees about each other is difficult in trust aware decision making problems. Since it complicates the process of properly assessing an agent. Is an agent honest if most of the time it provides a good service or if the witness information it provides is good?

6 Conclusion

In this paper, we have introduced a challenging problem of having interaction costs and budget limitations in trust and reputation systems. We investigated the performance of some simple algorithms, adapted from existing Budget-Limited Multi-Armed Bandit (BL-MAB) models. We evaluated these algorithms in a simulated environment with a central reputation provider. This is the first, but a very initial investigation into the use of witness information in trust-aware decision making when the decision maker is budget-limited, and where acquiring witness information is not cost-free. We have provided some evidence that strategic gathering of witness information can increase the number of successful interactions, despite this incurring costs on a limited budget. In future research, we will investigate varying service and witness information costs, and develop techniques to interleave exploration and exploitation.

References

1. Yu, H., Miao, C., An, B., Leung, C., Lesser, V.: A reputation management approach for resource constrained trustee agents. In: International Joint Conference on Artificial Intelligence (2013)
2. Jøsang, A., Ismail, R.: The beta reputation system. In: Proceedings of the 15th Bled Electronic Commerce Conference, vol. 5, pp. 2502–2511 (2002)

3. Regan, K., Poupart, P., Cohen, R.: Bayesian reputation modeling in e-marketplaces sensitive to subjectivity, deception and change. In: Proceedings of the National Conference on Artificial Intelligence, vol. 21, p. 1206 (2006)
4. Teacy, W.L., Luck, M., Rogers, A., Jennings, N.R.: An efficient and versatile approach to trust and reputation using hierarchical Bayesian modelling. Artif. Intell. **193**, 149–185 (2012)
5. Jøsang, A., Ismail, R., Boyd, C.: A survey of trust and reputation systems for online service provision. Decis. Support Syst. **43**(2), 618–644 (2007)
6. Sen, S., Ridgway, A., Ripley, M.: Adaptive budgeted bandit algorithms for trust in a supply-chain setting. In: Proceedings of the 2015 International Conference on Autonomous Agents and Multiagent Systems, pp. 137–144 (2015)
7. Tran-Thanh, L.: Budget-limited multi-armed bandits. Ph.D. thesis, University of Southampton (2012)
8. Etuk, A., Norman, T.J., Şensoy, M., Srivatsa, M.: How to trust a few among many. Auton. Agents Multi-agent Syst. **31**(3), 531–560 (2016)
9. Jøsang, A., Hayward, R., Pope, S.: Trust network analysis with subjective logic. In: Proceedings of the 29th Australasian Computer Science Conference, pp. 85–94 (2006)
10. Stein, W.E., Seale, D.A., Rapoport, A.: Analysis of heuristic solutions to the best choice problem. Eur. J. Oper. Res. **151**(1), 140–152 (2003)
11. Wang, D., Muller, T., Liu, Y., Zhang, J.: Towards robust and effective trust management for security: a survey. In: Proceedings of the 13th International Conference on Trust, Security and Privacy in Computing and Communications, pp. 511–518 (2014)
12. Wang, Y., Singh, M.P.: Formal trust model for multiagent systems. In: Proceedings of the 20th International Joint Conference on Artifical Intelligence, pp. 1551–1556 (2007)

Max-sum Revisited: The Real Power of Damping

Liel Cohen[(✉)] and Roie Zivan

Industrial Engineering and Management department, Ben Gurion University,
Beer-Sheva, Israel
{lielc,zivanr}@bgu.ac.il

Abstract. Max-sum is a version of Belief propagation, used for solving DCOPs. On tree-structured problems, Max-sum converges to the optimal solution in linear time. Unfortunately when the constraint graph representing the problem includes multiple cycles (as in many standard DCOP benchmarks), Max-sum does not converge and explores low quality solutions. Recent attempts to address this limitation proposed versions of Max-sum that guarantee convergence, by changing the constraint graph structure. Damping is a method that is often used for increasing the chances that Belief propagation will converge, however, it was not mentioned in studies that proposed Max-sum for solving DCOPs.

In this paper we investigate the effect of damping on Max-sum. We prove that, while it slows down the propagation of information among agents, on tree-structured graphs, Max-sum with damping is guaranteed to converge to the optimal solution in weakly polynomial time. Our empirical results demonstrate a drastic improvement in the performance of Max-sum, when using damping. However, in contrast to the common assumption, that it performs best when converging, we demonstrate that non converging versions perform efficient exploration, and produce high quality results, when implemented within an anytime framework. On most benchmarks, the best results were achieved using a high damping factor (A preliminary version of this paper was accepted as a two page extended abstract to a coming up conference.)

1 Introduction

Distributed Constraint Optimization Problem (DCOP) is a general model for distributed problem solving that has a wide range of applications in multi-agent systems. Complete algorithms for solving DCOPs [7,11] are guaranteed to find the optimal solution, but because DCOPs are NP-hard, solving optimally requires exponential time in the worst case. Thus, there is growing interest in incomplete algorithms, which may find suboptimal solutions but run quickly enough to be applied to large problems [20,21].

Whether complete or incomplete, DCOP algorithms generally follow one of two broad approaches: distributed search [7,20] or inference [2,11]. Max-sum [2] is an incomplete inference algorithm that has drawn considerable attention in recent years, including being proposed for multi-agent applications such as

© Springer International Publishing AG 2017
G. Sukthankar and J. A. Rodriguez-Aguilar (Eds.): AAMAS 2017 Visionary Papers,
LNAI 10643, pp. 111–124, 2017.
https://doi.org/10.1007/978-3-319-71679-4_8

sensor systems [16]. Max-sum is actually a version of the well known Belief propagation algorithm [19], used for solving DCOPs.

Belief propagation in general (and Max-sum specifically) is known to converge to the optimal solution for problems whose constraint graph is acyclic. Unfortunately, there is no such guarantee for problems with cycles [19]. Furthermore, when the agents' beliefs fail to converge, the resulting assignments may be of low quality. This occurs because cyclic information propagation leads to inaccurate and inconsistent information being computed by the agents. Unfortunately, many DCOPs that were investigated in previous studies are dense and indeed include multiple cycles (e.g., [7]). Our experimental study revealed that on various standard benchmark problem classes (uniform and structured), Max-sum does not converge and explores low-quality solutions.

Damping is a method that was combined with Belief propagation in order to decrease the effect of cyclic information propagation. By balancing the weight of the new calculation performed in each iteration and the weight of calculations performed in previous iterations, researchers have reported success in increasing the chances for convergence of Belief propagation when applied in different scenarios [5,12,17]. Nevertheless, Damping was not mentioned in the papers that adopted Max-sum for solving DCOPs and proposed extended versions of the algorithm [2,13,22]. To the best of our knowledge there are no published indications of the effect of damping on Max-sum, when solving DCOPs.

In this paper we contribute to the development of incomplete inference algorithms for solving DCOPs by investigating the effect of using damping within Max-sum. It is important to emphasize that the contribution and novelty of this work is not in proposing the use of damping, which is a well known method that has been studied by researchers in the graphical models community (see details in Sect. 2), but rather to investigate the unique properties of this method, when applied to Max-sum in order to improve its performance when used for solving DCOPs. More specifically we make the following contributions:

1. We prove that on tree-structured graphs, Damped Max-sum converges in weakly polynomial time. This result applies to a graph with a single cycle as well (under the restrictions specified in [18]). On a directed acyclic graph structure (as used in Max-sum_ADVP [22]) the convergence is also guaranteed in weakly polynomial time, but not necessarily to the optimal solution. This result is extremely significant in distributed scenarios where agents are not aware of the global topology, only of their own neighborhood, thus, they cannot avoid the use of damping when the graph has a structure that guarantees convergence.
2. We investigate the relation between the damping factor used and the success of the damping method in improving the solutions produced by Max-sum when solving DCOPs. On most standard DCOP benchmarks, the best results were achieved for high damping factor values. However, on graph coloring problems and other problems with similar constraint structure, a high damping factor resulted in a higher convergence rate, but also in lower quality solutions.

3. We demonstrate that, in contrast to the common assumption, the best performance is achieved when Max-sum with damping does not converge, but rather performs efficient exploration that can be captured when used within an anytime framework [21]. The combination of Damped Max-sum using a high damping factor and the anytime mechanism, outperforms all other versions of Max-sum, as well as local search DCOP algorithms, on various benchmarks.

2   Related Work

The graphical models literature includes many indications for the use of damping within Belief propagation (BP). We specify a number of studies that have some resemblance to our work and from which one can learn the common assumptions regarding the effect of damping on BP.

An attempt to apply damping to BP when solving both synthetic and realistic problems, represented by Bayesian networks, was presented in [8]. The results (with a rather small damping factor, 0.1) indicated that damping reduced oscillations and increased the chances of convergence. However, in many cases the algorithm converged to inaccurate solutions (i.e., did not approximate the optimal solution well). An investigation of the relation between the damping level and the convergence rate of BP when solving K-SAT problems, was presented in [12]. Results indicated that fastest convergence is achieved for damping factor of approximately 0.5, while larger damping factors (0.9) are better for reducing oscillations.

Lazic et al. report that damping increases the chances for convergence on maximum-a-posteriori (MAP) inference problems [5]. They find that a damping factor of 0.8 is enough to achieve convergence in most cases, although their results indicate that a high damping factor may increase the number of iterations required for convergence.

The most similar study to our own seems to be [10]. For bit error problems in communication channels the effect of damping on both the convergence and the quality of the result of BP was investigated. In contrast to the results we present, they report that the method is successful in producing high quality solutions for damping factors between 0.3 and 0.7 and that the best solutions were found when using a damping factor of 0.45.

An investigation of the effect of damping on convergence of BP solving clustering data problems was presented in [1]. The results indicate that when converging, the algorithm produces similar high quality results (regardless of the damping factor) and that only for very small damping factors the algorithm does not converge (up to 0.3). Again, they report that high damping factors slow convergence.

The conclusion from this short survey is that the effect of damping on BP is highly dependent on the problem being solved. Thus, there is merit in investigating the effect of damping when solving DCOP benchmarks. Furthermore, none of the papers mentioned (and any other we know of) reports the theoretical bounds we prove or suggests the possibility that damping can be used to balance exploration and exploitation of Max-sum, as we report in this paper.

Very few studies that use Max-sum for solving DCOP report the use of damping. One such paper used a damping factor of 0.5 and found the algorithm to be inferior to standard local search algorithms [9]. There was also an attempt to use damping for local search algorithms, which is obviously less relevant to our work [6].

3   Background

3.1   Distributed Constraint Optimization

Without loss of generality, in the rest of this paper we will assume that all problems are minimization problems. Our description of a DCOP is consistent with the definitions in many DCOP studies, e.g., [7,11].

A *DCOP* is a tuple $\langle \mathcal{A}, \mathcal{X}, \mathcal{D}, \mathcal{R} \rangle$. $\mathcal{A}$ is a finite set of agents $\{A_1, A_2, ..., A_n\}$. $\mathcal{X}$ is a finite set of variables $\{x_1, x_2, ..., x_m\}$. Each variable is held by a single agent. $\mathcal{D}$ is a set of domains $\{D_1, D_2, ..., D_m\}$. Each domain D_i contains the finite set of values that can be assigned to variable x_i. An assignment of value $d \in D_i$ to x_i is denoted by an ordered pair $\langle x_i, d \rangle$. $\mathcal{R}$ is a set of relations (constraints). Each constraint $C \in \mathcal{R}$ defines a non-negative *cost* for every possible value combination of a set of variables, and is of the form $C : D_{i_1} \times D_{i_2} \times \ldots \times D_{i_k} \to \mathbb{R}^+ \cup \{0\}$. A *binary constraint* refers to exactly two variables and is of the form $C_{ij} : D_i \times D_j \to \mathbb{R}^+ \cup \{0\}$.[1] A *binary DCOP* is a DCOP in which all constraints are binary. A *partial assignment* (PA) is a set of value assignments to variables, in which each variable appears at most once. *vars(PA)* is the set of all variables that appear in PA. A constraint $C \in \mathcal{R}$ of the form $C : D_{i_1} \times D_{i_2} \times \ldots \times D_{i_k} \to \mathbb{R}^+ \cup \{0\}$ is *applicable* to PA if $x_{i_1}, x_{i_2}, \ldots, x_{i_k} \in vars(PA)$. The *cost of a PA* is the sum of all applicable constraints to PA over the assignments in PA. A *complete assignment* (or a *solution*) is a partial assignment that includes all the DCOP's variables $(vars(PA) = \mathcal{X})$. An *optimal solution* is a complete assignment with minimal cost.

For simplicity we make the standard assumptions that all DCOPs are binary DCOPs in which each agent holds exactly one variable. These assumptions are commonly made in DCOP studies, e.g., [7].

3.2   Max-Sum

[2]Max-sum operates on a *factor-graph*, which is a bipartite graph in which the nodes represent variables and constraints [4]. Each variable-node representing a variable of the original DCOP is connected to all function-nodes that represent

---

[1] We say that a variable is *involved* in a constraint if it is one of the variables the constraint refers to.

[2] For lack of space we describe the algorithm and its extensions briefly and refer the reader to more detailed descriptions in [2,13,22].

constraints, which it is involved in. Similarly, a function-node is connected to all variable-nodes that represent variables in the original DCOP that are involved in the constraint it represents. Variable-nodes and function-nodes are considered "agents" in Max-sum, i.e., they can send and receive messages, and perform computation.

A message sent to or from variable-node x (for simplicity, we use the same notation for a variable and the variable-node representing it) is a vector of size $|D_x|$ including a cost for each value in D_x. In the first iteration all messages include vectors of zeros. A message sent from a variable-node x to a function-node f is formalized as follows: $Q^i_{x \to f} = \sum_{f' \in F_x, f' \neq f} R^{i-1}_{f' \to x} - \alpha$, where $Q^i_{x \to f}$ is the message variable-node x intends to send to function-node f in iteration i, F_x is the set of function-node neighbors of variable-node x and $R^{i-1}_{f' \to x}$ is the message sent to variable-node x by function-node f' in iteration $i-1$. α is a constant that is reduced from all costs included in the message (i.e., for each $d \in D_x$) in order to prevent the costs carried by messages throughout the algorithm run from growing arbitrarily.

A message sent from a function-node f to a variable-node x in iteration i includes for each value $d \in D_x$: $min_{PA_{-x}} cost(\langle x, d \rangle, PA_{-x})$, where PA_{-x} is a possible combination of value assignments to variables involved in f not including x. The term $cost(\langle x, d \rangle, PA_{-x})$ represents the cost of a partial assignment $a = \{\langle x, d \rangle, PA_{-x}\}$, which is: $f(a) + \sum_{x' \in X_f, x' \neq x, \langle x', d' \rangle \in a} Q^{i-1}_{x' \to f}.d'$, where $f(a)$ is the original cost in the constraint represented by f for the partial assignment a, X_f is the set of variable-node neighbors of f, and $Q^{i-1}_{x' \to f}.d'$ is the cost that was received in the message sent from variable-node x' in iteration $i-1$, for the value d' that is assigned to x' in a. x selects its value assignment $\hat{d} \in D_x$ following iteration k as follows: $\hat{d} = argmin_{d \in D_x} \sum_{f \in F_x} R^k_{f \to x}.d$.

4   Introducing Damping into Max-Sum

A common assumption regarding Belief propagation was that it is successful when it converges, and that its main drawback is that it fails to converge on problems in which the graph used for representing them includes multiple cycles. Thus, different methods were proposed in order to guarantee the convergence of Belief propagation, e.g., by revising the optimization function, or by changing the graph structure [13, 15, 22].

Damping is a less radical method that was proposed for increasing the chances that Belief propagation will converge [12, 14, 17]. However, in contrast to the methods mentioned above, introducing damping into Belief propagation is empirically found to increase the probability of convergence, but, to best of our knowledge, there is no theoretical guarantee or even an estimation or prediction method that can identify when Belief propagation with damping will converge.

In order to add damping to Max-sum we introduce a parameter $\lambda \in (0, 1]$. Before sending a message in iteration k an agent performs calculations as in standard Max-sum. Denote by $\widehat{m^k_{i \to j}}$ the result of the calculation made by agent A_i of the content of a message intended to be sent from A_i to agent A_j in iteration k. Denote by $m_{i \to j}^{k-1}$ the message sent by A_i to A_j at iteration $k-1$. The message sent from A_i to A_j in iteration k is calculated as follows:

$$m_{i \to j}^{k} = \lambda m_{i \to j}^{k-1} + (1 - \lambda)\widehat{m_{i \to j}^{k}} \tag{1}$$

Thus, λ expresses the weight given to previously performed calculations with respect to the most recent calculation performed. Moreover, when $\lambda = 0$ the resulting algorithm is standard Max-sum. We demonstrate further in this paper that a selection of a high value for λ (close to 1) increases the chances of the algorithm to converge.

In all our implementations damping was performed only by variable-nodes. This allowed us to analyze the level of damping with respect to n (the number of variables/agents).

5   Convergence Runtime Bounds

Standard Max-sum guarantees convergence in linear time to the optimal solution, when the constraint graph (and the corresponding factor-graph) is tree-structured. We first establish a weakly polynomial lower bound for this guarantee, i.e., that there exists a problem on which damping slows down the convergence by a factor of $log_{1/\lambda}(C)$, where C is the cost of the optimal solution plus ϵ and ϵ is the smallest difference between constraint costs (thus, C is the smallest possible cost for a solution, which is larger than the cost of the optimal solution). Next, we prove a (loose) upper bound on the time for convergence, which is also weakly-polynomial.

Let n be the number of variables in a problem and C as defined above.

Lemma 1. *There exists a scenario in which Max-sum with damping will converge on a tree-structured graph in no less than $2(n - 2) + log_{1/\lambda}(C)$.*

Proof: Consider a factor-graph with four variable-nodes, X_1, X_2, X_3 and X_4 and three function-nodes F_{12}, F_{23} and F_{34}, as depicted in Fig. 1. Each variable has two values in its domain, a and b. All functions include infinite costs for any non equal combination of value assignments. Function F_{23} includes for both equal combinations of both variables the cost 0. Function F_{12} includes a cost of $C > \epsilon$ if both agents assign a and zero cost if they both assign b. Function F_{34} includes a cost of $C - \epsilon$ if both agents assign b and zero cost if they both assign a. Obviously the optimal solution is when all variables assign b. However, in order for variable X_4 to realize that it should assign b, X_2, which receives cost C for its value a from F_{12} in every iteration, must perform $log_{1/\lambda}(C)$ iterations before it sends a message to F_{23} with a cost larger than $C - \epsilon$ for the assignment of a. This information must path to X_4 before it can learn that it is better to assign b than a, which requires 4 sequential messages. Obviously, if we add more variables to the chain (each with two values a and b), such that the two functions adjacent to the first and last variable-nodes in the chain are identical in their costs to F_{12} and F_{34}, and all other functions are identical in costs to F_{23}, the

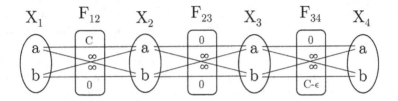

Fig. 1. Lower bound example

number of sequential messages will increase by 2 for each additional variable. Thus, a lower bound to this problem is $log_{1/\lambda}(C) + 2(n-2)$.   □

Proposition 1. *The guaranteed runtime for convergence for Max-sum with damping is at least, weakly polynomial.*

Proof: An immediate corollary from Lemma 1   □

In order to produce an upper bound on the number of steps that Damped Max-sum will perform before converging to the optimal solution, we note that the convergence of standard Max-sum on tree-structured graphs is achieved in linear time because each variable-node in the factor-graph can be considered as a root of a tree to which all other agents accumulate costs (similar to a DPOP running on a pseudo-tree with no back-edges, cf. [11]). Thus, each agent, after at most a linear number of steps, knows for each of the values in its variable domain, the costs of the best solution it is involved in (for simplicity and without loss of generality, we will assume no ties).

Let n be the number of variables in a problem represented by a tree-structured factor-graph G' and $\widehat{C}$ the maximal cost sent by an agent in standard Max-sum, solving the same problem. We use η to represent the largest *ignorable* difference for a problem, i.e., the largest number such that for each cost c sent in standard Max-sum by some agent when solving the same problem, if the agent would send cost $c' = c - \eta$, the receiving agent would perform exactly the same actions as when receiving c in standard Max-sum, i.e., select the same value assignments to calculate function costs, if the receiver is a function-node, or make the same selection of value assignment, if the receiver is a variable-node.

Lemma 2. *After at most $2(n-2)\cdot log_{1/\lambda}(\widehat{C}/\eta)$ steps of the algorithm, a variable-node X_i in G' can select its value assignment in the optimal solution.*

Proof: Allow each of the variable-nodes, from the farthest from X_i in G' to the closest, to perform $log_{1/\lambda}(\widehat{C}/\eta)$ steps, taking into consideration only the last message received from their neighbors, and allow each function-node receiving a message to perform a single step immediately. Obviously, after these steps are completed, X_i receives costs that allow it to select its assignment in the optimal solution.   □

Proposition 2. *Max-sum with Damping is guaranteed to converge to the optimal solution, on tree-structured graphs in weakly polynomial time.*

Proof: Immediate from Lemma 2. After $2(n-2) \cdot log_{1/\lambda}(\widehat{C}/\eta)$ steps, all variable-nodes can select their assignment in the optimal solution, thus, the convergence rate is polynomial in n, and $\widehat{C}/\eta$, i.e., weakly polynomial. $\qquad\square$

We note that similar proofs can establish that Max-sum with damping produces the optimal solution on graphs with a single cycle in weakly polynomial time (subject to some restrictions [18]) and that using damping in Max-sum_AD and Max-sum_ADVP [22] slows down the convergence in each phase to, at most, weakly polynomial time.

6   Experimental Evaluation

In order to investigate the advantages of the use of damping in Max-sum, we present a set of experiments comparing different versions of the algorithm, using different λ values with standard Max-sum and two versions that guarantee convergence: Bounded_Max-sum [13] and Max-sum_ADVP [22]. We also include in our experiments the results of the well known DSA algorithm (we use type C with $p = 0.7$ [20]), in order to give an insight on the quality of the results, in comparison with local search DCOP algorithms.

We evaluated the algorithms on random uniform DCOPs and on structured and realistic problems, i.e., graph coloring, meeting scheduling and scale-free. At each experiment we randomly generated 50 different problem instances and ran the algorithms for 5,000 iterations on each of them. The results presented are an average of those 50 runs. For each iteration we present the cost of the assignment that would have been selected by each algorithm at that iteration. All algorithms were implemented within the anytime framework proposed in [21], which allowed us to report for each of them the best result it traverses within 5,000 iterations. Also, in all versions of Max-Sum, we used value preferences selected randomly for the purpose of tie breaking, as was suggested in [2].

As mentioned above, the experiments were performed on four types of DCOPs, commonly used for evaluating DCOP algorithms, all formulated as minimization problems. Uniform random problems were generated by adding a constraint for each pair of agents/variables with probability p_1 and for each constrained pair, a cost for each combination of value assignments, selected uniformly between 1 and 10. Each problem included 100 variables with 10 values in each domain. Graph coloring problems included 50 agents and all constraints $R_{ij} \in \mathcal{R}$ were "not-equal" cost functions where an equal assignment of neighbors in the graph incurs a cost of 1 and non equal value assignments incur 0 cost. Following the literature, we used $p_1 = 0.05$ and three values (i.e., colors) in each domain [2,20,21]. Scale-free network problems included 50 agents, each holding a variable with 10 values in each domain, and were generated using the Barabási–Albert (BA) model. An initial set of 7 agents was randomly selected and connected. Additional agents were added sequentially and connected to 3 other agents with a probability proportional to the number of links per agent. Costs were independently drawn between 0 to 99. Similar problems were previously used to evaluate DCOP algorithms in [3]. Meeting scheduling problems included 90 agents, which scheduled 20 meetings into 20 time slots. When the time slots of two meetings do not allow participation in both, a cost equal to the number of agents assigned to both meetings was incurred. These realistic problems are identical to those used in [21].

Our experiments included various λ values, however, in order to avoid redundancy, we only present results with $\lambda \in 0.5, 0.7, 0.9$. This selection allows us to avoid graph density while presenting the trend of improvement of the algorithm when λ is closer to one.

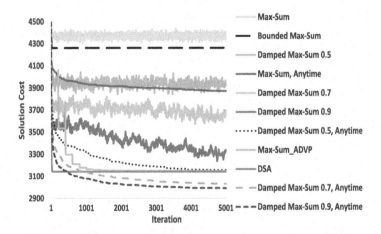

Fig. 2. Solution cost for random uniform problems with relatively low density ($p_1 = 0.1$).

Figures 2 and 3 present the solution costs found by all algorithms when solving uniform random problems containing 100 agents with a relatively low density ($p_1 = 0.1$) and with higher density of $p_1 = 0.7$ respectively. The results per iteration show that Damped Max-sum is inferior to DSA and the guaranteed convergence version Max-sum_ADVP. That been said, the anytime results of Damped Max-sum using high λ values (0.7 and 0.9) significantly outperform DSA and Max-sum_ADVP. This suggests that damping triggers efficient exploration by Max-sum, i.e., that in contrast to the assumptions made in the Belief propagation literature, the best results of Max-sum are not achieved when it converges but rather (like in the case of local search) when there is a balance between exploration and exploitation.

Figures 4, 5 and 6 present results on scale free nets, meeting scheduling and graph coloring problems, respectively. On scale free nets the trends are similar to the results obtained for uniform random problems. Damped Max-sum improves as more iterations are performed and explores solutions of higher quality. Towards the end of the run, the results per iteration of the version with $\lambda = 0.9$ produces in some iterations better solutions than DSA and similar to

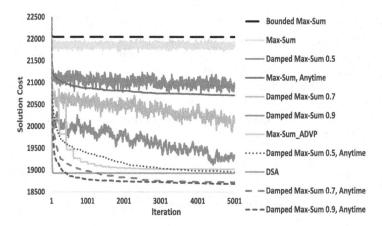

Fig. 3. Solution cost for random uniform problems with relatively high density $(p_1 = 0.7)$.

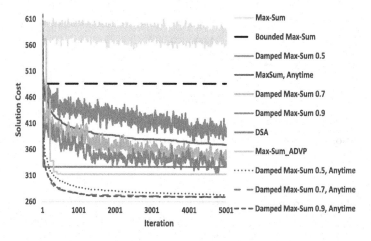

Fig. 4. Solution cost for scale free net problems.

Max-sum_ADVP. The anytime results outperform the converging algorithm significantly. On meeting scheduling and graph coloring problems, the results of the Damped Max-sum versions do not exhibit such an improvement, and seem to explore solutions of similar quality throughout the run. Interestingly, the $\lambda = 0.9$ version on graph coloring seems to perform limited exploration and traverse solutions with similar quality, while the 0.5 and 0.7 versions perform a higher level of exploration.[3]

---

[3] t-tests established that the Damped Max-Sum anytime solutions of all values of the parameter λ were better on average than the anytime solutions reported for standard Max-Sum, with statistical significance of p = 0.01, and better on average than DSA's solutions for λ values of 0.7 and 0.9 (except for the 0.9 version on graph coloring problems), with the same significance level.

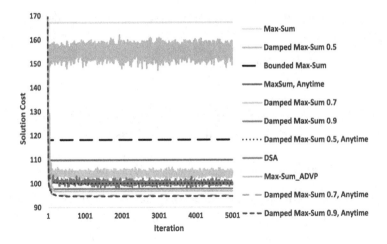

Fig. 5. Solution cost for meeting scheduling problems.

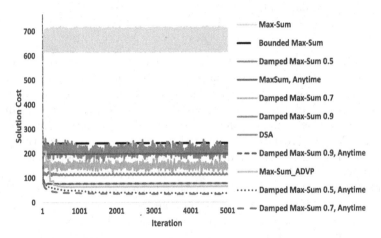

Fig. 6. Solution cost for graph coloring problems.

A closer look at Fig. 6 reveals that the $\lambda = 0.9$ version, after a small number of iterations, starts to perform limited oscillations that follow a strict pattern repeatedly. In contrast, the $\lambda = 0.5$ and $\lambda = 0.7$ versions perform rapid oscillations, which do not follow a specific pattern. Throughout the run, the average results per iteration of the $\lambda = 0.9$ version outperforms both the $\lambda = 0.5$ and $\lambda = 0.7$ versions. On the other hand, the corresponding anytime results of the $\lambda = 0.9$ version converge fast to a higher cost than the costs of the anytime solutions reported for the $\lambda = 0.5$ and $\lambda = 0.7$ versions. This is another indication of the relation between the level of exploration performed by Damped Max-sum and the quality of its anytime results.

Table 1. Convergence and anytime performance, for random uniform problems, $p_1 = 0.1$.

Problem count	Standard	0.5	0.7	0.9
Converged	0	2	7	20
% out of all 50	0%	4%	14%	40%
Anytime was better	50	48	44	33
% out of all 50	100%	96%	88%	66%

Table 2. Convergence and anytime performance, for graph coloring problems.

Problem count	Standard	0.5	0.7	0.9
Converged	1	6	8	49
% out of all 50	2%	12%	16%	98%
Anytime was better	49	44	43	37
% out of all 50	98%	88%	86%	74%

The results of our experiments indicate that, in contrast to the common assumption regarding the role of damping in improving Belief propagation, by increasing its convergence rate, the success of damping is in generating useful exploration of high quality solutions that can be captured by an anytime framework and outperform versions of Max-sum that guarantee convergence, as Max-sum_ADVP. In order to straighten this statement we present the convergence rate and anytime performance of the Max-sum versions for the uniform random problem settings and for the graph coloring problems (the convergence results of the meeting scheduling problems and the scale free nets showed similar trends to the uniform settings and were omitted for lack of space). Tables 1 and 2 present for standard Max-Sum and the Damped Max-Sum, the number of problems out of the 50 problems solved, on which each of the versions of the algorithm converged. In addition, the tables present the number of problems in which the anytime solution was better than the solution produced in the final iteration of the algorithm's run.

For the random problems (Table 1) the results indicate that the closer λ is to one, the higher are the chances of convergence of the Damped Max-Sum algorithm. The results for problem with higher density preserved the same trend and were omitted for lack of space. As for the anytime solutions reported, in problems for which the algorithm converged, it did not always converge to the best solution visited during the algorithm's run. The number of problems on which the algorithm converged to the best solution reached during the algorithm's run, increases when a higher value of λ is selected. Nevertheless, for all versions, the anytime results were better than the results in the last iteration of the algorithm on a significant portion of the problem instances.

The results in Table 2 strengthen our analysis of Fig. 6. On graph coloring problems, the $\lambda = 0.9$ has a much higher convergence rate than the $\lambda = 0.5$ and $\lambda = 0.7$ versions. However, its anytime results are better than the results in the last iteration in a fewer number of runs of the algorithm. Thus, on these problems a lower damping factor resulted in more effective exploration. In order to check whether this phenomenon was unique for graph coloring problems, we ran experiments in which we changed the constraint structure of all other benchmarks (random uniform, scale free and meeting scheduling) such that it was similar to the constraint structure in graph coloring, i.e., where for every pair of constrained variables, for each value in each domain there was a single value in the domain of the other variable with whom it was constrained. The results across all benchmarks were that the version with $\lambda = 0.9$ had higher convergence rate and produced results with higher costs than the version with $\lambda = 0.7$, as in graph coloring.

7 Conclusion

We investigated the effect of using damping within the Max-sum algorithm, the distributed version of Belief propagation, which was adopted for solving DCOPs.

In terms of computational bounds for convergence, we proved that on acyclic problems, where Max-sum is guaranteed to converge to the optimal solution, in the worst case damping slows the convergence to weakly polynomial time. Similar proofs can be applied to other structures on which Max-sum is guaranteed to converge, e.g., graphs with a single cycle and directed acyclic graphs (on which it converges, but not necessary to the optimal solution).

Our empirical study revealed that while damping improved the results of the algorithm drastically, in most cases it did not converge within 5000 iterations. However, when combined with an anytime framework, Damped Max-sum significantly outperforms the best versions of Max-sum, and a standard local search algorithm as well.

In future work we intend to deepen the investigation on the best selection of the parameter λ in Damped Max-sum, with respect to the problem structure.

References

1. Dueck, D.: Affinity propagation: clustering data by passing messages. Ph.D. thesis, University of Toronto (2009)
2. Farinelli, A., Rogers, A., Petcu, A., Jennings, N.R.: Decentralized coordination of low-power embedded devices using the max-sum algorithm. In: AAMAS, pp. 639–646 (2008)
3. Kiekintveld, C., Yin, Z., Kumar, A., Tambe, M.: Asynchronous algorithms for approximate distributed constraint optimization with quality bounds. In: AAMAS, pp. 133–140 (2010)
4. Kschischang, F.R., Frey, B.J., Loeliger, H.A.: Factor graphs and the sum-product algorithm. IEEE Trans. Inf. Theor. **47**(2), 181–208 (2001)

5. Lazic, N., Frey, B., Aarabi, P.: Solving the uncapacitated facility location problem using message passing algorithms. In: International Conference on Artificial Intelligence and Statistics, pp. 429–436 (2010)
6. Verman, A.B.M., Stutz, P.: Solving distributed constraint optimization problems using ranks. In: AAAI Workshop Statistical Relational Artificial Intelligence (2014)
7. Modi, P.J., Shen, W., Tambe, M., Yokoo, M.: Adopt: asynchronous distributed constraints optimizationwith quality guarantees. Artif. Intell. **161**(1–2), 149–180 (2005)
8. Murphy, K.P., Weiss, Y., Jordan, M.I.: Loopy belief propagation for approximate inference: an empirical study. In: Proceedings of the Fifteenth Conference on Uncertainty in Artificial Intelligence, UAI 1999, Stockholm, Sweden, 30 July–1 August 1999, pp. 467–475 (1999)
9. Okamoto, S., Zivan, R., Nahon, A.: Distributed breakout: beyond satisfaction. In: Proceedings of the Twenty-Fifth International Joint Conference on Artificial Intelligence, IJCAI 2016, New York, NY, USA, 9–15 July 2016, pp. 447–453 (2016)
10. Som, A.C.P.: Damped belief propagation based near-optimal equalization of severely delay-spread UWB MIMO-ISI channels. In: 2010 IEEE International Conference on Communications (ICC), pp. 1–5 (2010)
11. Petcu, A., Faltings, B.: A scalable method for multiagent constraint optimization. In: IJCAI, pp. 266–271 (2005)
12. Pretti, M.: A message-passing algorithm with damping. J. Stat. Mech. Theor. Exp. **11**, P11008 (2005)
13. Rogers, A., Farinelli, A., Stranders, R., Jennings, N.R.: Bounded approximate decentralized coordination via the max-sum algorithm. Artif. Intell. **175**(2), 730–759 (2011)
14. Som, P., Chockalingam, A.: Damped belief propagation based near-optimal equalization of severely delay-spread UWB MIMO-ISI channels. In: 2010 IEEE International Conference on Communications (ICC), pp. 1–5. IEEE (2010)
15. Sontag, D., Meltzer, T., Globerson, A., Jaakkola, T., Weiss, Y.: Tightening LP relaxations for map using message passing. In: UAI, pp. 503–510 (2008)
16. Stranders, R., Farinelli, A., Rogers, A., Jennings, N.R.: Decentralised coordination of mobile sensors using the max-sum algorithm. In: Proceedings of the 21st International Joint Conference on Artificial Intelligence, IJCAI 2009, Pasadena, California, USA, 11–17 July 2009, pp. 299–304 (2009)
17. Tarlow, D., Givoni, I., Zemel, R., Frey, B.: Graph cuts is a max-product algorithm. In: Proceedings of the 27th Conference on Uncertainty in Artificial Intelligence (2011)
18. Weiss, Y.: Correctness of local probability propagation in graphical models with loops. Neural Comput. **12**(1), 1–41 (2000)
19. Yanover, C., Meltzer, T., Weiss, Y.: Linear programming relaxations and belief propagation - an empirical study. J. Mach. Learn. Res. **7**, 1887–1907 (2006)
20. Zhang, W., Xing, Z., Wang, G., Wittenburg, L.: Distributed stochastic search and distributed breakout: properties, comparishon and applications to constraints optimization problems in sensor networks. Artif. Intell. **161**(1–2), 55–88 (2005)
21. Zivan, R., Okamoto, S., Peled, H.: Explorative anytime local search for distributed constraint optimization. Artif. Intell. **212**, 1–26 (2014)
22. Zivan, R., Peled, H.: Max/min-sum distributed constraint optimization through value propagation on an alternating DAG. In: AAMAS, pp. 265–272 (2012)

A Realistic Dataset for the Smart Home Device Scheduling Problem for DCOPs

William Kluegel[1], Muhammad A. Iqbal[1], Ferdinando Fioretto[2(✉)],
William Yeoh[1,3], and Enrico Pontelli[1]

[1] Department of Computer Science, New Mexico State University, Las Cruces, USA
{wkluegel,miqbal,wyeoh,epontell}@cs.nmsu.edu
[2] Department of Industrial and Operations Engineering,
University of Michigan, Ann Arbor, USA
fioretto@umich.edu
[3] Department of Computer Science and Engineering,
Washington University in St. Louis, St. Louis, MO, USA

Abstract. The field of Distributed Constraint Optimization has gained momentum in recent years thanks to its ability to address various applications related to multi-agent cooperation. While techniques for solving Distributed Constraint Optimization Problems (DCOPs) are abundant and have matured substantially since the field's inception, the number of DCOP realistic applications available to assess the performance of DCOP algorithms is lagging behind. To contrast this background we *(i)* introduce the Smart Home Device Scheduling (SHDS) problem, which describes the problem of coordinating smart devices schedules across multiple homes as a multi-agent system, *(ii)* detail the physical models adopted to simulate smart sensors, smart actuators, and homes' environments, and *(iii)* introduce a realistic benchmark for SHDS problems.

1 Introduction

Distributed Constraint Optimization Problems (DCOPs) [16,20,27] have emerged as one of the prominent agent models to govern the agents' autonomous behavior, where both algorithms and communication models are driven by the structure of the specific problem. Researchers have used DCOP algorithms to solve various multi-agent coordination and resource allocation problems, including meeting scheduling [13,29], power network management [12], and smart home appliances coordination [22].

Since the research field's inception, a wide variety of algorithms has been proposed to solve DCOPs. DCOP algorithms are typically classified as either *complete* or *incomplete*, based on whether they can guarantee to find an optimal solution or they trade optimality for shorter execution times [6]. In addition, each of these classes can be categorized into several groups, depending on the degree of locality exploited by the algorithms (e.g., full decentralization or partial

© Springer International Publishing AG 2017
G. Sukthankar and J. A. Rodriguez-Aguilar (Eds.): AAMAS 2017 Visionary Papers,
LNAI 10643, pp. 125–142, 2017.
https://doi.org/10.1007/978-3-319-71679-4_9

centralization) [11,14,21], the way local information is updated (e.g., synchronous [14,19,20] or asynchronous [5,10,16]), and the type of exploration process adopted (e.g., search-based [11,16,26,28], inference-based [5,20], or sampling-based [7,17,18]).

While techniques to solve DCOPs are abundant and have matured substantially since the field's inception, the number of realistic DCOP applications and benchmarks used to assess the performance of DCOP algorithms is lagging behind [9]. Typical DCOP algorithms are evaluated on artificial random problems, or simplified problems that are adapted to the often unrealistic assumptions made by DCOP algorithms (e.g., that each agent controls exactly one variable, and that all problem constraints are binary). To evaluate the performance of DCOP algorithms, it is necessary to introduce realistic benchmarks of deployable applications.

Motivated by these issues, we recently introduced the *Smart Home Device Scheduling (SHDS)* problem [8], which formalizes the problem of coordinating the schedules of smart devices (e.g., smart thermostats, circulator heating, washing machines) across multiple smart homes as a multi-agent system (MAS). The SHDS problem is suitable to be modeled as a DCOP due to the presence of both complex individual agents' goals, describing homes' energy price consumption, as well as a collective agents' goal, capturing reduction in energy peaks.

In this paper, we introduce a realistic synthetic benchmark for the SHDS problem for DCOPs. We report the details of the physical models adopted to simulate smart home sensors and actuators, as well as home environments, and describe how the actuator's actions affect the environments of a home (e.g., home's temperature, cleanliness, humidity). The dataset, the models, and the source code used to generate the SHDS dataset is available at https://github.com/nandofioretto/SHDS_dataset.

1.1 DCOP

A *Distributed Constraint Optimization Problem (DCOP)* [16,27] is described by a tuple $\langle \mathcal{X}, \mathcal{D}, \mathcal{F}, \mathcal{A}, \alpha \rangle$, where: $\mathcal{X} = \{x_1, \ldots, x_n\}$ is a set of *variables*; $\mathcal{D} = \{D_1, \ldots, D_n\}$ is a set of finite *domains* (i.e., $x_i \in D_i$); $\mathcal{F} = \{f_1, \ldots, f_e\}$ is a set of *utility functions* (also called *constraints*), where $f_i : \times_{x_j \in \mathbf{x}^{f_i}} D_i \to \mathbb{R}_+ \cup \{-\infty\}$ and $\mathbf{x}^{f_i} \subseteq \mathcal{X}$ is the set of the variables (also called the *scope*) relevant to f_i; $\mathcal{A} = \{a_1, \ldots, a_p\}$ is a set of *agents*; and $\alpha : \mathcal{X} \to \mathcal{A}$ is a function that maps each variable to one agent. f_i specifies the utility of each combination of values assigned to the variables in $\mathbf{x}^{f_i}$. A *partial assignment* σ is a value assignment to a set of variables $X_\sigma \subseteq \mathcal{X}$ that is consistent with the variables' domains. The utility $\mathcal{F}(\sigma) = \sum_{f \in \mathcal{F}, \mathbf{x}^f \subseteq X_\sigma} f(\sigma)$ is the sum of the utilities of all the applicable utility functions in σ. A *solution* is a partial assignment σ for all the variables of the problem, i.e., with $X_\sigma = \mathcal{X}$. We will denote with $\mathbf{x}$ a solution, while $\mathbf{x}_i$ is the value of x_i in $\mathbf{x}$. The goal is to find an optimal solution $\mathbf{x}^* = \text{argmax}_{\mathbf{x}} \mathcal{F}(\mathbf{x})$.

2   Scheduling Device in Smart Homes

A *Smart Home Device Scheduling (SHDS)* problem is defined by the tuple $\langle \mathbf{H}, \mathcal{Z}, \mathcal{L}, \mathbf{P}_H, \mathbf{P}_Z, H, \theta \rangle$, where: $\mathbf{H} = \{h_1, h_2, \ldots\}$ is a neighborhood of smart homes, capable of communicating with one another; $\mathcal{Z} = \cup_{h_i \in \mathbf{H}} \mathbf{Z}_i$ is a set of smart devices, where $\mathbf{Z}_i$ is the set of devices in the smart home h_i (e.g., vacuum cleaning robot, smart thermostat). $\mathcal{L} = \cup_{h_i \in \mathbf{H}} \mathbf{L}_i$ is a set of locations, where $\mathbf{L}_i$ is the set of locations in the smart home h_i (e.g., living room, kitchen); $\mathbf{P}_H$ is the set of state properties of the smart homes (e.g., cleanliness, temperature); $\mathbf{P}_Z$ is the set of devices state properties (e.g., battery charge for a vacuum robot); H is the planning horizon of the problem. We denote with $\mathbf{T} = \{1, \ldots, H\}$ the set of time points; $\theta : \mathbf{T} \to \mathbb{R}^+$ represents the real-time pricing schema adopted by the energy utility company, which expresses the cost per kWh of energy consumed by consumers. Finally, we use Ω_p to denote the set of all possible states for state property $p \in \mathbf{P}_H \cup \mathbf{P}_Z$ (e.g., all the different levels of cleanliness for the cleanliness property). Figure 1(right) shows an illustration of a neighborhood of smart homes with each home controlling a set of smart devices.

2.1   Smart Devices

For each home $h_i \in \mathbf{H}$, the set of smart devices $\mathbf{Z}_i$ is partitioned into a set of actuators $\mathbf{A}_i$ and a set of sensors $\mathbf{S}_i$. Actuators can affect the states of the home (e.g., heaters and ovens can affect the temperature in the home) and possibly their own states (e.g., vacuum cleaning robots drain their battery power when running). On the other hand, sensors monitor the states of the home. Each device $z \in \mathbf{Z}_i$ of a home h_i is defined by a tuple $\langle \ell_z, A_z, \gamma_z^H, \gamma_z^Z \rangle$, where $\ell_z \in \mathbf{L}_i$ denotes the relevant location in the home that it can act or sense, A_z is the set of actions that it can perform, $\gamma_z^H : A_z \to 2^{\mathbf{P}_H}$ maps the actions of the device to the relevant state properties of the home, and $\gamma_z^Z : A_z \to 2^{\mathbf{P}_Z}$ maps the actions of the device to its relevant state properties. We will use the following running example throughout this paper.

Example 1. Consider a vacuum cleaning robot z_v with location $\ell_{z_v} = \mathsf{living\_room}$. The set of possible actions is $A_{z_v} = \{\mathsf{run}, \mathsf{charge}, \mathsf{stop}\}$ and the mappings are:

$$\gamma_{z_v}^H : \mathsf{run} \to \{\text{cleanliness}\}; \mathsf{charge} \to \emptyset; \mathsf{stop} \to \emptyset$$
$$\gamma_{z_v}^Z : \mathsf{run} \to \{\text{battery\_charge}\}; \mathsf{charge} \to \{\text{battery\_charge}\}; \mathsf{stop} \to \emptyset$$

where $\emptyset$ represents a *null* state property.

2.2   Device Schedules

To control the energy profile of a smart home, we need to describe the behavior of the smart devices acting in the smart home during time. We formalize this concept with the notion of *device schedules*.

We use $\xi_z^t \in A_z$ to denote the action of device z at time step t, and $\xi_X^t = \{\xi_z^t \mid z \in X\}$ to denote the set of actions of the devices in $X \subseteq \mathcal{Z}$ at time step t.

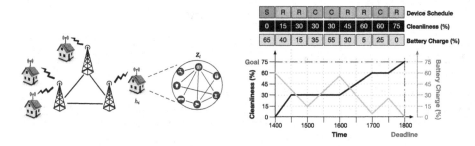

Fig. 1. Illustration of a neighborhood of smart homes (Color figure online)

Definition 1 (Schedule). *A schedule* $\xi_X^{[t_a \to t_b]} = \langle \xi_X^{t_a}, \dots, \xi_X^{t_b} \rangle$ *is a sequence of actions for the devices in* $X \subseteq \mathcal{Z}$ *within the time interval from* t_a *to* t_b.

Consider the illustration of Fig. 1(left). The top row of Fig. 1(left) shows a possible schedule $\langle R, R, C, C, R, R, C, R \rangle$ for a vacuum cleaning robot starting at time 1400 h, where each time step is 30 min. The robot's actions at each time step are shown in the colored boxes with letters in them: red with 'S' for stop, green with 'R' for run, and blue with 'C' for charge.

At a high level, the goal of the SHDS problem is to find a schedule for each of the devices in every smart home that achieve some user-defined objectives (e.g., the home is at a particular temperature within a time window, the home is at a certain cleanliness level by some deadline) that may be personalized for each home. We refer to these objectives as *scheduling rules.*

2.3 Scheduling Rules

We define two types of scheduling rules: *Active scheduling rules (ASRs)* that define user-defined objectives on a desired state of the home (e.g., the living room is cleaned by 1800 h). *Passive scheduling rules (PSRs)* that define implicit constraints on devices that must hold at all times (e.g., the battery charge on a vacuum cleaning robot is always between 0% and 100%). We provide a formal description for the grammar of scheduling rules in Sect. 3.4.

Example 2. The scheduling rule (1) describes an *ASR* defining a goal state where the living room floor is at least 75% clean (i.e., at least 75% of the floor is cleaned by a vacuum cleaning robot) by 1800 h:

$$\texttt{living\_room cleanliness} \geq 75 \texttt{ before } 1800 \tag{1}$$

$$z_v \texttt{ battery\_charge} \geq 0 \texttt{ always} \tag{2}$$

$$z_v \texttt{ battery\_charge} \leq 100 \texttt{ always} \tag{3}$$

and scheduling rules (2) and (3) describe *PSRs* stating the battery charge of the vacuum cleaning robot z_v needs to be between 0% and 100% of its full charge at all the times:

We denote with $R_p^{[t_a \rightarrow t_b]}$ a scheduling rule over a state property $p \in \mathbf{P}_H \cup \mathbf{P}_Z$, and time interval $[t_a, t_b]$. Each scheduling rule indicates a goal state at a location or on a device $\ell_{R_p} \in \mathbf{L}_i \cup \mathbf{Z}_i$ of a particular state property p that must hold over the time interval $[t_a, t_b] \subseteq \mathbf{T}$. The scheduling rule goal state is either a desired state of a home, if it is an ASR (e.g., the cleanliness level of the room floor) or a required state of a device or a home, if it is a PSR (e.g., the battery charge of the vacuum cleaning robot).

Each rule is associated with a set of actuators $\Phi_p \subseteq \mathbf{A}_i$ that can be used to reach the goal state. For instance, in our Example (2), Φ_p correspond to the vacuum cleaning robot z_v, which can operate on the living room floor. Additionally, a rule is associated with a sensor $s_p \in \mathbf{S}_i$ capable of sensing the state property p. Finally, in a PSRs the device can also sense its own internal states.

The ASR of Eq. (1) is illustrated in Fig. 1(left) by dotted red lines on the graph. The PSRs are not shown as they must hold for all time steps.

2.4   Feasibility of Schedules

To ensure that a goal state can be achieved across the desired time window the system uses a *predictive model* of the various state properties. This predictive model captures the evolution of a state property over time and how such state property is affected by a given joint action of the relevant actuators. We describe the details of the physical predictive models used to generate our benchmark set in Sect. 3.3.

Definition 2 (Predictive Model). *A predictive model Γ_p for a state property p (of either the home or a device) is a function $\Gamma_p : \Omega_p \times \times_{z \in \Phi_p} A_z \cup \{\perp\} \rightarrow \Omega_p \cup \{\perp\}$, where $\perp$ denotes an infeasible state and $\perp + (\cdot) = \perp$.*

In other words, the model describes the transition of state property p from state $\omega_p \in \Omega_p$ at time step t to time step $t + 1$ when it is affected by a set of actuators Φ_p running joint actions $\xi_{\Phi_p}^t$:

$$\Gamma_p^{t+1}(\omega_p, \xi_{\Phi_p}^t) = \omega_p + \Delta_p(\omega_p, \xi_{\Phi_p}^t) \qquad (4)$$

where $\Delta_p(\omega_p, \xi_{\Phi_p}^t)$ is a function describing the effect of the actuators' joint action $\xi_{\Phi_p}^t$ on state property p. We assume here, w.l.o.g., that the state of properties are numeric—when this is not the case, a mapping to the possible states to a numeric representation can be easily defined.

Notice that a recursive invocation of a predictive model allows us to predict the trajectory of a state property p for future time steps, given a schedule of actions of the relevant actuators Φ_p. Let us formally define this concept.

Definition 3 (Predicted State Trajectory). *Given a state property p, its current state ω_p at time step t_a, and a schedule $\xi_{\Phi_p}^{[t_a \rightarrow t_b]}$ of relevant actuators Φ_p, the predicted state trajectory $\pi_p(\omega_p, \xi_{\Phi_p}^{[t_a \rightarrow t_b]})$ of that state property is defined as:*

$$\pi_p(\omega_p, \xi_{\Phi_p}^{[t_a \rightarrow t_b]}) = \Gamma_p^{t_b}(\Gamma_p^{t_b - 1}(\dots (\Gamma_p^{t_a}(\omega_p, \xi_{\Phi_p}^{t_a}), \dots), \xi_{\Phi_p}^{t_b - 1}), \xi_{\Phi_p}^{t_b}) \qquad (5)$$

Consider the device scheduling example in Fig. 1(left). The predicted state trajectories of the *battery_charge* and *cleanliness* state properties are shown in the second and third rows of Fig. 1(left). These trajectories are predicted given that the vacuum cleaning robot will take on the schedule shown in the first row of the figure. The predicted trajectories of these state properties are also illustrated in the graph, where the dark grey line shows the states for the robot's battery charge and the black line shows the states for the cleanliness of the room.

Notice that to verify if a schedule satisfies a scheduling rule it is sufficient to check that the predicted state trajectories are within the set of feasible state trajectories of that rule. Additionally, notice that each active and passive scheduling rule defines a set of feasible state trajectories. For example, the active scheduling rule of Eq. (1) allows all possible state trajectories as long as the state at time step 1800 is no smaller than 75. We use $R_p[t] \subseteq \Omega_p$ to denote the set of states that are feasible according to rule R_p of state property p at time step t. More formally, a schedule $\xi_{\Phi_p}^{[t_a \rightarrow t_b]}$ satisfies a scheduling rule $R_p^{[t_a \rightarrow t_b]}$ (written as $\xi_{\Phi_p}^{[t_a \rightarrow t_b]} \models R_p^{[t_a \rightarrow t_b]}$) iff:

$$\forall t \in [t_a, t_b] : \pi_p(\omega_p^{t_a}, \xi_{\Phi_p}^{[t_a \rightarrow t]}) \in R_p[t] \tag{6}$$

where $\omega_p^{t_a}$ is the state of state property p at time step t_a.

Definition 4 (Feasible Schedule). *A schedule is feasible if it satisfies all the passive and active scheduling rules of each home in the SHDS problem.*

In the example of Fig. 1, the evaluated schedule is a feasible schedule since the trajectories of both the *battery_charge* and *cleanliness* states satisfy both the *active scheduling rule* (1) and the *passive scheduling rules* (2) and (3).

2.5   Optimization Objective

In addition to finding feasible schedules, the goal in the SHDS problem is to optimize for the aggregated total cost of energy consumed.

Each action $a \in A_z$ of device $z \in \mathbf{Z}_i$ in home $h_i \in \mathbf{H}$ has an associated energy consumption $\rho_z : A_z \rightarrow \mathbb{R}^+$, expressed in kWh. The aggregated energy $E_i^t(\xi_{\mathbf{Z}_i}^{[0 \rightarrow H]})$ across all devices consumed by h_i at time step t under trajectory $\xi_{\mathbf{Z}_i}^{[1 \rightarrow H]}$ is:

$$E_i^t(\xi_{\mathbf{Z}_i}^{[0 \rightarrow H]}) = \sum_{z \in \mathbf{Z}_i} \rho_z(\xi_z^t) \tag{7}$$

where ξ_z^t is the action of device z at time t in the schedule $\xi_{\mathbf{Z}_i}^{[0 \rightarrow H]}$. The cost $c_i(\xi_{\mathbf{Z}_i}^{[0 \rightarrow H]})$ associated to schedule $\xi_{\mathbf{Z}_i}^{[1 \rightarrow H]}$ in home h_i is:

$$c_i(\xi_{\mathbf{Z}_i}^{[1 \rightarrow H]}) = \sum_{t \in \mathbf{T}} (\ell_i^t + E_i^t(\xi_{\mathbf{Z}_i}^{[0 \rightarrow H]})) \cdot \theta(t) \tag{8}$$

where ℓ_i^t is the home background load produced at time t, which includes all non-schedulable devices (e.g., TV, refrigerator), and sensor devices, which are always active, and $\theta(t)$ is the real-time price of energy per kWh at time t.

The objective of an SHDS problem is that of minimizing the following weighted bi-objective function:

$$\min_{\xi_{\mathbf{Z}_i}^{[0 \to H]}} \quad \alpha_c \cdot C^{\text{sum}} + \alpha_e \cdot E^{\text{peak}} \tag{9}$$

$$\text{subject to:} \quad \forall h_i \in \mathbf{H}, R_p^{[t_a \to t_b]} \in \mathbf{R}_i: \quad \xi_{\Phi_p}^{[t_a \to t_b]} \models R_p^{[t_a \to t_b]} \tag{10}$$

where $\alpha_c, \alpha_e \in \mathbb{R}$ are weights, $C^{\text{sum}} = \sum_{h_i \in \mathbf{H}} c_i(\xi_{\mathbf{Z}_i}^{[0 \to H]})$ is the aggregated monetary cost across all homes h_i; and $E^{\text{peak}} = \sum_{t \in \mathbf{T}} \sum_{\mathbf{H}_j \in \mathcal{H}} \sum_{h_i \in \mathbf{H}_j} \left(E_i^t(\xi_{\mathbf{Z}_i}^{[0 \to H]})\right)^2$ is a quadratic penalty function on the aggregated energy consumption across all homes h_i. Since the SHDS problem is designed for distributed multi-agent systems, in a cooperative approach, optimizing E^{peak} may require each home to share its energy profile with every other home. To take into account data privacy concerns and possible high network loads, we decompose the set of homes $\mathbf{H}$ into neighboring subsets of homes $\mathcal{H}$, so that E^{peak} can be optimized independently within each subset. One can use coalition formation algorithms [23–25] to form such coalitions/subsets of neighboring homes. These coalitions can be exploited by a distributed algorithm to (1) parallelize computations between multiple groups and (2) avoid data exposure over long distances or sensitive areas. Finally, Constraint (10) defines the valid trajectories for each scheduling rule $r \in \mathbf{R}_i$, where $\mathbf{R}_i$ is the set of all scheduling rules of home h_i.

2.6   DCOP Mapping

One can map the SHDS problem to a DCOP as follows:

- AGENTS: Each agent $a_i \in \mathcal{A}$ in the DCOP is mapped to a home $h_i \in \mathbf{H}$.
- VARIABLES and DOMAINS: Each agent a_i controls the following set of variables:
  - For each actuator $z \in \mathbf{A}_i$ and each time step $t \in \mathbf{T}$, a variable $x_{i,z}^t$ whose domain is the set of actions in A_z. The sensors in $\mathbf{S}_i$ are considered to be always active, and thus not directly controlled by the agent.
  - An auxiliary interface variable $\hat{x}_j^t$ whose domain is the set $\{0, \ldots, \sum_{z \in \mathbf{Z}_i} \rho(\text{argmax}_{a \in A_z} \rho_z(a))\}$, which represents the aggregated energy consumed by all the devices in the home at each time step t.
- CONSTRAINTS: There are three types of constraints:
  - *Local* soft constraints (i.e., constraints that involve only variables controlled by the agent) whose costs correspond to the weighted summation of monetary costs, as defined in Eq. (8).
  - *Local* hard constraints that enforce Constraint (10). Feasible schedules incur a cost of 0 while infeasible schedules incur a cost of ∞.
  - *Global* soft constraints (i.e., constraints that involve variables controlled by different agents) whose costs correspond to the peak energy consumption, as defined in the second term in Eq. (9).

3 Model Parameters and Realistic Data Set Generation

This section describes the parameters and models adopted in our SHDS dataset. We first describe the structural parameters adopted to model the houses, which are used in turn to calculate the predictive models. Next, we describe the smart devices adopted in our dataset and we discuss their power consumptions and their effects on the house environments. We then describe the predictive models adopted to capture changes in the houses' environments and devices' states. Finally, we report the Backus-Naur Form (BNF) for the scheduling rules introduced in Sect. 2.3 and the pricing scheme adopted in our experiments.

3.1 House Structural Parameters

We consider three house sizes (small, medium, and large). The floor plans for the three house structures are shown in Fig. 2.

Fig. 2. Floor plans for a small (left), medium (center), and large (right) house

Our house structural model simplifies the floor plans shown in Fig. 2 by ignoring internal walls. This abstraction is sufficient to capture the richness of the predictive models introduced in Sect. 2.4. Table 1 reports the parameters of the houses adopted in our SHDS dataset. The house sizes are expressed in meters ($L \times W$). The wall's height is assumed to be 2.4 m and the window area denotes the area of the walls covered by windows. The overall heat transfer coefficient (also referred to as U-value) describes how well a building element conducts heat. It is defined as the rate of heat transfer (in watts) through one unit area (m^2) of a structure divided by the difference in temperature across the structure [15].

The material of the walls is constituted by a metal panel with R-11 insulation, and a gypsum board with an F01 layer (outside surface), an F08 steel siding layer with I04 insulation, and a G01 gypsum board layer. The walls' heat-transfer coefficient (U_{walls}) is 0.48 $\frac{W}{m^2 \cdot \,^\circ C}$. We consider vertical double glazed windows with $30 - 60$ mm of separation between glasses and whose heat-transfer coefficient ($U_{windows}$) is 2.8 $\frac{W}{m^2\,{}^\circ C}$. Additionally, we consider a wood roof with R-10 insulation board, wood deck, and suspended acoustical ceiling, and whose heat-transfer coefficient (U_{roof}) is 0.39 $\frac{W}{m^2\cdot{}^\circ C}$. Finally, we consider a 5.08 cm wooden door, with heat-transfer coefficient of 2.6 $\frac{W}{m^2\,{}^\circ C}$. These are commonly adopted materials in the US house construction industry [15]. We assume a background load consumption which accounts of a medium-size refrigerator (120 W), a wireless router (6 W), and a set of light bulbs (collectively 40 W) [15]. The heat gain from the background house appliances is computed according to [15] (Table 9.8). We consider the heat gain generated by two people and computed as in [15] (Table 9.7), assuming the metabolic rate of *light office work*.

Table 1. House structural parameters

Structural parameters	Small	Medium	Large	Structural parameters	Small	Medium	Large
House size (m)	6 × 8	8·× 12	12 × 15	U_{roof} (W/(m^2 °C))	1.1	1.1	1.1
Walls area (m^2)	67.2	96	129.6	Lights energy density (W/m^3)	9.69	9.69	9.69
Window area (m^2)	7.2	10	16	Background load (kW)	0.166	0.166	0.166
U_{walls} (W/(m^2 °C))	3.9	3.9	3.9	Background heat gain (W)	50	50	50
$U_{windows}$ (W/(m^2 °C))	2.8	2.8	2.8	People heat gain (Btu/h)	400	400	400

3.2 Smart Devices

In this section, we report the complete list of smart devices (sensors and actuators) adopted by the smart homes in our SHDS dataset.

Sensors. Table 2 reports the sensors adopted in our SHDS problem. For each sensor, we report an identifier (ID), the state property (see Sect. 2.1) it senses, and its location in the house. All sensors are considered to be constantly active, sensing a single state property at a location (e.g., an air temperature sensor is located in a room of the house, a charge sensor is located on a device).

Actuators. Table 3 reports the list of the actuators. It tabulates the type of actuator and its model, its possible actions, the power consumption (in kWh), the state properties affected by each of its action, and the effects (Δ) on the associated predictive models in the small, medium, and large house sizes. The latter represents the incremental quantity that affects the physical system, given the action of the actuator, as defined in Eq. (4). We detail the calculation of the house and devices physical models below.

ID	State property	Location	ID	State property	Location
01	Air temperature	House room	08	Dish cleanliness	Appliance
02	Floor cleanliness (dust)	House room	09	Air humidity	House room
03	Temperature	Appliance	10	Luminosity	House room
04	Battery charge	Appliance	11	Occupancy	House room
05	Bake	Appliance	12	Movement	House room
06	Laundry wash	Appliance	13	Smoke detector	House room
07	Laundry dry	Appliance			

3.3   Physical Models

In this section we describe the physical models used to compute the effects Δ of the actuators' actions on a predictive model (see Table 3). These values, in turn, are adopted within the SHDS predictive models as described in Eq. (4).

Battery (Dis)charge Model. The battery charge/discharge model adopted in our work for the battery-powered devices is as follows. For a given battery b with capacity Q_b (expressed in kWh), voltage V_b, and electric charge $E_b = \frac{V_b}{Q_b}$ (expressed in ampere-hour (Ah)), and assuming a 100% charging/discharging efficiency, the battery charge time b_α^+ and discharge time b_α^- are computed, respectively, as:

$$b_\alpha^+ = \frac{E_b}{C^+}; \qquad b_\alpha^- = \frac{E_b}{C^-}, \tag{11}$$

and expressed in hours. C^+ and C^- are, respectively, the charging amperage and the in-use amperage. In Table 4, we report the battery model parameters associated to our electric vehicle and to our robotic vacuum cleaner. These parameters are derived following the products' manuals [1,3], respectively. The effects Δ of the devices' action associated to the charging time and discharging time are computed by dividing the total charging time and discharging time by $|\mathbf{T}|$.

Air Temperature Model. The air temperature predictive model is computed following the standard principle of heating and ventilation [15], and described as follows. Let G be the ventilation conductance: $G = \dot{V}\rho_a\bar{h}$, where $\dot{V}$ is the air volume flow rate, whose value is set to 100, ρ_a is the density of the air, set to 0.75, and $\bar{h}$ is the specific heat of the air, set to 0.24, following [15]. The house heat loss coefficient h_{loss} is expressed as:

$$h_{\text{loss}} = U_{\text{walls}} \cdot A_{\text{walls}} + U_{\text{roof}} \cdot A_{\text{roof}} + U_{\text{windows}} \cdot A_{\text{windows}} + G \tag{12}$$

where U_{walls}, U_{roof}, and U_{windows} describe the heat transfer coefficients for the walls, roof, and windows of the house, respectively, and A_{walls}, A_{roof}, and

Table 3. List of actuators

Actuator	Model	Actions	Consumption (kWh)	State properties (ID)	Effects small (Δ)	Effects medium (Δ)	Effects large (Δ)
Heater	Dyson AM09	Off	0	{01}	$-\dfrac{L_h}{148.48\cdot T_A}$	$-\dfrac{L_h}{296.86\cdot T_A}$	$-\dfrac{L_h}{593.75\cdot T_A}$
		Fan	0.008	{01}	$-\dfrac{L_h}{148.48\cdot T_A}$	$-\dfrac{L_h}{296.86\cdot T_A}$	$-\dfrac{L_h}{593.75\cdot T_A}$
		Heat	0.025	{01}	$\dfrac{L_h}{148.48\cdot|T_Z-T_A|}$	$\dfrac{L_h}{296.86\cdot|T_Z-T_A|}$	$\dfrac{L_h}{593.75\cdot|T_Z-T_A|}$
AC	Bryant 697CN030B	Off	0	{01}	$\dfrac{L_h}{148.48\cdot T_A}$	$\dfrac{L_h}{296.86\cdot T_A}$	$\dfrac{L_h}{593.75\cdot T_A}$
		Fan	0.012	{01}	$\dfrac{L_h}{148.48\cdot T_A}$	$\dfrac{L_h}{296.86\cdot T_A}$	$\dfrac{L_h}{593.75\cdot T_A}$
		Cool	0.037	{01}	$\dfrac{L_h}{148.48\cdot|T_A-T_Z|}$	$\dfrac{L_h}{296.86\cdot|T_A-T_Z|}$	$\dfrac{L_h}{593.75\cdot|T_A-T_Z|}$
Water heater	Tempra 36	Off	0	{03}	{0}	{0}	{0}
		On	0.060	{03}	{9.90°C}	{8.94°C}	{6.83°C}
Vacuum bot	iRobot Roomba 880	Off	0	{02, 04}	{0.0%, 0.0%}	{0.0%, 0.0%}	{0.0%, 0.0%}
		Vacuum	0	{02, 04}	{0.676%, -0.21%}	{0.338%, -0.21%}	{0.168%, -0.21%}
		Charge	0.004	{04}	{0.33%}	{0.33%}	{0.33%}
Electric vehicle	Tesla Model S	Off	0	{04}	{0}	{0}	{0}
		48 amp wall charger	0.192	{04}	{0.226%}	{0.226%}	{0.226%}
		72 amp wall charger	0.283	{04}	{0.333%}	{0.333%}	{0.333%}
		Super charger	120	{04}	{2.326%}	{2.326%}	{2.326%}
Clothes washer	GE WSM2420 D3WW	Off	0	{06}	{0}	{0}	{0}
		Wash (Regular)	0.007	{06}	{1}	{1}	{1}
		Spin (Regular)	0.008	{06}	{1}	{1}	{1}
		Rinse (Regular)	0.008	{06}	{1}	{1}	{1}
		Wash (Perm-Press)	0.007	{06}	{1}	{1}	{1}
		Spin (Perm-Press)	0.007	{06}	{1}	{1}	{1}
		Rinse (Perm-Press)	0.008	{06}	{1}	{1}	{1}
		Wash (Delicates)	0.007	{06}	{1}	{1}	{1}
		Spin (Delicates)	0.007	{06}	{1}	{1}	{1}
		Rinse (Delicates)	0.008	{06}	{1}	{1}	{1}
Clothes dryer	*GE WSM2420 D3WW	Off	0	{07}	{0}	{0}	{0}
		On (Regular)	0.027	{07}	{1}	{1}	{1}
		On (Perm-Press)	0.024	{07}	{1}	{1}	{1}
		On (Timed)	0.028	{07}	{1}	{1}	{1}
Oven	Kenmore 790.91312013	Off	0	{05}	{0}	{0}	{0}
		Bake	0.037	{05, 01}	{1, 0.017°C}	{1, 0.009°C}	{1, 0.004°C}
		Broil	0.042	{05, 01}	{1.25, 0.02°C}	{1.25, 0.01°C}	{1.25, 0.005°C}
Dishwasher	Kenmore 665.13242 K900	Off	0	{08}	{0}	{0}	{0}
		Wash	0.006	{08}	{1}	{1}	{1}
		Rinse	0.009	{08}	{1}	{1}	{1}
		Dry	0.006	{08}	{1}	{1}	{1}

Table 4. Electric vehicle [3] and robotic vacuum cleaner [1] batteries' physical model.

	Tesla model S			iRobot Roomba 880
	Slow charge	Regular charge	Super charger	
V_b	240	240	240	120
E_b	354 Ah	354 Ah	354 Ah	3 Ah
C^+	48 A	72 A	500 A	1.25 A
C^-	60 A	60 A	60 A	0.75 A
b_α^+	7 hr 22 min	5 h	43 min	2 h 24 min
b_α^-	6 h	6 h	6 h	4 h

A_{windows} describe the areas of the walls, roof, and windows, respectively. Their values are provided in Table 1. If T_A is the current temperature and T_Z is a target temperature, then the heating load $\dot{L}_h$ is given by

$$\dot{L}_h = h_{\text{loss}}|T_Z - T_A| \tag{13}$$

The heating load defines the quantity of heat per unit time (in BTU) that must be supplied in a building to reach a target temperature T_Z, from the given temperature T_A. Given the heating load $\dot{L}_h$ and the heater capacity C of a heater/cooler, the time required for a device to operate so to reach the desired temperature is given by: $\frac{L_h}{C}$.

The heating/cooling load is also effected by the outdoor and indoor temperature difference. Consider the example where $T_A = 12\,°C$, $T_Z = 22\,°C$, and the outdoor temperature changes from T_A to $T_N = 8\,°C$. We can calculate the new load due to change in temperature using the following:

$$\dot{L}_n = \dot{L}_h \cdot \frac{|T_Z - T_N|}{|T_Z - T_A|}. \tag{14}$$

The above expression shows that an outdoor temperature drops of 4 °C, causes the heating load to increase by a factor of 1.4. In our model, to compute the change in temperature per time step (Δ) we use the heat-loss relationship:

$$\Delta = \frac{h_{\text{loss}}}{m \cdot c_p}, \tag{15}$$

where m is the mass of the air and c_p is the specific heat of air. In our model, m depends on volume flow rate of an air in the house, and $c_p = 1$ kJ/kg·K.

Water Temperature Model. The rise in the water temperature per unit of time (Δ value) is dependent on the difference in the water temperature flowing into the water heater and the amount of water flowing out of the water heater, as well as water usage. We considered an on-demand electric water heater (tankless). The water usage depends on household size and the activities of multiple users. In our model, to compute the rise and drop in water temperature, we adopted the highest potential peak in households water usage following [2,4], and corresponding to 26.50 l/min (small house), 29.34 l/min (medium house), and 38:38 l/min (large house). The rise in temperature is 18.33 °C for 14.31 l/min of water usage [2]. Thus the rise in temperature for our small, medium, and large house, are, respectively, 9.90 °C, 8.94 °C, and 6.83 °C.

Cleanliness Model. Our floor cleanliness model is computed using the following equation: $T = \frac{A}{0.313}$, where A represents the area of the room (in m^2) and T is the amount of time (in minutes) required by a robotic vacuum cleaner to vacuum the entire room. A robotic vacuum cleaner *iRobot Roomba 880* is estimated to cover a 17.84 m^2 room in 57 min [1] (which is approximately 0.313 m^2/min). In our proposed dataset we use three different areas: $A_{small} = 48$ m^2, $A_{medium} = 96$ m^2, and $A_{large} = 180$ m^2. Thus the estimated times to cover a 100% floor for the small, medium, and large houses are, respectively: $T = 153.35, 306.71$, and 575.08 min. The corresponding Δ value of Table 3, represents the percentage of floor covered in the time unit, and is computed as: $\Delta = \frac{100}{T}$.

All other predictive models (e.g., laundry wash, laundry dry, bake, dish cleanliness, etc.) simply capture the time needed for a device to achieve the required goal. The specifics for such values are provided in Sect. 4.

3.4 Scheduling Rules

We now report the complete Backus-Naur Form (BNF) describing the *scheduling rules* for a smart home $h_i \in \mathbf{H}$, introduced in Sect. 2.2.

$$\langle rules \rangle ::= \langle simple\ rule \rangle \mid \langle simple\ rule \rangle \wedge \langle rules \rangle$$
$$\langle simple\ rule \rangle ::= \langle active\ rule \rangle \mid \langle passive\ rule \rangle$$
$$\langle active\ rule \rangle ::= \langle location \rangle \langle state\ property \rangle \langle relation \rangle \langle goal\ state \rangle \langle time \rangle$$
$$\langle passive\ rule \rangle ::= \langle location \rangle \langle state\ property \rangle \langle relation \rangle \langle goal\ state \rangle$$
$$\langle location \rangle ::= \ell \in \mathbf{L}_i$$
$$\langle state\ property \rangle ::= s \in \mathbf{P}_H \mid s \in \mathbf{P}_Z$$
$$\langle relation \rangle ::= \leq \mid < \mid = \mid \neq \mid > \mid \geq$$
$$\langle goal\ state \rangle ::= sensor\ state \mid actuator\ state$$

In our dataset, the device states are mapped to numeric values, i.e., $\Omega_p = \mathbb{N}$, for all $p \in \mathbf{P}_H \cup \mathbf{P}_Z$.

3.5 Pricing Schema

For the evaluation of our SHDS dataset we adopted a pricing schema used by the Pacific Gas & Electric Co. for its customers in parts of California,[1] which

---

[1] https://goo.gl/vOeNqj.

accounts for 7 tiers ranging from $0.198 per kWh to $0.849 per kWh, reported in Table 5.

Table 5. Pacific gas & electric co. pricing schema

Time start	0:00	8:00	12:00	14:00	18:00	22:00
Time end	7:59	11:59	13:59	17:59	21:59	23:59
Price ($)	0.198	0.225	0.249	0.849	0.225	0.198

4   SHDS Dataset

We now introduce a dataset for the SHDS problem for DCOPs. We generate synthetic microgrid instances sampling neighborhoods in three cities in the United States (Des Moines, IA; Boston, MA; and San Francisco, CA) and estimate the density of houses in each city. The average density (in houses per square kilometers) is 718 in Des Moines, 1357 in Boston, and 3766 in San Francisco. For each city, we created a $200\,\text{m} \times 200\,\text{m}$ grid, where the distance between intersections is $20\,\text{m}$, and randomly placed houses in this grid until the density is the same as the sampled density. We then divided the city into k $(=|\mathcal{H}|)$ coalitions, where each home can communicate with all homes in its coalition. Finally, we ensure that there are no disjoint coalitions; this is analogous to the fact that microgrids are all connected to each other via the main power grid.

We generate a total of 624 problem instances, where, for each city, we vary the number of agents—up to 7532 for the largest instance, the number of coalitions from 1 to 1024, and the number of devices controlled by each house agent (from 2 to 20). The SHDS datasets is available at https://github.com/nandofioretto/SHDS_dataset.

Each home device has an associated active scheduling rule that is randomly generated and a number of passive rules that must always hold. The parameters used to generate active rules and passive rules are reported, respectively, in Tables 6 and 7. The time predicates associated with these rules are generated at random within the given horizon. Additionally, the relations r and goals states g_i are randomly generated by sampling from the sets corresponding, respectively, to the columns ⟨*relation*⟩ and ⟨*goal state*⟩ of Table 6.

Tables 9, report the results of the SHDS experiments for a subset of the Des Moines, Boston, and San Francisco instances, respectively, where we vary the number of agents (n)—up to 474 for the largest instances—and the number of devices controlled by each home (m), while retaining the number of coalitions $k = 1$. To solve these instances, we use an *uncoordinated* approach, where agents solve their private scheduling subproblem without coordinating their actions with those of other agents and, thus, disregarding the energy peak minimization objective. Each agent reports the best schedule found with a local Constraint Programming solver[2] as subroutine within a 10-s timeout. The row *obj*

---

[2] We adopt the JaCoP solver (http://www.jacop.eu/).

Table 6. Scheduling (active) rules

⟨location⟩	⟨state property⟩	⟨relation⟩	⟨goal state⟩	⟨time⟩
Room	Air temperature	$r \in \{>, \geq\}$	$g_1 \in [17, 24]$	⟨time⟩
Room	Floor cleanliness	$r \in \{>, \geq\}$	$g_2 \in [50, 99]$	⟨time⟩
Electric vehicle	Charge	$r \in \{>, \geq\}$	$g_3 \in [50, 99]$	⟨time⟩
Water heater	Temperature	$r \in \{>, \geq\}$	$g_4 \in [15, 40]$	⟨time⟩
Clothes washer	Laundry wash	$r \in \{\geq\}$	$g_5 \in \{45, 60\}$	⟨time⟩
Clothes dryer	Laundry dry	$r \in \{\geq\}$	$g_6 \in \{45, 60\}$	⟨time⟩
Oven	Bake	$r \in \{=\}$	$g_7 \in \{60, 75, 120, 150\}$	⟨time⟩
Dishwasher	Dish cleanliness	$r \in \{\geq\}$	$g_8 \in \{45, 60\}$	⟨time⟩

Table 7. Scheduling (passive) rules

⟨location⟩	⟨state property⟩	⟨relation⟩	⟨goal state⟩	⟨location⟩	⟨state property⟩	⟨relation⟩	⟨goal state⟩
Room	Air temperature	$\geq$	0	EV	Charge	$\leq$	100
Room	Air temperature	$\leq$	33	Water heater	Temperature	$\geq$	10
Room	Floor cleanliness	$\geq$	0	Water heater	Temperature	$\leq$	55
Room	Floor cleanliness	$\leq$	100	Clothes washer	Laundry wash	$\leq$	g_5
Roomba	Charge	$\geq$	0	Clothes dryer	Laundry dry	$\leq$	g_6
Roomba	Charge	$\leq$	100	Oven	Bake	$\leq$	g_7
EV	Charge	$\geq$	0	Dishwasher	Dish cleanliness	$\leq$	g_8

Table 8. Physical models: values and assumptions

Physical model	Parameter	Value (small house)	Value (medium house)	Value (large house)
Air temperature	$\dot{V}$	100	200	400
	m	148.48	296.86	593.75
	c_p	1.0	1.0	1.0
	ρ_a	0.75	0.75	0.75
	$\bar{h}$	0.24	0.24	0.24
	h_loss	352.24	544	764.75
	T_Z	22	22	22
	T_A	10	10	10
	$\dot{L}_n$	4226.88	6528	9177
Floor cleanliness	A	$48\,\mathrm{m}^2$	$96\,\mathrm{m}^2$	$180\,\mathrm{m}^2$
	T	$153.35\,\mathrm{min}$	$306.71\,\mathrm{min}$	$575.08\,\mathrm{min}$
	Δ	0.652%	0.326%	0.174%
Water temperature	Household size	2	3	4
	Liters/min usage	26.50	29.34	38.38
	Δ	$27.9\,^\circ\mathrm{C}$	$25.2\,^\circ\mathrm{C}$	$19.2\,^\circ\mathrm{C}$

Table 9. Des Moines, Boston, San Francisco

Instance	n	Obj	Avg. price ($)	Avg. energy (kWh)	Largest peak (kWh)
dm_7	7	29227.05	3.31	16.04	299.3
dm_21	21	81841.35	3.31	15.77	885.8
dm_35	35	136696.19	3.28	15.76	1479.5
dm_71	71	287989.80	3.32	15.96	3015.8
dm_251	251	1006807.18	3.32	15.92	10622.5
bo_13	13	50493.74	3.33	15.89	534.6
bo_40	40	163246.01	3.34	16.15	1722.50
bo_67	67	272651.41	3.33	16.03	2844.1
bo_135	135	534692.07	3.31	15.90	5694.7
bo_474	474	1890711.09	3.31	15.92	19969.5
sf_37	37	149964.95	3.33	16.01	1563.4
sf_112	112	450723.92	3.32	15.97	4778.3
sf_188	188	750741.31	3.31	15.89	7904.1
sf_376	376	1486321.71	3.30	15.84	15669.0

of Tables 9 reports the upper bounds for the SHDS objective function, while the rows *avg price*, *avg power*, and *largest peak*, report, respectively, the average cost of the schedule (in US dollars), the average energy consumption (in kWh), and the largest peak (in kWh) produced during the day. For our experiments, we set $H = 12$, and report a summary of the parameters' settings adopted in our smart homes physical models, in Table 8. In these experiments, we notice that a large portion of the houses power consumption is caused by charging electric vehicles' batteries.

5   Conclusions

With the proliferation of smart devices, the automation of smart home scheduling can be a powerful tool for demand-side management within the smart grid vision. In this paper, we described the *Smart Home Device Scheduling (SHDS)* problem, which formalizes the device scheduling and coordination problem across multiple smart homes as a multi-agent system, and its mapping to a Distributed Constraint Optimization Problem (DCOP). Furthermore, we described in great detail the physical models adopted to model the smart home's sensors and actuators, as well as the physical model regulating the effect of the devices actions on the house environments properties (e.g., temperature, cleanliness). Finally, we reported a realistic dataset for the SHDS problem for DCOPs which includes 624 instances of increasing difficulty. We hope that the MAS community will find this dataset useful for their empirical evaluations.

Acknowledgments. This research is partially supported by NSF grants 0947465 and 1345232. The views and conclusions contained in this document are those of the authors and should not be interpreted as representing the official policies, either expressed or implied, of the sponsoring organizations, agencies, or the U.S. government.

References

1. Roomba 880 specs. http://www.consumerreports.org/products/robotic-vacuum/ roomba-880-290102/specs/. Accessed 18 Feb 2017
2. Sizing a new water heater. https://www.energy.gov/energysaver/sizing-new-water-heater. Accessed 18 Feb 2017
3. Tesla model S specifics. https://www.tesla.com/models
4. Typical water used in normal home activities. http://www.pittsfield-mi.gov/ DocumentCenter/View/285. Accessed 18 Feb 2017
5. Farinelli, A., Rogers, A., Petcu, A., Jennings, N.: Decentralised coordination of low-power embedded devices using the Max-Sum algorithm. In: AAMAS, pp. 639–646 (2008)
6. Fioretto, F., Pontelli, E., Yeoh, W.: Distributed constraint optimization problems and applications: a survey. *CoRR*, abs/1602.06347 (2016)
7. Fioretto, F., Yeoh, W., Pontelli, E.: A dynamic programming-based MCMC framework for solving DCOPs with GPUs. In: Rueher, M. (ed.) CP 2016. LNCS, vol. 9892, pp. 813–831. Springer, Cham (2016). https://doi.org/10.1007/ 978-3-319-44953-1_51
8. Fioretto, F., Yeoh, W., Pontelli, E.: A multiagent system approach to scheduling devices in smart homes. In: AAMAS, pp. 981–989 (2017)
9. Freuder, E.C., O'Sullivan, B.: Grand challenges for constraint programming. Constraints **19**(2), 150–162 (2014)
10. Gershman, A., Meisels, A., Zivan, R.: Asynchronous forward-bounding for distributed COPs. JAIR **34**, 61–88 (2009)
11. Hirayama, K., Yokoo, M.: Distributed partial constraint satisfaction problem. In: Smolka, G. (ed.) CP 1997. LNCS, vol. 1330, pp. 222–236. Springer, Heidelberg (1997). https://doi.org/10.1007/BFb0017442
12. Kumar, A., Faltings, B., Petcu, A.: Distributed constraint optimization with structured resource constraints. In: AAMAS, pp. 923–930 (2009)
13. Maheswaran, R., Tambe, M., Bowring, E., Pearce, J., Varakantham, P.: Taking DCOP to the real world: efficient complete solutions for distributed event scheduling. In: AAMAS, pp. 310–317 (2004)
14. Mailler, R., Lesser, V.: Solving distributed constraint optimization problems using cooperative mediation. In: AAMAS, pp. 438–445 (2004)
15. Mitchell, J.W., Braun, J.E.: Principles of Heating. Ventilation and Air Conditioning in Buildings. Wiley, Hoboken (2012)
16. Modi, P., Shen, W.-M., Tambe, M., Yokoo, M.: ADOPT: asynchronous distributed constraint optimization with quality guarantees. Artif. Intell. **161**(1–2), 149–180 (2005)
17. Nguyen, D.T., Yeoh, W., Lau, H.C.: Distributed gibbs: a memory-bounded sampling-based DCOP algorithm. In: AAMAS, pp. 167–174 (2013)
18. Ottens, B., Dimitrakakis, C., Faltings, B.: DUCT: an upper confidence bound approach to distributed constraint optimization problems. In: AAAI, pp. 528–534 (2012)

19. Pearce, J., Tambe, M.: Quality guarantees on k-optimal solutions for distributed constraint optimization problems. In: IJCAI, pp. 1446–1451 (2007)
20. Petcu, A., Faltings, B.: A scalable method for multiagent constraint optimization. In: IJCAI, pp. 1413–1420 (2005)
21. Petcu, A., Faltings, B., Mailler, R.: PC-DPOP: a new partial centralization algorithm for distributed optimization. In: IJCAI, pp. 167–172 (2007)
22. Rust, P., Picard, G., Ramparany, F.: Using message-passing DCOP algorithms to solve energy-efficient smart environment configuration problems. In: IJCAI, pp. 468–474 (2016)
23. Sandholm, T., Larson, K., Andersson, M., Shehory, O., Tohme, F.: Coalition structure generation with worst case guarantees. Artif. Intell. **111**(1), 209–238 (1999)
24. Shehory, O., Kraus, S.: Methods for task allocation via agent coalition formation. Artif. Intell. **101**(1–2), 165–200 (1998)
25. Voice, T., Polukarov, M., Jennings, N.: Coalition structure generation over graphs. JAIR **45**, 165–196 (2012)
26. Yeoh, W., Felner, A., Koenig, S.: BnB-ADOPT: an asynchronous branch-and-bound DCOP algorithm. JAIR **38**, 85–133 (2010)
27. Yeoh, W., Yokoo, M.: Distributed problem solving. AI Mag. **33**(3), 53–65 (2012)
28. Zhang, W., Wang, G., Xing, Z., Wittenberg, L.: Distributed stochastic search and distributed breakout: properties, comparison and applications to constraint optimization problems in sensor networks. Artif. Intell. **161**(1–2), 55–87 (2005)
29. Zivan, R., Okamoto, S., Peled, H.: Explorative anytime local search for distributed constraint optimization. AI J. **212**, 1–26 (2014)

Computers That Negotiate on Our Behalf: Major Challenges for Self-sufficient, Self-directed, and Interdependent Negotiating Agents

Tim Baarslag[1]([⊠]), Michael Kaisers[1], Enrico H. Gerding[2],
Catholijn M. Jonker[3,4], and Jonathan Gratch[5]

[1] Intelligent and Autonomous Systems Group,
Centrum Wiskunde & Informatica, Amsterdam, The Netherlands
T.Baarslag@cwi.nl
[2] Agents, Interaction and Complexity Group,
University of Southampton, Southampton, UK
[3] Interactive Intelligence Group, Delft University of Technology,
Delft, The Netherlands
[4] LIACS, Leiden University, Leiden, The Netherlands
[5] Institute for Creative Technologies, University of Southern California,
Playa Vista, CA, USA

Abstract. Computers that negotiate on our behalf hold great promise for the future and will even become indispensable in emerging application domains such as the smart grid, autonomous driving, and the Internet of Things. Much research has thus been expended to create agents that are able to negotiate in an abundance of circumstances. However, up until now, truly autonomous negotiators have rarely been deployed in real-world applications. This paper sizes up current negotiating agents and explores a number of technological, societal and ethical challenges that autonomous negotiation systems are bringing about. The questions we address are: in what sense are these systems autonomous, what has been holding back their further proliferation, and is their spread something we should encourage? We relate the automated negotiation research agenda to dimensions of autonomy and distill three major themes that we believe will propel autonomous negotiation forward: accurate representation, long-term perspective, and user trust. We argue these orthogonal research directions need to be aligned and advanced in unison to sustain tangible progress in the field.

1 Introduction

Negotiation, the process of joint decision making, is pervasive in our society [35]. Whenever actors meet and influence each other to forge a mutually beneficial agreement, a form of negotiation is at work [76].

Negotiation arises in almost every social and organizational setting, yet many avoid it out of fear or lack of skill and this contributes to income inequality [9],

© Springer International Publishing AG 2017
G. Sukthankar and J. A. Rodriguez-Aguilar (Eds.): AAMAS 2017 Visionary Papers,
LNAI 10643, pp. 143–163, 2017.
https://doi.org/10.1007/978-3-319-71679-4_10

political gridlock [34] and social injustice [26]. This has led to an increasing focus on the design of autonomous negotiators capable of automatically and independently negotiating with others. This interest has been spurred since the beginning of the 1980s with the work of early pioneers such as Smith [66] and Sycara [67].

Automated negotiation research is fueled by a number of benefits that computerized negotiation can offer, including better (win-win) deals, and reduction in time, costs, stress and cognitive effort on the part of the user. Moreover, autonomous negotiation will soon become not just desired but *required* in instances where the human scale is simply too slow and expensive. For instance, with the world-wide deployment of the smart electrical grid and the must for renewable energy sources, flexible devices in our household will soon (re-)negotiate complex energy contracts automatically. Another example is the rise of the Internet of Things (IoT), which will introduce countless smart, interconnected devices that autonomously negotiate the usage of sensitive data and make trade-offs between privacy concerns, price, and convenience.

To properly fulfill its representational role in an ever-dynamic environment, a negotiation agent has to balance and adhere to different aspects of autonomous behavior, including self-reliance and the capability and freedom to perform its actions, while at the same time remaining interdependent in its joint activity with the user. While many successes have been achieved in advancing various degrees of autonomy in negotiating agents, it is readily apparent that fully-deployed and truly autonomous negotiators are still a thing of the future. Continued development will be required before agents will be able to forge even mundane agreements such as the personalized renewal of our energy or mobile phone contracts. This begs the obvious question: what is still lacking currently and what is needed for autonomous negotiators to be able to fulfill their promise?

This paper discusses the challenges and upcoming application domains for (almost) entirely autonomous negotiation on people's behalf, extending the vision set out in [8]. We describe the technological challenges associated with these future domains and provide a roadmap towards full autonomy, together with stops along the way, highlighting what we deem important solution concepts for enabling future autonomous negotiation systems. As a basis for our discussion, we provide a unifying view of autonomous negotiation based on three orthogonal dimensions of autonomy that research has focused on so far: being self-sufficient, self-directed, and interdependent. We argue that automated negotiation opportunities of tomorrow are calling for a combined effort to address these three pillars of a negotiator's autonomy.

This paper does not aim to survey all research or challenges in the field comprehensively, but rather presents pointers to what we consider important focal points for autonomous negotiation, now and in the future. We pinpoint and elaborate on the following major challenges for autonomous negotiation:

1. Domain knowledge and preference elicitation;
2. Long-term perspective; and
3. User trust and adoption.

Lastly, this paper also pays homage to the 2001 landmark publication by Jennings et al. [42] and asks what has happened, 16 years later, with the prospects and challenges of automated negotiation. We examine which main challenges have been addressed, and which stay relevant in a world that offers more opportunities for automated negotiation than ever before.

2   The Autonomy Diagonal of Negotiation

Autonomous negotiation is more than just *automated* negotiation; it is the freedom to negotiate independently. Rather than being uni-dimensional, autonomy incorporates at least two components [14]: *self-sufficiency* (the capability of the actor to take care of itself) and *self-directedness* (the freedom to act within the environment and the means to reach goals). Following [44] we distinguish a third dimension called *support for interdependence* – being able to work with others and influence and be influenced by team members.[1]

We can distinguish three strands of research in automated negotiation that each cluster around one of the three dimensions of autonomy (Fig. 1):

Self-sufficient: **Game theoretical approaches and trading bots.** The theory of games is a principal tool for studying negotiation and bargaining [72,76]. Game theory's dominant concern is with fully rational players and what each should optimally do. This approach is therefore called *symmetrically prescriptive* [63]. The focus is on either equilibrium strategies or protocols that can guarantee a good outcome for both players through mechanism design [76]. Agents have a reduced scope for self-directedness in such settings, as they are relatively simple and need to conform to certain strategies (e.g. to bid truthfully in an auction). Similarly, real-world trading bots mostly employ simple rule-based functions which have been hard-coded in advance. Examples of this type are among the most advanced autonomous negotiators in terms of self-sufficiency, such as high frequency trading agents for financial and advertising exchanges, and sniping agents used in eBay that place bids at the last possible second [39]. While these approaches are able to function without human intervention and can be highly self-sufficient, they are constrained in terms of freedom to direct the process.

Self-directed: **Negotiation analytical approaches.** Negotiation analysis *prescribes* how players should act given a *description* of how others will act. That is, this field is concerned with an *asymmetrical prescriptive/descriptive* view of autonomous negotiation [63]. Much research on what are often dubbed simply 'negotiation agents' (or 'heuristics' in game theory literature) falls into

---

[1] Note that the notion of autonomy is notoriously difficult to capture (see [44] for an overview). We are concerned here with those aspects especially relevant for negotiation and for their autonomy in relation to their environment; an alternative, more self-contained definition, for example, is an agent's ability to generate its own goals [51].

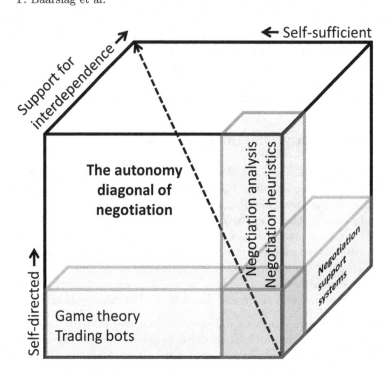

Fig. 1. By and large, negotiation research can be clustered around one of the three main orthogonal dimensions of autonomy: *self-sufficiency*, *self-directedness*, and *interdependence*. The efforts of the three need to be integrated to arrive at truly autonomous negotiators that can progress along the *autonomy diagonal*.

this category; e.g. all negotiation agents from the annual automated negotiation competition [5]. A key feature of this approach is the agent's ability to make judgment calls without intervention (i.e. to construct beliefs based on partial information and act in best response to these beliefs, typically over opponent types or strategies), while the agent's preferences are often considered externally given. This locates the negotiation analytical approach around the self-directed axis.

Interdependent: **Negotiation support systems.** Negotiation support systems are designed to assist and train people in negotiation. Some of these systems, such as the Inspire system [45], have been widely employed in real-life. However, while negotiation support systems enable interdependence by design, humans predominately supervise and make decisions on the appropriate outcome, which results in low self-sufficiency and self-directedness.

As can be gleaned from the fields indicated above, autonomous negotiation has garnered attention from different research directions and has managed to advance in key aspects of autonomous behavior. As a result, we now have negotiators that exist independently of their owner in the real world, delegated with a gamut of available strategies to freely choose among, and with the ability to engage in supportive interdependence; *just not all at the same time.*

The varied set of requirements for adequately autonomous negotiation may explain why it has proven difficult to extend the progress made in this field to truly representative negotiating agents. Of course we acknowledge that to a lesser degree, combined work on all dimensions has been performed (as depicted by the three-colored cube in Fig. 1); we simply argue that the main automated negotiation research lines have developed in parallel to one of the three autonomy directions. Research-wise, it is unquestionably a sound strategy to first explore the autonomy axes in separation. As Fig. 1 suggests, we can make substantive progress in autonomous negotiation by continuing to advance along *the autonomy diagonal*, which has inspired the focal points of the challenges we present in the next section (as summarized in Table 1).

Table 1. Overview of major challenges in autonomous negotiation and the main dimensions of autonomy to which they relate. Each challenge is subdivided in building blocks along with a solution roadmap and illustrative example applications.

Domain knowledge and preference elicitation (Sect. 3.1)
Addressing *self-sufficiency* & *interdependence*

Building blocks	Solutions roadmap	Applications
Preference elicitation on-the-fly	Value of information indicators, robust performance estimates	Privacy and IoT
Domain modeling	Separate user/agent domain models, expert mappings	Smart grids

Long-term perspective (Sect. 3.2)
Addressing *self-sufficiency* & *self-directedness*

Building blocks	Solutions roadmap	Applications
Repeated interactions	Temporally integrative negotiations, reputation metrics	Communities, smart homes, autonomous driving
Non-stationary preferences	Cost-efficient tracking, context-dependent models, preference dynamics	B2B, entertainment booking

User trust and adoption (Sect. 3.3)
Addressing *self-directedness* & *interdependence*

Building blocks	Solutions roadmap	Applications
Acceptability and participation	Co-creation, adjustable autonomy, transfer of control	Conflict resolution, customer retainment
Transparent consequences	Transparency and openness, worst-case bounds, risk measures	Sharing economy, decentralized marketplaces

3   Major Challenges

The various aspects of autonomy drive three major open challenges for autonomous negotiation, of which the overall theme can be summarized as *trusted and sustained representation*. We describe the challenges and their building blocks below, together with a number of explicit opportunities in each case (see Table 1 for an overview).

Note that many of these challenges intersect and cannot be entirely untangled; for example, adequate user preference extraction will not only increase the user model accuracy, but may also boost user trust. Therefore, just like autonomy itself, each challenge outlined here is *multi-dimensional*; i.e., each challenge pertains to at least two dimensions of autonomy, thereby providing the impetus to further advance along the autonomy diagonal.

3.1   Domain Knowledge and Preference Elicitation

A *negotiation domain* typically admits contracts that consist of multiple issues (e.g. price, amount, quality of service). The specific structure of a domain together with the *user preferences* associated with its outcomes (prescribed by e.g. a utility function or outcome orderings [4]) forms a *negotiation scenario*.

Individual preferences over specific scenarios provide the opportunity for joint improvement and trade-offs [19]. The co-dependence between user and agent requires that they synchronize their negotiation scenario model, which can be enhanced by imparting the agent with accurate and timely user preferences about the negotiation process and co-constructing the real-world intricacies of the domain.

Preference Elicitation On-the-Fly. In order to faithfully represent the user, an autonomous negotiator needs to engage with the user to make sure it constructs an accurate preference model (see e.g. [40]). However, users are often unwilling or unable to engage with a negotiation system, and hence prudence needs to be exercised when interacting with the user to avoid elicitation fatigue. This is especially important in domains where people are notably reluctant to engage with the system at length, for instance in privacy negotiations.

As a consequence, automated negotiators of the future are required to not only strike deals with limited available user information, but also to assess which additional information should be elicited from the user, while minimizing user bother [6]. This challenge is still as relevant (and for the most part still unaddressed) as when it was raised by Jennings et al. in [42]. However, as a way forward, we believe future research should particularly emphasize *preference elicitation on-the-fly* [7]: that is, active preference extraction *during* negotiation(s) (see Fig. 2). Potential benefits include a significantly reduced initial preference elicitation phase (which can otherwise be a nuisance in many negotiation support systems) and the ability to select the most informative query to pose to

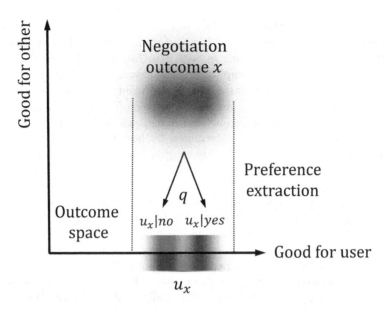

Fig. 2. A representative agent has a high uncertainty about the utility u_x of a negotiation outcome $x \in \Omega$ (in purple, prior to posing a query). Preference extraction through a query q (e.g. "is $u_x > 0.5$?") can reduce this uncertainty, against certain user bother cost, by distinguishing between bad outcomes ($u_x \mid no$, in red) and good ones ($u_x \mid yes$, in blue). (Color figure online)

the user at the most relevant time. For example, while negotiating, the system could dynamically decide to ask the user to rate specific negotiation outcomes, or to compare two of them.

To facilitate this, new performance-based metrics are required that can assess how supplementary preference information influences negotiation performance. Adaptive utility elicitation models provide a good starting point for representing probabilistic utility-based preferences that allow for incremental updating over time (e.g. by using Bayesian reasoning), in the vein of work by Chajewska et al. [16]. To continuously balance the expected negotiation payoff with the potential benefit of performing additional elicitation, the viability of a negotiation query can for instance be measured in terms of the expected value of information [12] in order to assess the marginal utility of altering belief states and to decide if a query is worth posing.

Another challenge is for a negotiation strategy to decide on actions effectively in light of its imprecise information state. Techniques for decision making under uncertainty could assist in this and could thereby give rise to novel negotiation strategy concepts, for instance by incorporating the notion of expected *expected* utility [13] to express the expected negotiation payoff over all possible instantiations of the user model.

Note that the above discussion largely follows the standard assumptions of rational choice theory: i.e. that people's preferences can be accurately elicited.

Most approaches adopt the perspective that the value of possible agreements is expressible by a (relatively) time- and context-invariant utility function over material outcomes – we revisit this in Sect. 3.2. Unfortunately, several idiosyncrasies of human psychology complicate these assumptions. While preference-elicitation methods can often extract coherent utility functions that capture people's rankings over possible agreements, people often have difficulty explicitly expressing their preferences. Further, a person's willingness to accept an agreement is also only partially determined by how they feel about the final agreement; these feelings are also highly sensitive to contextual factors, such as how the deal is reached and how it is described. Research on human negotiation emphasizes that people attend to many factors besides the final outcome, as identified, for example, by Curhan's Subjective Value Inventory [20].

Research also illustrates that elicited utility functions are highly sensitive to subtle contextual factors. For example, *framing effects* emphasize that preferences between outcomes can reverse depending on whether they are seen as losses or gains with respect to some reference point [70]. In a negotiation, the reference point is often the perceived value that the other party receives, even though this knowledge does not change the individual's objective outcome. As a result, outcomes can be readily manipulated simply by changing the form and nature of information conveyed [31]. More broadly, valuations in a negotiation are shaped by emotion, including emotions that arise from the process, but also beliefs about what other parties feel (see, e.g., [10]). Given the highly context-sensitive nature of on-the-fly preference elicitation, such considerations will have to be taken into account in its design and implementation.

Domain Modeling. The quality of the negotiation outcome depends not only on the faithfulness of the preference model of an autonomous negotiator, but also on the accuracy of the domain model. The old 'garbage in, garbage out' truism applies here, as the quality of the offered solution depends so heavily on a correct domain description.

However, domain modeling, and certainly formal modeling, is an expertise that cannot be expected from an arbitrary user. Therefore, users require either expert guidance, or explicit domain modeling support. Modeling in close cooperation with a domain expert runs the risk of perpetuating people's uncertainty about the model, thereby limiting their ability to make necessary adjustments. When modeling support is provided by the system, the knowledge representation language used will be inherently simple as it has to be understood by arbitrary negotiators. This is especially important in domains where users can employ automated negotiation without any expertise, such as in the smart grid, which can result in the wrong evaluation of bids. Highly accurate models, on the other hand, also have their disadvantages: they can display complex non-linearities [41,50], in which case even assessing the utility of a proposal can prove NP-hard [21].

This inspires the following open research question: what is the impact of simplifying the domain and preference models to facilitate layman understanding?

An answer might come from using two models, as suggested in [37]: an accurate, but complex model that serves as a reference for the agent, and a more comprehensive one for interacting with the user. Proper clarification and explanation could then be elicited from a process of co-creation [62] or participatory design [65] between modeling experts and domain experts. Ideally, a reflection phase should be included during and after negotiations, in which the human (and perhaps eventually the agent) can provide feedback to allow for long-term co-evolution.

The above points also apply to the appropriateness and understandability of the *negotiation protocol*, which governs the rules of the negotiation. A pre-negotiation phase provides the opportunity for the negotiation parties to engage in a debate about what protocol to employ and how to enforce the rules. To reduce the chance of parties exploiting loopholes in the rules, horizontal governance [68] approaches can be employed. Such techniques are applied in border customs regulations, where the responsibility for fairness is carried by all participants. A corresponding challenge is to construct a best practice repository for negotiation techniques [42]. This has been tackled at least partially through recent efforts in creating a negotiation handbook for negotiation protocols [52].

Whatever approach is chosen, experts in formal modeling will be needed to instantiate a domain model that sufficiently captures all salient features. Those experts are pivotal to the negotiation agent business model and will be responsible for mapping user-understandable interests to the negotiation issues within complex domains. These are likely to become future jobs; i.e., real estate agents informing procurement agents of the future. Relevant research areas, and courses for training these experts, will be on collaborative and supportive modeling.

3.2 Long-Term Perspective

Given the effort involved in domain modeling and preference elicitation, the opportunities for automated negotiation are even clearer in long-term scenarios where an agent frequently faces similar negotiation situations. Most research on negotiation agents, however, has focused on single encounters. The different challenges and opportunities for such long-term negotiations hinge on the volatility of both the opponent pool and the user's preferences.

Repeated Encounters. Given the efforts required to obtain an accurate user model, the benefits of autonomous agents become especially apparent when repeatedly dealing with similar situations, as is the case when negotiating multiple times with the same set of opponents. Indeed, there are many promising opportunities for applying negotiation in such repeated encounters. For example, in community energy exchange [2], agents can trade energy from storage and local renewable sources between neighboring homes and businesses to reduce peaks, carbon emissions and the load on the local network. These interactions would occur on a daily basis or even more frequently. Another example is the smart home, where different occupants have different needs and preferences and have to reach mutual agreements, e.g. about the trade-off between comfort and energy cost [59] and the use of IoT devices [57]. Other settings, in which the agent faces many different opponents, include self-driving vehicles, where vehicle-to-vehicle and vehicle-to-infrastructure negotiation will play an important role by, e.g., negotiating priority at intersections [71].

Negotiation opportunities for isolated encounters can be very limited, since often a resource (e.g. electricity or giving way) is needed without necessarily offering anything immediately in return (except possibly money or virtual currencies). In a single negotiation, the only truly interesting interactions revolve around multi-issue negotiation in which trade-offs can be made between the parties varying interests. However, explicitly considering the *temporal dimension* allows agents to receive or concede something now in return for conceding or receiving the same resource later. In other words, sequential, distributive negotiations can be turned into richer, multi-issue, integrative negotiations, with more scope to achieve win-win solutions (as presented in [53]; see Fig. 3). This is entirely analogous to how in single negotiations, package deals are more efficient than settling the issues independently due to the possibility of making fair trade-offs across issues [27]. Or likewise, how economic efficiency is enhanced when combinations of assets rather than individual items are considered [23]. By carefully bundling interdependent issues together, the exponential complexity of the resulting outcome space can in principle be mitigated (see e.g. [32]).

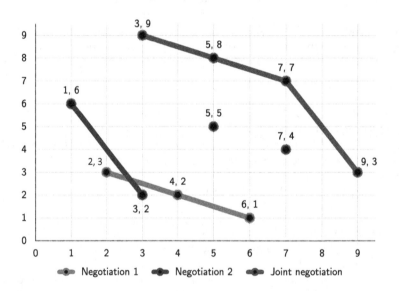

Fig. 3. By considering the Cartesian product of the outcome spaces, two sequential, distributive negotiations (one with 2 outcomes, in red; one with 3 outcomes, in blue) can be transformed to produce one integrative negotiation (with 6 outcomes, in purple). (Color figure online)

Another significant challenge for long-term reciprocal encounters is that future needs are often uncertain, and so it is difficult to commit to giving up or requesting specific future resources. Possible solutions involve money or virtual currencies which can be redeemed at a later stage and can undergo temporal discounting if necessary, but they do not take advantage of the distributive nature of multi-issue negotiation. They also introduce additional challenges: using actual money requires an exchange rate with the resources involved (and other dimensions such as the scarcity at the time they are requested), while it may not be desirable to introduce money in certain settings; e.g. when they rely, to some degree, on unincentivized cooperation and altruistic behavior. Virtual currencies (including distributed ledger approaches) can be traded bilaterally in a "like for like" manner, addressing the exchange problem, but then other issues arise, e.g. how much of a currency each agent receives to begin with, and what happens if an agent runs out.

Another possible solution is to rely on altruism and using trust ratings and reputation metrics to provide the desired incentives (e.g. using favors and ledgers [53]). In such cases, 'altruism' can be a self-interested strategy if this is reciprocated at a later state, possibly involving a different opponent. While reputation mechanisms are well-known to incentivize cooperation in the prisoner's dilemma, more research on this is needed in the context of (repeated) automated negotiation.

Unfortunately, negotiation methods that seek to establish a value-creating relationship by identifying efficient and fair (e.g., envy-free) agreements face, in addition to the above, a number of *psychological* challenges. People adopt a variety of interpretations as to what is fair and negotiations often involve disputes over which principle to apply [73]. For example, in the context of organ donation, the *equity principle* would allocate resources on the basis of ability, effort or merit, the *equality rule* would treat individuals the same, whereas the *principle of need* is achieved by allocating according to individuals medical condition, socio-economical status or other relevant needs. Even people's willingness to engage in negotiation is shaped by their views toward these principles [55]. Other complications involve moral constraints on certain exchanges. For example, it is considered morally repugnant to exchange money for bodily organs, so an agreement that combines material interests with sacred values may be seen as substantially worse than an independent evaluation of these elements would suggest [24].

Although these challenges might seem insurmountable, there are several ways to incorporate these biases into conventional computational methods. One approach is to incorporate psychological factors into the utility function, which can be done without violating the basic tenets of utility theory [28]. Some of the challenges with fairness can be addressed by making the process more transparent (Sect. 3.3). Another approach is to incorporate modest psychological extensions to rational methods. For example, framing effects can be handled through the use of prospect theory (e.g., [75]).

Non-stationary Preferences. While short-lived instantiations of representational agents may assume that there are some true and stationary preferences to be elicited from the user, in long-term negotiations, these very preferences may evolve over the course of weeks or months according to certain *preference dynamics*. For example, exposure to the view of wind generators can impact the preference profile over various renewable generation types [47]. This is related to the machine learning notion of *concept drift*, which expresses that statistical properties of a target variable (e.g. in a data stream) may change over time, possibly *abruptly* or *gradually*, which makes modeling challenging [69].

If an autonomous negotiator acts on elicited information for an extended period of time without accounting for existing drift in preferences, it may erroneously fulfill outdated design objectives. This leads to a plunge in user trust and adoption, or a de-facto shortened time of deployment. This is a typical example of opacity that can result from an excess of unchecked autonomy [56]. As a result, long-term negotiation requires increased co-dependence at the cost of throttled-down self-directedness; e.g., by repeated assessment of the preference representation quality, with intermittent elicitation actions whenever their anticipated benefits exceed their costs.

It is important to distinguish *complex preference models* from *dynamic preferences*, albeit the two provide complementary views on the same process. In representational negotiation, the target is to accurately model the users preferences, which may be elicited at a cost, and which the user applies to judge the agent's performance. The user may perceive an exogenous evolution in her preferences (e.g., in risk tolerance or fairness attitudes), or update her preferences actively based on experience – she thus maintains dynamic preferences, that may themselves be *learned* over time. In contrast, the agent may employ a complex preference model, describing user preferences dependent on possibly uncertain user state variables. Changes in user preference may thus be ascribed to updates in the belief over the user's state, based on dynamics or observed information. The crucial deviation from previous approaches is an acknowledgment of the possibility that preferences may not settle, but remain in a state of flux. Tracking can mitigate the effects of evolving negotiation preferences in order to facilitate sustained representation [15].

Assuming non-stationary preferences reframes the challenge posed in Sect. 3.1 of preference elicitation to *cost-efficient tracking of non-stationary preferences* in long-term negotiation. Possible applications range from secretary tasks (e.g., 'book a restaurant/hotel/holiday') to representational business-to-business (B2B) negotiations [58]. Inspiration for tackling this challenge may come from the area of news recommender systems, which has embraced context-dependent models [1] and preference dynamics [48] in response to the inherent need to capture fast-paced preference evolution. Such models have promising merit for being transferred to negotiation strategies that balance the preciseness of preference representation with relevant and timely but costly elicitation, extending preliminary work in that area [7]. Reinforcement learning techniques could provide another possible route way by which to deal with this challenge by extending research into negotiation with non-stationary opponents [36,54].

Beyond the passive modeling of dynamic user preferences, an opportunity for *managing user preferences* arises once a model of the user preference dynamics is available, e.g. through nudges and manipulation of cognitive biases [11,30]. If preferences are learned, then the agent can choose to guide the user's experience (with intermediate results of negotiated outcomes) to promote certain preference profiles for which higher utility can be achieved in the long run.

3.3   User Trust and Adoption

While the agent depends on the user for knowledge and guidance (as described in Sect. 3.1), the user relies on a self-directed agent for a good outcome. To alleviate unwillingness to relinquish control and to guarantee user satisfaction with and adherence to the final outcome, the user needs to trust the system through co-participation, transparency, and proper representation.

User Participation. Lessons learned from collaborative human-robot teams indicate that it is important to be able to escalate to the meta-level (i.e. have humans participate) when necessary [43]. The need for escalating to a higher authority applies whenever a negotiator represents a group or a company (e.g., a union, or stakeholder organizations in general). In such cases, the negotiator can only make deals that fall within certain margins. Take, for example, a helpdesk operator with a telecom provider, authorized to offer new deals on a contract renewal. She has only limited freedom in terms of the bounded range of possible deals she can sign off on; in fact, she does not even really possess the freedom to decide *whether* to negotiate. In case of doubt, the decision is escalated to a different authority level.

Similar to preference elicitation on-the-fly, user escalation should only occur through a minimum number of timely and pertinent questions (cf. [17,46,60]). As automated negotiators become more general and domain-independent [49], the need for a co-active design increases; i.e. one that requires the automated negotiator to be aware of the strengths and weaknesses of itself and that of the user, together with the ability to enhance the team model with domain-specific knowledge, preferred strategies, and interpretation of incoming bids.

The idea of collaborative control, or mixed-initiative control (see e.g. [29,43]) might become essential to achieve the best outcome in complex, real-life negotiations. In this envisioned line of research, each negotiation party consists of at least one human and one negotiation agent. The agent should do the brunt of the negotiation work to find possible agreements with the other negotiation parties and which can presented to their human partners for feedback and new input, which necessitates an understanding of their behavior [33], attitudes [77], and preferred interaction method [61]. The research challenge is to determine when, how, and how often to switch the initiative from human to agent and vice versa.

Transparent Consequences. There exists an inherent tension between increased self-directedness and trust, which dampens the adoption of increasingly autonomous negotiators: on the one hand, an autonomous negotiatior's relevance is directly proportional to its ability to impact the user independently in meaningful ways (e.g. fiscal, well-being, reputation, and so on); but, in turn, the user's trust and willingness to relinquish control is conditional on understanding the agent's reasoning and consequences of its actions. The two can be reconciled by making the outcome space more *transparent* to the user, and by enabling the user to specify the permissible means in the form of *principles*. The challenge is that the negotiation agent's reasoning abilities may very well exceed the domain insights of a nonspecialist user, thus requiring a translation from stochastic performance models of self-directed expert reasoning into laymen terms that adequately convey expectations and risks.

Note that we suggest transparency as the key concept here, which subsumes Jennings' notion of predictability [42]. Predictability is essential towards the user to instill trust, but can be disastrous towards the opponent because of the potential for exploitability. Unpredictable behavior is in fact desirable as a negotiation tactic as a confusing and randomization device, as long as the consequences are transparently explained to the user.

The uncertainty inherent in negotiation can be captured in performance models and risk metrics, where the complexity should be scaled to the criticality of the consequences for the user. If the performance intervals are sub-critical, then simple guarantees on the range of possible outcomes may suffice (such as price bounds provided by Uber for individual rides), leaving it up to the user to build and judge the average performance model; otherwise, measures of risk are required, such as Conditional Value at Risk (CVar) [64].

4   Concluding Observations

Autonomous systems that are capable of negotiating on our behalf are among society's key technological challenges for the near future, and their uptake is important for many critical economical application areas. In this paper, we present a roadmap to arrive at representative and trusted negotiators that are endowed with a long-term perspective. By continuing along this trajectory, negotiation research can address perhaps the biggest challenge of all: a co-active approach that can propel swift adoption of computerized negotiation by simultaneously advancing the autonomy of a negotiation agent in all its aspects.

On the other hand, the sensitive nature of negotiation requires keeping a watchful eye for potentially adverse effects of increased computer autonomy. For instance, autonomous negotiators need to encapsulate information locally as part of their decentralized nature, which entails an inherent privacy risk. Privacy concerns can be important enough to restrict negotiation information flow to representative entities (as illustrated, for instance, by the leaked memo controversy of Brexit negotiators [74]). This also means that even when it is possible from a user's comfort level, it is not necessarily desired to extract the maximum user knowledge possible. This reiterates the need for improved measures for the value of information in negotiation; e.g. a metric that encapsulates the increased value of accurate preference estimates to reach win-win outcomes. For example, if a desire for maternity leave is inconsequential to the outcome (e.g. when it is not part of the contract), it does not need to be known by the agent.

Another consideration is when negotiation (in the sense of exchanging offers and counter offers) is the appropriate choice, and when other mechanisms can or should be used. Often alternatives are available that could be more efficient or simpler to use. These include auctions, which are especially fitting in cases of competing settings and resource allocation problems, and voting protocols, which are a good way of reaching agreements when a consensus is needed. These approaches are often used in settings with only one issue to decide on (in case of voting), or where the main issue is a monetary payment for a commodity (in case of auctions). Another, much simpler, alternative to negotiation is to offer an exhaustive menu of choices and allow the other player to pick one of these (as in the case of e.g. insurance policies). The advantage of negotiation is the ability to strategize over information revelation and to personalize deals by reaching differentiated agreements over illiquid, customized contracts. If these features of negotiation are not taken advantage of, then other approaches might be preferable.

On a societal level, negotiation has potential benefits and costs. In terms of benefits, negotiation allows for much more efficient allocation of resources than fixed pricing schemes as it optimizes value with respect to an individual's willingness-to-pay [38] rather than appealing to the "average customer". This helps to reach win-win outcomes and to get closer to what economists call first-degree price discrimination. Negotiation has fallen out of favor in wealthier societies because the time and anxiety associated with it, except for very costly transactions such as salary negotiations and home purchases, yet automated negotiation agents can mitigate these concerns and generate value for society as a whole. Widespread adopting of negotiation technology could benefit members of society that are reluctant or unable to negotiate effectively and could potentially address friction costs as well as inequities across society. For example, women are especially averse to negotiating their salaries and this is a major contributor to gender pay inequality [9]. But negotiation technology could be abused in ways that outweigh or even undermine these potential benefits. For example, a benefit of fixed-pricing schemes is that they are transparent and applied uniformly, regardless of a persons gender, race, income, or negotiation skills. Indeed, Amazon's attempts at price discrimination have provoked lawsuits from consumer protection groups for exactly this concern [38]. More broadly, if negotiation agents are only available to the wealthy, they could exacerbate existing societal injustice. Regulations and ethical guidelines are needed to balance these benefits and costs.

In the end, the potency of autonomous negotiators is as much contingent on the acceptance by their users as by their counter-parties. Possible sources of resistance to adoption include established business models based on human inefficiencies (e.g., phone and media contracts) or anti-competitive practices (e.g., proprietary lock-in), which could become invalidated by autonomous (re-)negotiation. The most promising incubators of autonomous negotiators are ecosystems in which autonomous agents provide a unique source of societal value that is distributed over all stakeholders, as in the application of demand response for smart grids. Open platforms for value distribution have recently seen increased attention in flagship applications such as the cryptocurrency *bitcoin* and the decentralized world wide web *Blockstack* [3]. The digital API of these systems offers fertile grounds for a level playing field for competition and may soon provide a common interface for automated negotiators.

Finally, looking even further forward, it is worth noting that people negotiate differently through intermediaries than they would face-to-face. The literature on *representation effects* suggests that people may show less regard for fairness and ethical behavior when negotiating through a third (human) party [18]. Indeed, human lawyers are ethically permitted and, to some extent, expected to lie on behalf of their clients [31]. This raises the question as to whether agents should similarly lie on behalf of a user, e.g. by using argumentation and persuasion technology [25]. Analogous to recent research on ethical dilemmas in self-driving cars, people may claim that negotiation agents should be ethical, but sacrifice these ideals if it maximizes their profits. The natural dichotomy between recognizing the agent's autonomy and taking responsibility for its actions is best resolved by acknowledging user responsibility for the agent's design objectives (what should be achieved) and principles (how it should be achieved, as discussed in Sect. 3.3). This also illustrates an additional impetus for having humans understand the agent: feeling responsibility for the agent's actions implies an understanding what the agent is doing. Fortunately, some recent research on agent negotiators suggests that people may act more ethically when negotiating via computer agents [22], but far more research is needed to understand how *artificial representation effects* arise.

Acknowledgments. This research has received funding through the ERA-Net Smart Grids Plus project Grid-Friends, with support from the European Union's Horizon 2020 research and innovation programme. This work is part of the Veni research programme with project number 639.021.751, which is financed by the Netherlands Organisation for Scientific Research (NWO).

References

1. Adomavicius, G., Tuzhilin, A.: Context-aware recommender systems. In: Ricci, F., Rokach, L., Shapira, B. (eds.) Recommender Systems Handbook, pp. 191–226. Springer, Boston (2015). https://doi.org/10.1007/978-1-4899-7637-6_6
2. Alam, M., Gerding, E.H., Rogers, A., Ramchurn, S.D.: A scalable interdependent multi-issue negotiation protocol for energy exchange. In: 24th International Joint Conference on AI (IJCAI), pp. 1098–1104 (2015)
3. Ali, M., Nelson, J., Shea, R., Freedman, M.J.: Blockstack: a global naming and storage system secured by blockchains. In: 2016 USENIX Annual Technical Conference, pp. 181–194. USENIX Association (2016)

4. Aydoğan, R., Baarslag, T., Hindriks, K.V., Jonker, C.M., Yolum, P.: Heuristics for using CP-nets in utility-based negotiation without knowing utilities. Knowl. Inf. Syst. **45**(2), 357–388 (2015)

5. Baarslag, T., Aydoğan, R., Hindriks, K.V., Fuijita, K., Ito, T., Jonker, C.M.: The automated negotiating agents competition, 2010-2015. AI Mag. **36**(4), 115–118 (2015)

6. Baarslag, T., Gerding, E.H.: Optimal incremental preference elicitation during negotiation. In: Proceedings of the Twenty-Fourth International Joint Conference on Artificial Intelligence, IJCAI 2015, pp. 3–9. AAAI Press (2015)

7. Baarslag, T., Kaisers, M.: The value of information in automated negotiation: a decision model for eliciting user preferences. In: Proceedings of the 16th International Conference on Autonomous Agents and Multiagent Systems, AAMAS 2017. IFAAMAS (2017)

8. Baarslag, T., Kaisers, M., Gerding, E.H., Jonker, C.M., Gratch, J.: When will negotiation agents be able to represent us? The challenges and opportunities for autonomous negotiators. In: Proceedings of the Twenty-Sixth International Joint Conference on Artificial Intelligence, IJCAI 2017 (2017)

9. Babcock, L., Laschever, S.: Women Don't Ask: Negotiation and the Gender Divide. Princeton University Press, Princeton (2009)

10. Barry, B., Fulmer, I.S., Van Kleef, G.A.: I laughed, I cried, I settled: the role of emotion in negotiation. In: The Handbook of Negotiation and Culture, pp. 71–94 (2004)

11. Bazerman, M., Neale, M.: Nonrational escalation of commitment in negotiation. Eur. Manag. J. **10**(2), 163–168 (1992)

12. Boutilier, C.: A POMDP formulation of preference elicitation problems. In: Eighteenth National Conference on Artificial Intelligence, pp. 239–246. American Association for Artificial Intelligence, Menlo Park (2002)

13. Boutilier, C.: On the foundations of expected expected utility. In: Proceedings of the 18th International Joint Conference on Artificial Intelligence, IJCAI 2003, pp. 285–290. Morgan Kaufmann Publishers Inc., San Francisco (2003)

14. Bradshaw, J.M., Feltovich, P.J., Jung, H., Kulkarni, S., Taysom, W., Uszok, A.: Dimensions of adjustable autonomy and mixed-initiative interaction. In: Nickles, M., Rovatsos, M., Weiss, G. (eds.) AUTONOMY 2003. LNCS (LNAI), vol. 2969, pp. 17–39. Springer, Heidelberg (2004). https://doi.org/10.1007/978-3-540-25928-2_3

15. Cadilhac, A., Asher, N., Benamara, F., Lascarides, A.: Grounding strategic conversation: using negotiation dialogues to predict trades in a win-lose game. In: Proceedings of Empirical Methods in Natural Language Processing (EMNLP), pp. 357–368 (2013)

16. Chajewska, U., Koller, D., Parr, R.: Making rational decisions using adaptive utility elicitation. In: Proceedings of the Seventeenth National Conference on Artificial Intelligence, pp. 363–369 (2000)

17. Chu, W., Ghahramani, Z.: Preference learning with Gaussian processes. In: ICML, pp. 137–144 (2005)

18. Chugh, D., Bazerman, M.H., Banaji, M.R.: Bounded ethicality as a psychological barrier to recognizing conflicts of interest. In: Conflicts of Interest: Challenges and Solutions in Business, Law, Medicine, and Public Policy, pp. 74–95 (2005)

19. Coehoorn, R.M., Jennings, N.R.: Learning on opponent's preferences to make effective multi-issue negotiation trade-offs. In: Proceedings of the 6th International Conference on Electronic Commerce, ICEC 2004, pp. 59–68. ACM, New York (2004)

20. Curhan, J.R., Elfenbein, H.A., Xu, H.: What do people value when they negotiate? Mapping the domain of subjective value in negotiation. J. Pers. Soc. Psychol. **91**(3), 493 (2006)

21. de Jonge, D., Sierra, C., Sabaté, J.G.: Negotiations over large agreement spaces. Ph.D. thesis (2015)

22. de Melo, C.M., Marsella, S., Gratch, J.: Do as I say, not as I do: challenges in delegating decisions to automated agents. In: Proceedings of the 2016 International Conference on Autonomous Agents and Multiagent Systems, pp. 949–956. IFAAMAS (2016)

23. de Vries, S., Vohra, R.V.: Combinatorial auctions: a survey. Inf. J. Comput. **15**(3), 284–309 (2003)

24. Dehghani, M., Atran, S., Iliev, R., Sachdeva, S., Medin, D., Ginges, J.: Sacred values and conflict over Iran's nuclear program. Judgment Decis. Making **5**(7), 540 (2010)

25. Dimopoulos, Y., Moraitis, P.: Advances in argumentation based negotiation. In: Negotiation and Argumentation in Multi-agent Systems: Fundamentals, Theories, Systems and Applications, pp. 82–125 (2014)

26. Eisenberg, T., Lanvers, C.: What is the settlement rate and why should we care? J. Empirical Legal Stud. **6**(1), 111–146 (2009)

27. Fatima, S.S., Wooldridge, M., Jennings, N.R.: On efficient procedures for multi-issue negotiation. In: Fasli, M., Shehory, O. (eds.) TADA/AMEC 2006. LNCS (LNAI), vol. 4452, pp. 31–45. Springer, Heidelberg (2007). https://doi.org/10.1007/978-3-540-72502-2_3

28. Fehr, E., Schmidt, K.M.: The economics of fairness, reciprocity and altruism–experimental evidence and new theories. In: Handbook of the Economics of Giving, Altruism and Reciprocity, vol. 1, pp. 615–691 (2006)

29. Fong, T., Thorpe, C., Baur, C.: Collaborative control: a robot-centric model for vehicle teleoperation, vol. 1. Carnegie Mellon University, The Robotics Institute (2001)

30. Gelfand, M.J., Brett, J.M.: The Handbook of Negotiation and Culture. Stanford University Press, Stanford (2004)

31. Gratch, J., Nazari, Z., Johnson, E.: The misrepresentation game: how to win at negotiation while seeming like a nice guy. In: Proceedings of the 2016 International Conference on Autonomous Agents and Multiagent Systems, pp. 728–737. IFAAMAS (2016)

32. Hadfi, R., Ito, T.: Modeling complex nonlinear utility spaces using utility hyper-graphs. In: Torra, V., Narukawa, Y., Endo, Y. (eds.) MDAI 2014. LNCS (LNAI), vol. 8825, pp. 14–25. Springer, Cham (2014). https://doi.org/10.1007/978-3-319-12054-6_2

33. Haim, G., Gal, Y.K., Gelfand, M., Kraus, S.: A cultural sensitive agent for human-computer negotiation. In: Proceedings of the 11th International Conference on Autonomous Agents and Multiagent Systems - AAMAS 2012, Richland, SC, vol. 1, pp. 451–458. IFAAMAS (2012)

34. Hall, R.L.: Measuring legislative influence. Legislative Stud. Q. **17**, 205–231 (1992)

35. Harris, K.L.: Content analysis in negotiation research: a review and guide. Behav. Res. Meth. Instrum. Comput. **28**(3), 458–467 (1996)

36. Hernandez-Leal, P., Zhan, Y., Taylor, M.E., Enrique Sucar, L., de Cote, E.M.: An exploration strategy for non-stationary opponents. Auton. Agents Multi Agent Syst. **31**(5), 971–1002 (2017)

37. Hindriks, K., Jonker, C., Tykhonov, D.: Avoiding approximation errors in multi-issue negotiation with issue dependencies. In: Proceedings of the 1st International Workshop on Agent-based Complex Automated Negotiations (ACAN 2008), pp. 1347–1352 (2008)
38. Hinz, O., Hann, I.-H., Spann, M.: Price discrimination in e-commerce? An examination of dynamic pricing in name-your-own price markets. MIS Q. **35**(1), 81–98 (2011)
39. Hu, W., Bolivar, A.: Online auctions efficiency: a survey of eBay auctions. In: WWW, pp. 925–934 (2008)
40. Hunter, A.: Modelling the persuadee in asymmetric argumentation dialogues for persuasion. In: Proceedings of the 24th International Conference on Artificial Intelligence, IJCAI 2015, pp. 3055–3061. AAAI Press (2015)
41. Ito, T., Klein, M., Hattori, H.: A multi-issue negotiation protocol among agents with nonlinear utility functions. Multiagent Grid Syst. **4**(1), 67–83 (2008)
42. Jennings, N.R., Faratin, P., Lomuscio, A.R., Parsons, S., Wooldridge, M.J., Sierra, C.: Automated negotiation: prospects, methods and challenges. Group Decis. Negot. **10**(2), 199–215 (2001)
43. Johnson, M., Bradshaw, J.M., Feltovich, P.J., Jonker, C., van Riemsdijk, B., Sierhuis, M.: Autonomy and interdependence in human-agent-robot teams. IEEE Intell. Syst. **27**(2), 43–51 (2012)
44. Johnson, M., Bradshaw, J.M., Feltovich, P.J., Jonker, C.M., van Riemsdijk, B., Sierhuis, M.: The fundamental principle of coactive design: interdependence must shape autonomy. In: De Vos, M., Fornara, N., Pitt, J.V., Vouros, G. (eds.) COIN 2010. LNCS (LNAI), vol. 6541, pp. 172–191. Springer, Heidelberg (2011). https://doi.org/10.1007/978-3-642-21268-0_10
45. Kersten, G.E., Lo, G.: Negotiation support systems and software agents in e-business negotiations. In: The First International Conference on Electronic Business, Hong Kong, pp. 19–21, December 2001
46. Kingsley, D.C.: Preference uncertainty, preference refinement and paired comparison choice experiments. University of Colorado (2006)
47. Ladenburg, J.: Dynamic properties of the preferences for renewable energy sources a wind power experience-based approach. Energy **76**, 542–551 (2014)
48. Li, L., Zheng, L., Yang, F., Li, T.: Modeling and broadening temporal user interest in personalized news recommendation. Expert Syst. Appl. **41**(7), 3168–3177 (2014)
49. Lin, R., Kraus, S., Baarslag, T., Tykhonov, D., Hindriks, K.V., Jonker, C.M.: Genius: an integrated environment for supporting the design of generic automated negotiators. Comput. Intell. **30**(1), 48–70 (2014)
50. Lopez-Carmona, M.A., Marsa-Maestre, I., Klein, M., Ito, T.: Addressing stability issues in mediated complex contract negotiations for constraint-based, non-monotonic utility spaces. Auton. Agents Multi Agent Syst. **24**(3), 485–535 (2012)
51. Luck, M., D'Inverno, M., Munroe, S.: Autonomy: Variable and Generative, pp. 11–28. Springer, Boston (2003)
52. Marsa-Maestre, I., Klein, M., Jonker, C.M., Aydoğan, R.: From problems to protocols: towards a negotiation handbook. Decis. Support Syst. **60**, 39–54 (2014)
53. Mell, J., Lucas, G., Gratch, J.: An effective conversation tactic for creating value over repeated negotiations. In: Proceedings of the 2015 International Conference on Autonomous Agents and Multiagent Systems, AAMAS 2015, Richland, SC, pp. 1567–1576. IFAAMAS (2015)
54. Narayanan, V., Jennings, N.: Learning to negotiate optimally in non-stationary environments. In: Cooperative Information Agents X, pp. 288–300 (2006)

55. Neuberger, J., Ubel, P.A.: Finding a place for public preferences in liver allocation decisions. Transplantation **70**(10), 1411–1413 (2000)
56. Norman, D.A.: The 'problem' with automation: inappropriate feedback and interaction, not 'over-automation'. Philos. Trans. R. Soc. Lond. B Biol. Sci. **327**(1241), 585–593 (1990)
57. Perera, C., Wakenshaw, S.Y.L., Baarslag, T., Haddadi, H., Bandara, A.K., Mortier, R., Crabtree, A., Ng, I.C.L., McAuley, D., Crowcroft, J.: Valorising the IoT databox: creating value for everyone. Trans. Emerg. Telecommun. Technol. **28**(1), 1–17 (2017)
58. Radu, S.: A negotiation framework with strategies based on agent preferences. In: 2017 21st International Conference on Control Systems and Computer Science (CSCS), pp. 529–535, May 2017
59. Ramchurn, S.D., Vytelingum, P., Rogers, A., Jennings, N.R.: Putting the 'smarts' into the smart grid: a grand challenge for artificial intelligence. Commun. ACM **55**(4), 86–97 (2012)
60. Roijers, D.M., Vamplew, P., Whiteson, S., Dazeley, R.: A survey of multi-objective sequential decision-making. J. Artif. Intell. Res. **48**, 67–113 (2013)
61. Rosenfeld, A., Zuckerman, I., Segal-Halevi, E., Drein, O., Kraus, S.: Negochat: a chat-based negotiation agent. In: Proceedings of the 2014 International Conference on Autonomous Agents and Multi-Agent Systems, AAMAS 2014, Richland, SC, pp. 525–532. IFAAMAS (2014)
62. Sanders, E.B.-N., Stappers, P.J.: Co-creation and the new landscapes of design. Co-design **4**(1), 5–18 (2008)
63. Sebenius, J.K.: Negotiation analysis: a characterization and review. Manag. Sci. **38**(1), 18–38 (1992)
64. Shafie-khah, M., Fitiwi, D.Z., Catalão, J.P.S., Heydarian-Forushani, E., Golshan, M.E.H.: Simultaneous participation of demand response aggregators in ancillary services and demand response exchange markets. In: 2016 IEEE/PES Transmission and Distribution Conference and Exposition (T&D), pp. 1–5. IEEE, May 2016
65. Simonsen, J., Robertson, T.: Routledge International Handbook of Participatory Design. Routledge, Abingdon (2012)
66. Smith, R.G.: The contract net protocol: high-level communication and control in a distributed problem solver. IEEE Trans. Comput. **29**(12), 1104–1113 (1980)
67. Sycara, K.P.: Arguments of persuasion in labour mediation. In: Proceedings of the 9th International Joint Conference on Artificial Intelligence, San Francisco, CA, USA, vol. 1, pp. 294–296 (1985)
68. Torfing, J., Guy Peters, B., Pierre, J., Sørensen, E.: Interactive governance: advancing the paradigm. Publ. Adm. **91**(4), 1071–1082 (2013)
69. Tsymbal, A.: The problem of concept drift: definitions and related work. Technical report, Trinity College Dublin, Department of Computer Science (2004)
70. Tversky, A., Kahneman, D.: Loss aversion in riskless choice: a reference-dependent model. Q. J. Econ. **106**(4), 1039–1061 (1991)
71. Visintainer, F., Altomare, L., Toffetti, A., Kovacs, A., Amditis, A.: Towards manoeuver negotiation: Autonet2030 project from a car maker perspective. Transp. Res. Procedia **14**, 2237–2244 (2016)
72. Von Neumann, J., Morgenstern, O.: Theory of Games and Economic Behavior, Commemorative edn. (1 May 2007). Princeton University Press, Princeton (1953)
73. Welsh, N.A.: Perceptions of fairness in negotiation. Marq. L. Rev. **87**, 753 (2003)
74. Worthy, B.: Brexit and open government in the UK. Open Government Partnership (2016)

75. Yang, R., Kiekintveld, C., Ordonez, F., Tambe, M., John, R.: Improving resource allocation strategies against human adversaries in security games: an extended study. Artif. Intell. **195**, 440–469 (2013)
76. Peyton Young, H.: Negotiation Analysis. University of Michigan Press, Ann Arbor (1991)
77. Zhan, J., Luo, X., Feng, C., He, M.: A multi-demand negotiation model based on fuzzy rules elicited via psychological experiments. Appl. Soft Comput. (2017, in press)

A MaxSAT-Based Approach to the Team Composition Problem in a Classroom

Felip Manyà[1]([✉]), Santiago Negrete[1,2], Carme Roig[3], and Joan Ramon Soler[1]

[1] Artificial Intelligence Research Institute (IIIA, CSIC),
Campus UAB, 08193 Bellaterra, Spain
`felip@iiia.csic.es`
[2] Universidad Autónoma Metropolitana (DCCD, Cuajimalpa), Mexico City, Mexico
[3] INS Torres i Bages, Hospitalet de Llobregat, Barcelona, Spain

Abstract. Given a classroom containing a fixed number of students and a fixed number of tables that can be of different sizes, as well as a list of preferred classmates to sit with for each student, the team composition problem in a classroom (TCPC) is the problem of finding an assignment of students to tables in such a way that preferences are maximally-satisfied. In this paper, we formally define the TCPC, prove that it is NP-hard and define a MaxSAT model of the problem. Moreover, we report on the results of an empirical investigation that show that solving the TCPC with MaxSAT solvers is a promising approach.

1 Introduction

Given a classroom containing a fixed number of students and a fixed number of tables that can be of different sizes, as well as a list of preferred classmates to sit with for each student, the team composition problem in a classroom (TCPC) is the problem of finding an assignment of students to tables in such a way that preferences are maximally-satisfied. Our motivation behind this work is to solve a problem posed by the director of studies of a secondary school in the area of Barcelona, though this problem may be found in a wide range of situations and institutions.

In this paper, we formally define the TCPC, prove that it is NP-hard and define a MaxSAT model of the problem. Moreover, we report on the results of an empirical investigation that show that solving the TCPC with MaxSAT solvers is a promising approach.

To tackle the TCPC we use a MaxSAT-based problem solving approach, which is an active area of research in Artificial Intelligence, (see e.g. [2,5,7–12,15–17,20,21] and the references therein for previous and related work). MaxSAT-based problem solving is a generic problem solving approach for optimization problems which consists on first defining a MaxSAT model for instances of the problem to be solved, and then derive solutions to the encoded instances of the problem using an off-the-shelf MaxSAT solver. By a MaxSAT model we

© Springer International Publishing AG 2017
G. Sukthankar and J. A. Rodriguez-Aguilar (Eds.): AAMAS 2017 Visionary Papers,
LNAI 10643, pp. 164–173, 2017.
https://doi.org/10.1007/978-3-319-71679-4_11

mean a representation of the problem using the language of Boolean propositional logic. It is a declarative approach: we only need to define a model and from that model an optimal solution is automatically derived. Furthermore, the method is highly efficient because we may take advantage of the extremely efficient MaxSAT solvers which are publicly available.

It is commonly assumed that designing an algorithm to work directly on the original problem encoding should outperform approaches that require a translation via a generic intermediate formalism, such as a CSP, SAT or MaxSAT. However, this line of reasoning ignores the fact that generic solvers can benefit from many years of development by a broad research community. It is not easy to replicate this kind of effort in other domains.

In the present formulation of the problem, we consider the preferences of the students. Nevertheless, our approach could also be easily adapted to take into account other factors that can be relevant to the performance of a team such as personality, expertise, competence, competitiveness and human formation [4,6].

The rest of the paper is organized as follows: Sect. 2 defines the TCPC formally and proves that it is NP-hard. Section 3 gives some background on MaxSAT. Section 4 defines a MaxSAT model of the TCPC. Section 5 reports on the empirical investigation conducted. Section 6 gives some conclusions and future work.

2   The Team Composition Problem in a Classroom

Depending on the activity to be performed in a classroom at a given moment, the distribution of the students may need to be different. In the general case, we consider there is a fixed number of students and there is a list of preferred classmates to sit with for each student. Then, the goal is to partition students into teams, which may have different sizes, in such a way that the preferences of the students are maximally-satisfied.

The version of the TCPC that we use as a case study in this paper has the following constraints:

- The classroom has n students.
- The classroom has tables of 2 and 3 students with a combined capacity for n students.
- Each student has provided a list of classmates she would prefer to sit with.

The objective is to find an assignment of students to tables such that preferences are maximally-satisfied. Notice that the first two constraints are hard whereas the last one is soft. We will say that a solution is *fully-satisfied* if, and only if, all the students in the same table have the rest of the students of the table in their list of preferences. We will say that a solution is *maximally-satisfied* if, and only if, the number of students who have their preferences satisfied is maximized. Note that a fully-satisfied solution is also a maximally-satisfied solution.

Proposition 1. *Given n students, a classroom that has tables of 2 and 3 students with a combined capacity for n students, and a list of preferred classmates* *to sit with for each student, the problem of deciding if there is a fully-satisfied solution is NP-complete.*

Proof. This problem belongs to NP: we can check, in polynomial time, whether or not an assignment of students to tables is a fully-satisfied solution by inspecting the lists of preferences of the students.

We now prove that this problem is NP-hard by reducing the problem of partitioning a graph into triangles to it.

Given a graph $G = (V, E)$, where V is the set of vertices and E is the set of edges, that verifies that $|V| = 3q$ for some integer q, the partition of V into triangles consists on finding a partition of V formed by $V_1, \ldots, V_q$, each containing exactly 3 vertices, such that for each $V_i = \{u_i, v_i.w_i\}$, $1 \leq i \leq q$, the edges $\{u_i, v_i\}$, $\{u_i, w_i\}$ and $\{v_i, w_i\}$ belong to E. This problem is NP-complete [14].

That problem can be reduced to an instance of our problem without loss of generality by considering a classroom with $3q$ students, 0 tables of 2 and q tables of 3. For each edge $\{u, v\}$ on graph V, establish a preference of student u for student v and a preference of student v for student u. Note that this reduction takes polynomial time. Then, the problem of partitioning the vertices of a graph into triangles has a solution if, and only if, all the students in the classroom can be sat in such a way that all students preferences are fully-satisfied.   □

Corollary 1. *The TCPC is NP-hard.*

Proof. This follows from the fact that every fully-satisfied solution is also a maximally-satisfied solution.

3   The MaxSAT Problem

We assume readers have some familiarity with basic concepts of Boolean propositional logic. The most well-know problem of propositional logic is SAT: given a formula ϕ in Conjunctive Normal Form (CNF), decide whether there is a truth assignment that satisfies ϕ.

Reminder: a literal is a propositional variable or a negated propositional variable, a clause is a disjunction of literals, a CNF formula is a conjunction of clauses, and a truth assignment is a mapping that assigns 0 (false) or 1 (true) to each propositional variable. A CNF is satisfied by an assignment if it is true under the usual truth-functional interpretation of $\vee$ and $\wedge$ and the truth-values assigned to the variables.

An optimization variant of SAT is MaxSAT: given a CNF formula ϕ, MaxSAT consists of finding a truth assignment that maximizes the number of satisfied clauses of ϕ. However, in this paper we use the term MaxSAT in a broad sense: we allow to distinguish between hard and soft clauses, and allow to associate a weight to soft clauses (formally, hard clauses have an infinite weight). This more general formulation of MaxSAT is technically known as weighted partial MaxSAT [15], which is formally defined in the remaining of this section.

We start by defining a more general notion of clause. A weighted clause is a pair (c, w), where c is a clause and w, its weight, is a positive integer or infinity. A clause is hard if its weight is infinity; otherwise it is soft.

A weighted partial MaxSAT instance is a multiset of weighted clauses

$$\phi = \{(h_1, \infty), \ldots, (h_k, \infty), (c_1, w_1), \ldots, (c_m, w_m)\},$$

where the first k clauses are hard and the last m clauses are soft. For simplicity, in what follows, we omit infinity weights, and write $\phi = \{h_1, \ldots, h_k, (c_1, w_1), \ldots, (c_m, w_m)\}$. A soft clause (c, w) is equivalent to having w copies of the clause $(c, 1)$, and $\{(c, w_1), (c, w_2)\}$ is equivalent to $(c, w_1 + w_2)$.

Weighted partial MaxSAT for an instance ϕ is the problem of finding an assignment that satisfies all the hard clauses and minimizes the sum of the weights of the falsified soft clauses; such an assignment is called optimal assignment.

4   The MaxSAT Encoding

We show how the TCPC can be represented as a weighted partial MaxSAT instance. In other words, we show to model the TCPC in the weighted partial MaxSAT formalism. To illustrate how to model the problem, we will consider that the classroom has 28 students and there are 8 tables of 2 students and 4 tables of 3 students. This is a typical classroom distribution in secondary schools of the area of Barcelona.

First of all, we define the set of Boolean variables of our encoding:

$$\{x_{ij} | 1 \leq i < j \leq 28\} \cup \{x_{ijk} | 1 \leq i < j < k \leq 28\} \cup \{y_i | 1 \leq i \leq 28\}$$

These variables have the following intended meaning: x_{ij} is true iff students i and j sit together in a table of 2; x_{ijk} is true iff students i, j and k sit together in a table of 3; and y_i is true if student i sits in a table of 2 and is false if student i sits in a table of 3.

Using the previous Boolean variables, we create a Weighted Partial MaxSAT instance that encodes the constraints of the problem. The proposed encoding has the following hard clauses:

1. For each student i, where $1 \leq i \leq 28$, the encoding contains a set of hard clauses that encode the following cardinality constraint:
   (a) If $i = 1$, then

$$\sum_{j=2}^{28} x_{1j} + \sum_{j=2}^{27} \sum_{k=j+1}^{28} x_{1jk} = 1$$

   (b) If $2 \leq i \leq 27$, then

$$\sum_{j=1}^{i-1} x_{ji} + \sum_{j=i+1}^{28} x_{ij} + \sum_{j=1}^{i-1} \sum_{k=i+1}^{28} x_{jik} + \sum_{j=i+1}^{27} \sum_{k=j+1}^{28} x_{ijk} = 1$$

(c) If $i = 28$, then

$$\sum_{j=1}^{27} x_{j28} + \sum_{j=1}^{26} \sum_{k=j+1}^{27} x_{jk28} = 1$$

This cardinality constraint states that student i sits exactly in one table, and the table is either of 2 or of 3.

2. For each variable x_{ij}, the encoding contains the hard clauses $\neg x_{ij} \vee y_i$ and $\neg x_{ij} \vee y_j$. Note that $(\neg x_{ij} \vee y_i) \wedge (\neg x_{ij} \vee y_j)$ is equivalent to $x_{ij} \rightarrow y_i \wedge y_j$. This clause states that if x_{ij} is true, then students i and j sit in a table of 2.

3. For each variable x_{ijk}, the encoding contains the hard clauses $\neg x_{ijk} \vee \neg y_i$, $\neg x_{ijk} \vee \neg y_j$ and $\neg x_{ijk} \vee \neg y_k$. Note that $(\neg x_{ijk} \vee \neg y_i) \wedge (\neg x_{ijk} \vee \neg y_j) \wedge (\neg x_{ijk} \vee \neg y_k)$ is equivalent to $x_{ijk} \rightarrow \neg y_i \wedge \neg y_j \wedge \neg y_k$. This clause states that if x_{ijk} is true, then students i, j and k sit in a table of 3.

4. The encoding contains a set of hard clauses that encode the following cardinality constraints: $\sum_{i=1}^{28} y_i = 16$ and $\sum_{i=1}^{28} \neg y_i = 12$. These cardinality constraints state that there are 16 students sitting in tables of 2 and 12 students sitting in tables of 3.

   In practice, it is sufficient to add either the constraint $\sum_{i=1}^{28} y_i = 16$ or the constraint $\sum_{i=1}^{28} \neg y_i = 12$ because if there are exactly 16 (12) variables y_i, $1 \leq i \leq 28$, that evaluate to true (false), then the remaining 12 (16) variables must evaluate to false.

The encoding of a cardinality constraint of the form $x_1 + \ldots + x_n = k$ has $\mathcal{O}(n)$ clauses if one uses the encoding based on counters and defined in [22]. Other efficient encodings of cardinality constraints are described and analyzed in [1]. In our empirical investigation, we encode the previous cardinality constraints using PBLib[1], which is a C++ tool for efficiently encoding pseudo-Boolean constraints to CNF.

Since we considered two sizes of tables, we just need one variable y_i for each student. If we consider n different sizes, then we need $\lceil \log_2 n \rceil$ variables for each student. For example, for four different sizes, we need two variables (y_i, y_i') and each size is represented by one of the following conjunctions: $y_i \wedge y_i'$, $\neg y_i \wedge y_i'$, $y_i \wedge \neg y_i'$ and $\neg y_i \wedge \neg y_i'$.

The soft clauses of our encoding are the following weighted unit clauses:

1. For each variable x_{ij}, $1 \leq i < j \leq 28$, the encoding contains the weighted unit clause (x_{ij}, w_{ij}).

2. For each variable x_{ijk}, $1 \leq i < j < k \leq 28$, the encoding contains the weighted unit clause (x_{ijk}, w_{ijk}).

Let us explain how weights are assigned to the variables of the form x_{ij} and x_{ijk}. First of all, we build a directed graph $G = (V, E)$, where V contains a vertex i for each student i in the classroom, and E contains an edge (i, j) if student i wants to seat with student j. The weight associated with each student i in G,

---

[1] http://tools.computational-logic.org/content/pblib.php.

denoted by $w(i)$, is the out-degree of the vertex i of G.[2] The weight associated with the variable x_{ij}, denoted by w_{ij}, is $2(w(i) \times w(j))$, where $w(i)$ and $w(j)$ are the weights associated with vertices i and j, respectively, in the subgraph of G induced by the set of vertices $\{i, j\}$ (i.e.; the weight of student i and j in $G(\{i,j\})$). The weight associated with the variable x_{ijk}, denoted by w_{ijk}, is $3(w(i) \times w(j) \times w(k)/8)$, where $w(i)$, $w(j)$ and $w(k)$ are the weights associated with vertices i, j and k, respectively, in $G(\{i,j,k\})$. The value of $w(i) \times w(j)$ ranges from 0 to 1 and the value of $w(i) \times w(j) \times w(k)$ ranges from 0 to 8. This explains the fact that $w(i) \times w(j) \times w(k)$ is divided by 8. Moreover, we multiply the weights by 2 in the tables of 2 and by 3 in the tables of 3. In this way, we maximize the number of satisfied students.[3]

In the previous encoding, if the weight associated with a variable is 0, then the negation of this variable is added as a unit clause in the hard part. Moreover, an optimal solution corresponds to a fully-satisfied solution iff all the satisfied soft clauses of the form (x_{ij}, w_{ij}) and (x_{ijk}, w_{ijk}) have weight 2 and 3, respectively.

Observe that, for fully-satisfied instances, if we add to the hard part the negation of x_{ij} (i.e., the unit hard clause $\neg x_{ij}$) for each variable x_{ij} whose associated weight is different from 2 and the negation of x_{ijk} (i.e., the unit hard clause $\neg x_{ijk}$) for each variable x_{ijk} whose associated weight is different from 3, then we do not need to add any soft clause. Moreover, any satisfying assignment of the hard part allows us to derive a fully-satisfied solution. This case can be solved either with a SAT solver or with a MaxSAT solver fed with a MaxSAT instance that only contains hard clauses.

If there is no fully-satisfied solution, the objective is to find a solution that satisfies students as much as possible. Because of that, in the general case, we add the clauses (x_{ij}, w_{ij}) and (x_{ijk}, w_{ijk}) such that $w_{ij} \neq 0$ and $w_{ijk} \neq 0$ in the soft part of the encoding. In this way, we provide a solution that maximizes the number of satisfied students. In this case, we say that we have a maximally-satisfied solution.

Finally, it is worth mentioning that it is possible to define a MaxSAT encoding of the TCPC using the set of propositional variables $\{x_i^t | 1 \leq i \leq 28, 1 \leq t \leq 12\}$, where the intended meaning of x_i^t is that x_i^t is true iff student i sits at table t. However, all the experiments performed with encodings using this set of variables did not outperform the experiments performed with the encoding proposed in this section.

5   Experimental Results

We conducted an empirical investigation to assess how the MaxSAT-based approach to the TCPC works in practice on fully-satisfied instances. In the experiments, in order to analyze the scaling behavior, we considered different sizes of

---

[2] The out-degree of a vertex is the number of edges going out of a vertex in a directed graph.

[3] Since most of the MaxSAT solvers deal with weights that are positive integers, in the experiments we multiply the weights by 100 and take the integer part.

classrooms: the rows always have 2 tables of 2 and 1 table of 3, and the numbers of rows ranges from 1 to 20. So, the numbers of students per classroom ranges from 7 to 140. Besides, we assumed that each student gives a list of students she would like to sit with. We generated the preferences at random in such a way that we can guarantee that the generated instances have fully-satisfied solutions. We generated 50 different TCPC instances for each size of classroom, encoded them to weighted partial MaxSAT, and solved the resulting encodings with the exact MaxSAT solver WPM3 [7] using a cutoff time of 1 h. All the experiments were performed in a 2.3 GHz Intel PC with 1 GB RAM. The results obtained are shown in Tables 1 and 2.

Table 1 shows the results for the encoding that only contains hard clauses. Besides the hard clauses of Sect. 4, we add the unit hard clause $\neg x_{ij}$ for each variable x_{ij} whose associated weight is different from 2 and the unit hard clause

Table 1. Experimental results for the encoding without soft clauses: Students: number of students; Clauses: mean number of clauses per instance; Variables: mean number of variables per instance; and Time: mean time, in seconds, needed to solve an instance. The number of solved instances, within a cutoff time of 3600 s, is shown in parentheses.

Students	Clauses	Variables	Time
7	178	96	0.01 (50)
14	947	607	0.01 (50)
21	2675	1857	0.01 (50)
28	5888	4260	0.01 (50)
35	10841	8155	0.01 (50)
42	18036	13732	0.01 (50)
49	27685	21381	0.01 (50)
56	40282	31508	0.02 (50)
63	56130	44490	0.02 (50)
70	75187	60606	0.04 (50)
77	98640	80288	0.05 (50)
84	126205	103807	0.08 (50)
91	158597	131484	0.12 (50)
98	195963	163685	0.16 (50)
105	239214	200667	0.21 (50)
112	288402	242780	0.27 (50)
119	343816	290432	0.61 (50)
126	405198	343887	1.23 (50)
133	475062	403623	1.94 (50)
140	551134	469835	2.73 (50)

$\neg x_{ijk}$ for each variable x_{ijk} whose associated weight is different from 3. Table 2 shows the results for the encoding that has the hard clauses of the previous encoding but also the soft clauses of the form $(x_{ij}, 2)$ and $(x_{ijk}, 3)$.

Table 2. Experimental results for the encoding with soft clauses: Students: number of students; Clauses: mean number of clauses per instance; Soft clauses: mean number of soft clauses per instance; Variables: mean number of variables per instance; and Time: mean time, in seconds, needed to solve an instance. The number of solved instances, within a cutoff time of 3600s, is shown in parentheses.

Students	Clauses	Soft clauses	Variables	Time
7	178	7	96	0.01 (50)
14	947	18	607	0.01 (50)
21	2675	32	1857	0.01 (50)
28	5888	51	4260	0.05 (50)
35	10841	75	8155	3.26 (50)
42	18036	100	13732	346 (49)
49	27685	133	21381	1273 (10)

The empirical results show that the encoding without soft constraints finds optimal solutions quickly and scales well in practice. However, the encoding with soft constraints only finds optimal solutions quickly when the number of students is not greater than 35. In summary, the results show that MaxSAT allows one to find fully-satisfied solutions quickly using suitable encodings. For the TCPC, it is decisive to use efficient encodings for cardinality constraints.

6   Concluding Remarks

We have developed a method to encode the TCPC as a weighted partial MaxSAT problem, proved its NP-hardness, and carried out experiments to evaluate our approach using an exact MaxSAT solver. The results show that our method is useful because it does not need a dedicated algorithm; it is declarative, hence all stakeholders can be involved and understand the way the problem is specified; it is flexible because different classroom configurations can be solved with it; and it is efficient because it provides optimal solution in a reasonable amount of time. In the future, we plan to conduct a more exhaustive empirical investigation, model the problem using MinSAT [18,19] instead of MaxSAT, and explore the possibility of using our method to encode similar team composition problems. In practice, our method could be combined with profiling techniques [13] to solve the group formation problem in *Computer Supported Collaborative Learning* applications. Our contributions could also be applied to other projects have taken a different approach to solve related problems using other AI techniques (see [3,4,6] and the references therein for further details).

Acknowledgements. This work was supported by the Generalitat de Catalunya grant AGAUR 2014-SGR-118, and the MINECO-FEDER project RASO TIN2015-71799-C2-1-P. The second author is supported by grant PSPA-PNB-CGVyDI.324.2016 from Universidad Autónoma Metropolitana (Cuajimalpa), Mexico.

References

1. Abío, I., Nieuwenhuis, R., Oliveras, A., Rodríguez-Carbonell, E.: A parametric approach for smaller and better encodings of cardinality constraints. In: Proceedings of the 19th International Conference on Principles and Practice of Constraint Programming, CP, Uppsala, Sweden, pp. 80–96 (2013)
2. Abramé, A., Habet, D.: On the resiliency of unit propagation to max-resolution. In: Proceedings of the 24th International Joint Conference on Artificial Intelligence, IJCAI-2015, Buenos Aires, Argentina, pp. 268–274 (2015)
3. Alberola, J.M., del Val, E., Sánchez-Anguix, V., Palomares, A., Teruel, M.D.: An artificial intelligence tool for heterogeneous team formation in the classroom. Knowl. Based Syst. **101**, 1–14 (2016)
4. Alberola, J.M., del Val, E., Sanchez-Anguix, V., Julian, V.: Simulating a collective intelligence approach to student team formation. In: Pan, J.-S., Polycarpou, M.M., Woźniak, M., de Carvalho, A.C.P.L.F., Quintián, H., Corchado, E. (eds.) HAIS 2013. LNCS (LNAI), vol. 8073, pp. 161–170. Springer, Heidelberg (2013). https://doi.org/10.1007/978-3-642-40846-5_17
5. Alsinet, T., Manyà, F., Planes, J.: An efficient solver for weighted Max-SAT. J. Glob. Optim. **41**, 61–73 (2008)
6. Andrejczuk, E., Rodríguez-Aguilar, J.A., Roig, C., Sierra, C.: Synergistic team composition. In: Proceedings of the 16th Conference on Autonomous Agents and MultiAgent Systems, AAMAS, São Paulo, Brazil, pp. 1463–1465 (2017)
7. Ansótegui, C., Didier, F., Gabàs, J.: Exploiting the structure of unsatisfiable cores in MaxSAT. In: Proceedings of the Twenty-Fourth International Joint Conference on Artificial Intelligence, IJCAI, Buenos Aires, Argentina, pp. 283–289 (2015)
8. Ansótegui, C., Gabàs, J., Malitsky, Y., Sellmann, M.: MaxSAT by improved instance-specific algorithm configuration. Artif. Intell. **235**, 26–39 (2016)
9. Argelich, J., Li, C.M., Manyà, F., Planes, J.: The first and second Max-SAT evaluations. J. Satisfiability Boolean Model. Comput. **4**, 251–278 (2008)
10. Argelich, J., Li, C.M., Manyà, F., Planes, J.: Analyzing the instances of the MaxSAT evaluation. In: Sakallah, K.A., Simon, L. (eds.) SAT 2011. LNCS, vol. 6695, pp. 360–361. Springer, Heidelberg (2011). https://doi.org/10.1007/978-3-642-21581-0_29
11. Argelich, J., Manyà, F.: Exact Max-SAT solvers for over-constrained problems. J. Heuristics **12**(4–5), 375–392 (2006)
12. Bonet, M.L., Levy, J., Manyà, F.: A complete calculus for Max-SAT. In: Biere, A., Gomes, C.P. (eds.) SAT 2006. LNCS, vol. 4121, pp. 240–251. Springer, Heidelberg (2006). https://doi.org/10.1007/11814948_24
13. Costaguta, R.: Algorithms and machine learning techniques in collaborative group formation. In: Lagunas, O.P., Alcántara, O.H., Figueroa, G.A. (eds.) MICAI 2015. LNCS (LNAI), vol. 9414, pp. 249–258. Springer, Cham (2015). https://doi.org/10.1007/978-3-319-27101-9_18
14. Garey, M.R., Johnson, D.S.: Computers and Intractability: A Guide to the Theory of NP-Completeness. Freeman, San Francisco (1979)

15. Li, C.M., Manyà, F.: MaxSAT, hard and soft constraints. In: Biere, A., van Maaren, H., Walsh, T. (eds.) Handbook of Satisfiability, pp. 613–631. IOS Press (2009)
16. Li, C.M., Manyà, F., Planes, J.: New inference rules for Max-SAT. J. Artif. Intell. Res. **30**, 321–359 (2007)
17. Li, C.M., Manyà, F., Soler, J.R.: A clause tableaux calculus for MaxSAT. In: Proceedings of the 25th International Joint Conference on Artificial Intelligence, IJCAI-2016, New York City, NY, USA, pp. 766–772 (2016)
18. Li, C.M., Zhu, Z., Manyà, F., Simon, L.: Minimum satisfiability and its applications. In: Proceedings of the 22nd International Joint Conference on Artificial Intelligence, IJCAI-2011, Barcelona, Spain, pp. 605–610 (2011)
19. Li, C.M., Zhu, Z., Manyà, F., Simon, L.: Optimizing with minimum satisfiability. In: Artificial Intelligence, vol. 190, pp. 32–44 (2012)
20. Martins, R., Joshi, S., Manquinho, V., Lynce, I.: Incremental cardinality constraints for MaxSAT. In: O'Sullivan, B. (ed.) CP 2014. LNCS, vol. 8656, pp. 531–548. Springer, Cham (2014). https://doi.org/10.1007/978-3-319-10428-7_39
21. Morgado, A., Heras, F., Liffiton, M.H., Planes, J., Marques-Silva, J.: Iterative and core-guided MaxSAT solving: a survey and assessment. Constraints **18**(4), 478–534 (2013)
22. Sinz, C.: Towards an optimal CNF encoding of Boolean cardinality constraints. In: van Beek, P. (ed.) CP 2005. LNCS, vol. 3709, pp. 827–831. Springer, Heidelberg (2005). https://doi.org/10.1007/11564751_73

Heuristic Data Merging for Constructing Initial Agent Populations

Bhagya N. Wickramasinghe[✉], Dhirendra Singh, and Lin Padgham

RMIT University, 124, La Trobe Street, Melbourne, VIC 3000, Australia
{bhagya.wickramasinghe,dhirendra.singh,lin.padgham}@rmit.edu.au
https://www.rmit.edu.au

Abstract. In this paper, we explore an approach for developing an initial agent population that is suitable for integrating two component agent based models, representing conceptually the same agents. For some models the structure of the initial population is an important aspect of the model. When integrating two (or more) models that represent the same agents, we require a single integrated agent population (or unique mappings between the two populations). Obtaining such is not straightforward if we wish to preserve important structural characteristics of the component populations. We describe here a methodology inspired by work in constructing synthetic populations which are structurally similar to a real population. The approach uses the Iterative Proportional Fitting Procedure (IPFP) to combine two different data sets in a way that preserves the structure of each. We apply our approach to a specific case study and evaluate the quality of the resulting integrated population.

Keywords: Agent based modelling · Data merging · Model integration Synthetic population reconstruction

1 Introduction

This paper addresses the important issue of obtaining an initial population of agents suitable for use by two or more component simulations which are being integrated. In such a case each component's original initial population may have important structural characteristics, which as much as possible should be retained in the initial population to be used for the integration.

For example consider the two simulations, Linked Lives (LL) [16] and Wedding Doughnut (WD) [17], both developed as part of the Care Life Cycle project[1] which is a five-year research programme at the University of Southampton that commenced in October 2010. LL models the development of the UK population over 50 years, modelling health, births, deaths, marriages and associated changes

---

[1] http://www.southampton.ac.uk/clc.

© Springer International Publishing AG 2017
G. Sukthankar and J. A. Rodriguez-Aguilar (Eds.): AAMAS 2017 Visionary Papers,
LNAI 10643, pp. 174–193, 2017.
https://doi.org/10.1007/978-3-319-71679-4_12

in household composition and place of residence. The main purpose of the simulation is to estimate future health care needs in the UK, based on the assumption that where relatives are nearby, or in the same household, they will/can provide some of the carer needs.

Wedding Doughnut (WD) [17] also models the evolution of a population over time, and includes estimation of social health care needs. The main purpose of this simulation however is to explore the combination of detailed and accurate statistical demography, with agent based social simulation. The social simulation aspect is focussed on how relationship formation is influenced by peers, and how in turn family structures influence the need for social care.

Integrating these two components to take advantage of the more accurate demographic model and more sophisticated model of family relationship formation from WD, while retaining the modelling of household structures and population health from LL, should enable a better prediction of healthcare needs in the future, than either model alone. The work by Wickramasinghe et al. [23] shows one way in which the two models could be integrated at runtime. However it leaves open the issue of how to obtain an appropriate shared initial population. They use the initial LL population (as WD contains only a subset of the necessary information and cannot be used alone). By doing this they lose much of the value of WD's better demographics as the starting population of LL is significantly less accurate than that of WD, as illustrated in Fig. 1. This paper provides a method for obtaining an initial population that retains key aspects of the structure of two populations to be integrated: in this case the household structures of LL and the demographic structures of the agent population.

Agent Based modelling and Simulation (ABMS) is a powerful technique for exploring complex problems and is being used increasingly in areas such as emergency management, transport management systems (e.g. [1]), disease spread (e.g. [7]), and urban development (e.g. [21]). Complex simulations are time consuming and costly to develop, requiring both domain and technical expertise. As applications are extended and require inclusion of additional aspects, it is desirable to reuse and combine existing simulation models (components) where such exist. There are a number of approaches regarding how to combine multiple simulation components, such as HLA [5], OpenMI [13], OpenSim [18]. Whatever approach is used for the runtime integration, an initial shared and consistent start state is required. In the case where agents are part of multiple components, this requires a consistent initial agent population, which is appropriate for all components.

The inspiration for our approach to solving this problem comes from the literature on building synthetic populations to match various views on an underlying population, obtained for example from publicly available census tables. A technique which is commonly used is Iterative Proportional Fitting Procedure (IPFP) [4,6], an algorithm that iteratively converges to a fixed point to fill the cells of a matrix with values that result in correct summation in both dimensions. There is a large body of research around this procedure (which has a range of variations). We used a version incorporated into the R statistical package.[2]

---

[2] https://cran.r-project.org/web/packages/mipfp/index.html.

Our key idea is to regard the data from different components, representing conceptually the same agents, as analogous to different data or views regarding a single real population. IPFP, or its multi-dimensional variant if considering more than two components, can then be used to obtain distributions that conform to the marginal sums (constraints) from each component. An important difference is that the initial populations in two simulation components, while representing the same conceptual population in an integration, may not be derived from actual data of a single real population. For this reason it can be more challenging to achieve a suitable outcome, and additional algorithms are required to build an instantiated population, after the IPFP step.

We test and exemplify our approach using the two component simulations WD and LL described above. We have obtained the code of these simulations as well as the published descriptions, enabling us to test our approach using pre-existing simulations, developed independently from our own work. At the time that we obtained the two implemented components, there was no attempt being made to integrate them, although the researchers involved in the Care Life Cycle project felt it would be valuable to do so.

We present in Sect. 3 the approach we have used to obtain an integrated initial agent population. In Sect. 4 we describe the variations that we tried, and assess them based on statistical measures of equivalence to the original initial populations of each component, for those characteristics we wished to retain. In order to provide necessary background, we first describe in the following section some further information on the two component systems as well as brief overviews of synthetic population generation techniques and IPFP.

2   Background

2.1   Component Simulations

As discussed previously the core purpose of WD is to demonstrate the value of combining agent based simulation of social processes, with statistical demography. The social process modelled is that of relationship formation and is based on a substantially extended version of the wedding ring of Bilari et al. [3]. The demographics of the initial population are developed by taking the 1951 census data regarding structure of the population of the UK with regard to age, sex and marital status. This is then evolved using a variant of the Lee-Carter model of mortality and applying birth rates based on actual and predicted statistical data. Testing against 2011 census data showed a good match.

However, WD does not model geographical location and thus cannot be used for more detailed analysis of such things as relative need for health care support in different locations.

LL aims conceptually to model the UK population of 62 million. Due to the prohibitive computational cost they use a scaling factor of 1:10,000 to model a population of 6,200 agents. In order to obtain an initial population for the year 2000, LL starts with 375 arbitrary couples where individuals are aged between

20 and 40, and then runs the model for the 140 years needed to obtain a population of approximately 6,000 individuals, with plausible family and household structures. A fixed reproductive probability was used for all women aged 17–42, who are in any relationship. In order to obtain an improved match to actual data, this fertility level was set to be higher until 1965 and then gradually decreased to the empirically observed level. Mortality was modelled using a simple Gompertz-Makeham mortality model. The modelling of partnership formation is done by random pairing agents at age and sex specific rates, with some simple constraints that prevent partners having the same parents and disallow the male partner to be more than 5 years younger or 20 years older than the female partner. Divorces are modelled as age specific probabilities.

Agents move (probabilistically) based on partnership formation, relationship dissolution, adult children moving out of the parental home, arbitrary (low probability) moves of singles or families, and death of a partner.

Health degrades with age specific probability, and is linked to hours of care needed. There is a detailed model of how much care is needed for different levels of health, and how much care a relative can provide based on distance to the family member needing care and their own health status. Discrepancy between hours of care needed, and hours of care able to be provided, determines an estimate of social healthcare needs required.

As can be observed, both models have their strengths. LL covers more detail on geographical moves, health and the ability to provide health care. WD has more accurate demographic processes for birth and death, as well as a more developed social model of relationship formation. Both these simulations initialise their populations in ways that are important for the validity of the simulation. WD requires an initially sound demographic structure of the population if its more developed demographic processes are to produce valid results. LL requires an initial population with appropriate household structures and sizes incorporating individuals with varying health levels. Our task is to provide a single initial population that is suitable for both components.

2.2   Synthetic Population Construction Techniques

There is a substantial body of literature on techniques for developing a synthetic population which matches some actual observed population. Harland et al. [9] describe and compare several such techniques, all of which start with a sample set of anonymous but actual individuals, and generalise this to the full population by incremental improvement. The synthetic population is developed using various data sources, such as census tables and is constructed to match the actual population as closely as possible with regard to particular characteristics of interest.

Deterministic re-weighting and combinatorial optimisation are two popular synthetic population construction techniques. Deterministic re-weighting techniques such as IPFP [4,6] and GREGWT [19] produce the results by re-weighting an initial estimate produced by generalising a microdata sample. These techniques are deterministic and given the same input will always produce the same output. Combinatorial optimisation on the other hand is a stochastic approach [24]. These methods generally start with an initial estimate of households and individuals living in them, selected from a disaggregated sample from of the real population. The estimate is subsequently improved by swapping households in the estimate with random households from the sample until the household and individual distributions achieve expected accuracy with respect to aggregated marginals [15, 20].

The work discussed by Harland et al. [9] requires an actual sample of individuals for the population, as well as aggregated census type data. This is not available for the situation we are addressing, where there is not necessarily a specific population for which samples exist. Rather we are aiming to produce a synthetic population which has key characteristics of two component populations. In the particular WD and LL example, both components do aim to model the same underlying UK population, so in principle we could obtain a sample for that population. However this is not necessarily the case when integrating two components. As we are using WD and LL to exemplify and evaluate our general approach, it is not relevant to obtain such a sample.

2.3   Iterative Proportional Fitting Procedure

IPFP is the most commonly used deterministic re-weighting procedure for generating synthetic populations (e.g. [2, 14]). It iteratively adjusts cell values of a matrix so that they add up to target row and column totals (marginal totals) provided from the aggregated population data such as census tables. In each iteration, IPFP proportionally adjusts cell values to match the marginal sums, one dimension at a time, and is guaranteed to converge to the matrix marginals [8].

IPFP requires row and column sums to be equal. If the two data sources are inconsistent and row and column sums are not equal, frequencies can be converted to proportions. Secondly, IPFP relies on sample data to seed the matrix cells. Lovelace et al. evaluate the influence of two common problems related to the seed: the initial weights problem and zero cells problem [12]. The initial weights problem relates to certain agent categories being under/over represented in the seed. The zero cells problem relates to some agent categories not being represented at all in the sample, though observed in the actual population. In the latter case, the particular agent categories are always assigned zero in the final result. A significant finding in Lovelace et al.'s work is that influence of initial weights trend towards zero after 10 iterations. Based on the findings they conclude that it is more important to avoid the zero cell problem.

Iterative Proportional Updating [25] and Hierarchical Iterative Proportional Fitting [10] are two approaches similar to IPFP but extended to merging distributions at different aggregation levels, for example, merging household distributions and person level distributions. These approaches however are not applicable to this work as they rely on microdata samples, which are not available to us given the marginal distributions come from different component models. Though the both models used in this work capture the same person and household properties, the proposed methodology is intended to be applicable to models with different properties that conceptually influence characteristics of the merged population. For example integrating a model that captures personal income, age and marital status and another model that captures family structures (e.g. couple only, couple with children), where merged population is constructed considering the influence of personal attributes on family structures. In such situations the above two approaches become inapplicable due to unavailability of a common microdata sample that represents all the required aspects.

3   Approach

We describe here our suggested approach to producing an integrated initial population using two component simulations modelling the same conceptual agents in different ways.[3] We exemplify using the two components, WD and LL, previously described.

The starting point is the initial populations for the two components. LL requires an initialisation period, and is considered to be adequately initialised for the year 2000 after 140 iterations. WD is initialised with 1951 census data demographics, and is validated against 2011 census data. For our integration purposes we took the initial population for each component as that produced by each for the year 2000.

3.1   Obtaining the Marginal Distributions

The first step is to identify the key population aspects to be retained from the components being merged. We assume the agent is the central concept, but there may also be others that have inter-dependencies with the agents, such as families, households or organisations. We select from each component those characteristics which are expected to have dependencies, but where it is important to retain the original structure of that population. For example we may choose age from one component and marital relationships from another. Where a characteristic exists in both components, a decision must be made as to which to use, possibly based on perceived quality of the component data for that aspect. In our case study we decided to base age, gender and marital/parental relationships on WD, as empirical validation showed a better fit to actual data on age and gender than LL, while the more sophisticated modelling of relationships was also an advantage of WD. We independently assessed our initial populations for each, with respect to age distributions, against UK data for the year 2000 from the UK Office of National Statistics[4] and confirmed that WD was a better fit, as shown in Fig. 1. Data for which we wished to retain appropriate information from LL was that of household sizes. In choosing the characteristics from each population we must be careful not to choose characteristics with implicit dependencies that will necessarily cause inconsistencies. For example we should not take age from one component and date of birth from the other.

---

[3] We describe the procedure for two components, but multi-dimensional IPFP can be used for cases with three or four components.

[4] https://www.nomisweb.co.uk.

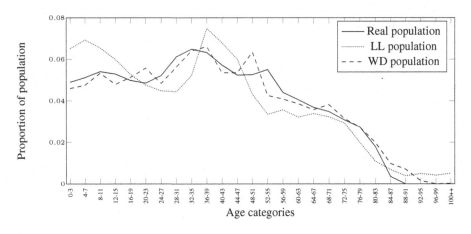

Fig. 1. Age category comparison of WD and LL with actual, year 2000

The attributes for each component must then be partitioned into suitable value ranges. This is partly determined by the representation in the relevant component. For example if a component represents an agent's salary as a \$10,000 dollar range, we cannot use any finer granularity than this, as the relevant information will not be available. We may however group values to obtain a coarser granularity than that used in the component (e.g. a \$20,000 dollar range). Trade-offs and implications regarding the granularity used are discussed in Sect. 4 in relation to the case study. The cells for which marginal distributions must be obtained are then determined by overlaying the partitions of each attribute on each other. For example a M/F gender attribute, combined with 5 age ranges of 25 years from 0–99, will result in 8 cells: a M and a F cell for each age category, as shown in Table 1. The bottom row then provides the distribution of the population across the various categories induced by the attributes and their values, the so called **"marginal distribution"**. So we have 130 male 0–24 years old, and 125 females in this age range.

Table 1. Example of marginal distributions for age and sex categories

M				F			
0–24	25–49	50–74	75–99	0–24	25–49	50–74	75–99
130	128	130	110	125	132	130	115

Two such marginal distributions then define the matrix whose cell values will be calculated by the IPF procedure, respecting the totals defined at the margins. To obtain the values for each marginal distribution we extract the data from the relevant initial population, for the categories defined by the cells, induced by the attributes we are interested in and the value categories we have defined for them.

In our case study the **column marginal distribution** was obtained from WD and consisted of 104 cells reflecting:

- gender (M/F),
- relationship (Single/Married) and
- age (26 categories in range 0–99, and 100+).

For some experimentation we added a parental attribute with 4 values (has children under 15, has children over 15, has children both under and over 15, has no children), giving 416 cells in the marginal distribution.

The **row marginal distribution** was obtained from LL, where we had 11 categories, representing number of people in households of size 1–11. This gave 1144 matrix cells (or 4576 if parental relationships were included) for the IPFP algorithm to determine values for.

If the initial population sizes are different this data may need to be normalised, though some IPFP packages (including the one we used) have this functionality inbuilt.

3.2   Obtaining Cell Values

Before running IPFP it is necessary to provide seed values for each cell in the matrix. Providing seed values that better represent the underlying population will allow IPFP to produce superior results. However it is possible to obtain results that adhere to the distribution constraints, even if 1 is used as the seed in all cells that are not impossible.

Given that there is no microdata sample that could be used for seeding, we experimented with two seed variations, one with 0's and 1's, respectively indicating impossible (e.g. married, under 15) and possible cells, and the other with approximate seed values obtained from calculations of categories in LL.[5]

Using IPFP the matrix cells are then populated with values that represent the characteristics of a merged agent population, which adheres to the structure of both the originally defined marginal distributions. This can then be used to build an initial population that adheres to the key structural characteristics of both source populations.

3.3   Building the Merged Population

In the simplest case, building the merged population involves instantiating the appropriate number of agents with the relevant characteristics, as defined by each matrix cell. However, in general, specific relationships may need to be established in heuristically appropriate ways, additional constraints may need to be enforced and attributes may need to be added and/or made more specific.

---

[5] This is further discussed in Sect. 4.

Relationships: The need to deal with relationships can arise when one of the marginal distributions concerns a grouping concept, such as in our example where the LL distribution deals with numbers of agents in households. Individuals must then be assigned appropriately to the groups, using values from the matrix. It can also be the case that some of the attributes refer to a relationship which must be specifically instantiated between agents in the population. An example also present in our case study, is that of marital status. Heuristics such as the allowable or preferred age difference between partners, and hard constraints such as only one marital relationship per agent, and minimum marriageable age, must guide the building of the instantiated initial population.

Attributes: Some necessary attributes of agents may not have been part of the structural merging procedure, but must be assigned before the initialisation is complete. An example in our case study is the health level of agents. Such attributes can be assigned in any suitable manner. As health level in both WD and LL is related to age, though the levels are more detailed in LL, we simply calculated the likelihood of the various health levels represented in LL for each age and gender category, and assigned accordingly. Some attributes assigned during the process based on matrix cell values may also need to be further refined. For example, age defined as a range, needed to be refined to a particular value within that range. Refinement may need to also take account of constraints such as age difference between marital partners, or between parent and child.

The integrated population must then be assigned into each component, ready for the execution of the components in the integrated simulation, maintaining synchronised and consistent agent representations by whatever method is being used. This may require further modification of attributes to ensure suitability for the particular component. This can include such things as translation of units of measurement, naming or aggregation/simplification of attribute values. An example in our case study was the illness/health attribute which has five levels in LL and was assigned five levels for the merged population. However WD has only a two level scale, ill or not ill. Consequently levels 1 and 2 in LL were assigned to not ill in WD, with levels 3–5 interpreted as ill.

Algorithm description: As mentioned earlier in assigning agents into households, or whatever other assignment of relationships between agents or entities must be done, certain constraints must be maintained. If the original data sources represent a real population, it is reasonable to assume that these constraints are realised in the actual population and are therefore implicit in the various data sources. In this case it should be possible to achieve assignments that allow exact adherence to IPFP cell values.[6] However this is not the case in our situation: there is no underlying "real" population. Rather we have two representations of some population where we are trying to conserve properties of each as much as we can. When applying the necessary hard and soft constraints (e.g. only one marital partner, parents must be at least 15 years older than their child, etc.)

---

[6] Exact adherence modulo rounding errors. We must of course round agent numbers obtained from percentages to be whole numbers.

there is no guarantee that the IPFP solution produced can be realised fully. We have developed an algorithm that aims to do "as good a job as *practically possible*" and we evaluate experimentally how good this actually is at preserving the desired structure in our case study. The algorithm is shown in Algorithm 1.

Algorithm 1. Grouping Algorithm

---

input : **U**: vector of desired counts per category

   R: 2D array of category rule vectors of size $|\mathbf{U}|$

output: **V**: vector of assigned agents per category

1   $\mathbf{F} \leftarrow$ getDistribution(**U**); $\mathbf{V} \leftarrow \mathbf{U}$; $\mathbf{V}' \leftarrow 0$

2   **while** $\mathbf{V}' \neq \mathbf{V}$ **do**

3     $\mathbf{V} \leftarrow \mathbf{V}'$

4   **for** *index c in* $\mathbf{V}'$ **do**

5       $R_c \leftarrow \mathbf{R}[c]$; $O \leftarrow 0$; $E \leftarrow 0$

6   **for** *index r in* R_c **do**

7         $O[r] \leftarrow \mathbf{V}' + R_c[r]$

8         $D \leftarrow$ getDistribution($O[r]$)

9         $E[r] \leftarrow$ getRMSDiff($D - \mathbf{F}$)

10   **end**

11       $W[c] \leftarrow O[argmin(E)]$

12   **end**

13     $\mathbf{V}' \leftarrow W[argmin(W)]$

14   **if** $\mathbf{V}' \neq \mathbf{V}$ **then**

15   // update relationships and attributes

16   **end**

17 **end**

18

The grouping algorithm operates row wise on the IPFP produced matrix of agent counts. Recall that rows represent household types from LL and the columns are agent categories from WD. This row wise operation is shown in Algorithm 1. Here, the input vector **U** contains the desired number of agents in each category–an IPFP output row. Vector **V** holds the allocated agents. An ideal algorithm would finish with $\mathbf{V} \leftarrow \mathbf{U}$, however, in our case, as mentioned before, there is no guarantee that this can be achieved, so the aim is to get **V** as close to **U** as practically possible.

The input **R** is a 2-dimensional array of *rule vectors*, where each row specifies a constraint for a given category. For instance, a rule for a "married male" category will contain a 1 for that category as well as a 1 for a female category that forms a suitable partner. Such a rule specifies that assigning an agent to the married male category must be accompanied by one other assignment to the specified female category. Several such rules may exist for the married male category (one per row in **R**) to capture the various *options* or combinations in which a relationship may be formed. As a minimum, each category has at least one corresponding rule in **R**.

In the following description, numbers in brackets indicate line numbers in Algorithm 1. The procedure starts by calculating F (the corresponding proportional distribution of each category in $\mathbf{U}$, adding up to 1) and assigning $\mathbf{V}$ and $\mathbf{V}'$ (a temporary vector) non-equal values (1), and then continues as long as $\mathbf{V}$ and $\mathbf{V}'$ are not equal (2). The algorithm contains two inner loops: one to operate on each element (category) of $\mathbf{V}'$ (4), and within that, another to operate on all rule options that apply to that category (6). The overall idea is to start with $\mathbf{V} \leftarrow 0$ and then proceed towards $\mathbf{V} \leftarrow \mathbf{U}$ by gathering, in each iteration of the outer loop, all legal allocations (all options across all categories), and then selecting one. Note that we pick the best option for a given category first (11), and then pick the best option across categories (13). The "best" option here is always the one that minimises the *root mean square error* between the desired distribution F and all possible resulting distributions from the options (6–11). The intuition is to proceed towards $\mathbf{U}$ as fast as possible, by picking the option that will reduce the error between $\mathbf{V}$ and $\mathbf{U}$ the most. Whenever a new option is chosen we also update any relationships and attributes relating to the impacted agents as needed (14–16).

Algorithm 1 stops when it can no longer assign agents to categories, resulting in some agents being left over (i.e., $\mathbf{U} - \mathbf{V}$). Assigning these leftover agents to any categories would end up increasing the error in the marginal distributions, so instead, these agents are discarded from the population. (Actually, we do a post-processing step before discarding, where we try to swap allocated and left-over agents, where doing so will allow us to reuse the swapped agent elsewhere.) This results in the usable population being smaller than desired ($\mathbf{V} < \mathbf{U}$), however, the structural makeup is as close to desired as possible.

4   Evaluation

4.1   Experimental Data

We produced 4 sets of population types, varying granularity of the marginal distribution categories and the seed values in the cells provided to the IPFP algorithm.

Coarse vs. fine granularity: The attributes which form the basis for the marginal distribution categories are gender, age, marital status and parental status. The coarse granularity data uses 26 age brackets (4 year intervals) and 2 categories each for gender and marital status, giving 104 categories. The fine granularity adds 4 categories regarding whether an individual has children. These categories are: 1. Has child(ren) under 15 (U15c); 2. Has child(ren) over 15 (O15c); 3. Has children both under and over 15 (UO15c); 4. Has no children (nc). Combining these denotations with R ("relationship") and S ("single) for marital status then gives the 8 categories RU15c, SU15c, RO15c, SO15c, RUO15c, SUO15c, Rnc, Snc. When combined with gender and age brackets this gives a total of 416 categories. Gender is denoted by suffixes, -m for male and -f for female. These category descriptors will be used when discussing detailed results.

Seed values: As described in Sect. 3.2, we experimented with a *simple seed* (0's and 1's) and an *informed seed* based on LL data.

Setup: Both WD and LL have built-in initial burn-in periods, where the starting population is allowed to evolve for some number of years (WD:1951–2000, LL: 1860–2000) before it is considered suitable. We first produced 100 initial WD populations and LL populations in this way. Due to burn-in, the initial population counts were different across runs but averaged around 4000 for WD, and 6000 for LL. We then produced coarse and fine level marginal distributions for each of these initial instances, and provided these to IPFP, seeded with a simple seed in one case and an informed seed in the other. This gave 400 IPFP tables, 100 in each setting of coarse granularity–simple seed (**CS**), coarse granularity–informed seed (**CI**), fine granularity–simple seed (**FS**), and fine granularity–informed seed (**FI**). These IPFP tables were used to produce the experimental population instances of size 4000.[7] Finally, we ran our assignment algorithm to produce 400 experimental population instances (100 in each setting) and collected the data to allow us to compare with the original WD and LL populations with respect to the characteristics we were trying to retain from each.

4.2 Evaluation Method

For each set of 100 merged population instances, we compared these with the set of 100 original WD or LL population instances on each of the relevant categories. We then assessed whether the populations produced by our approach were equivalent to the populations produced by WD or LL with respect to each relevant category. Finally we calculated the percentage of (relevant) categories for which each experimental population set (**CS, CI, FA, FI**) was equivalent to the WD (or LL) population set, giving an overall percentage equivalence. For assessing equivalence to WD there were 104 coarse (or 416 fine) categories, based on the demographic characteristics that we wished to retain from WD. For assessing equivalence to LL there were only 11 categories, as the household data was simply number of people in households of a given size (maximum size ever produced by LL was 11).

We considered two sets of populations equivalent with respect to some category (e.g. percentage of individuals in "married, 40–45 year-old males" category or percentage of "individuals in a household of size 4") if $p \leq 0.05$, with respect to the null hypothesis of them being different (standard 95% certainty). We assessed equivalence of WD to each of the 4 merged populations by assessing equivalence with respect to each of the categories in the row marginal distribution of the IPFP table (104 or 416 categories). We assessed equivalence of LL to each of these same merged populations, by assessing equivalence of LL with regard to each of the 11 categories of the IPFP column marginal distribution -

---

[7] As mentioned, IPFP rounding introduces errors. We rounded by taking the floor values which gave populations of around 3% less than 4000. This choice is not critical for us, however for a detailed discussion of rounding issues, see [11].

i.e. how similar was the distribution of households of varying sizes in the merged populations as compared to initial populations produced by LL.

We used the Two One Sided Test (TOST) [22] which is the standard statistical test for establishing equivalence (as opposed to the more usual procedures for establishing difference). TOST requires, in addition to the two distributions, input of the tolerable difference between means, the so-called epsilon value (ϵ). The larger this value, the easier it is to establish equivalence. We tested WD using two different ϵ values of 0.0015 and 0.002, representing 0.15% and 0.2% of the population, and LL using ϵ values of 0.002 and 0.0035. Choice of an appropriate epsilon is domain dependent and depends on how large a difference in mean should be allowed before the data is not considered equivalent. On average there are about 1400 households and 4000 agents in each population. The effect of one mis-categorised agent is therefore 0.00025 whereas the effect of one mis-categorised household is 0.000714, almost 3 times as much. This justifies our use of a slightly higher ϵ value.

4.3   Results

We discuss first the results for equivalence to WD, as these are more complex than for LL. We then provide similar data for LL.

Equivalence of Merged and WD on Demographics. Recall that we are comparing against 4 different merged populations: Coarse-Simple **CS** produced without considering parental relationships and using a 0 or 1 seed to represent possible vs impossible categories; Coarse-Informed **CI**, where we use the same categories as **CS** but use a seed based on LL distributions; Fine-Simple **FS**, where we add categories capturing parental relationships as described in Sect. 3.1; and Fine-Informed **FI**, where we use the extra parental relationships and seed based on LL distributions. Table 2 shows the % of categories equivalent for each of the four settings, and the two different ϵ values which we tested for.

Table 2. Equivalence of WD to each population set

	CS	FS	CI	FI
ϵ 0.0015	87.5%	75%	86.5%	81.25%
ϵ 0.002	96.15%	79.33%	92.3%	87.74%

Looking at Table 2 it is clear that the choice of the ϵ value has a substantial effect on results. What is a "reasonable" value depends on judgement with regard to the domain. One must assess whether the ϵ chosen results in actual numbers that intuitively are or are not equivalent. This will depend on what the categories represent, and also the raw numbers in the categories. Also of importance is which categories are not equivalent and whether that is expected to matter for the purpose of the integrated simulation. An interesting observation is that using the informed seed with the coarse granularity table appears to give slightly worse results than the simple seed. Further investigation across more studies is required to understand why this is. With fine granularity the informed seed leads to improvements. Also the coarse granularity performs better than the fine granularity, with both types of seed. The reason for this latter effect is that it is harder to meet the constraints in grouping with the finer granularity.

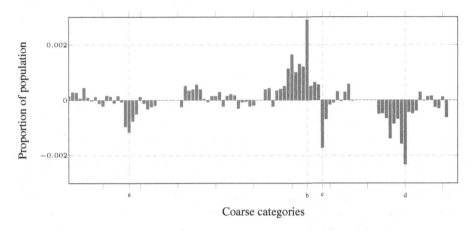

Fig. 2. Example over/under allocation in merged WD population with respect to original for 104 categories in CS.

Figure 2 shows the comparison of a single CS population instance against its corresponding WD original. The x axis represents the 104 coarse categories while the y axis represents the over/under allocation in the CS population as compared to the original, with respect to those categories, expressed as a proportion of the population. A positive bar represent categories where CS had more agents than the original, while negative bars represent the opposite case. A zero-height bar represents an exact match and includes empty categories. Only selected labels are shown on the x axis and these are discussed in the following text. The ϵ range of ±0.002 is also shown. In this instance, 102 out of 104 categories are equivalent (only bars b and d are not). Note that this is for a single example instance. Across all 100 instances of CS, 96.15% of categories are equivalent (Table 2).

The two non-equivalent categories b and d in Fig. 2 refer to the categories "Single female (S-f), Age 44–47" and "In relationship female (R-f), Age 44–47" respectively. In this example the difference can be attributed solely to a number of single females in the given age group for whom a suitable partner could not be found. The merged population therefore has less females in category d compared to the original (negative bar at d). These females end up in category b resulting in more females here than in the original (a corresponding positive bar at b).

A total of 37 agents were discarded in this example from a total of 3978 agents, or around 0.93% of the population (the average discarded agents for CS

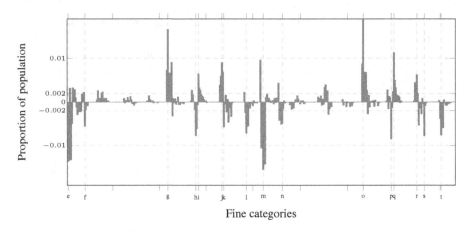

Fig. 3. Example over/under allocation in merged WD population with respect to original for 416 categories in FS.

across all 100 instances was 0.6%). Of these, 14 are from 4-member households. Out of that 5 agents are from S-f age 60–63 (label c) and 4 from S-m age 60–63 (label a). The rest are spread in other categories. The discarded agents in a and c have failed to form parental relationships (the only legal relationship) because there are no suitable agents left in the same household type. Though there are other agents in these two clusters, their age gaps are too small for a parental relationship.

Figure 3 shows an example instance fine granularity (FS). Here several clusters of agent categories exhibit significant differences. Two of those clusters, around labels e and m, mainly consist of under-15 single males and females, i.e., children. Another two important clusters are around labels f and n, which represent older single males and females with no children. Categories that fall under these labels have limited options when forming relationships and many are discarded because of that; about 56% of under-15 agents and more than 20% of "single males and females aged over 64, with no children", in total that is about 96% of all the discarded agents. All up in this instance, 427 out of the 3887 agents were discarded, or around 11% of the population (the average discarded agents for FS across all 100 instances was 13.42%).

We find that categories associated with under-15s, such as RU15c-m & RU15c-f aged 28–39 (h and p), and RUO15c-m & RUO15c-f aged 36–51 (l and t), are often less represented in the merged population. On the other hand, categories that do not need under-15 children often have more agents than required: Rnc-m & Rnc-f aged 16–35 (g and o), and RO15c-m & RO15c-f aged 32–47 (labels j and r) are four such clusters. This is possibly caused by not having enough agents aged under 15 in the population. As a result, agents that are supposed to be in "with under 15 children" (*U15c or *UO15c) categories end up in "no under 15 children" (*nc and *O15c) categories. However, there are a few notable exceptions. Categories RU15c-m aged 44–47 and RU15c-f aged 40–43

(i and q) have more agents in the merged than in the original. Two other such examples are agents aged 40–47 in RO15c-m and RO15c-f categories (k and s).

Equivalence of Merged and LL on Household Sizes. To establish the level of equivalence of our merged populations to LL with respect to distribution of household size categories, we followed a similar procedure, though with many fewer categories required. Each merged population (CS, CI, FS and FI) was compared to the LL population with respect to the 11 household size categories. Table 3 summarizes these results. Here we see the over-representation of 1 person households. The reason for this is that 1 person households can always be successfully formed, while a range of other size households sometimes cannot be formed due to relationship constraints (between couples and between parent and child). We see here most categories have some under-allocation. This results in 1 person households being over-represented in terms of percentage of all household types.

Figure 4 shows an example of over and under representation in one example merged population as compared to the original LL population, for CS. Here 10 out of the 11 categories, or 90.9%, are equivalent for $\epsilon = 0.0035$ (also shown). On average, for the same setting, 72.73% of the categories are equivalent for $\epsilon = 0.002$ (Table 3).

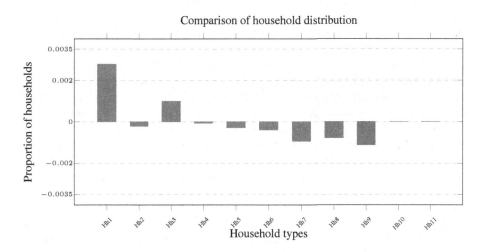

Fig. 4. Example over/under allocation in merged LL population with respect to LL for 11 household categories in CS.

Similarly to the WD results we see from Table 3 that using the coarse granularity to produce the merged population gives the best results, with an equivalence of 90.9% in the best case ($\epsilon = 0.0035$ **CS**). As with WD, use of fine granularity produces worse results, and in this case the deterioration is even greater than with WD. The explanation however is the same and has to do with the

Table 3. Equivalence of LL to each population set

	CS	FS	CI	FI
ϵ 0.002	72.73%	27.27%	54.55%	27.27%
ϵ 0.0035	90.9%	45.45%	81.82%	36.36%

increased number of constraints that must be met, resulting in larger numbers of discarded agents and households not able to be formed. In WD we saw that use of a simple seed gave better results for a coarse granularity population, while the informed seed gave better results for the fine granularity. For LL we continue to see a substantially superior performance with simple seed and coarse granularity (**CS** vs. **CI**), while there is no difference (but very poor results) for fine granularity (**FS** vs. **FI**). Based on these results we would use coarse granularity and simple seed in this case. However this is an area requiring further investigation across different applications to understand the general principles regarding what will give best results.

5   Discussion and Conclusion

In this work we have developed a process for obtaining a single initial population that can be used by two components in an integrated agent based simulation where both components model the same individuals conceptually. We provide a way to substantially retain structural elements of the original populations which are considered important. Our method is based on IPFP which has been widely used for building synthetic populations from different data sources representing the same population. We use the IPFP produced table to build the merged population following constraints necessary for the domain, such as individuals have only one marital partner, parents are older than children by at least X years, etc. In real populations these constraints are implicit in the actual data and so it should be possible to find a solution fully respecting the IPFP table. However, in our case this may not be so as there is no underlying "real" data. Our algorithm attempts to provide a solution which is as good as practically possible.

We have evaluated our technique using 400 different experimental populations and 100 initial populations generated from each of the components whose structure we are attempting to retain on some of the demographic characteristics. We have then run 4,248 TOST tests of equivalence using the allowable difference of ϵ equal 0.0015 and 0.002 for WD tests and 0.002 and 0.0035 for LL. Using coarse categories and simple seed we obtained 96.15% equivalence to WD ($\epsilon = 0.002$), and 90.9% equivalence to LL ($\epsilon = 0.0035$).

The equivalence of the original LL populations to the original WD populations ($\epsilon = 0.002$, coarse categories) was only 39.42%. Consequently it is clear that with this approach we have developed a more satisfactory initial population, respecting aspects of both components, than if we had simply imposed one component's initial population on the other. The approach is general, in that it can be applied to any two (or more) components which have overlapping populations which must be synchronised prior to executing a simulation using both components. Maintaining the synchronisation can of course also be challenging, but whatever approach is used to achieve that, a suitable initial population is required.

Although IPFP seems to provide a good start for building the integrated population, there is no guarantee, once additional constraints from the domain are applied, that a solution of actual agents which respects the original distributions exists. This problem is not as acute when synthesizing a population to match data from a single actual population, in that any domain constraints are implicitly respected within the data. In that case it is a matter of how good the algorithms are in forming the synthetic population. In our case when we are combining the characteristics of two different populations, for the purpose of integrating multiple aspects of a situation, there may well be an upper bound on the level of equivalence possible between the integrated population and each original. In further work we plan to analyse ways in which we can determine such a potential upper bound. If it is too low, this may be an indication of inherent problems with regard to the validity of integrating the components.

We also plan to explore whether alternative population synthesis techniques can be modified to address our problem, as well as analysing how the algorithm which builds the population from the statistical data plus required constraints, can be improved. We will further explore the optimal granularity of categories and the effect on equivalence, as well as exploring additional case studies.

While further work and investigation is important for a full understanding, we believe, on the basis of these results that we have developed a valuable approach to the problem of establishing an initial population for components when developing an integrated simulation from pre-existing pieces. Being able to integrate existing component simulations to form a more complex system is very important as simulation development is time consuming and costly, involving also significant domain expertise. Re-use is therefore increasingly important as we aim to address more and more real and complex systems. This work provides an important piece in being able to achieve re-use and the formation of new simulations by combining existing ones.

Acknowledgements. This research was funded in part by the Australian Research Council, SJB Urban and the (Melbourne) Metropolitan Planning Authority through Linkage Project grant LP130100008.

References

1. Balmer, M., Raney, B., Nagel, K.: Adjustment of activity timing and duration in an agent-based traffic flow simulation. In: Timmermans, H.J.P. (ed.) Progress in Activity-Based Analysis, pp. 91–114. Elsevier, Oxford, UK (2005)
2. Beckman, R.J., Baggerly, K.A., McKay, M.D.: Creating synthetic baseline populations. Transportation research part a: policy and practice **30**(6), 415–429 (1996)

3. Billari, F., Aparicio Diaz, B., Fent, T., Prskawetz, A., Prskawetz, A.: The "wedding-ring" an agent-based marriage model based on social interaction. Demogr. Res. **17**(3), 59–82 (2007)

4. Bishop, Y.M.M., Fienberg, S.E., Holland, P.W.: Discrete Multivariate Analysis: Theory and Practice. MIT, Cambridge (1975)

5. Dahmann, J.S., Kuhl, F.S., Weatherly, R.M.: Standards for simulation: as simple as possible but not simpler the high level architecture for simulation. Simulation **71**(6), 378–387 (1998)

6. Deming, W.E., Stephan, F.F.: On a least squares adjustment of a sampled frequency table when the expected marginal totals are known. Ann. Math. Stat. **11**(4), 427–444 (1940)

7. Dunham, J.B.: An agent-based spatially explicit epidemiological model in MASON. J. Artif. Soc. Soc. Simul. **9**(1), 3 (2005)

8. Fienberg, S.E.: An iterative procedure for estimation in contingency tables. Ann. Math. Stat. **41**(3), 907–917 (1970)

9. Harland, K., Heppenstall, A., Smith, D., Birkin, M.: Creating realistic synthetic populations at varying spatial scales: a comparative critique of population synthesis techniques. J. Artif. Soc. Soc. Simul. **15**(1), 1 (2012)

10. Kirill, M., Axhausen, K.W.: Hierarchical IPF: generating a synthetic population for Switzerland. In: 51st Congress of the European Regional Science Association, January 2011

11. Lovelace, R., Ballas, D.: Truncate, replicate, sample: a method for creating integer weights for spatial microsimulation. Comput. Environ. Urban Syst. **41**, 1–11 (2013)

12. Lovelace, R., Ballas, D., Birkin, M.H., van Leeuwen, E.: Evaluating the performance of iterative proportional fitting for spatial microsimulation: new tests for an established technique. J. Artif. Soc. Soc. Simul. **18**(2), 21 (2015)

13. Moore, R.V., Tindall, I.: An overview of the open modelling interface and environment (the OpenMI). Environ. Sci. Pol. **8**, 279–286 (2005)

14. Namazi-Rad, M.-R., Huynh, N., Barthelemy, J., Perez, P.: Synthetic population initialization and evolution-agent-based modelling of population aging and household transitions. In: Dam, H.K., Pitt, J., Xu, Y., Governatori, G., Ito, T. (eds.) PRIMA 2014. LNCS (LNAI), vol. 8861, pp. 182–189. Springer, Cham (2014). https://doi.org/10.1007/978-3-319-13191-7_15

15. Namazi-Rad, M.R., Mokhtarian, P., Perez, P.: Generating a dynamic synthetic population - using an age-structured two-sex model for household dynamics. PLoS ONE **9**(4), 94761 (2014)

16. Noble, J., Silverman, E., Bijak, J., Rossiter, S., Evandrou, M., Bullock, S., Vlachantoni, A., Falkingham, J.: Linked lives: the utility of an agent-based approach to modeling partnership and household formation in the context of social care. In: Winter Simulation Conference (WSC), Berlin, Germany, pp. 93:1–93:12. IEEE, 9–12 December 2012

17. Silverman, E., Bijak, J., Hilton, J., Cao, V.D., Noble, J.: When demography met social simulation: a tale of two modelling approaches. Artif. Soc. Soc. Simul. **16**(4), 9 (2013)

18. Singh, D., Padgham, L.: Opensim: a framework for integrating agent-based models and simulation components. In ECAI 2014–21st European Conference on Artificial Intelligence, Prague, Czech Republic, pp. 837–842, 18–22 August 2014

19. Tanton, R., Vidyattama, Y., Nepal, B., McNamara, J.: Small area estimation using a reweighting algorithm. J. Roy. Stat. Soc. Ser. A (Stat. Soc.) **174**(4), 931–951 (2011)

20. Voas, D., Williamson, P.: An evaluation of the combinatorial optimisation approach to the creation of synthetic microdata. Int. J. Population Geogr. **6**(5), 349–366 (2000)
21. Waddell, P.: Urbansim: modeling urban development for land use, transportation and environmental planning. J. Am. Plann. Assoc. **68**(3), 297–314 (2002)
22. Walker, E., Nowacki, A.S.: Understanding equivalence and noninferiority testing. J. Gener. Intern. Med. **26**(2), 192–196 (2011)
23. Wickramasinghe, B.N., Singh, D., Padgham, L.: Synchronising agent populations when combining agent-based simulations. In: Spring Simulation Multiconference, Alexandria, USA (2015)
24. Williamson, P., Birkin, M., Rees, P.H.: The estimation of population microdata by using data from small area statistics and samples of anonymised records. Environ. Plann. A **30**(5), 785–816 (1998)
25. Ye, X., Konduri, K., Pendyala, R.M., Sana, B.: A methodology to match distributions of both household and person attributes in the generation of synthetic populations. In: 88th Annual Meeting of the Transportation Research Board (2009). 9600(206)

Norm Conflict Identification Using Deep Learning

João Paulo Aires$^{(\boxtimes)}$ and Felipe Meneguzzi

School of Computer Science, Pontifical Catholic University of Rio Grande do Sul,
Porto Alegre, Brazil
`joao.aires.001@acad.pucrs.br, felipe.meneguzzi@pucrs.br`

Abstract. Contracts represent agreements between two or more parties formally in the form of deontic statements or norms within their clauses. If not carefully designed, such conflicts may invalidate an entire contract, and thus human reviewers invest great effort to write conflict-free contracts that, for complex and long contracts, can be time consuming and error-prone. In this work, we develop an approach to automate the identification of potential conflicts between norms in contracts. We build a two-phase approach that uses traditional machine learning together with deep learning to extract and compare norms in order to identify conflicts between them. Using a manually annotated set of conflicts as train and test set, our approach obtains 85% accuracy, establishing a new state-of-the art.

Keywords: Norms · Contracts · Deep learning · Natural language

1   Introduction

Regulations are often applied to social members in a society in order to minimize conflicting behaviors [18]. Such regulations also known as social norms, define expected behaviors accepted for society members and that ensure that individuals act according to a socially acceptable behavior. Besides regulating entire societies, social norms are also used to regulate interactions in smaller groups, and are often present in social relationships involving agreements over products and services. A common way to formalize a set of norms applied to an agreement is through contracts. In human societies, contracts are semi-structured documents written in natural language, which are used in almost every existing formal agreement. Contracts define the parties involved in the agreement, their relations, and the behavior expected of each party within clauses. When written in natural language, contracts may use imprecise and possibly vague language to define parties, obligations and objects of its clauses, leading to inconsistencies. Such inconsistencies may create, in the long run, unforeseen legal problems for one or more of the involved parties. To identify and solve such conflicts and inconsistencies, the contract maker needs to read the entire contract and identify

© Springer International Publishing AG 2017
G. Sukthankar and J. A. Rodriguez-Aguilar (Eds.): AAMAS 2017 Visionary Papers,
LNAI 10643, pp. 194–207, 2017.
https://doi.org/10.1007/978-3-319-71679-4_13

each conflicting pair of norms. As conflicts tend to have a large number of norms, the task of identifying norm conflicts is quite difficult for human beings, which makes it error-prone and takes substantial human effort.

Our main contributions in this work are two: first, an approach to address the problem of identifying and quantifying potential normative conflicts between natural language contract clauses; and second, a corpus containing normative conflicts[1]. We process raw text from contracts and identify their norms. Then, we train a convolutional neural network to classify norm pairs as conflict or non-conflict. We evaluate our approach using a dataset of contracts in which conflicts have been deliberately but randomly introduced between the norms, obtaining an accuracy around 85% in conflict identification for a 10-fold cross validation.

2   Norms and Contracts

Norms ensure that individuals act according to a defined set of behaviors and are punished when they are perceived not to be complying with them given a social setting [1]. Norms provide a powerful mechanism for regulating conflict in groups, governing much of our political and social lives. They are often represented using deontic logic, which has its origins in philosophical logic, applied modal logic, and ethical and legal theory. The aim of deontic logic is to describe ideal worlds, allowing the representation of deviations from the ideal (i.e. violations) [27]. Thus, deontic logic and the theory of normative positions are very relevant to legal knowledge representation, and consequently they are applied to the analysis and representation of normative systems [16]. Norms often use deontic concepts to describe permissions, obligations, and prohibitions. A prohibition indicates an action that must not be performed, and, if such action is carried out, a violation occurs. Conversely, a permission indicates an action that can either be performed or not, and no violation occurs in either case. In most deontic systems, a prohibition is considered to be equivalent to the negation of a permission, thus, an action that is not permitted comprises a prohibition. Although these two modalities are sufficient to represent most norms, obligations are also commonly employed in norm representation. An obligation represents an action that must be performed, and it is equivalent either to the negation of a permission not to act or a prohibition not to act.

In contracts, norms are defined within clauses and are often directed to one or more parties of the contract. A contract is an agreement that two or more parties enter voluntarily when it is useful to formalize that a certain duty comes into existence by a promise made by at least one of the parties. The creation of a contract formalizes what each party expects from the other, creating a warranty that each party will fulfill their duties [22] and legally enforceable obligations between these parties. These enforceable obligations are defined by a set of norms, which are responsible for describing any expected behavior from the parties.

With the use of the Internet, electronic contracts arise as a new way to represent formal agreements and are increasingly explored for commercial services.

---

[1] https://goo.gl/3Hbl1r.

An electronic contract is very similar to a traditional paper-based commercial contract, following the same rules and structure [20]. Almost all types of contract can be represented electronically, leading to the need of managing such contracts, dealing with the representation and evaluation of agreements. In this work, we deal with contracts written in natural language, thus, the task of analyzing and evaluating norms is traditionally done by human readers. As more contracts are required to codify an increasing number of online services which span over multiple countries and different legal systems, the tasks of writing and verifying contracts by humans become more laborious, taking substantial time [10].

2.1   Norm Conflicts

Sadat-Akhavi [23] describes four causes for a norm conflict to arise. The first cause is when the same act is subject to different types of norms. Thus, two norms are in conflict "if two different types of norms regulate the same act, i.e., if the same act is both obligatory and prohibited, permitted and prohibited, or permitted and obligatory". For example, consider a norm n1 that states that company X must pay product Z taxes, and a norm n2 that states that company X may pay product Z taxes. The second cause is when one norm requires an act, while another norm requires or permits a 'contrary' act. In this case, there is a normative conflict if "two contrary acts, or if one norm permits an act while the other norm requires a contrary act" [23]. For example, consider a norm n1 that states that Company X shall deliver product Z on location W, whereas norm n2 states that company X must deliver product Z on location Q. The conflict arises in the moment that one tries to comply with one norm and, at the same time, is non-complying with the other. The third case defines a cause of conflict when a norm prohibits a precondition of another norm. For example, norm 1 obliges company X to perform α in location θ, whereas norm 2 prohibits company X to be in location θ. In this case, company X cannot comply with norm 1 since been in location θ implies in a violation of norm 2. Finally, Sadat-Akhavi defines a cause of conflict when one norm prohibits a necessary consequence from another norm. For example, norm 1 states that company X shall/may replace its material supplier each year and the process shall not last more than two weeks, whereas norm 2 states that company X cannot be without a material supplier. In this case, the process of replacing the material supplier (norm 1) implies to company X an amount of time without a material supplier, complying with such norm makes company X violate norm 2.

3   Deep Learning

Deep learning is a branch of machine learning that tries to solve problems by automatically finding an internal representation based on hierarchical layers [12]. Such layers can extract complex features from data as they get deeper, which makes feature design from human engineers unnecessary [3]. There are multiple architectures of deep neural networks that achieve this type of learning, such as, convolutional neural networks (CNN) [4], recurrent neural networks (RNN) [15], and autoencoders [26].

3.1 Convolutional Neural Networks

Convolutional neural networks were first introduced by LeCun *et al.* [4]. They modify the usual neural network by adding successive convolutional layers before the fully connected neural network output layer, as illustrated in Fig. 1. A convolutional layer uses the convolution mathematical operator to modify specific regions of input data using a set of kernels, substantially diminishing the number of neural connection weighs a learning algorithm must adjust close to the input features. A convolution can be viewed as an operation between two functions that produces a third one. Each kernel of a convolutional layer has a defined size and contains a value for each cell; these values, called weights, multiply the values from the input features resulting in a new feature map. The kernel goes through the input multiplying every matrix cell, as illustrated in Fig. 2. The result of applying multiple convolutions to an input is a set of feature maps with specific information from the input.

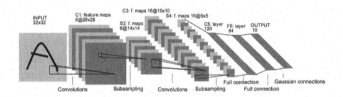

Fig. 1. Abstract representation of a CNN (extracted from LeCun *et al.* [4])

In order to reduce the dimensionality of features resulting from convolutions, convolutional networks often contain pooling layers between successive convolutional layers. These layers have a single kernel without weights that goes through the input aiming to down-sample the size of the image, much in the same way resizing an image reduces its dimensions, as illustrated in Fig. 3. They can be either a max pooling or a mean pooling, the former outputs the highest value among the ones in the kernel size and the later outputs the mean value among the ones in the kernel. LeCun *et al.* use this type of neural network to identify handwritten numbers from zip codes in real U.S. mail. From then on, convolutional neural networks have been used extensively to solve image processing problems. More recently, researchers have used CNNs to solve classical natural language processing problems ([11,28]), such as part-of-speech tagging, named entity recognition, and sentiment analysis. In most cases, approaches using CNNs have matched and surpassed previous approaches using rule-based and probabilistic approaches. The key challenge in applying CNNs to text processing is finding a suitable matrix representation for the input text.

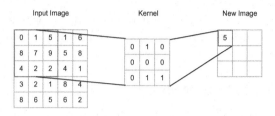

Fig. 2. Convolution example

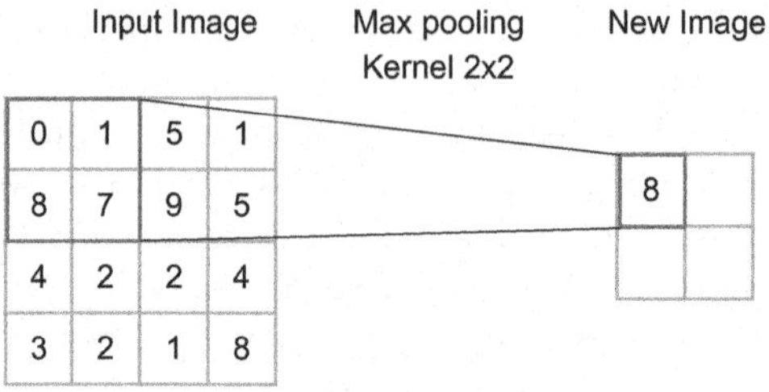

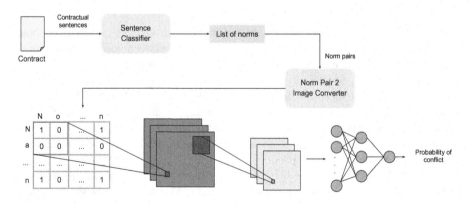

Fig. 3. Pooling example

4   Conflict Detection Approach

Our approach to identifying potential conflicts between norms in contracts is divided into two phases. In the first one, we identify norms within contractual sentences by training a Support Vector classifier using a manually annotated dataset. In the second part, we classify norm pairs as conflicting or non-conflicting using a CNN. Figure 4 illustrates the architecture of our approach.

Fig. 4. Architecture of the norm conflict identifier

4.1 Norm Identification

The first step towards norm conflict identification is to identify which sentences in a contract contain deontic statements (norms). For this task we consider contract sentences to be of two exclusive types: norm sentences and non-norm sentences. In order to separate norm sentences from the rest of the contract text, we train a classifier based on Support Vector Machines (SVM) using a manually annotated dataset. We created the dataset using real contracts extracted from the *onecle* website[2], specifically contracts of the manufacturing domain[3]. We manually annotated the sentences in each contract as being either norm or non-norm, resulting in a set of 699 norm sentences and 494 non-norm sentences from a total of 22 contracts, which we use as both train and test sets.

4.2 Norm Conflict Identification

In order to identify norm conflicts, we use the concepts introduced by Sadat-Akhavi [23]. Unlike the four causes for conflicts, Sadat-Akhavi identifies three main types of conflicts, which are:

- Permission x Obligation;
- Permission x Prohibition; and
- Obligation x Prohibition.

We base our conflict identification on these three conflict types in addition to the first and second causes of norm conflict defined by Sadat-Akhavi. Thus, in this work, we consider norm conflicts to be:

- Pairs of norms with different deontic concepts applied to the same actions and the same parties; and
- Pairs of norms where the obliged action of one clause is either prohibited or permitted in another clause.

The key challenge in processing text using CNNs is to generate a representation suitable for the matrix-format input required for the convolutional layers. Here, we take inspiration from recent work that deals with natural language. The first sentence representation, created by Zhang and LeCun [28], in which they use a CNN to deal with natural language processing problems. Their approach aims to, among other tasks, classify the sentiment (positive, negative, and neutral) of product reviews from Amazon. Since CNNs are designed to process images, the solution they propose to translate a sentence into an image is to create a matrix representation with the review characters as lines and the alphabet as columns. Thus, given a cell $\{i, j\}$, they assign 1 when the ith character is equal to the jth, otherwise, they assign 0. Figure 5 illustrates their sentence representation using as example a sentence that begins with 'above'. The resulting matrix has 1 where letters are equal (such as cell $1, 1$ and $2, 2$) and 0 otherwise.

---

[2] http://contracts.onecle.com/.

[3] http://contracts.onecle.com/type/47.shtml.

Alphabet

		a	b	$\cdots$	x	y	z
	a	1	0	$\cdots$	0	0	0
	b	0	1	$\cdots$	0	0	0
Sentence	o	0	0	$\cdots$	0	0	0
	v	0	0	$\cdots$	0	0	0
	e	0	0	$\cdots$	0	0	0

Fig. 5. Sentence representation by Zhang and LeCun

The second work is from Kim [17], which uses a sentence representation to classify sentences in different natural language processing problems. Here, the representation is a matrix in which the lines are the words of a sentence and columns are the word embedding of each word. An embedding is a representation that turns words into vectors of floating point numbers. Such representation may have a variable size and carries semantic information from each word. In Kim's approach, the resulting matrix is a group of word embedding lines. Figure 6 illustrates this sentence representation.

Embedding

	I	0.9	0.5	$\cdots$	0.6	0.1	0.2
	like	0.1	0.2	$\cdots$	0.5	0.5	0.6
Sentence	the	0.1	0.3	$\cdots$	0.2	0.9	0.1
	new	0.7	0.3	$\cdots$	0.4	0.1	0.2
	device	0.6	0.4	$\cdots$	0.8	0.3	0.7

Fig. 6. Sentence representation by Kim

One of the key aspects in norm conflicts is that both norms tend to be very similar in that usually both norms refer to the same party/parties with similar actions, and only the modality of the sentence differs. Thus, the similarity distance between two sentences often indicates how norm pairs are likely to conflict. Consequently, we rely on training examples that consist of binary images created from each pair of norms denoting the distance between these norms. Thus, we created a pair-of-norms representation using a matrix to denote similar characters in each norm. Given two norms α and β, our matrix consists of the characters from α in its lines and the characters from β in its columns, as Fig. 7 illustrates. Given a cell $\{i, j\}$, we assign 1 to it when the ith character of α is equal to the jth character of β and 0 otherwise. For this work, we limit the lengths

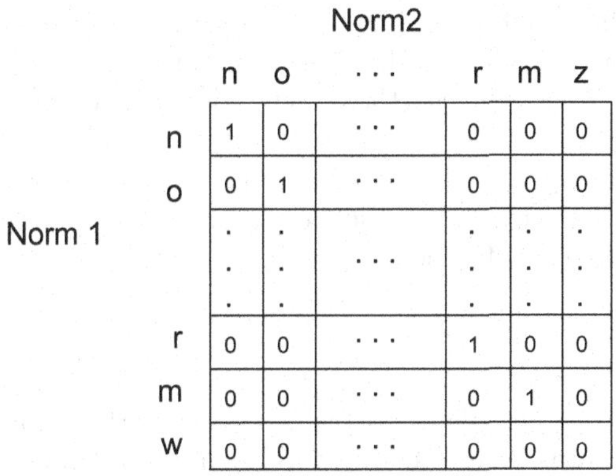

Norm2

	n	o	···	r	m	z
n	1	0	···	0	0	0
o	0	1	···	0	0	0
·	·	·		·	·	·
·	·	·	···	·	·	·
·	·	·		·	·	·
r	0	0	···	1	0	0
m	0	0	···	0	1	0
w	0	0	···	0	0	0

(Norm 1 labels the rows)

Fig. 7. Norm pair representation in our approach

of both norms to 200 characters, which is the mean length of norms from our dataset and truncate overlong sentences (which, as we see in the experiments, seems to have no effect in accuracy). Using this representation we train a CNN to generate a model to classify norm pairs as conflicting and non-conflicting.

5 Experiments

5.1 Norm Conflict Dataset Annotation

To evaluate our approach to detect potential conflicts between norms, we required a corpus with contracts containing real conflicts. However, since we found no such corpus available, we created a dataset with semi-automatically generated norm conflicts using a set of real non-conflicting norms as a basis. To assist in the creation of conflicts, we developed a system to assist human users to insert conflicts randomly in a contract, while still maintaining language syntactic correctness. In order to create such conflicts, we relied on the assistance of two volunteers each of which was responsible for inserting two different types of conflict. Each volunteer was asked to create one of the two causes of conflict. We asked the first volunteer to insert conflicts that have only differences in the modal verb, e.g. changing an obligation modal verb ('must') for a permission one ('may'). This volunteer created 94 conflicts in 10 different contracts, totaling 13 conflicts between Permission x Prohibition, 36 conflicts between Permission x Obligation, and 46 conflicts between Obligation x Prohibition. We asked the second volunteer to insert conflicts that contain deontic conflicts and modifications in the norm actions. This volunteer created 17 conflicts in 6 different contracts, totaling 2 conflicts between Permission x Prohibition, 6 conflicts between Permission x Obligation, and 4 conflicts between Obligation x Prohibition.

We developed a semi-automatic process conflict creation within a system that, when prompted, selects a random norm from a random contract, makes a copy of it, and asks the user to modify it. After user modification, the system creates a new contract containing both the original norm and the modified copy, ensuring that a semantically similar, but conflicting, clause is present in the resulting contract. Thus, we use these new contracts to identify the inserted conflicts.

From the contracts we used to create conflicts, we selected all sentences not used in the conflict creation to produce a set for the non-conflicting norm class. This set has a total of 204,443 norm pairs.

5.2 SVM

To create the sentence classifier, we trained a support vector machine (SVM) classifier using the dataset described in the Norm Identification section. SVM is often used to classify datasets with few training examples with multiple features and a binary classification task since it creates a hyperplane that tries to find the best division between two classes [14]. In order to train the SVM, we turn each sentence into a bag-of-words representation [13], which represents the frequency of words from a fixed dictionary in sentence. Using this representation, the SVM learns from the frequency each word appears in a class.

5.3 CNN

To create the norm conflict identifier, we train a CNN using norm pairs from the dataset described in Norm Conflict Dataset Annotation section. In this work, we use the classical *LeNet* CNN, developed by LeCun *et al.* [4]. The network architecture consists of two convolutional layers followed by a max pooling layer and two fully-connected neural networks. Each convolutional layer has 32 kernels that are responsible for extracting features from the input image. The network receives as input an image representation of each norm pair.

6   Results

6.1   Sentence Classifier

To evaluate our sentence classifier, we divided our manually annotated dataset into train and test set. We use a 80/20 division, which results in 954 sentences in the train set and 238 sentences in the test set. Both sets are balanced according to the number of elements in each class, i.e., 559 norm sentences and 395 non-norm sentences in the train set, and 139 norm sentences and 98 non-norm sentences in the test set. To compare the SVM with other linear models, we test the same dataset with two other classifiers: Perceptron and Passive Aggressive. Perceptron is a well-known linear model, which can be better explained as a neuron in a neural network [19]. It processes the input by multiplying it using a set of weights. The result goes to an activation function, which defines the input class. Passive Aggressive [2] is a linear model that has its name based on its weight update rule that, in each round, can be passive, when the hinge-loss result of its update

Table 1. Results for sentence classifier

Classifier	Prec.	Rec.	F-Score	Acc.
Perceptron	0.89	0.88	0.88	0.87
Pass. Agr	**0.92**	0.88	0.90	0.89
SVM	0.88	**0.94**	**0.91**	**0.90**

is zero, and aggressive, when it is a positive number. Table 1 shows the results for each classifier.

As we can see, SVM obtains the best result for the task with an accuracy of 90%. The passive aggressive algorithm has a similarly good accuracy and has the best precision in comparison to the others. However, since SVM obtains a better overall result, we use it as our sentence classifier.

6.2 Norm Conflict Identifier

To evaluate the norm conflict identifier, we used a 10-fold cross-validation step dividing our dataset into train, validation, and test. Since we have a total of 104 norm pairs with conflicting norms and 204,443 conflict-free norm pairs, the first step is to create a balanced dataset. Thus, we reduced the number of non-conflicting norm pairs to 104, which gives us a total of 208 samples. Each fold has 10% of the data, which is around twenty samples, ten of each class. In each round, we use eight folds to train, one to validate, and one to test. To prevent overfitting, we use the early stopping technique that monitors the accuracy in the train and validation set. When the accuracy in the validation set starts to decrease and the train accuracy keeps increasing, an overfitting is detected, resulting in the termination of the training phase. We show the accuracy results for each fold and the mean accuracy overall in Table 2.

Table 2. Results for the norm conflict identifier

Fold	0	1	2	3	4	5	6	7	8	9	Mean
Accuracy	0.85	0.85	0.76	0.95	0.85	0.76	0.71	0.95	0.95	0.80	0.84

7 Related Work

Since our approach merges information retrieval, which is the extraction of information from unstructured data, and contract reasoning, which is manipulation and reasoning over contract elements, in this section we compare our approach to recent work that deals with similar concepts applied to contracts.

Rosso et al. [21] propose an approach to retrieve information from legal texts. Their approach uses JIRS[4] (Java Information Retrieval System), a system that

---

[4] http://sourceforge.net/projects/jirs/.

measures distances between sentences using n-grams, to develop a solution for three problems: passage retrieval in treaties, patents, and contracts. In the first problem, they want to answer questions from treaty documents. Given a question about the content of the treaty, they use JIRS to measure the distance between the question and the text in the treaty, thus, they can rank the best answers to each question by their similarity. To the second problem, they develop an approach to help patent creators identify similar patents. As in the first problem, given a set of patents and a new one, they use JIRS to measure how similar the new patent is to existing ones. To the third problem, they develop an approach to identify conflicts between norms in contracts. To do so, they create a contract example between an airline and a ground operations company with a defined set of norms applied to both parties. They divide the process of conflict identification into three steps, first, they translate every norm in contract to a formal contract language ($\mathcal{CL}$ [7]), which they call Contract Language clauses. Second, they analyse the clauses using a model checker performed by the contract analysis tool $CLAN$ [8]. From the identified conflicts, they use JIRS to translate the sentences from $\mathcal{CL}$ to natural language. Although this work also tries to identify norm conflicts, it differs from ours in two points. First, our work tries to identify normative conflicts dealing directly with natural language, whereas in their work they use the approach proposed by Fenech *et al.* [8], which uses a single contract that has its norms *manually translated* into the controlled language $\mathcal{CL}$. Second, to identify norm conflicts, $CLAN$ uses a series of predefined rules, whereas in our approach we rely on a convolution neural network that processes matrix of distances between pairs of norms automatically extracting the information needed to classify them.

Curtotti and McCreath [5] propose an approach to annotate contracts using machine learning and rule-based techniques. They aim to classify each component of contractual sentences based on their structure. To extract data for machine learning, they create a hand-coded tagger and manually correct its outcome. As data, they use the Australian Contract Corpus [6] with 256 contracts, containing 42910 sentences and a vocabulary of 14217 words. In their experiments, they randomly select 30 contracts and divide them into three sets, one for train and two for test. Using different classifiers to compare the results, they obtain 0.86 of F-score. Instead of classifying each clause structure with a different class, in this work we want to identify norm clauses. However, we can use Curtotti and McCreath annotation for a further work with a deeper contract analysis.

Gao and Singh propose two different solutions for problems concerning information extraction from contracts. In the first one, they propose an approach to extract exceptions within norms in contracts [10]. They use a corpus with 2,647 contracts from the Onecle repository[5] as data for processing. As result, Enlil obtains an F-score of 0.9 in classifying contracts using a manually annotated corpus. Although Gao and Singh work is similar to ours by dealing with contractual norms, we have different ends. In our work, we use norms to find potential

---

[5] http://contracts.onecle.com.

conflicts, whereas they use them to identify exceptions within a contract. However, we can use their concept of exception in a new approach to identify conflicts with a high-level of detail, since exceptions in norms may induce to new types of conflicts.

In their second work, Gao and Singh [9] develop a hybrid approach for extracting business events and their temporal constraints from contracts. Using different machine learning algorithms they obtain an F-score of 0.89 for event extraction and 0.9 for temporal constraints. This, similar to the first work, is an approach to extract information from contracts. The main difference between their work and ours is that they try to identify temporal elements from norms. This is also an improvement we can apply to the norm conflict identification process.

Vasconcelos et al. [25] propose an approach to deal with normative conflicts in multi-agent systems. They develop mechanisms for detection and resolution of normative conflicts. To resolve conflicts they manipulate the constraints associated to the norms' variables, removing any overlap in their values. In norm adoption, they use a set of auxiliary norms to exchange by the ones applied to the agent. In norm removal, they remove a certain norm and all curtailments it caused, bringing back a previous form of the normative state. Figueiredo and Silva's work [24] consist of an algorithm for normative conflict detection using first-order logic. They use the Z language to formalize the conflict types and then identify them between norms. Both approaches from Vasconcelos et al. and Figueiredo and Silva propose a solution for norm conflicts applied to normative multi-agent systems. The main difference between their work and ours is that we make the identification of potential conflicts between norms from contracts written in natural language. It creates the need for a different approach since natural language is not structured. However, an alternative approach would be the translation of natural language to first-order-logic and use one of these approaches to identify conflicts.

8   Conclusion and Future Work

In this work, we developed a two-phase approach to identify potential conflicts between norms in contracts. Our main contributions are: (1) a dataset with manually annotated normative and non-normative sentences from real contracts; (2) a machine learning model to classify contractual sentences as normative and non-normative; (3) a manually annotated dataset with contracts containing conflicts between norms; (4) and a deep learning model to classify norm pairs as conflicting and non-conflicting. We evaluate both models and we obtain an accuracy of 90% for the sentence classifier and around 85% for the norm conflict identifier.

As future work, we aim to develop two different approaches. First, we aim to develop a pre-processing step in the norm conflict identification to identify elements that may improve the detection of conflicts, such as temporal information. Second, to fairly compare our results with the work proposed by Fenech et al. [8], we aim to create an approach to translate natural language to $\mathcal{CL}$ (contract language) and use *CLAN* to discover conflicts.

Acknowledgements. We gratefully thank Google Research Awards for Latin America for funding our project.

References

1. Axelrod, R.: An evolutionary approach to norms. Am. Polit. Sci. Rev. **80**(4), 1095–1111 (1986)
2. Crammer, K., Dekel, O., Keshet, J., Shalev-Shwartz, S., Singer, Y.: Online passive-aggressive algorithms. J. Mach. Learn. Res. **7**, 551–585 (2006)
3. Cun, L., Bengio, Y., Hinton, G.: Deep learning. Nature **521**(7553), 436–444 (2015)
4. Cun, L., Boser, B., Denker, J.S., Henderson, D., Howard, R.E., Hubbard, W., Jackel, L.D.: Handwritten digit recognition with a back-propagation network. In: Advances in Neural Information Processing Systems, pp. 396–404. Morgan Kaufmann, Massachusetts (1990)
5. Curtotti, M., Mccreath, E.: Corpus based classification of text in Australian contracts. In: Proceedings of the Australasian Language Technology Association Workshop, Melbourne, Australia, pp. 18–26 (2010)
6. Curtotti, M., McCreath, E.C.: A corpus of Australian contract language: description, profiling and analysis. In: Proceedings of the 13th International Conference on Artificial Intelligence and Law, ICAIL 2011, pp. 199–208. ACM, New York, NY, USA (2011)
7. Fenech, S., Pace, G.J., Schneider, G.: Automatic conflict detection on contracts. In: Leucker, M., Morgan, C. (eds.) ICTAC 2009. LNCS, vol. 5684, pp. 200–214. Springer, Heidelberg (2009). https://doi.org/10.1007/978-3-642-03466-4_13
8. Fenech, S., Pace, G.J., Schneider, G.: CLAN: a tool for contract analysis and conflict discovery. In: Liu, Z., Ravn, A.P. (eds.) ATVA 2009. LNCS, vol. 5799, pp. 90–96. Springer, Heidelberg (2009). https://doi.org/10.1007/978-3-642-04761-9_8
9. Gao, X., Singh, M.P.: Mining contracts for business events and temporal constraints in service engagements. IEEE Trans. Serv. Comput. **7**(3), 427–439 (2013)
10. Gao, X., Singh, M.P., Mehra, P.: Mining business contracts for service exceptions. IEEE Trans. Serv. Comput. 5(3), 333–344 (2012)
11. Gillick, D., Brunk, C., Vinyals, O., Subramanya, A.: Multilingual language processing from bytes. arXiv preprint arXiv:1512.00103 (2015)
12. Goodfellow, I., Bengio, Y., Courville, A.: Deep Learning. MIT Press, Cambridge (2016). (In Preparation)
13. Harris, Z.S.: Distributional Structure, pp. 775–794. Springer, Dordrecht (1970)
14. Hearst, M.A., Dumais, S.T., Osman, E., Platt, J., Scholkopf, B.: Support vector machines. IEEE Intell. Syst. Appl. **13**(4), 18–28 (1998)
15. Jain, L.C., Medsker, L.R.: Recurrent Neural Networks: Design and Applications, 1st edn. CRC Press Inc, Boca Raton, FL, USA (1999)
16. Jones, A.J.I., Sergot, M.J.: Deontic logic in the representation of law: towards a methodology. Artif. Intell. Law **1**(1), 45–64 (1992)
17. Kim, Y.: Convolutional neural networks for sentence classification. In: Moschitti, A., Pang, B., Daelemans, W. (eds.) Proceedings of the 2014 Conference on Empirical Methods in Natural Language Processing, EMNLP 2014, 25–29 October 2014, Doha, Qatar, A meeting of SIGDAT, a Special Interest Group of the ACL, pp. 1746–1751. ACL (2014)

18. Meneguzzi, F., Rodrigues, O., Oren, N., Vasconcelos, W.W., Luck, M.: BDI reasoning with normative considerations. Eng. Appl. Artif. Intell. **43**, 127–146 (2015)
19. Minsky, M., Papert, S.: Perceptrons. In: Anderson, J.A., Rosenfeld, E. (eds.) Neurocomputing: Foundations of Research, pp. 157–169. MIT Press, Cambridge (1988)
20. Prisacariu, C., Schneider, G.: A formal language for electronic contracts. In: Bonsangue, M.M., Johnsen, E.B. (eds.) FMOODS 2007. LNCS, vol. 4468, pp. 174–189. Springer, Heidelberg (2007). https://doi.org/10.1007/978-3-540-72952-5_11
21. Rosso, P., Correa, S., Buscaldi, D.: Passage retrieval in legal texts. J. Logic Algebraic Program. **80**(3–5), 139–153 (2011)
22. Rousseau, D.M., McLean Parks, J.: The contracts of individuals and organizations, vol. 15. JAI Press Ltd. (1993)
23. Sadat-Akhavi, A.: Methods of Resolving Conflicts Between Treaties. Graduate Institute of International Studies (Series), V. 3, M. Nijhoff (2003)
24. da Silva Figueiredo, K., da Silva, V.T.: An algorithm to identify conflicts between norms and values. In: Balke, T., Dignum, F., van Riemsdijk, M.B., Chopra, A.K. (eds.) COIN 2013. LNCS (LNAI), vol. 8386, pp. 259–274. Springer, Cham (2014). https://doi.org/10.1007/978-3-319-07314-9_14
25. Vasconcelos, W.W., Kollingbaum, M.J., Norman, T.J.: Normative conflict resolution in multi-agent systems. Auton. Agents Multi-Agent Syst. **19**(2), 124–152 (2009)
26. Vincent, P., Larochelle, H., Bengio, Y., Manzagol, P.A.: Extracting and composing robust features with denoising autoencoders. In: Proceedings of the 25th International Conference on Machine Learning, ICML 2008, pp. 1096–1103. ACM, New York, NY, USA (2008)
27. von Wright, G.H.: Deontic Logic, New Series, vol. 60. Oxford University Press on behalf of the Mind Association, Oxford (1951)
28. Zhang, X., Cun, L.: Text understanding from scratch. CoRR abs/1502.01710 (2015)

Identifying Affordances for Modelling Second-Order Emergent Phenomena with the $\mathcal{WIT}$ Framework

Pablo Noriega[1], Jordi Sabater-Mir[1(✉)], Harko Verhagen[2], Julian Padget[3], and Mark d'Inverno[4]

[1] IIIA-CSIC, Barcelona, Spain
{pablo,jsabater}@iiia.csic.es
[2] Stockholm University, Stockholm, Sweden
verhagen@dsv.su.se
[3] Department of Computer Science, University of Bath, Bath, UK
j.a.padget@bath.ac.uk
[4] Goldsmiths, University of London, London, UK
dinverno@gold.ac.uk

Abstract. We explore a means to understand second order emergent social phenomena (*EP2*), that is, phenomena that involve groups of agents who reason and decide, specifically, about actions – theirs or others' – that may affect the social environment where they interact with other agents. We propose to model such phenomena as socio-cognitive technical systems that involve, on one hand, agents that are imbued with social rationality (thus socio-cognitive) and, on the other hand, a social space where they interact. For that modelling we rely on the WIT framework that defines such socio-cognitive technical systems as a trinity of aspects (the social phenomenon, the simulation model and the implementation of that model). In this paper we centre our attention on the use of *affordances* as a useful construct to model socio-cognitive technical systems. We use the example of reputation emergence to illustrate our proposal.

1 Introduction

There is a rich discussion within the COIN[1] community about the properties and uses of open regulated multiagent systems that may be brought to bear upon the modelling of second order emergent phenomena (*EP2*). Such social

---

[1] COIN is the acronym Coordination, Organisations, Institutions and Norms, which has been adopted by a community of researchers, mostly within multiagent systems, who focus on these four topics. The COIN community typically organises two workshops each year leading to an annual volume of collected papers, published by Springer LNCS. The first COIN workshop took place in 2005 alongside AAMAS in Utrecht.

G. Sukthankar and J. A. Rodriguez-Aguilar (Eds.): AAMAS 2017 Visionary Papers,
LNAI 10643, pp. 208–227, 2017.
https://doi.org/10.1007/978-3-319-71679-4_14

phenomena involve agents that not only decide about their own actions but also about the actions of others and on the effect those actions have in the social environment where they interact. Although some $EP2$ have been explained as complex systems, it has been argued that agent-based simulation modelling may prove useful not only for explaining emergent features but also to understand motivational, strategic and organisational features that are ascribed to the individuals involved in these phenomena and the outcomes of their activity within a given social environment.

The $\mathcal{WIT}$ framework is one way to analyse and describe those multiagent systems. The $\mathcal{WIT}$ framework postulates that coordination support frameworks for open regulated MAS are the amalgam of three aspects: (i) $\mathcal{W}$: a socio-technical system that constitutes actual coordination of a particular collective activity in the real *world*; (ii) $\mathcal{I}$: an abstract or *institutional* specification of the conventions that articulate the interactions in that system; and (iii) $\mathcal{T}$: the *technological* elements that implement the institutional conventions and enable the use of the system in practice. The $\mathcal{WIT}$ framework postulates also the type of relationships that should exist between those three aspects and how to characterise classes of socio-cognitive technical systems by linking $\mathcal{I}$ with $\mathcal{T}$ through the correspondence between metamodels for agents and social spaces and the platforms that implement those metamodels.

We claim that the use of the $\mathcal{WIT}$ framework provides the relevant foundations to deal effectively with the problem of modelling $EP2$. In this paper we use a specific example of the emergence of reputation to make a first step in this direction. Namely, when rumours about the behaviour of an individual circulate within a group, the reputation of that individual may change. When members of the group perceive that change, they may react by sending messages that reinforce or attenuate reputation change. Therefore, as in other $EP2$, the perceived signals influence the behaviour of individuals, which in turn influences how that reputation evolves.

Informed by the $\mathcal{WIT}$ framework, here we focus our attention on the abstract features that are needed to model both socio-cognitive agents and their social space. In particular we use the $\mathcal{WIT}$ framework (Sect. 2) to elucidate the *affordances* required for modelling $EP2$. We approach this goal by working through three levels of refinement, each level being more specific than the previous. At the first, we put forward a primary list of *affordances* required for a generic $EP2$ (Sect. 4). At the second we choose a second order emergent phenomenon – reputation – to explore, and informed by the primary list and the characteristics of the phenomenon we build a second, more specific, list of affordances (Sect. 4.2). Finally, at the third level, we focus on a specific scenario that utilises the social phenomenon analysed at the second level. Again, using the primary and secondary lists, we build a third list that considers the particularities of the scenario (Sect. 4.3). We conclude with a brief discussion of future work (Sect. 5).

2   Socio-cognitive Technical Systems. The $\mathcal{WIT}$ Framework

A socio-cognitive technical system (SCTS) is an open regulated multiagent system where agents – that may be human or software – interact in a shared virtual (online) space. We distinguish SCTS from other MAS by making explicit some assumptions about the agents that participate and the form that participation takes. To make this more precise we reproduce in Notion 1 the definition set out in [13]. We then use that as a starting point to put forward three (new) associated notions:

Notion 2: The social space in which a SCTS is situated and in particular the state of that social space that participants may perceive;

Notion 3: How the views that characterise the $\mathcal{WIT}$ framework can capture perspectives on SCTS, while providing a potentially helpful separation of concerns, as well as drawing attention to the interfaces between $\mathcal{W}$, $\mathcal{I}$ and $\mathcal{T}$;

Notion 4: How the "correct" interaction between $\mathcal{W}$, $\mathcal{I}$ and $\mathcal{T}$ leads to a definition of a coherent SCTS.

Notion 1 (SCTS). *A* Socio-cognitive technical system (SCTS) *is a multiagent system that satisfies the following assumptions:*

A.1 *System. A socio-cognitive technical system is composed by two ("first class") entities: a* social space *and the* agents *who act within that space. The system exists in the real world and there is a boundary that determines what is inside the system and what is out.*

A.2 *Agents. Agents are entities who are capable of acting within the social space. They exhibit the following characteristics:*

A.2.1 *Socio-cognitive. Agents are presumed to base their actions on some internal decision model. The decision-making behaviour of agents, in principle, takes into account social aspects because the actions of agents may be affected by the social space or other agents and may affect other agents and the space itself [3].*

A.2.2 *Opaque. The system, in principle, has no access to the decision-making models, or internal states of participating agents.*

A.2.3 *Hybrid. Agents may be human or software entities (we shall call them all "agents" or "participants" where it is not necessary to distinguish).*

A.2.4 *Heterogeneous. Agents may have different decision models, different motivations and respond to different principals.*

A.2.5 *Autonomous. Agents are not necessarily competent or benevolent, hence they may fail to act as expected or demanded of them.*

A.3 *Persistence. The social space may change either as effect of the actions of the participants, or as effect of events that are caused (or admitted) by the system.*

A.4 *Perceivable. All interactions within the shared social space are mediated by technological artefacts—that is, as far as the system is concerned only those actions that are mediated by a technological artefact that is part of the system may have effects in the system. Note that although such actions might be described in terms of the five senses, they can collectively be considered percepts.*

A.5 *Openness. Agents may enter and leave the social space and a priori, it is not known (by the system or other agents) which agents may be active at a given time, nor whether new agents will join at some point or not.*

A.6 *Constrained. In order to coordinate actions, the space includes (and governs) regulations, obligations, norms or conventions that agents are in principle supposed to follow.*

¶

SCTS abound, and some typical examples are: (i) classical hybrid online social systems like *Facebook* [14], (ii) socio-cognitive technical systems like online public procurement systems and electronic institutions for various kinds of trading (e.g. EverLedger's diamond provenance system) [1,7], (iii) massive on-line role playing games [22], and (iv) agent based simulation systems [22], in particular the like of those we discuss in Sects. 3 and 4.

A key feature of all SCTS, that is common to these examples, is that they are state-based systems, in the following sense:

Notion 2 (State of the social space). *A SCTS involves autonomous entities that interact in a common restricted environment that we call the social space, so that:*

B.1 *At any point in time the social space is in a "state" that consists of all the facts that hold in the social space at that point in time. Such state is unique and, therefore, common to all participants.*

B.2 *The state of the social space changes either through the actions of individuals that comply with the conventions that regulate the SCTS, or through events that are acknowledged by the STSC conventions.[2]*

¶

In order better to characterise SCTS and develop guidelines for their design, we proposed an abstract framework – the $\mathcal{WIT}$ *framework* [13] – whose distinctive contribution is the realisation that every SCTS can be understood as a composition of three "aspects": an actual functioning system in the real world ($\mathcal{W}$), the institutional description of the system ($\mathcal{I}$) and the technological artefacts that support the operation of the system ($\mathcal{T}$). This realisation provides a separation of concerns for each aspect that is convenient for description and

---

[2] We mean exogenous events that affect the behaviour of the system *in a relevant way* and should therefore be accounted for in the description and implementation of the system. For example, rainfall, a new exchange rate, the passage of time.

design of SCTS (for an illustration of these claims see [14]). In Sect. 3, we show
how these ideas apply to simulation systems.

As we suggested above, one can see the system that simulates a particular
second order emergence phenomenon as a particular SCTS. In this case, $\mathcal{I}$ would
the specification of a model of the given phenomenon, $\mathcal{T}$ the implementation of
that specification and $\mathcal{W}$ would be the simulated emergent phenomenon. Thus,
in $\mathcal{W}$ one deals with issues concerned with the proper implementation of data
structures and algorithms; as well as the interfaces that allow the visualisation of
the simulated phenomenon. In $\mathcal{I}$ one is concerned with the expressiveness of the
formalism used to model emergent phenomena and whether the understanding
that one has of the social phenomenon is faithfully transcribed in that formalism.
Finally, $\mathcal{W}$ is the simulated phenomenon one wishes to study and therefore one
is concerned with the means to define the variable behaviour of agents (human
or artificial) and the exogenous events and how to interpret outcomes of those
interactions.

These intuitions are firmed up in the next set of definitions (cf. [13]). Notion 3
says that the three views may be characterised by their core ontologies, a *compatibility* relationship and their particular notion of state. Notion 4 states that the
three compatibility notions are "aligned" so that the state of the three aspects
evolve coherently.

Notion 3 ($\mathcal{WIT}$ views). *The $\mathcal{WIT}$ framework characterisation of a SCTS $\mathcal{S}$
is the triad $\langle \mathcal{W}, \mathcal{I}, \mathcal{T} \rangle$, where:*

C.1 $\mathcal{W} = \langle W, \succ \rangle$, *is the view of $\mathcal{S}$ as a running system situated in the (real)
world. It comprises:*

    C.1.1 *A domain ontology W, that captures the intuition that only certain
facts, events and actions that happen in the physical world are relevant for the system;*

    C.1.2 *The $\mathcal{W}$-compatibility relationship, $\succ$, corresponds to the intuition
that relevant actions are "feasible" in $\mathcal{W}$, only if the proper conditions hold, and if a relevant action is feasible its effects will be
relevant as well;*

    C.1.3 *$(\mathcal{S}_{\mathcal{W}t})$, the state of $\mathcal{W}$ at time t, is the set of all facts that are relevant
in $\mathcal{W}$ at time t:*

$$\mathcal{S}_{\mathcal{W}t} = \{\alpha \mid W \succ \alpha\} \tag{1}$$

C.2 $\mathcal{I} = \langle I, \propto \rangle$, *the institutional view of $\mathcal{S}$ is the abstract representation of the
system and the conventions that govern the actions that may take place in
$\mathcal{W}$ and their effects. It comprises:*

    C.2.1 *An institutional ontology I that captures the intuition that the insti-
tutional representation of $\mathcal{S}$ involves an ontology formed by "institutional" assertions and actions that corresponds to the relevant facts,
events and actions in W;*

    C.2.2 *The $\mathcal{I}$-compatibility relationship $\propto$ picks up the intuition that
attempted institutional actions will be "admissible" in $\mathcal{I}$, only if*

they comply with the prevailing conventions; and when an attempted action is admitted, its effects will be admitted in $\mathcal{I}$ as well.

C.2.3 *The state of $\mathcal{I}$ at time t, is the set of all expressions that are admitted ("hold") in $\mathcal{I}$ at time t:*

$$\mathcal{S}_{\mathcal{I}t} = \{\psi \mid W \propto \psi\} \tag{2}$$

C.3 $\mathcal{T} = \langle T, \bowtie \rangle$, *the technological view of $\mathcal{S}$ is the implementation of the system according to $\mathcal{I}$ that receives inputs from and produces outputs in $\mathcal{W}$. It includes:*

C.3.1 *a collection of data structures of the implementation of $\mathcal{S}$ whose values change when an "acceptable" input is processed in $\mathcal{T}$.*

C.3.2 *The $\mathcal{T}$-compatibility relationship $\bowtie$ catches the intuition that the values of some variables change when the system processes an acceptable input.*

C.3.3 *The state of $\mathcal{T}$ at time t, is the set of values of the relevant variables in $\mathcal{T}$ at time t:*

$$\mathcal{S}_{\mathcal{T}t} = \{\phi \mid W \bowtie \phi\} \tag{3}$$

¶

An important feature of the $\mathcal{WIT}$ characterisation is that one would like to express that only those actions that are *compatible* with the conventions of the system can change the state of the system. For that purpose we need to establish some sort of alignment between actions in $\mathcal{W}$, $\mathcal{I}$ and $\mathcal{T}$ and use the three *compatibility relationships* $(\succ, \propto, \bowtie)$ to indicate that the corresponding state changes if only if the attempted action is compatible with the prevailing state of the context. In particular, we postulate that if an SCTS is properly specified and deployed, the three $\mathcal{WIT}$ views are "coherent" in the sense that their corresponding states evolve as intended. In other words, when an action is attempted, in $\mathcal{W}$ –which is expressed as an attempted input in $\mathcal{T}$ – its effects in $\mathcal{W}$ should be the ones prescribed in $\mathcal{I}$, which ought to be the ones that are computed in $\mathcal{T}$ and are reflected in $\mathcal{W}$, as pictured in Fig. 1. The following notion approximates such alignment:[3]

Notion 4 (Coherence). *Let f_{wi}, f_{it} and f_{wt} be three "bijections" between the $\mathcal{WIT}$ views of a SCTS $\mathcal{S}$; and let α, ψ and ϕ be actions in $\mathcal{W}$, $\mathcal{I}$ and $\mathcal{T}$, respectively, such that $\psi = f_{wi}(\alpha)$ and $\phi = f_{it}(\psi)$ and $\phi = f_{wt}(\alpha)$.*

---

[3] In Notion 4 we postulate that the views are coherent when they are sort of *isomorphic*. This is an elusive concept in the sense that unless one has a precise specification of each view it is impossible to define the intended "bijections". However, the alignment can be made precise when one has a precise description of the domain language used in $\mathcal{W}$, the corresponding action, norm and communication languages used in $\mathcal{I}$; and, in turn how those are transcribed into actual code in $\mathcal{T}$ through some specification language. See [7,12] for an example.

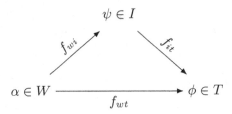

Fig. 1. The three "bijections" of Notion 4

The $\mathcal{WIT}$ views are coherent *iff for every time t,*

$$(\mathcal{S}_{\mathcal{W}t} \succ \alpha) \Leftrightarrow (\mathcal{S}_{\mathcal{I}t} \propto \psi) \Leftrightarrow (\mathcal{S}_{\mathcal{W}t} \bowtie \phi) \tag{4}$$

¶

It is worth noting that beyond the mapping of actions and effects that support the coherence of the three views, there are other relationships between views as depicted in Fig. 2. The following remarks give an indication of what these relationships stand for. Although we will not deal with these matters in detail here, we should note that they support design and methodological concerns (as suggested in [14]). In that spirit we illustrate the interrelationship between views in Sect. 3.

D.1 We call the $\mathcal{I}$ view *institutional* following the usage of Searle [20]. Thus we expect to have a bottom-up "corresponds" relationship from $\mathcal{W}$ to $\mathcal{I}$ that serves to create the "institutional reality". This is usually achieved through "constitutive norms" that transform (and legitimise) relevant brute facts and actions into the "corresponding" institutional facts and actions.

D.2 The intended coherence between the two aspects also entails a top-down "corresponds" relationship that converts (or anchors) the institutional effects of institutional facts and actions into the corresponding relevant brute facts and action. Thus, it also works as a prescriptive relationship (from $\mathcal{I}$ to $\mathcal{W}$).

D.3 Notice that the "corresponds" relationships presume that the representation in $\mathcal{I}$ of $\mathcal{W}$ is adequate (all relevant entities are properly represented and all pertinent institutional entities are properly reflected in relevant brute entities).

D.4 Once $\mathcal{I}$ is understood as a *prescription* of the intended behaviour of $\mathcal{S}$, it is used to *specify* the software that implements it. Thus the top-down "implements" relationship. Conversely, the actual behaviour of the implemented system in $\mathcal{T}$ should comply with the institutional conventions in $\mathcal{I}$.

D.5 Notice that the "implements" correspondence presumes that the specification is accurate and the implementation correct.

D.6 $\mathcal{T}$ enables $\mathcal{W}$ because Notion 1 postulates that all STSC are online systems. Thus, every relevant event that takes place in $\mathcal{W}$ and any action that is

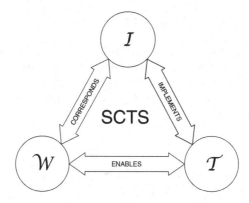

Fig. 2. The WIT trinity: The ideal system, $\mathcal{I}$; the technological artefacts that implement it, $\mathcal{T}$, and the actual world where the system is used, $\mathcal{W}$

attempted in $\mathcal{W}$ may affect the state of the $\mathcal{S}$ only, when wrapped as a message, it is deemed a valid input in $\mathcal{T}$. Conversely, changes in the state of $\mathcal{S}$ become actual brute facts in $\mathcal{W}$ if they are presented as outputs from $\mathcal{T}$.

D.7 Notice, finally, that those input-output connections between $\mathcal{W}$ and $\mathcal{T}$ presume that information is not lost or corrupted, that interfaces are ergonomic and correct, and that transfer of information is made according to the conventions stipulated in $\mathcal{I}$.

3   Simulation of *EP2* with the $\mathcal{WIT}$ Framework

In broad terms, we want to build simulation systems to study second-order emergent social phenomena. As discussed in Sect. 4, these phenomena involve individuals that may recognise that a macro phenomenon is emerging and, as a consequence, this phenomenon and the emergence process itself can be intentionally supported, initiated, changed or contrasted by the same individuals. In other words, individual agents decide what to do in view of their own motivations and preferences but also taking into account what others may or may not do and the effects of their own actions and the actions of others. Thus, in order to model *EP2* we need socio-cognitive agents. Moreover, since these agents do not act in a void but in a social environment that provides them with cues, opportunities and means to interact with other agents, we also need a persistent, regulated social space. In fact, since all the assumptions we postulate in Notion 1 apply to the systems where of second order phenomena emerge, we may use the $\mathcal{WIT}$ framework to characterise these systems.

Indeed, once we commit to a SCTS representation of the social phenomenon, a rough $\mathcal{WIT}$ characterisation is straightforward: the $\mathcal{I}$ view is the abstract model of a social phenomenon (we'll refer to it as $\mathcal{M}$) and $\mathcal{T}$ is the corresponding working computational model (we'll call it $\mathcal{P}$). Finally, $\mathcal{W}$ is the simulated (virtual) environment ($\mathcal{V}$) where one inputs experimental data and observes the social phenomenon.[4]

We may get a more refined characterisation of simulation systems by qualifying the relationships between $\mathcal{V}$, $\mathcal{M}$ and $\mathcal{P}$. Figure 3 adapts our original $\mathcal{WIT}$ trinity (Fig. 2) to simulation, and splits in two each of the relationships between views in order to clarify the character of those relationships when the framework is used for simulation.

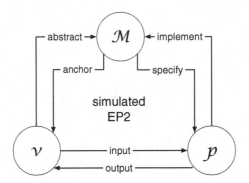

Fig. 3. A refinement of the WIT trinity for the simulation of second order emergence phenomena. The $\mathcal{W}$ view becomes a simulated virtual world $\mathcal{V}$ where one studies the emergent phenomenon, $\mathcal{I}$ becomes the conceptual model of the social phenomenon, $\mathcal{T}$ is, now, the implementation of the model that runs the virtual world and interrelationships between views are instrumental.

The process of design and construction of a simulation is (as usual) a cyclic process that normally (i) starts with a vague understanding of the phenomenon that is (ii) reflected in an abstract model ($\mathcal{M}$), which is in turn (iii) implemented ($\mathcal{P}$) to produce (iv) the virtual world ($\mathcal{V}$) where actual simulation runs take place. (v) The simulated phenomenon is progressively refined by testing the implementation of the model through the virtual world. What is distinctive of the WIT approach can be summarised along three lines:

Metamodels and affordances. We postulated [13] that a metamodel consists of *a collection of languages, data structures and operations that serve to represent* the agents and the social space of a given SCTS with an appropriate level of detail and accuracy. The model, hence, would be a *representation* of a phenomenon through a particular abstract or symbolic notation specific of the metmodel. A notation that, consequently, will be useful as long as it has the expressiveness needed to capture the relevant features of the phenomenon at the appropriate level of detail.

---

[4] Experimental data inputs consist of an initial state—including a population of agents with their own profiles and data—that is uploaded into $\mathcal{P}$, and then events—generated somehow—and actions taken by agents. By extension, the presence of human actors in $\mathcal{V}$ would make this a participatory simulation.

The closer the metamodel is to the phenomenon one wishes to understand, the easier it is to instantiate it. The more distant the metamodel is, the wider variety of systems that would be fit to model and the more detailed the effort of tailoring to the particular system. One way to make this proximity precise is to refer to the "affordances" of the metamodel [15]. In [13], we defined an *affordance* to be a property that enables coherent change of states in a SCTS. Namely,

Notion 5. *An* affordance *is a property of the SCTS (of individual agents or of social space) that supports effective interactions of agents within an SCTS.*

We postulated three essential affordances of every SCTS: *Awareness*, which provides participating entities access to those elements of the shared state of the world that should enable them to decide what to do, *Coordination*, so that the actions of individuals are conducive to the collective endeavour that brings them to participate in the SCTS and *Validity* that preserves the proper correspondences of the tripartite view.

Those affordances may be achieved through several means and will be reflected in the features that can be directly expressed by the languages and constructs of the metamodel. Those features include, for instance, the description of the entities ("ontology") that are involved in the representation of a state of the system, the primitive actions that agents may take, the way actions are taken by agents and their are reflected and perceived in the social space, the possibility of organising certain interactions in a subcontext of the whole social space, whether the conventions that regulate interactions are regimented or may be enforceable and through what means, etc.[5]

Platforms. The implementation of the model is facilitated when that implementation is associated with the metamodel. This is the purpose of developing a suit of software tools—a *platform*—that is powerful enough to capture all the distinctive features of the metamodel and consequently enables the designer to move smoothly from a precise instantiation of the model to the code that runs it. The ideal situation would be to have a specification language that is used to make the model precise and generates the corresponding executable code.

There are several proposals of metamodels for socio-cognitive technical systems and a few of them are accompanied by a corresponding platform, see [1] for thorough descriptions of some of the most developed and examples of their application.

Methodological considerations. An important goal for coupling metamodel and platform is that one can get assurances about the correctness of the implementation and the completeness of the specification.

Notwithstanding that interplay, one is still confronted with the choice of platform and metamodel and making sure that the correctness and completeness hold. There is a good discussion of this matter, with respect to socio-cognitive

---

[5] See Sect. 4 for a more detailed list.

technical systems in [11] and a complementary one in [13]. Sect. 4 deals with these matters.[6]

We do not yet have a metamodel for modelling directly second order emergence and we find no platform that is convenient enough to model *EP2* specifically.

In the next section we take the first steps in that direction, following a bottom-up approach. Thus, rather than trying to adapt an available metamodel & platform framework like electronic institutions [7]—that is too general—we proceed from a rather specific phenomenon (a scenario where reputation emerges among a closed group of individuals through the exchange of a given class of messages (Sect. 4.3) and identify those features and affordances that are needed for a convenient representation, and move upwards towards affordances for reputation and for *EP2* in general. From those we intend to develop formalisms and specification languages that make those affordances operational. Similarly, we will start from an ad-hoc implementation of the affordances towards a platform that is closely linked to the resulting metamodels.

4   Affordances for Modelling Second Order Emergence

This section describes a three-stage top-down process to uncover tentative lists of individual and social space affordances, firstly at a generic level (Sect. 4.1), second at the level of a class of particular phenomena, namely reputation (Sect. 4.2), and thirdly in the case of a specific reputation model (Sect. 4.3). We emphasise this is not the only such answer: its purpose is primarily to illustrate how one might go about affordance identification, rather then being definitive either about process or outcome.

4.1   Second Order Emergence

At the core of the old debate on micro foundations (individualism) versus macro properties (structuralism) of societal systems – also known as the micro-macro link problem – we find the notion of *emergence* and how the micro and macro levels interact. Specifically we have to differentiate between two different approaches to the *emergence* of social phenomena.

Following a *generativist paradigm* [8], we can approach the emergence of social phenomena as a process that goes from micro to macro, from the individuals and their local behaviour to the macro structures that *emerge* as a result of the local interactions. In this approach

---

[6] In [22] we elaborated on the convenience of separating design ($\mathcal{M}$) and implementation ($\mathcal{P}$) concerns and also the advantage of building a metamodel that facilitates design and a corresponding platform that supports implementation. We also discussed the advantage of having a "design environment" to deal separately with the definition and management of simulations.

"the only action takes place at the level of individual actors, and the 'system level' exists solely as emergent properties characterising the system of action as a whole." [4]

This is known as *first order emergence* and is the main approach followed in current state-of-the-art social simulations:

"Given some macroscopic explanandum – a regularity to be explained – the *canonical agent-based experiment*[7] is as follows: Situate an initial population of autonomous heterogeneous agents in a relevant spatial environment; allow them to interact according to simple local rules, and thereby generate – or 'grow' – the macroscopic regularity from the bottom up." [8]

This, however, is only half the story. To what extent do macro-level properties exercise some kind of causal influence on the micro-level individuals' behaviour? [5]. In many cases, in a real human society, many of the macro structures that start to appear as a result of the individual's local behaviour have an effect on macro-level attributes (for example, the creation of ghettos may imply the increase of the crime rates and, as a consequence, devaluation of houses in that area[8]). The modification of those macro-level attributes, at the same time, has an effect in the individual's local behaviour modifying it (what is known as a *'downward causation'* [5]). This change in the individual's behaviour influences again how the macro structures emerge; how the emergence of the new macro structures modify the macro-attributes; and so on.

The scenario is even more complex if we consider that individuals may recognise that the phenomenon is emerging and, as a consequence, this phenomenon (and the emergence process itself) can be intentionally supported, maintained, changed or contested by the same agents. This is what is known as *second-order emergence*. Many important social phenomena are characterised by *second order emergence*. Examples of these phenomena go from social movements like the African-American civil rights movement, the Arab spring or the 15-M movement in Spain, to relevant social constructs like *reputation*, which is the basis of the exercise in Sects. 4.2 and 4.3.

Affordances for Second Order Emergence
What are the generic affordances that allow (are necessary for) *second order emergence*? As we have said above, the main characteristic of *second order emergence* is the capacity of the individuals at the micro level to detect that the social

---

[7] When we talk about social simulation we have to talk invariably about *agent-based social simulation* (ABSS). The main characteristic of a social simulation is that the simulated *individuals* are not entities whose aggregated behaviour can be adequately described using mathematical equations. Every individual is unique and interacts with the other individuals and the environment in an autonomous way. This particularity is what makes the multiagent systems paradigm the predominant approach in social simulation nowadays. From now on, we will use the terms social simulation and agent-based social simulation interchangeably.

[8] We only make reference to Schelling's dynamics example for sake of reader familiarity, rather than to engage in debate about its appropriateness or correctness.

phenomenon that will show up in the macro level is starting to emerge. This means that the individuals (or at least some of them) know about the existence of that phenomenon and, more importantly, know about the signals that identify its emergence in a given society. On the one hand, the *social space* makes more or less explicit these signals to the individuals. On the other hand, individuals need to have the capacity to perceive them and again, more importantly, of interpreting them as indicators of the emergence of the social phenomenon. Invariably, this goes through the capacity to anticipate what the other individuals will do in the future, in other words, the individual has to operate with a theory of mind. Theory of Mind is "the ability to understand others as intentional agents [6], and to interpret their minds in terms of intentional concepts such as beliefs and desires" [10]. Having a theory of mind has been recognised by several authors as a fundamental requirement of an architecture of the social mind [2,21].

The detection of the emergence of a social phenomenon is only the first stage of *second order emergence*. Once the individuals at the micro level become aware of the emergence process, they should have the capacity to influence it. This implies some kind of capacity for action embedded in the individual that at the same time is facilitated by the *social space*.

That said, a tentative list of generic affordances necessary for a *second order emergence* scenario can be summarised as follows:

Individual affordances

1. Cognitive capabilities to understand the emergent social phenomenon.
2. Theory of mind. Anticipate what others intend to do, how they will do it and what are they motivations.
3. Sensor capabilities to detect the signals that the *social space* makes available and that are associated with the emergence of the social phenomenon.
4. Cognitive capabilities to interpret the signals as indicators of the emergent process.
5. Actuator capabilities to influence the emergent process.

Social space affordances

1. A shared ontology of objects, agents, actions and events.
2. Some sort of social model to represent roles, groups, organisations and their relationships.
3. Some sort of governance or coordination support.
4. Perception channels adapted to the sensor capabilities of the individuals.
5. Actuation channels adapted to the actuator capabilities of the individuals.

4.2 Reputation

While the affordances we enumerated are generic for modelling second order emergence phenomena (*EP2*), if one wants to model a specific phenomenon, one may profit from the availability of affordances that are specific to the particular phenomenon. Thus we look into a well-known social construct: reputation.

Reputation can be defined as "what a *social entity says* about a target regarding his/her/its behaviour and characteristics". A social entity is "a group which is irreducible to the sum of its individual members, and so must be studied as a phenomenon in its own right" [19]. The definition postulates that whoever is saying something about the target is not an individual, but a social entity. An individual is just a messenger of what is supposed to be the opinion of the social entity (in fact, the messenger does not even have to be a member of that social entity to spread a reputation). This is a key aspect because it allows reputation to be an efficient mechanism to spread social evaluations by reducing fear of retaliation [17].

The next important element in the definition above is the action of "saying". Reputation exists because an evaluation circulates. Without communication, reputation cannot exist. You can have the members of a community sharing a belief. This belief however is not a reputation until it starts to circulate. In fact, communication is so important for reputation that there is a specific type of communication specialised for building reputation values: *gossip*.

When messages start circulating and people realise that a reputation on a target is starting to form, many times they will start performing actions (in the form of new rumours, support messages, shame messages, etc.) that are intended to influence the formation of that reputation. Therefore, as in any second order emergent phenomenon, the perceived signals that a reputation is emerging influence the behaviour of the individuals, that at the same time influence how that reputation emerges.

Affordances for Reputation

First of all, the individual needs to have a reputation model. This model has to go beyond the traditional computational models of reputation [18] that focus only on how reputation is evaluated. The individual has to be able to influence reputation so it has to know how it spreads (how gossip works), how it is evaluated and what are the elements that lead to the emergence of reputation or its undermining. Notice that this level of knowledge about reputation requires a theory of mind (when will the other individuals spread a reputation value?, who will be receptive to a specific reputation value?). It is also important that the individual knows about the utility of reputation: what is it good for? How can reputation favour/limit the achievement of my goals?

From the previous definition of reputation, it is clear that the nentity social group is essential for reputation and needs to be present at both levels, individual and *social space*. An individual needs to be able to detect social groups and determine the membership to those groups. At the same time, the *social space* can make more or less explicit this membership to the rest of members of the society. Linked to this capacity and as part of the reputation model, the individual has to be able to understand social relations and how they influence reputation and its spreading.

Finally, we reiterate that reputation depends on communication, so the individual has to be able to communicate with other individuals and the *social space* has to enable and support this communication.

Our proposed tentative list of affordances at this level of abstraction is the following:

Individual affordances

1. A [complete] model of reputation (including a "reputation oriented" theory of mind).
2. Notion of group. Capacity to detect groups. Understanding of social relations.
3. Capacity to communicate with other individuals (receive and send messages).

Social space affordances

1. Support for group formation and identification.
2. Communication channels.
3. Messages of different types.

4.3   Reputation Scenario

After identifying the affordances for second order emergence in general (Sect. 4) and those for the specific and illustrative second order phenomenon of reputation (Sect. 4.2), the next level of concretisation in our exercise is to identify the affordances associated to a specific scenario related with the social phenomenon. A scenario is a particular environment (that can include a physical space, a set of possible actions, behavioural restrictions, etc.) where the social phenomenon is present and relevant. The scenario that we will use to illustrate this third step is an idealised environment to study the spread of rumours and the formation of reputation. Notice that this is one of many possible scenarios and that the affordances identified at this level are strongly related to the particularities of the scenario.

The individuals in our scenario are directed by motivations. Each individual has a set of basic needs that he/she/it tries to satisfy. The set of needs that are relevant for a specific agent determine its personality and the kinds of actions the individual is motivated to perform in the world. In our scenario, the kinds of actions that an individual can perform are actions that influence the reputation of others.

The world where the agents evolve is divided in what we call *social contexts*. A *social context* is a physical space where individuals perform a social activity. For example, your home is a *social context* where you interact with the individuals that belong to your family in domestic activities, the gym is a *social context* where you interact with people that, like you, enjoy practising sport. Each *social context* has different characteristics that facilitate or restrict social interaction.

In our scenario, at every turn the individuals are randomly assigned to a *social context*. Once in a *social context*, an individual can approach or avoid other individuals present in that *social context*. We want to simulate the dynamics of individuals that have different motivations to approach or avoid other individuals in the same *social context*. These dynamics take into account the preferences of each pair of individuals. First, all the individuals express their intention to approach or avoid other members present in the *social context*. Second, with these intentions the system calculates the *communication groups* (groups of individuals that at some moment will be together to exchange messages) that will be formed in that *social context* using the following rules:

Given a pair of agents (A, B):

1. If one of the two agents has explicitly expressed its intention to avoid the other, the system will take care that they never meet. This simulates the situation when an individual wants explicitly to run away from another.
2. If A wants to approach B and (i) B also wants to approach A or (ii) B has not expressed any intention related with A, the system will place the agents in a common *communication group*. This simulates the situation when an individual wants to approach another individual and the latter either agrees on that approach or he/she is indifferent.
3. If neither A nor B have expressed any intention related to the other, the system will randomly decide to place them in a common *communication group* or not. This simulates the chance approach of one individual to another.

Notice that an individual can be in more than one *communication group* at the same time. Think that the *communication groups* do not necessarily happen at the same time (see Algorithm 1). As an example, imagine agents A, B and C. We have the following intentions (A approach B) (A approach C) (B avoid C). In this scenario, the system will generate two *communication groups*: $[A, B]$ and $[A, C]$ and will never generate a communication group with both B and C (see Algorithm 1 for the details about how we calculate the *communication groups*).

Individuals in a *communication group* can exchange messages (*rumours*) and can listen to the messages exchanged by the other individuals in that group. As a result of a received or heard *rumour*, an individual can react and send a *support* message (reinforcing the original *rumour*) or a *shame* message (expressing his/her disapproval of the original *rumour*). The message-reaction cycle is repeated until all the individuals in that *communication group* have had the opportunity to send a message, after which the group is dissolved. When all the groups are dissolved, the system asks again about the intentions of approaching or avoiding other individuals in that *social context* and this generates a new set of *communication groups*. This is repeated n times, after which the system starts a new turn. The sequence of a turn in the reputation scenario is illustrated in Algorithm 1.

Affordances for the Reputation Scenario

Our proposed list of affordances at this level of abstraction follows the guidelines established at the previous level (Sect. 4.2) taking into account the specific scenario described above:

Individual affordances

1. Agent architecture directed by motivations with a "reputation oriented" theory of mind.

Data: *SocialContexts*: Set of social contexts; *Agents*: Set of agents;

Each agent in *Agents* is assigned randomly to a social context in *SocialContexts*;
foreach *SC in SocialContexts* **do**

   repeat

      Each agent in *SC* evaluates which other agents in *SC* wants to
approach, to *avoid* or is indifferent about it (*neutral*);
The environment collects from each agent the list of intentions
(*approach | neutral | avoid*) towards the rest of the agents in *SC*;
The environment assigns a *distance* between each pair of agents in *SC*
according to the following table:

intention(A → B)	intention(B → A)	distance(A,B)
approach	*approach | neutral*	0
approach | neutral | avoid	*avoid*	1
neutral	*neutral*	random(0,1)

The environment creates the communication groups that will happen in
that *SC* Taking the graph where the nodes are the agents in *SC* and
the edges connect any pair of agents at distance 0, the *communication
groups* are defined as the maximal cliques of that graph.
foreach *CG in SC* **do**

      repeat

         The environment chooses randomly one agent from those that
want to send a *rumour*;
The selected agent sends the *rumour*;
The other agents send reactions to that *rumour* till no one has
anything to say;

      until *no agent wants to send a new rumour*;

   end

   until *n times*;

end

Algorithm 1. A turn in the reputation scenario.

2. Capability to decide which individuals to avoid or to approach (according to
the individual's internal motivations and the personality of individuals in the
communication group).
3. Reasoning mechanisms to decide when to send a {*rumour* ‖ *support* ‖ *shame*}
message (according to the individual's internal motivations an the personality
of individuals in the communication group).
4. Capability to send a {*rumour* ‖ *support* ‖ *shame*} message.

Social space affordances

1. Creation of *social contexts*.
2. Creation of *communication groups*.
3. Make explicit to each agent in a *social context* which are the other members
of the society in the same *social context*.
4. Make explicit to each agent in a *communication group* the other members of
the society in the same *communication group*.

5. Enable movement of individuals according to the scenario rules.
6. Communication channel between agents that belong to the same communication group.
7. Enforce the communication protocol in a *communication group*.

5   Closing Remarks

Our long-term aim is the creation of a conceptual model, leading to a family of computational frameworks, that can support the creation and exploration of complex socio-cognitive technical systems. In this paper we begin to address the questions arising from how to observe, understand and model the ways in which actors engage with social processes, for which they do not necessarily have existing conventions or norms to guide their behaviour, and which by their actions affect the emergence and properties of the nascent process. We put forward the $\mathcal{WIT}$ framework as a way to structure the dissection and understanding of three perspectives on the action space, coupled with a three step methodology for the refinement of the individual and social space affordances, taking reputation as the target social phenomenon for this particular exercise.

In earlier work [13,14], our focus was on the framework alone, as we sought to establish the characteristics of the perspectives of $\mathcal{W}$orld, $\mathcal{I}$nstitution and $\mathcal{T}$echnology and their inter-relationships, as set out in Notion 1. This in turn was informed by our experience in developing electronic institutions – from the earliest conceptual versions [9] to its current metamodels and implementation platforms and numerous applications [12,16] – which give us confidence that the $\mathcal{WIT}$ approach is sufficient to the task and also that we should aim for an *EP2* metamodel that is powerful (capture a large class of *EP2*), intuitive (so non-experts can use it to simulate *EP2*) and easy to use. The additional notions of the state of the social space (Notion 2), the views afforded by $\mathcal{WIT}$ (Notion 3) and coherence between those views (Notion 4), flesh out the framework in order to focus on how the framework may be applied to simulation in a straightforward manner.

We have sought to illustrate our exploration of *EP2* by taking the case of reputation. First, because it is an *EP2* that is well-known to social scientists and also one with which we already have experience. Second, because, as was the case with auctions, we believe that it contains archetypal *EP2* features. Thus, our expectation in choosing it, is that it can take us towards a conceptual framework that is generic enough to be applied for modelling of a wide class of *EP2*, as well as specific enough for particular *EP2*, and that it is practical for implementing *EP2* although it might be quite impractical for modelling other social coordination artefacts.

We illustrate our analysis of reputation through the three-step process outlined in Sect. 4, which takes a top-down route from generic through class to instance, to identify the individual and social space affordances that appear to be sufficient in the case as presented here, while also providing pointers for future work and other case studies.

Acknowledgements. This research has been supported by project MILESS (Ministerio de economía y competitividad - TIN2013-45039-P - financed by FEDER) and SCAR project (Ministerio de economía y competitividad - TIN2015-70819-ERC). We also thank the Generalitat de Catalunya (Grant: 2014 SGR 118).

References

1. Aldewereld, H., Boissier, O., Dignum, V., Noriega, P., Padget, J. (eds.): Social Coordination Frameworks for Social Technical Systems. LGTS, vol. 30. Springer, Cham (2016). https://doi.org/10.1007/978-3-319-33570-4
2. Castelfranchi, C.: Cognitive architecture and contents for social structures and interactions. In: Sun, R. (ed.) Cognition and Multi-agent Interaction, pp. 355–390. Cambridge University Press, Cambridge (2006)
3. Castelfranchi, C.: InMind and OutMind; Societal Order Cognition and Self-Organization: The role of MAS, May 2013. http://www.slideshare.net/sleeplessgreenideas/castelfranchi-aamas13-v2. Invited talk for the IFAAMAS "Influential Paper Award". AAMAS 2013. Saint Paul, Minn. US
4. Coleman, J.S.: Foundations of Social Theory. Belknap Press, Cambridge (1990)
5. Conte, R., Andrighetto, G., Campennì, M., Paolucci, M.: Emergent and immergent effects in complex social systems. In: Proceedings of AAAI Symposium, Social and Organizational Aspects of Intelligence, pp. 8–11 (2007)
6. Dennett, D.: The Intentional Stance. MIT Press, Cambridge (1989)
7. d'Inverno, M., Luck, M., Noriega, P., Rodriguez-Aguilar, J.A., Sierra, C.: Communicating open systems. Artif. Intell. **186**, 38–94 (2012)
8. Epstein, J.M.: Generative Social Science: Studies in Agent-Based Computational Modeling. Princeton University Press, Princeton (2006)
9. Esteva, M., Padget, J., Sierra, C.: Formalizing a language for institutions and norms. In: Meyer, J.-J.C., Tambe, M. (eds.) ATAL 2001. LNCS (LNAI), vol. 2333, pp. 348–366. Springer, Heidelberg (2002). https://doi.org/10.1007/3-540-45448-9_26
10. Harbers, M., van den Bosch, K., Meyer, J.-J.: Modeling agents with a theory of mind: theory-theory versus simulation theory. Web Intell. Agent Syst. **10**(3), 331–343 (2012)
11. Jones, A.J.I., Artikis, A., Pitt, J.: The design of intelligent socio-technical systems. Artif. Intell. Rev. **39**(1), 5–20 (2013)
12. Noriega, P., de Jonge, D.: Electronic institutions: the EI/EIDE framework. In: Aldewereld, H., Boissier, O., Dignum, V., Noriega, P., Padget, J. (eds.) Social Coordination Frameworks for Social Technical Systems. LGTS, vol. 30, pp. 47–76. Springer, Cham (2016). https://doi.org/10.1007/978-3-319-33570-4_4
13. Noriega, P., Padget, J., Verhagen, H., d'Inverno, M.: Towards a framework for socio-cognitive technical systems. In: Ghose, A., Oren, N., Telang, P., Thangarajah, J. (eds.) COIN 2014. LNCS (LNAI), vol. 9372, pp. 164–181. Springer, Cham (2015). https://doi.org/10.1007/978-3-319-25420-3_11
14. Noriega, P., Verhagen, H., d'Inverno, M., Padget, J.: A manifesto for conscientious design of hybrid online social systems. In: Cranefield, S., Mahmoud, S., Padget, J., Rocha, A.P. (eds.) COIN-2016. LNCS (LNAI), vol. 10315, pp. 60–78. Springer, Cham (2017). https://doi.org/10.1007/978-3-319-66595-5_4
15. Norman, D.A.: Affordance, conventions, and design. interactions **6**(3), 38–43 (1999)

16. Padget, J., ElDeen Elakehal, E., Li, T., De Vos, M.: InstAL: an institutional action language. In: Aldewereld, H., Boissier, O., Dignum, V., Noriega, P., Padget, J. (eds.) Social Coordination Frameworks for Social Technical Systems. LGTS, vol. 30, pp. 101–124. Springer, Cham (2016). https://doi.org/10.1007/978-3-319-33570-4_6

17. Pinyol, I., Paolucci, M., Sabater-Mir, J., Conte, R.: Beyond accuracy. reputation for partner selection with lies and retaliation. In: Antunes, L., Paolucci, M., Norling, E. (eds.) MABS 2007. LNCS (LNAI), vol. 5003, pp. 128–140. Springer, Heidelberg (2008). https://doi.org/10.1007/978-3-540-70916-9_10

18. Pinyol, I., Sabater-Mir, J.: Computational trust and reputation models for open multi-agent systems: a review. Artif. Intell. Rev. **40**(1), 1–25 (2013)

19. Ruben, D.H.: The existence of social entities. Philos. Q. **32**, 295–310 (1982)

20. Searle, J.R.: What is an institution? J. Inst. Econ. **1**(01), 1–22 (2005)

21. Sun, R.: Desiderata for cognitive architectures. Philos. Psychol. **17**(3), 341–373 (2004)

22. Verhagen, H., Noriega, P., d'Inverno, M.: Towards a design framework for controlled hybrid social games. In: Verhagen, H., Noriega, P., Balke, T., de Vos, M. (eds.) Social Coordination: Principles, Artefacts and Theories (SOCIAL.PATH), AISB 2013 Convention Proceedings, Exeter, UK, 3 April 2013, pp. 83–87. The Society for the Study of Artificial Intelligence and the Simulation of Behaviour (2013)

A Personal Medical Digital Assistant Agent for Supporting Human Operators in Emergency Scenarios

Angelo Croatti$^{(\boxtimes)}$, Sara Montagna, and Alessandro Ricci

DISI, University of Bologna, Via Sacchi 3, Cesena, Italy
{a.croatti,sara.montagna,a.ricci}@unibo.it

Abstract. In this paper we present Trauma Tracker, a project – in cooperation with the Trauma Center of a hospital in Italy – in which agent technologies are exploited to realise Personal Medical Digital Assistant Agents (PMDA) supporting a Trauma Team in trauma management operations. This project aims at exploring the fruitful integration of software personal agents with wearable/eyewear computing, based on mobile and wearable devices such as smart-glasses. The key functionality of Trauma Tracker is to keep track of relevant events occurring during the management of a trauma, for different purposes. The basic one – discussed in detail in this paper – is to have an accurate documentation of the trauma, to automate the creation (and management) of reports and to enable offline data analysis, useful for performance evaluation and to improve the work of the Trauma Team. Then, tracking is essential to conceive more involved assisting functionalities by the PMDA, from monitoring and warning generation to suggesting actions to perform— fully exploiting the hands-free interface of wearable technologies. This goes towards the idea – envisioned in the paper – of *augmented physicians* working in *augmented hospitals*, in which software personal agents are exploited along with enabling technologies from wearable and pervasive computing, augmented reality, to create novel smart environments to support individual and cooperative work of healthcare professionals.

1 Introduction

In the last decade, information and communication technologies (ICT) witnessed an impressive progress, in particular mobile and *wearable* ones, making the visions about pervasive computing in hospitals [2, 27, 48] more and more a reality. Nowadays Personal Digital Assistants (PDA) and tablets are widely deployed in various healthcare contexts [18]. Modern smartphones are powerful computing

This paper has already been published in:

© Springer International Publishing AG 2017

S. Montagna et al. (Eds.): A2HC/A-HEALTH 2017, LNAI 10685, pp. 59–75, 2017.
https://doi.org/10.1007/978-3-319-70887-4_4

© Springer International Publishing AG 2017
G. Sukthankar and J. A. Rodriguez-Aguilar (Eds.): AAMAS 2017 Visionary Papers,
LNAI 10643, pp. 228–244, 2017.
https://doi.org/10.1007/978-3-319-71679-4_15

devices, featuring a variety of onboard sensors (camera, GPS, NFC reader,...), a robust support for pervasive interaction with an ecosystem of Bluetooth-enabled external devices and wireless networking. This makes it possible to design complex mobile computing applications, eventually interacting with services in local area networks and on the Internet/cloud.

Besides mobile computing, technologies for *wearable computing* [20] and *eyewear computing* [5] are achieving a level of maturity that makes it possible to exploit them out of labs, in real-world professional contexts. In particular, smart-glass technologies – e.g., Vuzix m300, Epson Moverio BT-200, Microsoft Hololens – allow to designing a new generation of (pervasive) software systems exploiting different degrees of Mixed and Augmented Reality [43]. These devices are basic bricks to realise *hands-free* or *use-on-the-go* systems [40,41], in which users can, e.g., asynchronously perceive information, data generated by the application without the need of changing the focus of their current activity and limiting as much as possible the use of hands to act/interact with the device.

The development of these technologies allows for devising new kind of *software personal agents*, assisting healthcare professionals in doing their job. In this paper we refer to this agent technology as Personal Medical Digital Assistant agent (PMDA). A main healthcare context where this kind of technology can be useful is the *emergency*. In this context, agent technologies have been already proposed e.g. for emergency coordination.

In this paper, we present and discuss a further novel case, concerning the development of a PMDA for *trauma documentation and management*. The project – called Trauma Tracker – is being developed in cooperation with the Emergency Department, a Trauma Center, of a hospital in Italy. The first prototype of Trauma Tracker has been implemented using BDI-based (Belief-Desire-Intention) agent technologies—a version of the JaCaMo platform [3] running on Android-based mobile and wearable devices.

Trauma Tracker has been designed in a modular way, to support increasing levels of functionalities and services. The base level concerns tracking events and data, for documentation purposes—which is the focus of this paper. A first validation of the system has been carried on by the trauma team, remarking both the benefits with respect to the current practice, and current limits, providing feedbacks for further development of the system. Upper levels concern functionalities more oriented to real-time *assistance*, from the reactive generation of warnings to more proactive form of assistance (e.g., suggesting the actions to perform), exploiting the hands-free capabilities of wearable technologies such as the smart-glasses. This goes towards the vision of *augmented physicians* working in *augmented hospitals*, in which software personal agents are exploited along with enabling technologies from wearable and pervasive computing, and augmented reality, to create novel PMDA and smart environments for assisting healthcare professionals.

The remainder of the paper is organised as follows. In Sect. 2 we provide a background and overview on related work about agent technologies applied to emergency. After that, in Sect. 3 we introduce the Trauma Tracker project, the levels of support which is meant to provide and its coarse-grained architecture, including – as a key component – the PMDA. Then, in Sect. 4, we discuss in detail the *Tracking Level* of Trauma Tracker, which is the one developed to tackle the trauma documentation problem. In particular, we discuss in the design and prototype implementation of the PMDA using JaCaMo and a first evaluation. After that, in Sect. 5 we discuss the level of assistance that we aim at building on top of the tracking level, envisioning the idea of *augmented physicians* working in *augmented hospitals*. Finally, in Sect. 6 we draw some conclusions, briefly depicting our ongoing and future work.

2   Agents in Heathcare Emergency Scenarios

The unquestioned benefit of the introduction of ICT into healthcare systems is already recognised worldwide since ICT successfully addresses the vast set of characteristics and situations proper of the healthcare scenario —such as mobility, time-critical, distribution and large-scale coordination, context-awareness, decision-making, interoperability, complexity. Last-generation ICT infrastructures and services, especially the emergence of wearable and mobile technologies, opened new frontiers in healthcare by efficaciously supplying the work of hospital staff, doctors, and patients. The so-called *e-Health* [52] and *m-Health* [38] improved the quality of health-services, providing technologies for different purposes, such as acquiring and sharing patient data through Electronic Medical Records (EMR), automating administrative health-related processes, providing telemedicine services, remote and mobile monitoring, and much more [28,50].

In particular, the adoption of the agent paradigm seems to be particularly suited to improve the performance of an ICT infrastructure in terms of interoperability, scalability and reconfigurability. Literature refers a wide range of applications of the agent framework in e-Health for different purposes. A comprehensive review is provided in [15], where the main categories of applications identified are: *(i)* Medical data management: accessing, integrating and sharing patient' data from different remote sources is crucial for easing the work of physicians and for statistical analysis purposes [28,49]; *(ii)* Decision support systems: supporting physicians in their fast-paced work can reduce human errors, and safe time [6]; *(iii)* Planning and resource allocation: scheduling decisions on the allocation of professional and physical resources must be coordinated by planning techniques [46]; *(iv)* Remote care: mainly devoted to remote patient monitoring, it allows on one side patients with reduced mobility to not travel towards healthcare facilities for vital signs check-up, on the other side physicians to observe the dynamic of the patient's health and provide opportune recommendations tailored to the patient [44]. Moreover, the literature proposes the development of agent systems for *chronic diseases management*, such as diabetes, respiratory illnesses, and cardiovascular diseases [36]. The goal is to develop applications enabling a shift of the control of chronic illness from the caregiver to the patients themselves, namely the *self-management* of chronic diseases [23]. In this context an agent-based platform enables: *healthcare professionals* to be continuously updated on the patient's health by receiving data such as vital signs measures decreasing the occasions for patients to travel to health facilities; *patients* to be supported in daily decisions by instructions delivered by the application that is based on the elaboration of such data.

In this paper, we discuss specific issues related to the Emergency Department (ED), that is one of the most critical and challenging hospital departments, since it requires reactivity, quick and coordinated response, fast-paced and accurate decision-making. In this scenario, there are three key issues that may be tackled by the agent technology. First of all, the fast-paced sequence of events during a trauma resuscitation leaves little time for physicians to reason about the best treatment and care. A PMDA can thus support human operators by autonomously providing suggestions on the best choice. This would reduce human errors while saving time and increasing team performance. Secondly, an accurate documentation of trauma resuscitation seems to be crucial to improve the quality of trauma care where, according to [14] "Quality of trauma care can be defined as achieving the best possible outcome for a given set of clinical circumstances". Third, agent technologies – in particular Multi-Agent Systems – can be exploited to support the coordination among the various actors involved in the trauma management. An example is presented in [10], about the Ubimedic2 agent framework for supporting rescue operations. [28] presents CAS-COM, a distributed multi-agent system for the execution of smart emergencies by providing efficient remote healthcare in case of unexpected events. Within the platform distributed data and information can be retrieved and make available to physicians everywhere, thus enabling easier and faster choices.

The trauma tracker project focuses on the first two issues. The PMDA is a *software personal agent* assisting the activity of the Trauma Team. Personal assistants are a well-known application of software agents [19,21,25]. Existing proposal and technologies have been developed for different kind of purposes and capabilities, from scheduling joint activities [22,37,51], monitoring and reminding users of key timepoints [7,47], sharing information, assisting in negotiation decision support [17]. Compared to SPAs discussed in literature, the PMDA in our project have two main specific coarse-grained features:

- the kind of assistances requires the continuous observation of both the dynamic state of the context where the physician is acting, and also what specifically the physician is *doing* and *perceiving* in that context;
- to be able to provide assistance while the physician is carrying on her practical activity, *without distracting or interrupting her action.*

From a technological point of view, the design of these agents can benefit from the availability of wearable technologies such as smart-glasses, and, more generally, from the fruitful interaction with the research developed in the context of wearable and eyewear computing [5].

3   The Trauma Tracker Project

Trauma Tracker has been conceived and designed by taking in consideration the structure and work organisation of the Trauma Team. The team leader – the so called *Trauma Leader*, usually a senior official – is in charge of producing the documentation paper. However this is just one of the several functions she/he has. During trauma resuscitation Trauma Leaders supervise the work of their teams and are actively involved in the actual resuscitation, and only *after* that work is finished they produce the report. That is, they recall and write down in prose the main facts of the trauma resuscitation process, documenting from memory and not real-time. This is the typical situation of hospital emergency departments in Italy—besides the specific trauma center considered in this paper. Therefore, in this case, the availability of a system based on mobile and wearable technologies for trauma tracking and assistance, not only would improve the accuracy of the trauma documentation, but also significantly reduce the cognitive burden of the trauma team – of the Trauma Leader in particular – to create the reports. Nevertheless, such a system is useful also when a *scribe* or *recorder* is available in the Trauma Team, usually a nurse, like it happens in hospitals in Europe and US—to support her work.

3.1   Levels of Support

The Trauma Tracker project has a twofold general objective. A short-term one is enabling a systematically and as-much-as possible seamlessly tracking all the trauma managed in the Trauma Center, to increase both the quality and quantity of the collected data and to provide a flexible and comprehensive way to manage and analyse such data, structured in reports. This is the job of the Tracking Level, which is the base level of Trauma Tracker. The design and prototype development of this level, as well as its first validation, will be discussed in Sect. 4.

A medium-term one is to introduce different kind of *assistance* to support the Trauma Team during the management of a trauma. Such assistance ranges from monitoring to suggesting. This level will be discussed in Sect. 5.

3.2   Coarse-Grained Architecture

The coarse-grained general architecture of TraumaTracker, represented in Fig. 1, is agent and service oriented, and includes four main parts:

- The PMDA, referred as *Trauma Assistant Agent*.
- a set of Web-based services deployed in the hospital local area network, referred as GT^2 *infrastructure*.
- a set of pervasive services, provided by devices deployed in the physical environment of the hospital, referred as GT^2 *pervasive*.
- a set of Web-apps, enabling users to access and interact with some of the GT^2 *infrastructure* services, referred as GT^2 *apps*.

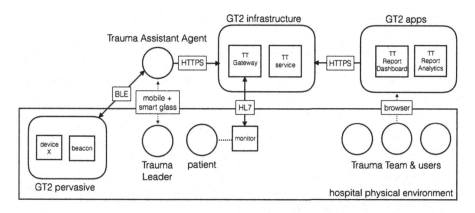

Fig. 1. Trauma tracker coarse-grained architecture.

The *Trauma Assistant Agent* runs on the mobile (a tablet) and wearable (smart-glasses) used by the Trauma Leader. It interacts with the services of the GT^2 *infrastructure* and GT^2 *pervasive*. The GT^2 *infrastructure* includes a set of web services that are exploited by the *Trauma Assistant Agent* and by the web-apps. The GT^2 *pervasive* currently includes a set of beacons placed in all rooms involved in the management of a trauma, to enable the room-level localisation for the PMDA.

A specific set of services in GT^2 *infrastructure* and apps in GT^2 *apps* is available to support the functionalities of the levels identified above. Currently, these services include (1) the *TT Report Management Service* – that provides a RESTful APIs for collecting and managing trauma reports and accessing to related statistical data – and (2) the *TT Vital Signs Monitor Service* – that provides APIs for dynamically retrieving the vital signs parameters of a patient under trauma, and services to realise continuous monitoring. Data collected by these services are made available to other hospital applications running on the same infrastructure, in an open ecosystem perspective. Finally, GT^2 *apps* currently includes a *TT Report Dashboard*, a web application that allows users – e.g., the member of the Trauma Team – to access the trauma documentation i.e. the reports, to manage, print and export them, as well as to do basic statistics.

In the next section we consider in detail the design and implementation of the Tracking Level, focusing in particular on the Trauma Assistant Agent.

4   The Tracking Level

The Tracking Level tackles the trauma documentation problem. In this section, we first discuss this problem in more detail, then we describe the design and implementation of the Trauma Tracker prototype, focusing in particular on the Trauma Assistant Agent, and finally we discuss its evaluation.

4.1   The Trauma Documentation Problem: Details

The documentation of a trauma, known in the literature as *trauma documentation*, is meant to be acquired during the process of trauma resuscitation, reporting where and when crucial events occurred, which and when treatments are given, procedures are performed, and finally it should report repeated vital signs measures. The documentation is crucial because it is used to make the most informed choice for patient medication and management, and later to evaluate the work of team members by producing data and statistics such as: time of team activation, primary assessment, arrival time of attending physician.

There reasons that make this task – i.e., producing an accurate documentation in the context of trauma resuscitation – challenging are manyfold [35]. First of all, trauma resuscitation is a fast-paced process, and very few time is left for documenting the process whilst some of the data to be documented are instead time-consuming. Secondly, multiple events happen simultaneously. To treat severe injuries, potentially life-threatening, team members perform concurrent tasks and parallel activities. Monitoring all of them is not trivial. Finally, the person in charge of documenting is often multitasking, his/her resources are not completely dedicated to the documentation task but he/she also performs other activities.

Nowadays most of the EDs adopt *handwritten paper records and flow sheets* for acquiring data [24,35]. The process of data acquisition is mainly conducted during the trauma resuscitation – or sometimes immediately after by collective memory and verbal communication – by the *recorder*, a person with that specific function. Papers are then sent to central bureau where data are manually entered from the sheets into a computerised databank. The overall procedure produces incomplete or even wrong documentation for two main reasons: *(i)* data acquisition is often inaccurate and crucial data are lacking. This is due to several reasons, some of which are due to the intrinsic characteristics of the context, as cited above: multitasking of the person in charge of acquiring data, parallel activities of the different members of the team, multiple data to be recorded, retrospective documenting from collective memory; *(ii)* manual transfer of data from paper to electronic format can introduce oversights. Furthermore, it is expensive in terms of time spent to complete the overall procedure and of workload.

The main objective of the Tracking Level of Trauma Tracker is then to help human operators – the Trauma Leader in particular – in producing an accurate trauma documentation, minimising as much as possible the human intervention and burden.

4.2   Trauma Assistant Agent Tasks

In the Tracking Level, the main tasks of the Trauma Assistant Agent are: *(i)* tracking events occurring in the emergency rooms related to a specific patient, inferring as much as possible data from the context (e.g., the place where a procedure is performed), and *(ii)* at the end of the trauma management, producing and sending a report to be sent to the *TT Report Management Service*.

Event tracking is mainly a reactive activity, in which the Trauma Assistant Agent:

- keeps track of the actions performed by the trauma team. These actions can be either procedures (e.g., endotracheal intubation, thoracic drainage, application of a tourniquet and many others) or drug/blood product infusion (e.g., millilitres of crystalloids or hypertonic solution, adrenaline, atropine, pools of cryoprecipitates, etc.);
- allows the trauma leader to take snapshots, record video or audio annotation, to be included in the report, exploiting the camera equipped with the smart-glasses;
- allows to retrieve, display and track the current value of patient's vital signs— by interacting with the *TT Vital Signs Monitor Service* service. These data must be automatically retrieved and annotated *(i)* when a procedure or the administration of a particular drug are performed; *(ii)* periodically, with a period that depends of the specific location of the patient in the emergency room (i.e. the period of vital signs monitoring could be different if the patient is currently in shock-room rather than in the TAC room).

Every event/note tracked by the agent includes both temporal (date and time) and spatial (location, specific room) information.

At the beginning of the trauma management, the system provides an easy-to-use form to annotate, in a qualitative way, the state of health in which the patient is (i.e. if his heart rate is normal rather than bradycardic or tachycardic, if the patient is breathing spontaneously or not, if external bleeding are present, and many others). Then, the system allows to annotate important variations to the patient vital signs (i.e. the patient that was hypoxic has returned to have a normal oxygen saturation). Finally, when the trauma management is completed, the Trauma Leader can annotate the final destination of the patient (i.e. emergency room observation area, ICU, mortuary). After that, the full report about the trauma – including also photos, videos, vocal notes – is automatically sent and stored on a server, exploiting the hospital WiFi Local Area Network.

An important and challenging aspect of the agent is the strategy used to keep track of the actions performed on the patient by the trauma team. Currently, this occurs by reacting to commands that are explicitly requested by the Trauma Leader, either exploiting the user interface provided on the smartphone device where the agent is running, or as speech commands. The UI must be necessarily very simple and effective, minimizing the number of interactions and taps required to specify the action performed.

4.3   Design and Implementation

The Trauma Assistant Agent is designed upon the BDI (Belief-Desire-Intention) agent model/architecture. The BDI has been originally introduced to design real-time intelligent system assisting humans in critical operations [30], featuring the capability of integrating a goal-oriented behaviour – i.e., the agent has explicit

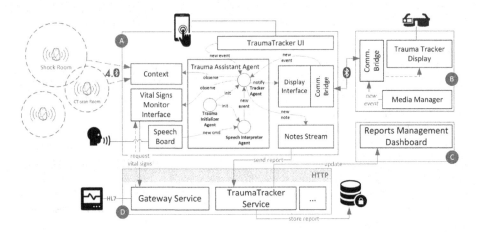

Fig. 2. Trauma Tracker System Logical Architecture. Parts (A) and (B) represent the Trauma Leader subsystem and in particular the Trauma Assistant Agent, Part (C) is the Reports Management subsystem and, finally, Part (D) represents the GT^2 infrastructure.

goals to achieve and for that purpose it selects and executes plans – and a reactive behaviour – i.e., while executing the plans it can promptly react to events occurring in the environment, eventually executing further plans to handle them. This model/architecture makes it possible to easily design a Trauma Assistant Agent with the reactive capabilities required by the Tracking Level, yet being ready for designing and implementing more pro-active features required by the Assisting Level.

In BDI computational models/languages [29], such reactive capabilities can be effectively modelled in terms of a set of predefined *plans* that are triggered by events occurring in the environment. In our case, such events are about actions carried on by the Trauma Team on the patient, multi-media annotation requests by the Trauma Leader (snapshots, video, vocal notes), and events concerning changes of: Patient's vital parameters, the location (room) where the Trauma is taking place, the Trauma Team organisation (e.g., the change of the Trauma Leader).

Besides BDI, the A&A conceptual model [26] has been adopted to model and design the *agent environment*. This is useful to modularise the set of percepts and actions available to agents into dynamic modules called *artifacts*, which represents – from the agent point of view – resources and tools that can be used to do its job. In particular:

- a TraumaTracker UI artifact is used to collect and make observable to the Trauma Assistant Agent the stream of events about actions performed by the Trauma Team and requests from the Trauma Leader;
- a Display Interface artifact provides actions to display messages and information to be perceived by the Trauma Leader (either through the tablet or the smart-glasses);

- a Context artifact keep tracks and makes it observable the current location of the Trauma Leader (i.e., the room), exploiting a BLE beacon-based localisation infrastructure deployed in the hospital environment, part of the GT^2 *pervasive*;
- a Vital Signs Monitoring Interface artifact keeps track of and makes it observable the updated data about patient's vital signs, interacting with *TT Vital Signs Monitor Service* service.
- a Notes Stream artifact to persistently store the stream of notes carrying information about the events and providing other functionalities related to report generation and delivery to the *TT Report Management Service* service.

Figure 2 shows a sketch of the architecture of Trauma Tracker, with in evidence the agents and artifacts involved.

4.4   Prototype Implementation

The Trauma Assistant Agent has been implemented using JaCaMo, a BDI-based multi-agent oriented programming platform, which integrates the Jason agent programming language (to program BDI agents), the CArtAgO environment programming framework (to program agents' environment) and MOISE organization framework (to specify MAS organization) [3]. In particular, a version of JaCaMo running on mobile and wearable devices has been exploited, based on JaCa-Android [34], which introduces an agent-oriented programming model to design, develop and run agent-based applications on top of the Google Android platform.

Even if at the logical level the Trauma Assistant Agent is a single conceptual high-level agent, the implementation in JaCaMo includes multiple Jason agents that work together inside an environment composed of a set of resources and services wrapped inside a proper set of CArtAgO artifacts. In particular, current design includes three Jason agents (see Fig. 2, part A), each one in charge of a different task:

- The *Trauma Initializer Agent*, responsible for initializing the tracking phase and collecting (and store) all preliminary information, essential for reports creation, including the identity of the trauma leader and the patient's initial health status.
- The *Tracker Agent*, which is the core of the Trauma Assistant Agent, encapsulating most of its functionalities. This Jason agent is in charge of keeping track of the trauma events – by reacting to events generated by corresponding artifacts (TraumaTracker UI, Context and Vital Signs Monitoring Interface) – and of incrementally building the report and making the Trauma Leader aware of specific information when needed – by using actions provided by the other artifacts (Note Stream and Display Interface).
- The *Speech Interpreter Agent*, responsible for the interpretation of speech commands. In particular, this agent recognises if a particular command may be accepted in that particular instant of the trauma management process –

according to the actions work-flow – and, if so, translate it into an appropriate event to be perceived by the Tracker Agent.

The full source code of the project is available on a public repository[1].

4.5 Evaluation

A first qualitative validation of the system has been carried on by the trauma team in a simulated environment, focusing in particular on the usability of the user interface (UI) and the responsiveness of the system. The basic configuration of the system – using the mobile devices only, without wearable technologies – appears to be ready and robust enough for being experimented in the real-world, providing already clear and measurable benefits – in terms of saved time and accuracy of the data – with respect to the current paper-based practice. So the next step, in this case, will be a further validation stage, in which the system is gradually introduced in the current practice, starting from the management of less critical trauma. Besides, this further stage will be essential to realise a more rigorous quantitative analysis and validation of the approach.

The adoption of smart-glasses – e.g., the intermediate configuration of the system – proved to be valuable to show information about vital signs in particular when the Trauma Leader is far from the vital signs monitor, and to take snapshots/video. As expected, the key benefit is to enable a first form of hands-free support, so that the Trauma Leader can take a snapshot or perceive information about the parameters without changing her focus and distracting from the scene. A critical point to be tackled before moving to the next validation stage is about the physical head mounting of the smart-glasses. On the one hand, current setting proved to be stable enough to deal with (abrupt) Trauma Leader's movements; on the other hand, we need to improve the flexibility in allowing the Trauma Leader to dynamically and seamlessly raise/drop the smart-glasses in some moments (to get them back, then), as well as reducing the effort (and time) needed to adjust the device.

Not surprisingly, the aspect that needs to be strongly improved in order to be usable in the trauma real-world settings is speech recognition. Currently, the performance is acceptable only for recognising basic commands used sporadically. This is not unexpected, since we are not using in the prototype specific speech recognition engine but the one available with the basic Android platform, functioning in offline mode. We expect to improve this aspect by investigating speech recognition technologies specifically tailored to the medical context.

5   From Tracking to Assistance – Vision and Challenges

Besides tackling the trauma documentation problem, the Tracking Level is the base layer to devise on top different levels of assistance, which calls for designing more complex and interesting kind of PMDA agents. In this section we discuss

---

[1] https://bitbucket.org/pslabteam/traumatracker.

the main ideas that we have about and that will be experimented in the Trauma Tracker Project.

5.1 From Monitoring and Warning Generation to Suggestions and Workflow

A first level of assistance is about the automatic generation of *warnings* that are displayed on the smart-glasses, about situations that the Trauma Leader may want to be notified without necessarily interrupting her activity flow. Situations may concern both the current state of the patient or its evolution – e.g., a warning could be generated if/when the value v of a vital parameter dynamically tracked by the system falls outside some predefined range $[min, max]$ –, and the temporal flow of actions carried on by the Trauma Team – e.g. some time t has elapsed after the administration of some drugs.

Situations can be modelled as predicates over the full context, including tracked information, current time and place where the Trauma Leader is, the identity trauma leader, and so on. This account for designing a PMDA which is capable of reasoning – at real-time – about the knowledge related to the temporal stream of data about the actions performed by the Trauma Team and about the evolution of the patient, and produce warnings. Such reasoning can be driven by rules defined by the Trauma Team. By exploiting the BDI model, such rules can be encoded into plans, reacting to relevant events and checking for the condition over beliefs encoding the context.

The kind of assistance discussed so far can be considered essentially *reactive*, i.e. the PMDA observes and reacts to events and situations occurring during the trauma management so as to notify warnings. A further kind of assistance which can be considered more *pro-active* accounts for a PMDA capable of reminding and suggesting the workflow of steps to follow in peculiar cases that require an ad-hoc treatment. In those cases, the trauma protocols and workflow to be adopted can be encoded in terms of goals and plans of the PMDA agent, yet preserving its reactive capabilities.

5.2 Integrating Cognitive Personal Assistant Agents with Cognitive Systems

In the model discussed so far, the generation of warnings and suggestions by the PMDA is based solely on the *local* knowledge about the ongoing trauma. A further step is to consider for that purpose also the *corpus* of knowledge related to trauma management and the documentation about the trauma done in the past, a big data collecting information from different hospital and trauma centers, and the use if *cognitive computing* techniques [13] to get insights from that Big Data. "cognitive computing" has been recently introduced by IBM [16] to refer to a set of tools and techniques – including Big Data and Analytics, machine learning, Internet of Things, Natural Language Processing, causal induction, probabilistic reasoning, and data visualization – which makes it possible to devise a "cognitive system" which is capable of learn, remember, analyse, resolve problems in specific contexts—healthcare and life science are a primary one [8]. The reference example developed by IBM of Cognitive System is Watson [16]. An interesting open research issue is then the design of PMDA that combines the capabilities of *cognitive agents* and the support of cloud-based *cognitive services* (Cognition-as-a-Service [39]) provided by cognitive systems such as Watson.

5.3   Towards Augmented Physicians Working in Augmented Hospitals

As already mentioned in the paper, wearable technologies promotes the design and use of hands-free or *on-the-go* interfaces [40, 41], that avoid as much as possible distracting the user from what she is doing – if not desired – and providing an information and suggestion flow which is seamlessly perceived and exploited by the user in her activity. This fosters a new perspective on the personal assistant running on this devices, like the PMDA.

Software Personal Agents explored in literature so far are based on the metaphor that of a *personal assistant* who is *collaborating with the user* in the same work environment [19]. The user interface of SPAs developed so far is mainly desktop or mobile, in which the SPA is often represented as a separate entity to interact with and to which the user delegates tasks. With wearable computing and handsfree interface, the SPA can be conceived more as *an extension of the self* [42], whose perceptions, beliefs, and possibly goals could be thought to be an extension of the user's ones, making the interaction more implicit and effective. Conceptually, the PMDA becomes an extension of the physician (*augmented physician*), augmenting her cognitive and practical capabilities.

This perspective goes toward the design of interface agents that – in spite of agent autonomy – should make the user always "feel in control" [11]. A main feature that could characterise this kind of personal agents would the capability to "see what the user sees" – by means of the camera on the eyewear device – and, more generally, to know what the user is perceiving about her context, given the sensors equipped with the device(s) worn by the user. This allows to frame a kind of pro-active assistance in which SPAs reason not only about the context of the user, but about what the user is perceiving – and not perceiving – from that context, what she is looking at, etc.

The definition and development of this kind of personal agents introduce interesting new research challenges for the agent community, partially tackled in related research context about eyewear computing [5], cognition-aware computing [4], activity-based computing [45] and context-aware computing [9]. These agents are meant to build dynamically a model about what the user is perceiving, and use this knowledge along with the information about user's goals, the state of ongoing activity, the actual state of the physical environment, to provide a pro-active and smart assistance, possibly anticipating and notifying problems and suggesting actions to do.

The full power of this idea can unleashed when the environment where the users are situated is *augmented* too, to provide functionalities and services that can be exploited by the Personal Medical Digital Assistant agents. Such augmentation can include two different levels, integrated:

- a software infrastructure layer running on computing devices embedded in hospital physical objects and environment;
- an augmented/mixed reality layer, composed by augmented entities enriching the physical reality, to be shared and perceived by the human users.

In literature, the first level is explored by research works on *pervasive healthcare*, applying pervasive computing to the healthcare domain, including hospital environments [1]. In our case, this means the possibility for a PMDA agent to interact with hospital objects, devices and appliances turned into smart things in an Internet-of-Things (IoT) perspective, including output devices such wall displays. A further case which is relevant for the agent community is about adopting agents also for modeling and engineering the pervasive software layer, as investigated by research work in literature exploring agent-based ambient intelligence [12,32,33].

The second level concerns enriching the physical reality with *holograms* perceived by users by means of proper wearable devices (AR-enabled smart-glasses, visors), eventually shared among multiple users situated in the same augmented environment. Such virtual entities can range from simple information related to specific physical objects to virtual user interfaces and full-fledge animated virtual objects, eventually enriching the functionality of the physical environment. In our case, the Personal Medical Digital Assistant agent could be able to interact with holograms, eventually creating them according to the need.

The intertwining of these two augmentation levels leads to the idea of *augmented hospital* where (mobile) augmented reality technologies are integrated with pervasive ones so as to create novel kinds of smart environments [31], providing more advanced functionalities to support individual and cooperative work.

6 Conclusion and Future Work

Currently, the TraumaTracker prototype implements just the tracking functionality, which is however useful already to improve the quality of the trauma documentation and to automate the generation of trauma reports. Next steps will be devoted to develop and integrate higher functionality levels, along the vision depicted in Sect. 5. In particular, the very first next step will be to provide functionalities in terms of real-time assistance to the Trauma Leader/team, fully exploiting the hands-free characteristics of the system. The first kind of assistance which is being implemented is about the automatic generation of warnings that are displayed on the smart-glasses, about situations that the Trauma Leader may want to be notified without necessarily interrupting her activity flow. The modular design adopted for the Trauma Assistant Agent makes it possible to implement the extensions without substantially change the behaviour of the existing internal agents. For instance, we plan to implement the new assistance functionalities as a new Jason Monitoring Agent, which observes and reasons about the notes created in the Notes Stream artifact, generating proper warnings to be displayed through the Display Interface artifact.

Finally, our medium-term research objective accounts for *(i)* fully exploring the idea of an agent-based augmented hospital sketched in Sect. 5, starting from exploring the design of an augmented environment improving the work of healthcare professionals involved in trauma management, and *(ii)* devising proper models and architectures that allow to integrate cognitive agents – taking JaCaMo as reference technology – with cognitive computing systems, like Watson.

References

1. Bardram, J.E., Christensen, H.B.: Pervasive computing support for hospitals: an overview of the activity-based computing project. IEEE Pervasive Comput. **6**(1), 44–51 (2007)
2. Bardram, J., Baldus, H., Favela, J.: Pervasive computing in hospitals, pp. 48–77. CRC Press (2006)
3. Boissier, O., Bordini, R.H., Hübner, J.F., Ricci, A., Santi, A.: Multi-agent oriented programming with jacamo. Sci. Comput. Program. **78**(6), 747–761 (2013)
4. Bulling, A., Zander, T.O.: Cognition-aware computing. IEEE Pervasive Comput. **13**(3), 80–83 (2014)
5. Bulling, A., Cakmakci, O., Kunze, K., Rehg, J.M.: Eyewear computing – augmenting the human with head-mounted wearable assistants (Dagstuhl Seminar 16042). Dagstuhl Rep. **6**(1), 160–206 (2016). http://drops.dagstuhl.de/opus/volltexte/2016/5820
6. Burstein, F., Zaslavsky, A., Arora, N.: Context-aware mobile agents for decision-making support in healthcare emergency applications. In: Workshop on Context Modeling and Decision Support (2005)
7. Chalupsky, H., Gil, Y., Knoblock, C.A., Lerman, K., Oh, J., Pynadath, D.V., Russ, T.A., Tambe, M.: Electric elves: applying agent technology to support human organizations. In: Proceedings of the Thirteenth Conference on Innovative Applications of Artificial Intelligence Conference, pp. 51–58. AAAI Press (2001)
8. Chen, Y., Argentinis, J.E., Weber, G.: IBM Watson: how cognitive computing can be applied to big data challenges in life sciences research. Clin. Ther. **38**(4), 688–701 (2016)
9. Dey, A.K.: Understanding and using context. Pers. Ubiqui. Comput. **5**(1), 4–7 (2001)
10. Domnori, E., Cabri, G., Leonardi, L.: Ubimedic2: an agent-based approach in territorial emergency management. In: 2011 5th International Conference on Pervasive Computing Technologies for Healthcare (PervasiveHealth) and Workshops, pp. 176–183, May 2011
11. Don, A., Brennan, S., Laurel, B., Shneiderman, B.: Anthropomorphism: from Eliza to terminator 2. In: Proceedings of the SIGCHI Conference on Human Factors in Computing Systems, CHI 1992, pp. 67–70. ACM, New York (1992)
12. Hagras, H., Callaghan, V., Colley, M., Clarke, G., Pounds-Cornish, A., Duman, H.: Creating an ambient-intelligence environment using embedded agents. IEEE Intell. Syst. **19**(6), 12–20 (2004)
13. Hurwitz, J., Kaufman, M., Bowles, A.: Cognitive Computing and Big Data Analytics. Wiley, Indianapolis, IN (2015)

14. Civil, I.D.S.: What is quality care in trauma? Injury **38**(5), 525–526 (2007)
15. Isern, D., Sánchez, D., Moreno, A.: Agents applied in health care: a review. Int. J. Med. Inf. **79**(3), 145–166 (2010)
16. Kelly, J.E.: Computing, cognition and the future of knowing, iBM Research and Solutions, white paper (2015)
17. Li, C., Giampapa, J.A., Sycara, K.P.: Bilateral negotiation decisions with uncertain dynamic outside options. IEEE Trans. Syst. Man Cybern. Part C **36**(1), 31–44 (2006)
18. Lindquist, M.A., Johansson, E.P., Petersson, I.G., Saveman, B.I., Nilsson, C.G.: The use of the personal digital assistant (PDA) among personnel and students in health care: a review. J. Med. Internet Res. **10**(4), e31 (2008)
19. Maes, P.: Agents that reduce work and information overload. Commun. ACM **37**(7), 30–40 (1994)
20. Mann, S.: Wearable computing as means for personal empowerment. In: Proceedings of the First International Conference on Wearable Computing (ICWC), Fairfax, VA. IEEE Computer Society Press, May 1998. http://www.eyetap.org/wearcam/icwc98/keynote.html
21. Mitchell, T.M., Caruana, R., Freitag, D., McDermott, J., Zabowski, D.: Experience with a learning personal assistant. Commun. ACM **37**(7), 80–91 (1994)
22. Modi, P.J., Veloso, M., Smith, S.F., Oh, J.: CMRadar: a personal assistant agent for calendar management. In: Bresciani, P., Giorgini, P., Henderson-Sellers, B., Low, G., Winikoff, M. (eds.) AOIS 2004. LNCS (LNAI), vol. 3508, pp. 169–181. Springer, Heidelberg (2005). https://doi.org/10.1007/11426714_12
23. Newman, S., Steed, L., Mulligan, K.: Self-management interventions for chronic illness. Lancet **364**(9444), 1523–1537 (2004)
24. O'Connor, T., Raposo, E.A., Heller-Wescott, T.: Improving trauma documentation in the emergency department. J. Trauma Nurs. **21**(5), 238–243 (2014)
25. Okamoto, S., Scerri, P., Sycara, K.: Toward an understanding of the impact of software personal assistants on human organizations. In: Proceedings of the Fifth International Joint Conference on Autonomous Agents and Multiagent Systems, AAMAS 2006, pp. 630–637. ACM, New York (2006)
26. Omicini, A., Ricci, A., Viroli, M.: Artifacts in the A&A meta-model for multi-agent systems. Auton. Agents Multi Agent Syst. **17**(3), 432–456 (2008)
27. Orwat, C., Graefe, A., Faulwasser, T.: Towards pervasive computing in health care – a literature review. BMC Med. Inf. Decis. Making **8**(1), 26 (2008)
28. Poggi, A., Bergenti, F.: Developing smart emergency applications with multi-agent systems. Int. J. E-Health Med. Commun. **1**(4), 1–13 (2010)
29. Rao, A.S.: AgentSpeak(L): BDI agents speak out in a logical computable language. In: Van de Velde, W., Perram, J.W. (eds.) MAAMAW 1996. LNCS, vol. 1038, pp. 42–55. Springer, Heidelberg (1996). https://doi.org/10.1007/BFb0031845
30. Rao, A.S., Georgeff, M.P.: BDI agents: from theory to practice. In: Lesser, V.R., Gasser, L. (eds.) 1st International Conference on Multi Agent Systems (ICMAS 1995), pp. 312–319. The MIT Press, San Francisco, 12–14 June 1995
31. Ricci, A., Piunti, M., Tummolini, L., Castelfranchi, C.: The mirror world: preparing for mixed-reality living. IEEE Pervasive Comput. **14**(2), 60–63 (2015)
32. Rodríguez, M.D., Favela, J., Preciado, A., Vizcaíno, A.: Agent-based ambient intelligence for healthcare. AI Commun. **18**(3), 201–216 (2005)
33. Sadri, F.: Ambient intelligence: a survey. ACM Comput. Surv. **43**(4), 36:1–36:66 (2011)

34. Santi, A., Guidi, M., Ricci, A.: JaCa-Android: an agent-based platform for building smart mobile applications. In: Dastani, M., El Fallah Seghrouchni, A., Hübner, J., Leite, J. (eds.) LADS 2010. LNCS (LNAI), vol. 6822, pp. 95–114. Springer, Heidelberg (2011). https://doi.org/10.1007/978-3-642-22723-3_6

35. Sarcevic, A.: "Who's scribing?": documenting patient encounter during trauma resuscitation. In: Proceedings of the SIGCHI Conference on Human Factors in Computing Systems, CHI 2010, pp. 1899–1908. ACM, New York (2010)

36. Shankararaman, V., Ambrosiadou, V., Loomes, M., Panchal, T.: Patient care management using a multi-agent approach. In: 2000 IEEE International Conference on Systems, Man, and Cybernetics, vol. 3, pp. 1817–1821 (2000)

37. Shintani, T., Ito, T., Sycara, K.: Multiple negotiations among agents for a distributed meeting scheduler. In: Proceedings of the Fourth International Conference on MultiAgent Systems (ICMAS 2000), Washington, DC, USA, p. 435. IEEE Computer Society (2000)

38. Silva, B.M., Rodrigues, J.J., de la Torre Díez, I., López-Coronado, M., Saleem, K.: Mobile-health: a review of current state in 2015. J. Biomed. Inf. 56, 265–272 (2015)

39. Spohrer, J., Banavar, G.: Cognition as a service: an industry perspective. AI Mag. 36(4), 71–86 (2015)

40. Starner, T.: The challenges of wearable computing: Part 1. IEEE Micro 21(4), 44–52 (2001)

41. Starner, T.: The challenges of wearable computing: Part 2. IEEE Micro 21(4), 54–67 (2001)

42. Starner, T.: Project glass: an extension of the self. IEEE Pervasive Comput. 12(2), 14–16 (2013)

43. Starner, T., Mann, S., Rhodes, B., Levine, J., Healey, J., Kirsch, D., Picard, R.W., Pentland, A.: Augmented reality through wearable computing. Presence Teleoper. Virtual Environ. 6(4), 386–398 (1997)

44. Su, C.J., Wu, C.Y.: JADE implemented mobile multi-agent based, distributed information platform for pervasive health care monitoring. Appl. Soft Comput. 11(1), 315–325 (2011)

45. Davies, N., Siewiorek, D.P., Sukthankar, R.: Activity-based computing. IEEE Pervasive Comput. 7(2), 20–21 (2008)

46. Taboada, M., Cabrera, E., Iglesias, M.L., Epelde, F., Luque, E.: An agent-based decision support system for hospitals emergency departments. Procedia Comput. Sci. 4, 1870–1879 (2011)

47. Tambe, M.: Electric Elves: what went wrong and why. AI Mag. 29(2), 23–27 (2008)

48. Tentori, M., Hayes, G.R., Reddy, M.: Pervasive computing for hospital, chronic, and preventive care. Found. Trends® Hum. Comput. Inter. 5(1), 1–95 (2012)

49. de la Torre, A.B., Lluch-Ariet, M., Pegueroles-Vallés, J.: Security analysis of a protocol based on multiagents systems for clinical data exchange. In: 2013 Seventh International Conference on Complex, Intelligent, and Software Intensive Systems, pp. 305–311, July 2013

50. Varshney, U.: Mobile health: four emerging themes of research. Decis. Support Syst. 66, 20–35 (2014)

51. Wagner, T., Phelps, J., Guralnik, V., VanRiper, R.: Coordinators: coordination managers for first responders. In: Proceedings of the Third International Joint Conference on Autonomous Agents and Multiagent Systems, AAMAS 2004, Washington, DC, USA, vol. 3, pp. 1140–1147. IEEE Computer Society (2004)

52. Whitten, P., Holtz, B., LaPlante, C.: Telemedicine: what have we learned? Appl. Clin. Inf. 1(2), 132–141 (2010)

Author Index